Hospitality Marketing

Hospitality Marketing
Principles and Practice

SECOND EDITION

David Bowie and Francis Buttle

AMSTERDAM BOSTON HEIDELBERG LONDON NEW YORK OXFORD PARIS
SAN DIEGO SAN FRANCISCO SINGAPORE SYDNEY TOKYO

Butterworth-Heinemann is an imprint of Elsevier

Butterworth-Heinemann is an imprint of Elsevier
The Boulevard, Langford Lane, Kidlington, Oxford, OX5 1GB, UK
30 Corporate Drive, Suite 400, Burlington, MA 01803, USA

First edition 2004
Reprinted 2006, 2007, 2008
Second edition 2011

British Library Cataloguing in Publication Data
A catalogue record for this book is available from the British Library

Library of Congress Cataloging-in-Publication Data
A catalog record for this book is available from the Library of Congress

ISBN: 978-0-08-096791-2

For information on all Butterworth-Heinemann publications
visit our website at www.elsevierdirect.com

Printed and bound in Spain

11 12 13   10 9 8 7 6 5 4 3 2

Working together to grow
libraries in developing countries

www.elsevier.com | www.bookaid.org | www.sabre.org

ELSEVIER   BOOK AID International   Sabre Foundation

For Julie, Olive, James
and Rowan, Cherry and James
DB

For my parents Bill and Mary,
and Dale and Nick
FB

Contents

Preface

Most readers of this textbook will be university undergraduate or college students studying hospitality and/or tourism marketing for the first time. Our main objective in writing the book has been to provide you with an easy-to-read text, which presents a review of modern marketing theory in the context of the hospitality industry. Examples from the industry are provided to illustrate real-life practice and give you a better understanding of hospitality marketing.

The book has the following special features:

- A unique structure, which examines marketing activities before, during and after the customers' experience of the hospitality encounter. This helps you to understand what has to be done to attract customers, provide them with an experience that meets their expectations, and motivate them to return.

- Fifteen chapters, one for each of the key elements you need to understand about marketing.

- Each chapter contains learning activities, which include Internet searches of relevant company websites and visits to hospitality units as a customer to collect information – you will then need to analyze and evaluate your findings.

- Its own website (www.elsevierdirect.com/companions/ 9780080967912) which contains a student section with further information, case studies and hospitality contact details. For tutors, there is a separate section, which provides additional teaching materials.

Structure

The structure of the book is divided into the following sections:

- *Part A: Introduction.* A single chapter, which introduces the key concepts of marketing in the hospitality industry, including market demand, the marketing concept, the special characteristics of service industries, the PESTE environment and the hospitality marketing mix.

- *Part B: Pre-encounter marketing.* This part of the text consists of eight chapters and discusses all the marketing activities that companies have to carry out to attract customers to experience the hospitality offer. Chapters include marketing research; understanding and segmenting customers; competitive strategies; developing, locating, pricing, distributing and communicating the offer.

- *Part C: Encounter marketing.* This section comprises three chapters, which are concerned with managing the customer experience while consuming the hospitality offer. They include managing the physical environment, managing the service process and managing customer contact employees.

- *Part D: Post-encounter marketing.* These two chapters discuss post-encounter marketing and explain the importance of customer satisfaction and developing mutually beneficial relationships with key customers.

- *Part E: The marketing plan.* The final chapter builds on the previous chapters, and explains how to write a marketing plan for a hospitality business.

Learning features

Each chapter contains the following features to aid understanding:

- *Chapter Objectives*: Each chapter begins with bullet points highlighting the main features and learning to be covered in the chapter.

- *Activities*: Short practical activities located at appropriate 'break' points throughout the chapter, which enable the reader to assess their understanding and marketing experience.

- *Headlines*: Highlights, appearing in blue type, throughout the chapter, which bring important points to the attention of the reader.

- *Marketing Insights*: Marketing anecdotes and observations to contextualize learning.

- *Case Studies*: International companies and scenarios are used to illustrate how the theories work in real world situations.

- *Conclusion*: Condenses the main themes of the chapter enabling the reader to check learning and understanding.

- *Review Questions*: Appear at the end of each chapter allowing readers to test their knowledge, understanding and to put the theory into practice.

Each chapter contains online sources to help students explore the good examples of hospitality marketing in practice.

Acknowledgements

We would like to thank the following people who have provided advice, materials and support throughout the writing of this book:

Professor Levent Altinay, Rowan Aragues, Richard Arman, Martin Armistead, Pauline and David Baldwin, Ian Baldwin, Lisa Basford, Nina Becket, Emma Benney, Dr David Bowen, James Bowie, Dr Maureen Brookes, Cathy Burgess, Pamela Carvell, Francesca Castelli, Atesh Chandra, George Chattis, Dr Jackie Clark, Julia Clarke, Grant Clendining, John Clifford, Richard Coates, Steve Conway, Andrew Creese, Professor Liz Doherty, Thierry Douin, Cherry Fleet, Louise Flemming, Chris Grant, John Griffin, Professor Peter Harris, Dr Rebecca Hawkins, Sam Harrison, Stuart Harrison, David Hayes, Klaus Kabelitz, Anna Karwata, John Kennedy, Nick Lander, Professor Conrad Lashley, Philip Lassman, Erik Marsh, Alasdair McNee, Nicky Michellietti, Professor Victor Middleton, Kathy and Ian Mitchell, Sophie Mogford, Peter Mygind, Razia Ghulam-Nabi, Christina Norton, Dr Alex Paraskevas, Geoff Parkinson, Mark Patterson, Philip Pickering, Rupert Power, Jonathan Raggett, Nick Read, Nick Rich, Mike Rimmington, Clive Robertson, Dr Angela Roper, Honour Schram de Jong, Richard Shepherd, Donald Sloan, Paul Simmons, Renu Snehi, Cris Tarrant, Gerard Tempest and Gary Yates.

The authors acknowledge the help of Roberto Daniele, Kate Ringham and Kate Varini from the Department of Hospitality, Leisure and Tourism Management, Oxford Brookes University, Oxford, UK in preparing chapters 7 and 8.

PART A

Introduction

C H A P T E R **1**

Introduction to hospitality marketing

INTRODUCTION

In this chapter, you will be introduced to the key concepts of marketing. We start by explaining what marketing is reviewing different definitions of marketing, defining the marketing concept and discussing management orientations. We then discuss the macro- and micro-environments in which hospitality companies operate, the special characteristics of service, and the hospitality marketing mix.

Whether we recognize it or not, we are all involved, willingly or unwillingly, in marketing. We come in contact with marketing practice every day as customers making buying decisions and at work, even if we do not have a job in marketing. Although marketing has a powerful influence in modern life, it is often misrepresented and misunderstood.

Students learning about marketing for the first time can be confused, because academic definitions of marketing differ from the everyday use of the term. Students can also be confused about the role of marketing, since marketing is both a business philosophy and a management practice.

Activity 1.1

- Write down what you think 'marketing' means before reading the chapter.
- Write down what you think marketers do.
- List the jobs that you think marketers are responsible for.

We will review your ideas at the end of this chapter and see whether they have changed!

WHAT IS MARKETING?

One set of marketing definitions suggests that marketing is primarily a business philosophy that puts the customer first. From this perspective, the primary goal of hospitality businesses should be to create and retain satisfied customers. This perspective proposes that satisfying customers' needs and wants should be at the center of an organization's decision-making processes. Professional marketers believe that true customer focus is the responsibility of everybody in the organization. Adopting this philosophy requires a total management commitment to the customer, and companies that pursue this approach can be described as having a *customer orientation*.

Definitions of marketing

Early definitions of marketing centered on the exchange/transaction process. Kotler (2010) proposes that in order to satisfy people's needs and wants, products and services are exchanged in mutually rewarding transactions, generally but not exclusively, using the monetary system. Kotler originally suggested that this exchange process, now known as transaction marketing, is a core concept in marketing and is a 'value-creating process which leaves both parties better off than before the exchange took place'.

Another set of definitions suggests that marketing is a management process aimed at delivering customer satisfaction. Examples of this approach include the definitions offered by the Chartered Institute of Marketing in 1976 and the American Marketing Association (2007). These definitions introduce a crucial aspect of marketing management – planning, which is discussed in greater detail later in this textbook but is implicit in all of an organization's marketing activities.

Earlier definitions of marketing have been criticized on the grounds that the transactional focus is on generating first-time sales only. Relationship marketing evolved as a response to that criticism and has become more widely appreciated as academics and practitioners recognize the lifetime value of a customer can be high, even if the value of each transaction is relatively low. Relationship marketing is the development of mutually beneficial long-term relationships between suppliers and customers. In hospitality markets, a 'relationship marketing' approach has seen the major hotel groups focus their marketing activities on frequent travellers in an attempt at encouraging repeated and recommended business.

A definition proposed by the Chartered Institute of Marketing in a 2007 discussion paper called 'Shape the Agenda', presents a wordy and more complex definition whilst retaining the core idea that marketing is a strategic business function with a focus on managing customer demand.

Marketing insight 1.1

Different Perspectives of Marketing (1976–2007)

'Marketing is the management process responsible for identifying, anticipating and satisfying customer requirements profitably'.

(Chartered Institute of Marketing, 1976)

'In services, every contact between customers and employees includes an element of marketing'.

(Carlzon, 1987)

Relationship marketing aims to 'identify and establish, maintain and enhance, and where necessary, terminate relationships with customers and other stakeholders, at a profit so that the objectives of all parties involved are met; and this is done by mutual exchange and fulfillment of promises'.

(Grönroos, 1994)

'Marketing's central purpose is demand management ... and marketers ... need to manage the level, timing and composition of demand'.

(Kotler, 1999)

(Continued)

'Marketing is the strategic business function that creates value by stimulating, facilitating and fulfilling customer demand. It does this by building brands, nurturing innovation, developing relationships, creating good customer service and communicating benefits. With a customer-centric view, marketing brings a positive return on investment, satisfies shareholders and stakeholders from business and the community, and contributes to positive behavioral change and a sustainable business future'.

(Chartered Institute of Marketing, 2007)

'Marketing is the activity, set of institutions, and processes for creating, communicating, delivering, and exchanging offerings that have value for customers, clients, partners, and society at large'.

(American Marketing Association, 2007)

Creating memorable experiences

Another view of marketing proposes that satisfying customers is no longer enough in a competitive environment. Companies compete by 'creating memorable experiences' to 'wow' customers and generate positive word of mouth to build repeat and recommended business (Pine & Gilmore, 1999). Creating memorable experiences in hospitality is a combination of marketing planning, company culture and individual employees' spontaneous responses to customer requirements. Memorable moments provide long-lasting and remarkable experiences that demonstrate a genuine commitment to customers by the company and its employees. These moments can be trivial, like clearing light snowfall from the cars parked in the lot, or they can be linked to emotional events, like the special attention that should be given to honeymooners and couples celebrating romantic anniversaries. Creating memorable moments can be applicable in any hospitality sector, and at any price point and can happen at any time – but not all businesses can realistically strive to compete on this basis. Albrecht (1992) suggests that there are four product levels that companies can offer from the basic, expected, desirable to ultimately the unanticipated (see Fig. 1.1); but only the fourth level – the unanticipated – is where companies are competing strategically to deliver memorable experiences.

1 At the basic level, a company provides essential core attributes (e.g. a clean bed) that customers need. If this basic level is not provided, customers will not buy the product – if the bed is not clean, customers will not be satisfied and might check out of the hotel. A hospitality firm that only offers a basic level of value is not competitive and is unlikely to generate significant repeat and recommended business.

2 At the expected level, a company provides attributes that customers expect and take for granted – for example, efficient check in, a clean bed and availability of a bar/restaurant might be examples

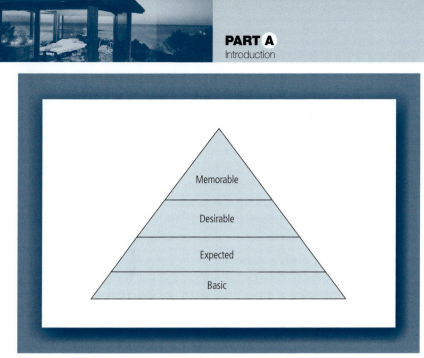

Figure 1.1 The hierarchy of customer value *Adapted from Albrecht (1992)*

of the attributes expected from a mid-scale hotel. A hospitality company providing attributes at the expected level is only providing an average standard service; there is nothing better about the service offer compared with the competition. Customers may only be moderately satisfied, and there is no incentive to return or recommend this company.

3 At the desirable level, a company provides attributes that customers know of but do not generally expect. The friendliness of the staff, the quality of the food and the efficiency of the service are examples of attributes that customers know but do not always expect. Companies providing the desirable offer are competing more effectively than most of their competitors.

4 At the memorable level, hospitality operators offer customers memorable experiences that demonstrate outstanding service quality. Companies aiming to deliver memorable experiences can leverage a significant competitive advantage over their competitors. Fairmount Hotels are a collection of luxury properties that strives to deliver 'authentic local experiences and warm, memorable service' (www.fairmount.com); whilst Jonathan Raggett of Red Carnation Hotels encourages his employees to deliver *TNT – Tiny Noticeable Touches*.

The marketing concept

To summarize the various approaches and definitions of marketing, we present the following core principles

1 Marketing is the business philosophy that places the customer at the center of a hospitality organization's purpose. Increasingly,

hospitality companies recognize that developing long-term relationships with customers is mutually beneficial.

2 There is an exchange activity between hospitality organizations and their customers, which should be mutually rewarding.

3 The central purpose of marketing is to manage demand.

4 Marketing is a management process that focuses on planning for the future success of the organization.

5 There are a set of marketing tools, which marketers use in understanding customers' needs and wants and in developing appropriate products, and services to satisfy or delight customers.

Companies that place a customer at the center of their thinking are said to have adopted the marketing concept. A key feature of marketing orientated companies is that they have an external focus and are constantly researching their customer needs and wants, their competitors and the environment in which they operate.

Managing demand

All the different definitions can seem quite confusing, particularly when many people who work in marketing are actually involved in increasing sales using many different forms of promotional activities such as online and offline advertising, sales promotion and publicity. Most hospitality marketers are employees in sales, sales promotion, print and publicity, direct mail, advertising, public relations, customer relations, marketing research, and online sales and marketing roles such as guest user interface (GUI) management, web product development, website sales, search engine optimization, database management, daily web operations and content management.

So how can we bridge the gap between the various philosophies and definitions of marketing and the roles that marketers occupy?

The key concept that underpins marketing theory and practice is *the management of demand*. After a lifetime devoted to developing marketing theory and promoting the benefits of marketing, Kotler (1999) stated that 'marketing's central purpose is demand management' and marketers need 'to manage the level, timing and the composition of demand'. This definition of marketing seems to explain most accurately what marketers do and why they do it.

What is a market?

Originally, a market was a meeting place, where people could buy and sell produce and, of course, this type of market still exists today. In modern societies, a 'market' is much more complex, but still reflects the core principle of bringing together buyers and sellers with common interests. This modern concept of the market is based on groups of people who have similar needs and wants (actual and potential consumers or customers), and companies that aim to satisfy those needs and wants better than their competitors (an industry). *Needs* can range from the basic requirements for survival – food, shelter, safety – to much more complex social needs, such as belonging and recognition.

Wants are how different people choose to satisfy their needs; wants are shaped by culture and personality. People with similar needs, for example, the need to travel for a family event and stay overnight, can have different wants – some will want to stay with relatives while others want to have the independence of their own hotel accommodation. Obviously, a major limitation on how people can satisfy their wants is the amount they can afford to pay.

Consumers have to make buying choices based on their own resources or buying power. Consumers will often buy the best bundle of benefits provided by a product for the price that can be afforded. The aggregated purchase decisions of *all* the individuals buying a product (or service) are described as *market demand*. Market demand is normally measured using two criteria:

1 The number of units sold, which is a reflection of the number of people buying the product or service; this is called the volume
2 How much people have paid for the product; this is called the value.

Individuals can choose different ways to satisfy similar needs. Not everyone wants the same bundle of benefits and this creates sub-markets, or market segments, within the overall market. In hospitality markets, luxury, mid-market and budget market segments represent different bundles of benefits sought by different groups of customers. Over a period of time, the volume and the value of market segments can increase or decrease depending on a wide range of factors.

Market supply can also be measured and this is called the *industry capacity*. In the hotel market, the number of hotels and bedrooms in an area is called the *market capacity*. If the number of hotels and bedrooms is increasing, because new hotels or bedroom extensions have been built, then the market capacity increases. In the hospitality industry, market supply is often categorized under the same headings as market demand segments; thus, the luxury, mid-market and budget classifications are also used to describe the different types of operations serving those market segments. Other ways of categorizing hospitality market supply include

- Tourist board, motoring or other organization ratings for hotels and restaurants (e.g. star rating classification)
- Purpose of travel (leisure or business)
- Niche markets (e.g. youth action adventure holidays, conferences or gourmet food).

The level of market demand and the amount of industry capacity are the crucial factors underpinning the profitability of hospitality firms:

- When market demand is consistently high and industry capacity is low, the hospitality business should be operating at high capacity and be profitable.
- When market demand falls (e.g. in a recession) and industry capacity is high, the hospitality business will be operating in a highly competitive environment and sales and profitability will normally fall.

Categories of demand

We have suggested that one way to think about marketing is to view it as the art and science of managing customer demand. Because demand states vary, so does the task of marketing. Table 1.1 provides a list of eight categories of demand and the marketing response. When demand states 1–4 occur, actual demand is lower than the desired level of demand and the hospitality marketer is primarily interested in facilitating and stimulating more demand. Negative demand exists when consumers dislike a product – for example, an unpopular food or drink product. The marketing response is to encourage demand by educating consumers about the positive features of, or benefits from, the product. You can often witness free tastings of food and drink products in supermarkets and wine shops, which enable potential customers to see, taste and buy the product.

When there is no demand, the marketing task is to create demand. Raising awareness by advertising and public relations activity to demonstrate a product's positive attributes may help to educate consumers and encourage them to try the product.

Table 1.1 Demand management		
	Category of demand	Marketing task
1	Negative demand	Encourage demand
2	No demand	Create demand
3	Latent demand	Develop demand
4	Falling demand	Revitalize demand
5	Irregular demand	Synchronize demand
6	Full demand	Maintain demand
7	Overfull demand	Reduce demand
8	Unwholesome demand	Destroy demand

Source: Kotler P. Marketing Management, 11th ed., 2003, p. 6.

Latent demand means that demand would exist if there were a suitable product/service. The development of domestic short breaks as a hotel product was originally based on consumers' increasing affluence and available leisure time.

When demand is falling, the task is to revitalize demand. This situation can occur when a product/service is beginning to lose its appeal. Marketers need to research the reasons why the product no longer meets consumers' needs, reformulate the offer and re-launch it to stimulate consumer interest and revitalize demand.

Irregular demand is widespread in hospitality; it takes the form of seasonal demand. In these situations, companies strive to develop marketing strategies to synchronize demand over the high and low seasons, often using price-led promotions.

Full demand occurs when actual demand matches the desired demand; here, the marketing task is to maintain current demand. In hospitality markets, full demand rarely occurs, since competitors are likely to enter attractive markets and disturb the equilibrium.

If there is too much (or overfull) demand, the service operation will not be able to cope and there is likely to be considerable customer dissatisfaction. The hospitality marketer will aim to reduce demand either by increasing prices or by managing the booking/queuing process to prevent overfull demand. A long-term solution to overfull demand is to increase capacity by building more bedrooms or extending the seating area in a restaurant, but managers need to be confident that overfull demand will be sustained.

Unwholesome demand can occur when illegal activities such as drug taking, unlawful gambling or prostitution are taking place on the hospitality premises. Management clearly has a legal and ethical duty to try and inhibit or destroy unwholesome demand; however, this can be a difficult situation when customers are willingly involved.

Market demand in hospitality

Market demand in hospitality falls into four broad categories:

1 Business travel demand includes all those journeys business people make to meet customers and suppliers, and attend conferences, exhibitions and seminars. Business travel does not include the daily journeys people make when commuting to and from work.
2 Leisure travel demand includes journeys which people make away from home for amusement, entertainment or relaxation – for example, holidays, weekend breaks or same-day visits. A major component of leisure travel is visiting friends and relatives and this is described using the acronym 'VFR'.
3 Domestic travel demand includes all the travel generated within a country by people living in that country – so, for example, the

Table 1.2 Categories of demand in hospitality

Purpose of Travel	Domestic	International
Business	Domestic business demand	International business demand
Leisure	Domestic leisure demand	International leisure demand

domestic demand for business travel in Australia is all business journeys taken in Australia by people living in Australia.

4 International travel demand includes all the journeys generated to a country from people living in other countries. France is one of the most popular tourist destinations and attracts international visitors from all over the world.

Some types of travel do not fit easily into these broad categories. People often combine business and holidays in the same trip. However, these are convenient descriptions that tourist and hospitality organizations use. Table 1.2 summarizes these descriptors of market demand in hospitality.

MANAGEMENT ORIENTATIONS

Five different management philosophies have been identified in free market economies (see Fig. 1.2). Some of these 'orientations' have been linked to specific economic conditions and to certain periods in economic history. Hospitality organizations, like other businesses, could adopt any one of the following orientations, regardless of the economic circumstances.

Product or service orientation

The product or service orientation is not linked to any specific economic era or to specific market conditions. Companies adopting a product orientation believe that their customers can *only* be satisfied with a particular type of product or service and that the basis of corporate success is product or service excellence. Management concentrates on developing better versions of the *existing* product, but fails to recognize that customers could be satisfied better by different *types* of products. For example, hospitality companies with a product orientation include the famous restaurants with celebrity chefs, who serve what they think customers should want regardless of what the customers actually want! Chefs like this lose touch with customer preferences and become obsessed with their product.

Theodore Levitt's (1960) famous article 'Marketing myopia' warned companies that a product orientation could lead to failure.

Starting point	Focus	Means	End
Product or service orientation			
Existing hospitality product/service	Maintain and improve existing product concept	Minor improvements and adaptations of existing marketing mix	Profit dependent upon stable market conditions
Production orientation			
Innovative, strong, hospitality products	Satisfying high demand	New technology generating mass production at low prices	Profit through mass sales
Selling orientation			
Existing hospitality product/service	Existing and new facilities	Aggressive selling and promotional tactics	Profit through sales volume
Marketing orientation			
Business and leisure markets	Business and leisure customer needs and wants	Integrated marketing (including marketing research)	Profit through customer satisfaction
Societal-marketing orientation			
Business and leisure markets AND the needs and wants of the community and environment	Socially concerned hospitality business activities	Integrated marketing which takes into account the needs and wants of consumers and society	Profit through enhanced image and customer satisfaction

Figure 1.2 Marketing orientations *Adapted from Kotler, Bowen, & Makens, 2003*

The product management focus is inward looking. Although a company can prosper with a product orientation, changes in consumer tastes and fashion can quickly undermine a product-oriented company.

Operations or production orientation

Originally developed by Henry Ford, a production orientation is appropriate when there is a rising demand for strong, innovative products. If demand exceeds supply, management concentrates on generating volume to satisfy the growing demand. Improved technologies generate economies of scale, which allows management to reduce prices further and grow the market.

The production orientation is based on conditions of mass production and limited consumer choice. This leads to an inward-looking focus as management strives to control costs, to improve quality and efficiency and to increase volume. Critically, from a marketing concept perspective, the needs and wants of customers can be forgotten in the interests of organizational efficiency. Providing customers are satisfied with the low-cost, mass-produced product, then a production orientation is appropriate.

There are many examples of product innovation generating strong demand in the fast-food industry. When American fast-food operations entered the major cities of countries such as China and Russia, they generated high demand for what was considered an innovative foreign food product. This meant that McDonald's adopted a production orientation. McDonald's management's main focus was on achieving operational efficiency by improving their food supply chain and training staff to service the high demand. Airline, contract and welfare food service operations also have a production focus because of the mass markets they serve, with varying degrees of success.

There are also examples of hospitality organizations using a production orientation ineffectively. Sometimes, the standard operations manuals in the large hotel corporations that detail rules and procedures for every aspect of the hotel operation can stifle intuitive employee responses to customer care. This bureaucratic approach inhibits innovation, making hospitality managers focus on the systems and paperwork instead of on customers. Smaller companies can also neglect customers by adopting an operations focus. Simplifying the production process for operational convenience can lead to limited customer choice – for example, small sandwich shops can easily limit the choice of fillings to reduce waste and thereby lose customers by not offering sufficient choice.

Selling orientation

Companies adopt the selling orientation when their products are competing in markets, where supply exceeds demand and growth is low or declining. A critical issue for management is surplus capacity combined with a high fixed capital investment in buildings and plant. This combination can force management to focus on high sales volume and aggressive sales generation to strive to make a decent return on investment. Despite this apparent external focus on sales generation, the management is still essentially inward looking, since it is concentrating on selling the existing product to potential customers and is not focusing on identifying and then satisfying customer needs and wants.

Companies with a selling orientation tend to accept every possible sale or booking, regardless of its suitability for the business or other customers. By mixing incompatible customer segments, hospitality companies can fail to deliver customer satisfaction, which is ultimately self-defeating. Long-term, profitable relationships with

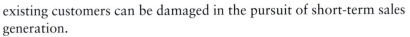

existing customers can be damaged in the pursuit of short-term sales generation.

A sales orientation is endemic in the hospitality industry, as many marketing programs are really only sales promotions aimed at filling bedrooms, bars and restaurants – regardless of customers' needs and wants.

Although selling is a vital element of hospitality marketing, sales strategies should be integrated into the marketing plan and should be consistent with a marketing orientation.

Marketing orientation

Marketing-oriented businesses have adopted the marketing concept and put customer focus at the heart of the business. It is an alternative to the selling orientation and designed to cope with similar economic conditions (i.e. surplus capacity leading to a fiercely competitive environment). Companies adopting the marketing orientation recognize that customers have considerable choice. Marketing-oriented businesses accept that to maintain long-term profitability they need to understand and serve customers better than their competitors.

Marketing-oriented businesses carry out marketing research and develop an integrated approach to marketing, ensuring that all marketing activities are coordinated and contribute to deliver customer satisfaction. A marketing orientation is an outward-looking management philosophy, which responds to changes in the business environment and considers the business from a customer perspective. As customers' needs and wants change, so the business adapts accordingly.

The advantage of a marketing orientation is that the business focus is on developing long-term relationships with customers, based on an intimate understanding of their needs and wants and the market-satisfying capabilities of competitors. The adoption of a marketing orientation suggests that companies are seeking long-term profits, as opposed to increasing profits in the short term at the expense of long-term customer satisfaction.

At its most advanced level, a marketing orientation becomes focused on the satisfaction of individual customers, whether organizations or people. Companies that tailor their offer to meet the needs of individual customers are said to be practicing one-to-one marketing. In hospitality, databases containing customer-related data such as guest history, demographics, contact details and preferences increasingly enable hotel companies to personalize services and communications to satisfy individual customers. This one-to-one style of marketing is predicted to become more important in the future.

> **Activity 1.2**
>
> Compare the sustainability credentials of Hilton Hotels on their 'about us' webpage and the Kandalama Eco Hotel:
>
> Hilton Hotels at www.hiltonworldwide.com.
>
> Kandalama Eco Hotel at www.heritancehotels.com.
>
> List the sustainability policies of each company and identify any similarities and differences.

Societal marketing orientation

In the 1980s, the marketing orientation was criticized for its narrow focus on customers and its lack of concern for environmental and social issues. The original marketing orientation ignored the potential conflict between consumers' wants and society's needs. The societal marketing orientation was a response to these criticisms and recognizes that commercial organizations have a wider responsibility than simply looking after customers. A societal marketing orientation suggests that companies should become proactive in the community, adopting a 'good neighbor' policy, and being attentive to environmental and cultural considerations, whilst running a sustainable business.

More recently, consumers concern for environmental issues such as animal welfare, climate change and ethical food production has generated considerable interest in companies' sustainable business practices. The leading hospitality corporations have adopted a range of policies to reduce their carbon footprint and enhance their societal credentials as good 'corporate citizens'. Due to their size and scale, there are inherent difficulties for global players to adopt a coherent sustainable strategy, but smaller hospitality organizations founded by eco-minded entrepreneurs are more able to operate on a sustainable basis.

A number of hospitality organizations have genuinely adopted a societal marketing approach. One example is Prêt à Manger (see Case study 1.1). Other organizations claim to adopt a societal marketing approach, but are really only putting a spin on the corporate behaviours that are designed to gain positive publicity. The distinction between a genuine societal marketing approach and a superficial approach lies in the core values of the organization. If the entire organizational culture is clearly committed to a sustainable business model and demonstrates this in all its activities, then it has adopted a societal marketing approach.

A company's orientation may be formally adopted in a written planning statement, informally agreed by the management team or simply implied in the way the business is run. Many hospitality

Case study 1.1 Prêt à Manger

Prêt à Manger, a sandwich shop founded in 1986 by Julian Metcalfe and Sinclair Beecham in south London, is now a major brand in the United Kingdom with over 200 units. There are also approximately 25 units in the United States, primarily in New York and eight units in Hong Kong. The company's success is rooted in the values of its owners who are 'passionate about food'. Prêt's mission statement explains their business proposition: 'to create handmade, natural food, avoiding the obscure chemicals, additives and preservatives common to so much of the 'prepared' and 'fast' food on the market today'. The mission, website and packaging materials consistently promote examples of their suppliers, who are named along with details of their free-range farms and organic husbandry, and staff who work in interesting jobs ensuring the natural quality of the produce. All sandwiches are freshly made on each shop premises, and unsold sandwiches are offered free to the homeless – in 2010, Prêt gave away 1.7 million products to homeless charities in the United Kingdom.

Prêt's human resource management practices are better than most in their sector, including competitive pay and very good promotion prospects. Prêt has ambitious sustainability targets to reduce the business's impact on the environment and is proactive in charity support for homeless people. In 2001, McDonald's purchased a stake in the business, which helped Prêt to become more successful in the United States. The McDonald's stake was subsequently sold to a private equity firm in 2008 and Prêt remains privately owned. This helps the management team to retain their unique approach to marketing. Prêt's management orientation is clearly based on a societal marketing approach and continued expansion in the United Kingdom, the United States and Hong Kong suggests that its mission works.

Source: Prêt à Manger – look at Prêt's website for more details: www.pret.com

companies may not even be aware of their business orientation. Clearly recognizing which orientation a company is using will enable managers to better understand their operation. Opinions differ on whether a specific orientation is appropriate for any given economic situation. Some experts maintain that a marketing orientation is the only appropriate orientation, whilst others suggest that the economic situation should determine which orientation to adopt. Companies can adopt different orientations at different stages of their growth, whilst global companies can adopt different orientations depending on which country they are operating in.

ENVIRONMENTAL INFLUENCES ON HOSPITALITY ORGANIZATIONS

Since marketing is an outward-looking business philosophy, marketers in hospitality companies need to understand and adapt to changes in the business environment. Both macro- and micro-environmental factors influence the practice of marketing in a hospitality business.

The macro-environment

The macro-environment of a business includes all the political, economic, socio-cultural, technological and environmental (PESTE) forces that impact on its customers and operations; therefore, it is known as the PESTE environment. Hospitality companies have limited, if any, control over PESTE influences; but major changes in even one PESTE factor can significantly impact on the business, either for better or worse. PESTE factors are constantly changing. These changes affect consumers, drive market demand and influence the competitive environment. Figure 1.3 provides an overview of the environmental influences on hospitality organizations.

Political

The political direction of a country determines how consumers and commercial organizations can act. The political philosophy of government can either stimulate or stifle economic, social and technological development. Although Western nations generally foster an open economy, encouraging tourism and creating a positive climate for hospitality businesses, some countries – for example Zimbabwe – restrict international access and inhibit the development of tourism and hospitality businesses. Political and governmental decisions are constantly changing the environment in which we live and work, and impact on hospitality marketing activity in a variety of ways.

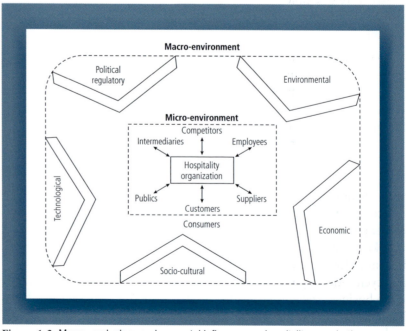

Figure 1.3 Macro- and micro-environmental influences on hospitality organizations

For Europeans, the political environment includes the European Union as well as their own national and local governments. Decisions about the Single European Market and the Euro currency are examples of European political regulation.

The political environment includes the legal/regulatory environment, which covers any legislation that influences the marketplace. Examples include the following:

- Planning regulations (permission for building hotel, restaurant and leisure extensions or developing new properties), which alter the industry capacity,
- Licensing laws, which regulate the opening times of licensed premises,
- Local, regional or national government taxes that impact on prices (Value Added Tax and General Sales Tax rates and excise duty on alcoholic drinks) and, therefore, influence the demand for hospitality products,
- Regulation of marketing communications. Different countries have a variety of nation-specific regulations for advertising, direct mail and the use of databases for marketing purposes.

Economic

The economic environment includes all those activities that influence the wealth and income of the population. Examples of economic influences are

- State of the economy
- Structure of employment and the level of unemployment
- Rate of inflation
- Exchange rate.

These factors combine to influence business confidence, consumers' disposable income and consumer confidence, which play a significant role in changing demand for hospitality services. When business and consumer confidence is high, hospitality markets thrive; when business and consumer confidence is low, hospitality markets decline and firms are prone to failure. The global financial crisis that began in 2009 had a significant influence on the hospitality industry. Upscale hotels struggled to maintain occupancy levels as corporate clients cut costs, including travel budgets. Paradoxically, some economy food service operations reported improved sales as customers traded down to cheaper dining-out and take-away food service options.

A key economic factor is the business cycle, which influences demand. Hospitality firms need to respond to the stages in the business cycle. Although hospitality businesses all trade at the same stage of the business cycle, firms will respond differently according to their financial and marketing strengths, and their leadership. The stages of the hospitality business cycle (see Fig. 1.4) are as follows.

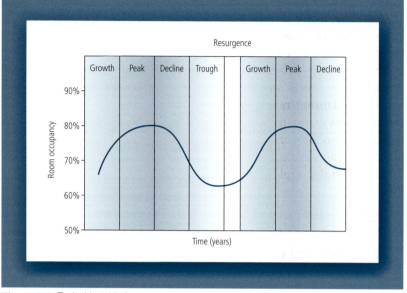

Figure 1.4 Typical hotel industry cycle

- *Growth*: Occupancy and room rates increase in response to grow-ing demand, there is a strong positive cash flow (which means that capital is available for further investment), property values increase and hoteliers have high business confidence.
- *Peak*: Occupancy and room rates remain strong, and funds are still available for investment; however, growth tends to slow.
- *Decline*: Occupancy begins to decrease. If the decrease is gradual, room rates are increased in line with inflation. Investors sense the higher risk in declining occupancy and seek increased returns before agreeing to invest in hotel businesses, property values begin to fall, the rate of decline becomes more rapid as occupancy falls, price competition becomes more intense and achieved room rates fall and the rate of decline can become faster as the industry moves toward recession.
- *Trough*: There is a large imbalance of supply and demand during a recession; low occupancy, low room rates and a slump in property values means that highly geared (over-borrowed) companies are put into receivership. There is a bottoming out period as demand gradually stabilizes and then slowly begins to increase.
- *Resurgence*: There is a gradual resurgence, and the cycle starts all over again.

A major recurring problem for the hospitality industry is that hotel development projects are funded in the growth and peak stages of the business cycle but, because of the time lag between gaining invest-ment funds and planning permission, many hotels open for busi-ness just as the cycle peaks. Hence, additional new build capacity is added to the stock just as demand falls, creating further problems for the industry. Capacity does not really diminish during periods of declining and low demand. From a hospitality marketing perspective, companies' response to the business cycle during a downturn period and a recession is problematic. Companies engage in major cost-cutting activities; marketing employees and expenditure are often significantly reduced; and financially weaker brands are vulnerable to takeover. During resurgent and growth periods, marketing activity increases as companies respond to the growth in hospitality demand. Although nobody can accurately predict the precise timing of a stage in the business cycle, it is vital for hospitality managers and owners to understand the implications of each stage.

Socio-cultural

The socio-cultural environment influences consumers' purchase and consumption behaviour. A country's socio-cultural environment is a complex product of its geography, climate, history, religion and ethnic make-up. We are influenced by the values of our own culture, even though we are not aware of this all the time. Indeed, cultural differences between countries provide hospitality marketers with some of the greatest challenges when developing global brands.

One of the key aspects of a country's hospitality industry, which is heavily influenced by national culture, is eating and drinking habits. Each country and region has developed its own cuisine based on factors, such as the climate, which dictates the produce available. The growth of international travel for business and leisure purposes has widened people's cultural knowledge and encouraged the development of new food and beverage concepts.

Demographic changes (changes in the make-up of a population) also make a significant impact on market demand in hospitality. Examples include the following:

- The number of older people living in Western countries is growing, changing the demand characteristics for holidays
- The increase in the number of single people (caused by people marrying later and more people getting divorced) is changing the demand characteristics for eating out.

Hospitality marketers need to be aware of socio-cultural and demographic trends to ensure their companies adapt to changes in markets and remain competitive.

Technological

The technological environment in hospitality is closely associated with innovation and developments in information communications technology (ICT). ICT developments have a major influence on all industries. Improvements in the technological environment influencing the hospitality industry include the following:

- The development of inter-connected property management systems, computerized reservation systems, global distribution systems and networks (GDS), the Internet and mobile technologies to facilitate on-line booking
- The rapid adoption of the Internet and online environment by consumers searching and booking hospitality and travel products
- The development of in-hotel computerized systems that has reduced energy consumption and improved in-room comfort and security for guests.
- Improvements in kitchen equipment, which has enhanced food production techniques.

The current rate of technological change is super-fast, and new developments are constantly altering the technological environment.

Environmental

Environmental factors have become more important in all parts of the world as people recognize the impact tourists have on the planet. In particular, mass tourism has become much more controversial. Tourism stands accused of the following. It

- encourages new hotel and leisure developments,
- erodes natural habitats,
- threatens the integrity of indigenous cultures,
- uses up scarce resources,
- generates air, noise and carbon pollution, and
- creates waste disposal problems.

Although the concept of sustainable tourism is much publicized, and 'green' pressure groups lobby government and hospitality companies to improve the industry's environmental policies, the hotel and restaurant industry does not have a good reputation in this area, apart from a small number of environmentally aware companies.

Interaction of PESTE factors

Some factors in the macro-environment will affect all the PESTE variables, and each individual element of the PESTE can influence other elements. This means that analyzing the macro-environment can be confusing, since it is difficult to separate the impact of each influence. For example, demographic changes are forecast to become a major influence on economic, social and political factors later in the twenty-first century. National population changes affect a country's economy. Global and national changes in population affect socio-cultural

forces and influence the composition and character of travel markets. Countries react politically to migration pressures, and demographic changes can also stimulate the creation of pressure groups that lobby government on behalf of their interests. Thus, one driver of change influences several PESTE factors, and each of the PESTE factors interacts with the others.

The micro-environment

The micro-environment includes internal company factors (customers, employees, suppliers and intermediaries) and external factors (the direct competitors operating in the same locations and the various 'publics' with which a company interacts). Unlike the PESTE framework for the macro-environment, there is no recognized formula or mnemonic to describe the micro-environment. Hospitality companies have more influence over the micro-environment than over the macro-environment.

Customers

Hospitality companies typically target a broad mix of customers, including business and leisure hotel residents, non-resident diners and drinkers. Managing the customer mix to ensure that all the different types of customers are satisfied or delighted is one of the major challenges for marketing. Over time, customers can change their needs and wants, so companies have to monitor and respond to these changes.

Employees

For most hospitality organizations, the local labour market is a key resource. The availability and quality of skilled employees who have been educated and can be easily trained is an important factor in delivering a quality service. Because employees interact with customers, they have a major influence on the level of customer satisfaction.

Suppliers

The hospitality company's performance is dependent on its suppliers. Although marketers are not directly involved in operational purchase decisions, marketing should have an input in setting quality standards and specifications. The hospitality marketer will certainly be responsible for handling relationships with external marketing communication and marketing research agencies.

Intermediaries

Intermediaries, also called distributors, are those companies who advise, influence and make bookings for customers. They include both online and offline organizations like search engines, travel agents, tour operators, conference placement agencies and specialist online retailers. Intermediaries are important links in the distribution channel from the customer to the hospitality outlets. Marketing managers needed to cultivate good relationships with actual and potential intermediaries.

Competitors

The competitive environment includes different kinds of competitors:

- Direct competitors – these are businesses offering a similar product or service, which is aimed at the same customer group. Direct competitors operate in the same geographic location and in the same (or adjacent) product category. For hotels, a three-star provincial business hotel could have a local competitor set including all three-star hotels and possibly some two- and four-star hotels within a 10-mile radius or 15 min travel time. Watching, knowing and anticipating what your competitors are doing is vital for hospitality marketing success.
- Competitors offering substitute products – these are offers that potential consumers can choose instead of a hospitality product but satisfies the same need (e.g. staying at home and cooking a prepaid convenience meal instead of going out to a restaurant).
- Indirect competition – this includes all those companies and non-profit organizations that are competing for consumers' disposable income (e.g. choosing between buying a new car or going on an exotic holiday).

The competitive environment in many hospitality markets has become more intense in recent years. The actions and reactions of competitors have radically changed market structure, influenced consumer behaviour and altered market demand.

Publics

The location of a hospitality premises and the size/scale of the company will determine the character of the organizations (also called publics) with which the organization interacts. These publics will include

- Local government authorities (who enforce health and safety, hygiene and planning regulations)
- Businesses and people who live or work in the neighbourhood (some of whom may also be customers)

- Community, educational, religious, social and voluntary institutions
- Leisure, sporting and tourism attractions
- Local media.

Local publics can exert considerable influence on a hospitality business. Developing effective public relations and fostering good relationships with local publics is part of the marketing task.

SPECIAL CHARACTERISTICS OF SERVICES MARKETING

Services, such as those of hospitality organizations, possess a number of special characteristics that present challenges to marketing practitioners. These special characteristics are seasonality, intangibility, perishability, inseparability, variability, interdependence, supply exceeding demand and high fixed costs. You can use the mnemonic *SIPIVISH* to remember the characteristics.

Seasonality

Seasonality refers to the fluctuations and demand in any given period. In hospitality operations, seasonality can occur at

- Different seasons of the year
- Different months of the year
- Different times of the week and even
- Different times of the day.

The demand for business accommodation is highest during the middle of the week, outside the peak holiday periods of Easter, summer and Christmas/New Year. Country hotels can have a poor mid-week winter business but achieve high occupancies at the weekends, when city hotels can be quiet. Restaurants can be full with customers on a busy Saturday night and empty on a Monday evening. However, over time seasonality can change according to changing consumer trends. For example, many city hotels have seen busier weekends due to an increase in weekend conference demand and better marketing of city leisure breaks. Case study 1.2 illustrates a seasonal business.

The under- or over-utilization of capacity creates operational difficulties. Sudden unexpected increases in customers can lead to production problems, unacceptable waiting times and dissatisfied customers. The profitability of hospitality companies suffers during low season periods, hence, one of the challenging roles for marketing is to increase demand in low season periods and to deflect over demand from peak periods to other times.

Case study 1.2 Seasonality at The Eden Project, Cornwall, England

The Eden Project is a unique environmental visitor attraction. The iconic build began in Cornwall in 1998 in what had previously been an open cast mine for china clay. The attraction officially opened on March 2001 and provides three climatic zones – Temperate, Mediterranean and Tropical – referred to as Biomes. The latter two Biomes are maintained in a greenhouse setting. The tropical Biome is the largest display greenhouse in the world.

The Eden Project mission is to promote the understanding and responsible management of the vital relationship between plants, people and resources, leading to a sustainable future for all. Therefore, Eden aims to entertain and communicate important environmental messages, provide a memorable day out and inspire visitors. Apart from the natural plant domains, there are a wide range of activities all year round including art and music events and a summer program for families. The site and seasonal events attract over 1 million visitors annually.

The Eden Project is open every day of the year except the 24th and 25th December. Visitor numbers can range from 300 on a weekday in January to 14,500 on the busiest day in the summer. Visitor flow is predictable and driven by traditional holiday periods; approximately 70% of visitors visit between the Easter holidays and the October school half term. Although a sophisticated planning system accurately forecasts the number of visitors on a weekly basis, visitor flow through the week (day by day) is less predictable. During the peak summer period of the school holidays, many tourists take a week long break travelling from home to Cornwall and back at the weekends, resulting in busy days Monday to Thursday. However, due to the vagaries of the British weather, it is much more difficult to forecast daily visitor numbers more than a week in advance. If the weather is warm and sunny, holidaymakers will stay at the beach; but if it rains, then they look for indoor attractions like the Eden Project. For example, on a sunny week in August, the forecast might be for an average of 6000 visitors per day between Monday and Thursday, but if there are days of heavy rain, then an extra 4000–6000 visitors will suddenly arrive at Eden on each of those rainy days. From a catering perspective, nearly all these extra visitors will combine a visit to the Biomes with the need to eat and drink.

The Eden Project provides several cafes and restaurants with the focus on fresh, local and tasty food. All the cafes and restaurants are Eden managed, and there are no franchised outlets. Menus cater for omnivore, vegetarian, vegan and gluten free consumers. Wherever possible, food is freshly prepared – for example, all the sandwiches are made fresh each day. In Jo's Café, customers can learn about the food they eat and its impact on their own health as well as the environment. Organic and fair trade products are sourced wherever possible and more than 80% of catering produce is sourced from local suppliers. There are four priorities when sourcing food products – quality, price, seasonality and Cornishness. Eden's interpretation of the 'triple bottom line' is to ensure that products are environmentally sound, socially acceptable and economically viable. Indeed, Eden spends around £10 million each year with approximately 2000 local suppliers.

So, how does the Eden Project team cope on these busy days? If there are more visitors than expected, then many of the catering and front-of-house employees will be helped by other employees who do not normally work in operations. The behind the scenes employees will receive an email asking for their assistance at short notice. Predictable busy days are classed as 'tricky days'. At the start of the season, each back-of-house employee has to select five tricky days out of a list of 30 potentially busy days, stating when they will be available to support their front-of-house colleagues. Additionally, because of the proximity and strong relationship of their local suppliers, if Eden suddenly requires extra food produce, the suppliers will readily help out.

If the team has over-estimated visitor numbers, then any produce that cannot hygienically be used the next day is composted in a closed aerobic food compost system. Indeed, annually 64% of all waste across the site is recycled, of which 9% is food based. Of that 9% food waste, the vast majority is what is left on consumer plates or peelings from food preparation.

The Eden Project is another good example of a societal marketing approach with a strong focus on environmental and sustainable values. You can access their website at www.edenproject.com and also access case study videos on YouTube.

Source: The Eden Project

Intangibility

Almost everything that is marketed comprises a mix of tangible and intangible components. If you were to buy a car (which is clearly tangible), it comes with a service warranty (which is intangible). If you buy a take-away meal, the burger, bun and fries are tangible, but someone would have prepared the food and provided the counter service, which is intangible. Services are intangible-dominant products, that is, they are principally made up of intangible components. Since services are intangible dominant, it means that they cannot be experienced – they cannot be heard, seen, smelt, tasted or touched – prior to being consumed. Unlike shopping for a laptop computer or buying a motorcar, hospitality consumers cannot really examine competing hotel, restaurant or leisure services without entering into a purchase contract and experiencing the product. For example, they cannot stay overnight in a hotel and test out the rooms without being expected to pay first.

Marketing intangibles create difficulties for the service provider. Customers often sense a higher level of risk and also find it difficult to assess the quality of intangibles. Customers need to be provided with information to help them to choose an appropriate hospitality outlet to satisfy their particular needs and wants. The challenge for marketers is how to provide such information in a way that will encourage customers to choose *their* offer without raising customer expectations too high and then failing to deliver customer satisfaction. The role of marketing communications in the design of effective promotional material to generate appropriate bookings whilst managing customer expectations is crucial.

Perishability

Everyone working in hospitality knows that you cannot sell last night's bedroom tonight. Hotels and restaurants have a fixed number of rooms and seats available each day or night. Unlike manufactured products, which can be stored in warehouses, services cannot be stored; this feature of service industries is called 'perishability'. The difficulty for hospitality companies is how to manage their capacity (the inventory) with a fluctuating demand pattern.

Hospitality managers recognize that managing the inventory is a critical issue in optimizing customer satisfaction, sales and profitability. The key marketing principle is to ensure that the price at peak demand times is set to deliver the maximum return to the company, provided it is compatible with customer satisfaction. In low season periods, the aim is to generate additional sales by developing attractive promotions. Managing the booking process to ensure that the business achieves this balance is essential.

Inseparability

Hospitality services are consumed as they are produced – they are inseparable. The simultaneous production and consumption of services mean that hospitality employees are an important part of the hospitality product. When you check into a hotel, the receptionist produces that check-in service at the same time that you consume it. Customers have to be present to consume hospitality services and because they are present and sometime interact with other customers, they also become a part of the other customers' experiences. Customers can exert significant influence on another customer's experience of the hospitality product, either by enhancing or spoiling the experience for other customers. These factors mean that customer interaction with hospitality staff and other hospitality guests provides a variety of opportunities to influence customer satisfaction positively or negatively.

Ways to manage the problems of inseparability include the following.

* Ensuring that customer segments are compatible
* Ensuring that the operations system is suitable for the projected market demand
* Adopting appropriate booking policies
* Organizing effective queuing systems
* Training staff effectively.

Variability

Partly as a result of inseparability, hospitality operations suffer from considerable fluctuations in the standards of delivery of the service.

This is called variability. Variability is influenced by service inputs such as people, products and technologies. Services comprise a high element of interaction between customers and staff; indeed, every service performance can be described as a unique event. Human interaction cannot be standardized, and consequently it is impossible for service companies to deliver a totally non-variable experience. Inputs such as fresh produce vary in availability and quality making consistent food production a challenge. Furthermore, technologies sometimes malfunction.

The difficulties arising out of variability are considerable:

- Imagine that the same customers order the same meal that is cooked by the same chef and served by the same staff, in the same restaurant, at the same time of the week. The resulting meal experience can be very different from one week (possibly perfect) to the next (possibly disastrous)!
- Again, two different sets of customers could be served the same meal, at the same time, in the same restaurant and by the same staff, but because of their different knowledge, experience and feelings, they could have very different experiences.

Some customers may be highly knowledgeable about food and wine. These 'expert' customers, with their different understanding of service and quality, may be highly critical of the meal experience compared with less knowledgeable customers who may have really enjoyed the occasion. Companies respond to this problem of variability by trying to standardize their operations and training their staff to perform according to the company's standard operating procedures.

Interdependence

Tourists make a variety of travel purchase decisions in one trip, and their overall satisfaction with a visit is based on a complex set of evaluations of different elements, including the travel arrangements, accommodation, attractions and facilities of a destination. The choice of hospitality products is only one element on which the consumer needs to decide. Hotel accommodation sales in particular are influenced by the consumer's choice of other tourism products. Most significant is the tourist's choice of destination. Visitors may base their decision to travel to a particular destination on the range of attractions, the ease and accessibility of transport to and from the area, the image of the destination, the price and word of mouth recommendations made by family, friends and associates. This means that the generation of demand for some hospitality operations is directly connected to the demand for complementary tourism products – so this type of demand is interdependent.

The response to interdependency is that individual businesses, regardless of the tourism sector they operate in, their size or ownership have to cooperate in the promotion of their destination. Destination marketing organizations work closely together with local government and tourism authorities to promote demand for tourism in their own particular area.

Supply exceeds demand

The hospitality industry is frequently described as a fragmented industry with low barriers to entry. It is relatively easy to obtain finance and buy or build a hospitality company. Indeed, many of today's great brands (Hilton, Marriott and McDonald's) were originally small companies developed by visionary entrepreneurs.

Although regulations vary in different countries, governments have generally welcomed the development of tourism. The last 10 years have witnessed a dynamic building period, with massive investment in new resorts, hotels, restaurants, cruise ships, leisure facilities and casino operations culminating in excess capacity in most sectors of the industry and in many parts of the world. In good economic times, record numbers of people travel for business and leisure purposes, but the growth in hospitality capacity has not always been matched by a sufficient growth in demand. When supply exceeds demand, the competitive environment becomes more intense and price competition can affect all firms' profitability.

High fixed costs

The cost structure of hospitality firms influences marketing activity. Hospitality businesses are capital, labour and energy intensive. Typical hospitality firms have high property costs and also employ large numbers of staff, many of who are full-time, permanent employees. These costs do not change; they are 'fixed' regardless of the number of customers using the premises. During periods of low demand, high fixed costs erode the profitability of the business. Companies need to generate sales to help make a contribution towards the fixed costs. The marketing response to seasonality and high fixed costs is to design new offerings and attractively priced promotions to stimulate sales in the low season.

THE ROLE OF MARKETING MANAGEMENT IN HOSPITALITY

The marketing manager's tasks range across research, planning, implementation and control of all activities that impact on customer experience, including:

1 Research and analysis in the needs and wants of current customers and selected target markets, changes in the PESTE environment, the actions of competitors.

2 Planning and budgeting marketing strategies to achieve agreed marketing objectives that may include sales revenues, profits, occupancy, revenue per available room (RevPAR), bar and food spend, new customer acquisition, customer retention and market share.

3 Implementing marketing strategies by designing, developing and rolling out new product concepts, setting brand standards, designing and executing online and integrated marketing communication campaigns. Many of these activities are accomplished through the marketing mix (see below).

4 Monitoring and control of marketing strategies by ensuring that marketing objectives are being achieved during a campaign; ensuring that marketing activities are carried out within the agreed budget; understanding the reasons why there are any variances between targeted performance and actual performance, and commissioning marketing research to evaluate marketing performance.

5 Influencing other departments to become more focused on the customer, including influencing operations departments to make or buy what customers want to experience, and human resources departments to recruit the right type of people for customer-contact positions.

Some of these marketing activities will be carried out in-house by the company's own marketing personnel; other activities will be delegated to specialist marketing and publicity agencies.

The hospitality marketing mix

The term *marketing mix* is used to describe the tools that the marketer uses to influence demand. The marketing mix is a core concept in marketing. The hospitality marketing mix adopted in this text is based on the eight marketing activities shown in Fig. 1.5.

Product/service offer

Hospitality products and services are primarily designed to satisfy the needs and wants of business and leisure travellers. Examples include the following:

- Accommodation – a bed, bedroom, cabin or suite, in a hotel, inn, chalet, apartment, timeshare, cruise ship, hospital;
- Food and beverage – a drink, sandwich, fast food, family meal, gourmet dinner, in a café, cafeteria, restaurant, bar, aeroplane, motorway service station or ship, at an attraction or leisure center;
- Business services – a meeting, conference, communication bureau in a hotel or conference center;

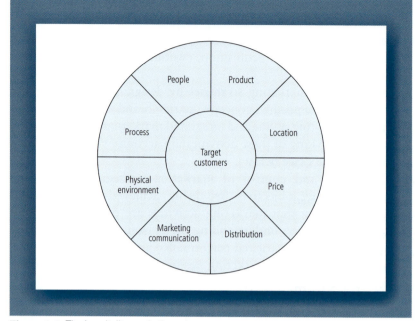

Figure 1.5 The hospitality marketing mix

- Leisure – a short break, domestic holiday or international holiday, in a hotel, resort, self-catering accommodation, camping and cara-van site or a cruise.

Marketing, working with operations, should play a role in devel-oping the product and service offers to ensure that the needs of customers are the focus of product development.

Location

Finding a suitable location to offer the chosen service is absolutely critical for a hospitality organization. Location decisions focus on where the hospitality business should build, buy, franchise or rent the site(s) from which it operates.

Price

The pricing decisions a hospitality organization makes include the following:

- Setting the tariff, rack rates and best available online rate
- Agreeing the level of discounts for key accounts
- Pricing all-inclusive packages (conferences, functions and leisure breaks)
- Developing special priced promotions to increase sales during low season periods.

Pricing decisions influence demand, which are crucial in driving profitability, and play an important role in presenting the 'image' the hospitality firms wants to project to customers and stakeholders.

Distribution

Distribution in hospitality is concerned with how a company can make it timely and convenient for a potential customer to book hospitality products directly from the hospitality company or through intermediaries. The impact of ICT and the online environment has radically transformed hospitality distribution channels and will continue to change relationships between hospitality providers and travel agents, tour operators, conference placement houses and incentive houses.

Marketing communications

Marketing communication covers all the tools that hospitality firms can use to communicate with customers, employees and other stakeholders. It is also known as promotion and is popularly described as 'marcom'. Communication is a core activity of most marketing and sales departments. The key elements of marketing communications in hospitality are

- Brand/corporate identity
- Online marketing (website design; search engine marketing; affiliate marketing and advertising)
- Personal selling (the sales team)
- Print and publicity material (e.g. brochures)
- Advertising
- Direct marketing
- Sales promotion
- Publicity
- Merchandising
- Sponsorship.

Physical environment

The physical environment (or physical evidence) consists of the tangible features of the hospitality offer – the external appearance of the premises (the landscaping, lighting and signage) and the internal layout (decor, furniture and furnishings). The physical environment can influence what customers believe and feel about the service, and how they behave. The ambience or atmosphere of a property is significantly influenced by conditions in its physical environment. The physical environment also impact on service operations staff.

Process

Because of the simultaneous production and consumption prevalent in hospitality services, the processes through which customers buy and consume hospitality products are of critical importance to marketers. Important processes include booking, checking in and checking out, queuing systems and service operations. Marketers need to ensure that the organization's service delivery processes are efficient, customer friendly and competitive.

People

In the services marketing mix, 'people' includes both employees and other customers. We have already discussed how hospitality customers interact with each other whilst on the premises – indeed, in certain hotel and holiday environments, a good rapport between customers is an essential ingredient of the successful product. Managing the customer mix and ensuring that target markets are compatible play a key role in delivering customer satisfaction. Hospitality is a service, where the interaction between customers and employees is also a critical element of the customer experience. Therefore, marketing needs to have an input into human resources aspects of the operation, and this is called *internal marketing*.

Hospitality brands and the integrated marketing mix

Brands are central to the marketing of multi-unit hospitality businesses. Hospitality companies develop branded concepts and then blend the elements of the marketing mix to provide target customers with a better brand offer than their competitors (see Case study 1.3). It is crucial that each element of the marketing mix is consistent with all the other elements. For example, a luxury hotel brand cannot be successfully located in a 'down market' area, and a cheap and cheerful restaurant cannot successfully promote gourmet dining. Those hospitality companies that do not provide a consistent marketing offer confuse customers by sending out mixed messages.

Thinking independently about each element of the marketing mix helps you to understand the complexity of the marketing offer. However, it should be remembered that customers form opinions based on their overall impression of the offer, and this can be influenced by 'minor items' such as the comfort of the pillow or the price of a drink, as well as by overarching considerations such as the general quality of service. If you reflect on all the different elements of the marketing mix, it becomes clear that marketers need to work closely with operations (on product, process and physical environment decisions), with finance (on pricing and marketing communication budget decisions) and with human resources (on staff recruitment and retention). In smaller, single-unit operations, where the owner/manager is close to the business and is responsible for all these decisions, the integration of marketing with other departments is easier. In large-scale, multi-unit national and international operations, such cooperation is much more difficult to achieve. Effective marketing is dependent on all the departments in a hospitality business working closely together.

Case study 1.3 Premier Inn – an integrated approach to marketing

In the 1980s, market demand for better-quality, low-cost accommodation in the United Kingdom grew significantly and Travelodge (the original developer of the concept) expanded rapidly. In 1987, Whitbread developed a competitor concept, called Travel Inn, which imitated the market leader in most aspects. By the late 1990s and despite intense competition from Accor, Days Inn, and Express by Holiday Inn, Travel Inn overtook Travelodge to become the market leader. In 2004, Travel Inn acquired Premier Lodge for over £500 million and increased the number of hotels by approximately 130 – the new brand was initially badged as Premier Travel Inn to reflect both brand names.

In 2007, the Premier Inn brand was created following extensive consumer and customer market research. A new brand identity was created, which retained the equity of the previous incarnation. A new strapline was developed: 'Everything's Premier But the Price' and the brand experience was refreshed through significant investment in the product offer and a multi-million pound advertising campaign:

- *Product* – low-cost, mid-market accommodation standards, with standardized bedrooms. Each room has en-suite bathrooms, king-size Hypnos beds (Hypnos also make beds for Queen Elizabeth 11), high-quality Fogarty duvets and pillows, flat screen digital TVs and Wi-Fi access. There are self-check-in kiosks at many sites to speed up arrivals and every site has a bar/restaurant serving an 'all you can eat' cooked breakfast, all day snacks and lunch/dinner menu.

- *Location* – there are over 590 sites in the United Kingdom and internationally there are sites in Dubai and in Bangalore, India. Premier Inn has developed a sophisticated approach to site selection using an in-house computer model with an extensive database of 1600 British cities and their catchment areas (see the case study, which discusses Premier Inn's location strategy in more detail in Chapter 6 Locating the offer). All sites are either located adjacent to Whitbread branded restaurants such as Beefeater, Table Table, Brewers Fayre, Taybarns and Thyme or on occasions, alongside franchise partners.

(Continued)

- *Price* – Premier Inn moved from a fixed price strategy to dynamic pricing to boost RevPAR.
- *Distribution* – Premier Inn operates a direct sales model using a computerized reservation system with links from its website and a telesales customer contact center. Premier Inn does not partner with third-party booking agents with the exception of one exclusive agreement.
- *Marketing communication* – the brand identity uses a strong, vibrant purple as the brand colour, which respondents in the focus groups suggested drove perceptions of high quality. There is considerable investment in point-of-sale material to promote offers in the reception, bedrooms and bar/restaurants. A TV, press and poster advertising campaign was launched in the spring of 2008 using a well-known and liked British comedian, Lenny Henry, as a celebrity endorsement. The ongoing campaign has helped to rapidly boost brand awareness, visits to the website, room occupancy and RevPAR.
- *Physical evidence* – the external signage was changed to incorporate the new brand identity, and on an ongoing basis, an extensive internal maintenance program is designed to keep product standards consistent. Each of the 43,000 rooms is refurbished every 3 years to maintain high levels of comfort and décor.
- *Process* – Premier Inn is a simple product with simple operating processes that prides itself on offering quality service levels in reception with outstanding levels of housekeeping. The food operation is predominantly managed by Whitbread branded restaurants either within or adjacent to the hotel.
- *People* – Premier Inn aims to recruit local, friendly staff who know the area; a key service performance metric is friendly service. The company has an 'Investors in People' UK government training award.

Investment in the Premier Inn brand has been rewarded by continued growth, increased brand awareness and many awards for marketing excellence. The aim is to increase the number of beds from 43,000 in 2010 to 55,000 in 2015. The well-established 100% money-back Good Night Guarantee, that promises comfortable surroundings, quality rooms and friendly staff was a first in the UK market, continues to be a key differentiator in the market place. Premier Inn's integration of all the elements of the marketing mix provides a consistent marketing offer, which is customer focused and financially successful.

Visit the Premier Inn website at www.premierinn.com.

Sources: Premier Inn.

The three marketing mixes

Because of the perishability and inseparability of hospitality products, marketers need to produce three marketing mixes, each aimed to influence demand at different times.

Before the customer comes to the property to experience the meal or the accommodation, the marketer is faced with identifying and influencing customer expectations and trying to generate a first-time purchase. The first marketing mix is therefore called the *pre-encounter marketing mix*, because it happens before the customer has the encounter with the service provider.

The second marketing mix occurs at the point of sale and consumption and is, therefore, called the *encounter marketing mix*. The task of this marketing mix is to produce a service encounter that meets or exceeds the customer's expectations, produces customer satisfaction and promotes positive word of mouth.

The third marketing mix is known as the *post-encounter marketing mix*, because it is designed to influence customers after the service experience, with a view to create a long-term relationship.

Different parts of the eight-element marketing mix are important at each stage – before, during and after the encounter. Before the encounter, marketing communications such as advertising, selling, pricing and brochures influence expectations. Marketers need to understand the product/service expectations of customers as they design offers for the customers. They must also make products easy to buy by establishing appropriate distribution channels.

During the encounter, customers come in contact with the people element of the marketing mix (employees and other customers), processes and physical evidence at locations where the service is produced and consumed.

After the encounter, hospitality marketers will want to communicate with customers to find out what they thought of the experience, to identify and satisfy customer complaints, and to encourage the customer to come back. Therefore, marketing communications are used to build future demand from existing customers. Table 1.3 summarizes what is important at each stage of the customer relationship with the firm.

Table 1.3 Marketing before, during and after the encounter			
	Pre-encounter marketing mix	Encounter marketing mix	Post-encounter marketing mix
Product/service offer	√	√	
Location	√	√	
Price	√	√	
Distribution	√		
Marketing communications	√	√	√
Physical environment	√	√	
Process	√	√	√
People		√	

The symbol '√' indicates which element is important in a particular marketing mix.

CONCLUSION

A popular misconception is that marketing is the same as selling and advertising. This chapter will have shown you that there is much more to marketing than promotion. Indeed, effective marketing encompasses virtually every aspect of the hospitality organization.

In this chapter, we have explained

- That marketing is a business philosophy that places the customer at the center of the hospitality organization;
- The essential purpose of marketing, which is to manage demand;
- How marketing-led companies seek to satisfy customers better than competitors;
- Why marketers need to scan the PESTE and micro-environment to understand future changes in the marketplace;
- The special characteristics of hospitality (SIPIVISH) and why marketers need to understand them;
- The hospitality marketing mix, which comprises eight factors that need to be integrated and consistent to ensure brand integrity;
- How marketers work to influence demand before, during and after the service encounter.

Activity 1.3

Look back to Activity 1.1

- Compare what you wrote about the meaning of 'marketing' with the definitions we have presented in this chapter. How different are the academic definitions to popular ideas about marketing?
- Reflect on what you think marketers do: have you changed your original ideas since reading his chapter?
- Can you now list more of the employment opportunities in marketing?

REVIEW QUESTIONS

Now check your understanding of this chapter by answering the following questions:

1 Identify three different definitions of marketing and explain the differences between them.
2 Discuss the advantages and disadvantages of each management orientation. Provide examples of each management orientation from your own experience of the hospitality industry (either as a customer or as an employee).
3 Discuss the external and internal factors that might influence a hospitality organization you know.

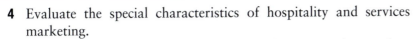
4 Evaluate the special characteristics of hospitality and services marketing.

5 Describe briefly the role of each element of the hospitality marketing mix.

References and Further Reading

Albrecht, K. (1992). *The only thing that matters*. Harper Business Books.

American Marketing Association. (October 2007). http://www.marketingpower.com/aboutama/pages/definitionofmarketing.aspx.

Brown, S. (2001). *Marketing: The retro revolution*. Sage.

Carlzon, J. (1987). *Moments of truth*. Ballinger Publishing.

Chartered Institute of Marketing (2007). *Shape the Agenda: Tomorrow's word, re-evaluating the role of marketing,* October 2007.

Grönroos, C. (1994). From marketing mix to relationship marketing: towards a paradigm shift in marketing. *Management Decision, 32,* 4–20.

http://www.fairmount.com.

Kotler, P. (1999). *Kotler on marketing*. Simon and Schuster.

Kotler, P. (2003). *Marketing management*. Prentice Hall.

Kotler, P., & Armstrong, G. (2010). *Principles of marketing*. Pearson Education.

Kotler, P., Bowen, J., & Makens, J. (2009). *Marketing for hospitality and tourism* (5th ed.). Prentice Hall.

Levitt, T. (1960). Marketing myopia. *Harvard Business Review*, *38*, 45–56.

Pine, J., & Gilmore, J. H. (1999). *The experience economy*. Harvard Business School Press.

PART B

Pre-encounter Marketing

CHAPTER

Marketing research

Chapter objectives

After going through this chapter, you should be able to:
- Explain the role marketing research plays in decision-making in the hospitality industry
- Identify sources of marketing information available to hospitality organizations
- Define secondary and primary data collection
- Explain the differences between qualitative and quantitative research methods
- Recognize how bias and sampling errors can distort marketing research findings
- Describe how hospitality organizations conduct online research.

②

INTRODUCTION

This chapter explains how marketing research provides the foundation for taking effective marketing decisions. We introduce the marketing information system as the starting point for marketing research activity and then review the wide range of internal and external information sources available for hospitality managers. Both secondary and primary data collection techniques, and qualitative and quantitative data, are discussed with relevant examples. Finally, we explain the marketing research process and how hospitality organizations can conduct research via the Internet.

You will probably be aware of marketing research activities in general terms. You may have been interviewed and carried out some primary research, and you will certainly know about surveys and opinion polls in the media. In fact, marketing research is a major industry that impacts on our everyday lives.

Activity 2.1

Before reading the rest of the chapter, try to think about the role of marketing research.

- Why do you think hospitality companies carry out research?
- What do you think are the main uses of research in the hospitality sector?
- List the marketing research activities you have heard about.

When you have completed the chapter, carry out this activity again and then compare your answers.

MARKETING RESEARCH

Managers are paid to make decisions. The purpose of marketing research is to inform and improve their decision-making by reducing uncertainty. Marketing research can be defined as the systematic gathering and analysis of data to provide relevant information to aid decision-making.

Marketing research is a planned process that follows a sequence of logical steps. Initially, the research objectives need to be agreed and the information sources are identified. Data are collected using a number of scientific methods, and then quantitative and qualitative data are analysed. The analysis is then evaluated and interpreted to provide useful information to aid decision-making. However, marketing research is not an exact science and cannot eliminate all risk in management decision-making.

You may have noticed that the term *marketing research* has been used – not market research. There is a difference.

- *Market research* is the term used to describe the investigation of consumer and organizational markets – the size and structure of a market, its consumption patterns and the demographic profile of consumers
- *Marketing research* has a much wider application including research into all the marketing mix variables and the macro (PESTE) and micro-environments.

Professional marketers use the term 'marketing research' to cover all aspects of research activity, including consumer and market behaviour.

International marketing research

The international dimensions of major hospitality companies mean they need to carry out research in various country markets. This presents unique problems because of the cultural and technological differences between countries (Usunier & Lee, 2009).

Issues include the following:

- Translation difficulties (e.g. it is usual for English-speaking researchers to compile questionnaires in English, have a native speaker to translate the questions to the local language and then have another English speaker to back-translate it to English; this process checks whether translation has changed the meaning of any questions)
- Variations in customer behaviour because of different cultural backgrounds
- Variations in customers' product knowledge
- Difficulties in obtaining comparable samples (some countries are unable to provide reliable lists of the population, such as electoral rolls)
- Different cultural responses to market research surveys (in some cultures, women are discouraged from participating in surveys or some types of question are regarded as intrusive)
- Differences in the infrastructure – some countries have poor postal systems, and not all consumers have access to mobiles, telephones and the Internet.

Companies carrying out international marketing research need to be aware of these difficulties and should employ specialist local research agencies to provide appropriate in-country advice. Case study 2.1 provides an example of global marketing research.

Case study 2.1 **Global marketing research at IHG**

In 2005, InterContinental Hotels Group (IHG) conducted, what is still, the largest and most comprehensive research project ever undertaken by an organization within the hospitality industry. IHG needed to review the strategic position and juxtaposition of its portfolio of brands to fit the needs of contemporary consumers. The company also recognised that its largest and most established brand, Holiday Inn, was in need of rejuvenation.

IHG combined qualitative and quantitative research including focus groups, in-depth interviews and quantitative surveys with regular hotel users and non-users, including people who stayed with family and friends or in hostel accommodation. Over 18,000 consumers from the United States, Canada, China, Germany and the United Kingdom participated in the research. The central objective was to understand how consumers viewed and selected the hotels they used, whether it was for business or leisure purposes. The focus was on the customer journey – from selection and booking, in-hotel experience to check out and even post-stay communications. The research benchmarked IHG brands and competitors on current and desired brand attributes.

The results enabled IHG to develop detailed consumer profiles for each segment of the hotel and lodging market. Matrices were developed to plot the IHG hotel portfolio against competitor brands in detail, such that the marketing team could clearly visualize the relationship among current brand attributes, consumer segments and competitor offers. This visualization helped IHG to map the future desired position for each of their brands and identified gaps in the market where new brands, such as Hotel Indigo, a branded boutique concept, might be developed. Most importantly, the research helped the brand managers of Holiday Inn and Holiday Inn Express to focus on improving brand conformance across the world and provided a strategic direction to reinvigorate these brands.

The 2-year research project culminated in a detailed plan to enhance the guest experience at Holiday Inn and Express and to improve the consistency of that experience – since contemporary consumers expect consistency across all the hotels in these branded chains. The findings also drove product enhancements such as improved food and beverage, public area design and pillow menus. In the past, only a few luxury hotel brands offered a choice of pillow, but Holiday Inn and Express introduced a choice of pillow as an in-room requirement for the brand standards. As a part of the re-launch, the iconic Holiday Inn logo, unchanged since 1952, was given a refreshed look, which helped hotel owners, management, employees and consumers to more closely identify with the re-branding.

Since 2007, US$ 1 billion has been invested in upgrading and revitalizing all Holiday Inn branded hotels around the world. At the time of writing, 2500 hotels have been re-launched and 430,000 rooms have been refreshed. Since Holiday Inn and Express is a franchise, IHG needed to obtain the support of the hotel owners (the franchisees) to invest in these improvements. Crucially, the original research played a major role in helping to inform and convince the franchisees about the need to invest in the hotels to improve brand performance. Before an existing franchisee was allowed to participate in the re-launch program, a Holiday Inn or Express had to pass more than 50 quality thresholds to ensure that the property quality and unit management was serious about the commitment to new brand standards.

There is a time-lag in monitoring the success of major hotel brand investments, but initial research is positive. Holiday Inn and Express have seen significant improvements in property guest satisfaction scores and gradually image perceptions already suggest that target consumers believe these brands are places they want to stay in. Holiday Inn looks after 100 million guests every year, and forecast growth is strong. IHG recognizes that marketing research is critical in developing an appropriate marketing offer to hospitality consumers. Research is an on-going company activity to ensure that IHG remains competitive in the world of hospitality.

Source: IHG

Criticisms of marketing research

Academics and practitioners have criticized modern marketing research for a number of reasons (Brown, 2001), including the following:

- The focus on collecting data and performing statistical analysis, which does not provide new insights for the business or inform decision-making
- Flawed marketing research methodologies that introduce unacceptable levels of bias or error
- The emphasis on research stifles creativity in marketing.

Despite these criticisms, major hospitality companies recognize the importance of marketing research and carry out extensive customer and competitor research on a continuous basis.

MARKETING INFORMATION SYSTEMS

Hospitality managers need relevant, accurate, current and reliable information to be able to make effective decisions that will influence the future of the business. Small, single-unit, owner-operated companies normally rely on informal approaches to data collection and interpretation. Owner–managers can easily talk to customers to judge levels of customer satisfaction, intention to return or to obtain clues about how to improve performance. They can visit and/or discuss what is happening in their own environment with local competitors, suppliers and community leaders. Larger organizations need to develop more sophisticated *marketing information systems* to ensure that corporate executives understand the more complex environments in which they are operating (see Fig. 2.1). This is because marketing managers in larger companies are separated geographically, and sometimes culturally, from the markets they serve. The marketing information system helps marketers to identify trends and plan for the future, utilizing

- existing data from internal company sources (accounts and sales, guest history and customer satisfaction) and

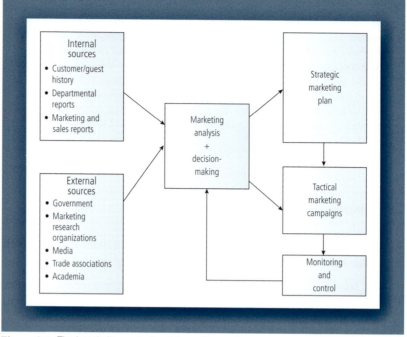

Figure 2.1 The hospitality marketing information system.

- data collected from external sources and marketing research activities (brand perceptions, consumer trends, competitor innovations and corporate reputation).

The major hospitality companies have invested significant capital in developing computerized databases, linked to guest history, to create systems capable of tracking customer segments and identifying emerging trends. The process of interrogating databases is called *data mining*.

Because larger companies routinely monitor their marketing environments, most of this marketing information will be collected on a scheduled, regular basis. However, there are occasions when there is a requirement for specific marketing information. On these occasions, a dedicated marketing research project needs to be commissioned and undertaken. This is known as *ad hoc* marketing research. Hospitality managers will use *ad hoc* marketing research to help them make decisions on questions such as

- Should the restaurant increase the number of vegetarian items on the menu? (a review of eating preferences is needed)
- Should the company open a new retail fast food unit in the airport? (a feasibility study will need to be undertaken)
- Should the conference center redefine its market position? (an internal audit and external competitive analysis is needed).

SOURCES OF INFORMATION

There are two sources of information in marketing research: internal and external.

Internal

Internal information is held by, and within, the organization. Accommodation businesses, such as cruise ships and hotels, are fortunate to hold a wealth of information about customers because of legal requirements regarding them to acquire and retain residents' personal details. However, one of the problems with this internal data is that departments other than the marketing department compile records for their own use. For example, the accounting department provides analysis in a format that is not always useful to marketers. Other departments need to have a clear understanding of the information needs of marketing managers and a commitment to provide it. The internal data for accommodation outlets are given in Table 2.1.

Other types of hospitality outlets have less opportunity to collect personal information, but can still utilize internal data effectively. Restaurants and bars do not normally hold such extensive details on customers, apart from an email list of regulars; but Electronic Point of Sale (EPOS) computer systems are used in chain operations to

Table 2.1	Internal data for accommodation outlets
Customer records	Hotel guest registration details (in most countries it is a legal requirement to record the name, address and length of stay of all residents)
Guest history	Source of booking (direct, travel agent, local company, website); method of reservation (phone, letter, fax, email, Internet, intranet, walk-in); type and number of guests (corporate, private, tour operator); customer feedback; any special requests
Departmental reports	Weekly/monthly accounts recording actual performance, against budget, for sales, occupancy, yield; non-residential sales (food and beverage, banqueting, conference, leisure outlets)
Marketing and sales reports	Customer satisfaction feedback questionnaires and surveys; customers' written compliments and complaints; sales force information from key accounts and intermediaries; monitoring of loyalty club activity; mystery customer surveys; brand conformance audits; brand performance surveys

monitor customer food preferences and purchase patterns, which do provide essential marketing data.

External

External information can be collected via the Internet and publications from a large number of sources, such as

- International and national government organizations. The World Tourism Organization, International Monetary Fund, United Nations and European Union publish a wide variety of useful marketing data and analysis. However, you should be aware that direct comparisons of key statistics between different countries are not always accurate due to cultural, sampling or respondent bias
- UK government publications such as the Annual Abstract of Statistics; the National Census, which was carried out every 10 years; the Social Trends Survey and VisitBritain (Britain's tourist authority)
- Marketing research organizations such as Mintel, Keynote and the Economist Intelligence Unit; management consultancies such as BDRC Continental, Deloitte, PKF and TRI, which produce commercial market reports on major sectors of the hospitality industry (e.g., hotels and holidays)
- Trade associations, such as the Institute of Hospitality, the American Hotel Sales and Marketing Association, and Hotel Marketing Association (part of the Chartered Institute of Marketing), which provide market information and services for members; sometimes these reports are also sometimes made available to the public
- Publicly quoted companies publish annual accounts for shareholders, which are also available to the public; annual accounts provide essential information about companies' marketing strengths and strategies, often the Chief Executive Officer's (CEO) report will contain information about the future plans of the business
- Useful company and market information is found in the industry's trade press (*Caterer and Hotelkeeper, Hotels' Magazine*), the financial press (*Financial Times, New York Times*) and surveys on media expenditure by companies such as Nielsen
- Universities and academic publishers produce journals reporting on current academic research; the journals discuss academic theory and provide insights into current industry practice (e.g., *Cornell Hotel and Restaurant Administration Quarterly, International Journal of Contemporary Hospitality Management* and the *Journal of Vacation Marketing*).

Marketers analyse data collected from the marketing information system and use the information as a basis for developing and refining the organization's strategic marketing plan.

SECONDARY AND PRIMARY DATA COLLECTION

Marketing researchers distinguish between secondary and primary data.

Secondary (or desk) data

Secondary data are data that have already been collected. Most of the external sources listed earlier in this chapter are examples of secondary data. It is relatively easy to obtain secondary data since the information has already been published.

However, there are limitations to secondary data. First, the data have been collected and analysed by another organization, which will have had its own reasons for carrying out the research and its own research objectives. This means that the information may not be appropriately accurate or completely relevant. Some organizations, including government bodies and pressure groups, may deliberately manipulate data to present findings to pursue their own agendas. Other organizations may have inadvertently introduced bias into their data collection due to poor research methods leading to flawed findings.

Another limitation of desk research is that the information is generally available to other organizations, including competitors, the media and pressure groups, and so offers little by way of competitive advantage. Finally, secondary data and analysis can often be 'dated' because of the long time between carrying out the research and publishing the findings. When carrying out secondary research, it is essential to check the date of the research and verify the credibility of the source of the material and to validate the research methods employed.

Despite these limitations, secondary research is usually the starting point for a research project and provides useful background information cost-effectively.

Primary data

Primary data consist of original information collected by an organization for a specific purpose. The data have not been published before. The organization conducting or commissioning the research determines the research objectives and research questions. The data are collected directly to provide answers to those questions.

Primary research is usually more costly than the secondary research. However, the advantages of primary research include the following:

- The ability to frame the research questions to the needs of the organization
- Research is current and not dated
- The research is confidential to the commissioning organization.

Primary data can enable a hospitality company to gain a competitive advantage if its rivals are not carrying out similar research.

Marketing insight 2.1

Closed and open questions

There are two major types of questions used in research: closed questions and open questions.

Closed questions provide a number of alternative answers from which the respondent chooses one answer. Examples include questions about the respondent's age, sex, employment, income or about the frequency with which a respondent visits a restaurant, drinks coffee or takes a holiday. Closed questions use a structured format, and this creates a data set that can be efficiently analysed using statistical methods. The research findings are described as 'hard' data and provide numerical information. If the research uses a quantitative approach then closed questions are essential.

Open-ended questions allow respondents to provide their own answers, without any guidance. Examples of open questions include 'Where would you stay tonight if this hotel was fully booked?' and 'How did you feel about the quality of service?' The response to an open question allows the respondent to use their own words to describe their experience, feelings and opinions. The research findings provide 'rich' data that are used in qualitative research.

Researchers usually ask a combination of both closed and open questions and combine qualitative and quantitative analysis.

QUALITATIVE AND QUANTITATIVE DATA

Qualitative data

Qualitative research aims to provide a deep understanding of people's contextualized behaviour. It aims to explain how and why people behave as they do. As such, it examines beliefs, perceptions, motives, attitudes and opinions. This type of research can provide deep insights into consumers' responses to an organization, its products, services, brands and image. Qualitative research in hospitality uses observation, in-depth interviews, focus groups (also known as group discussions) and qualitative questions in surveys.

Observation is a powerful research tool. Simply sitting in a reception lobby, or quietly observing the service at an event, and watching the customer/employee interaction can provide insights into the efficiency of the service operation, the friendliness of the service staff and the level of customer satisfaction.

In-depth interviewing enables a researcher to ask respondents open-ended questions, often in a semi-structured format. A semi-structured format typically involves the researcher creating a research protocol (a list of topic areas and ideal question running in order) in advance of the interviews and then asking questions in an informal, conversational way. The interviews can take place face-to-face, by telephone or through email. Face-to-face interviews allow the researcher to get close to the interviewee, which helps the researcher to note and react to the interviewee's body language and to probe with more searching questions in order to obtain more complete or honest responses. However, face-to-face interviewing is more time consuming and more expensive to conduct than telephone or email interviews.

Focus group discussions use group dynamics to explore important marketing issues. The researcher invites a number of people (usually, not more than 10) to participate in the discussion, which is normally held in a neutral environment. Depending on the purpose of the discussion, the invitees may be existing customers, potential customers, former customers or employees. A small reward is often offered for participation. A moderator hosts the discussion, which is conducted in a friendly, informal, even 'chatty' way. Focus groups start by discussing broad issues and then begin to focus on the core topic of the research. The researcher asks the participants' permission to record the session to enable further analysis. The group dynamics enable a skilled moderator to draw out different perspectives from each member of the group, as well as the group's collective views.

Questionnaires often include questions that generate qualitative and quantitative data. The qualitative questions are open ended, thus enabling the respondents to give opinions using their own words. We discuss quantitative questions in the next section.

Although qualitative research provides rich, detailed information based on consumers' personal experience and uses their own words, there is a methodological limitation to the technique. Respondents who are willing to participate by giving an interview or joining a focus group cannot be considered as a truly representative sample. Many hospitality customers are too busy, or not sufficiently interested, to give up their valuable time to participate. The inducements to participate – if any – are modest. Although the findings are valuable, they cannot be generalized, and other forms of marketing research need to be used to corroborate the qualitative research.

Sometimes, however, qualitative research is performed after quantitative research. This happens when quantitative research has discovered interesting information that needs further investigation.

For example, a customer satisfaction survey may indicate that a high percentage of customers do not like the food service in a hotel. Qualitative research can explore the reasons behind the statistic.

Quantitative data

Quantitative research uses a wide range of methods to obtain and analyse numerical data. Quantitative research counts numbers, in terms of either volume or value. For example, the number of customers, passengers, residents, diners, room nights, room occupancy; a restaurant unit's sales; or a hotel chain's room sales. If data are numeric then the research is quantitative. Quantitative research techniques are founded upon statistical theory. It is important that the correct statistical method is adopted to reduce possible error and bias. There are four main classes of error in the marketing research.

Sampling errors

The most common form of sampling error is sample bias. To be valid, the research has to be based on a representative sample of the population of interest to the researcher. An analysis based on a mid-week survey conducted in a shopping center in the morning would be biased because it excludes many people who are at work.

Respondent errors

People can change their behaviour when asked participate in marketing research. Some people may give answers which they think are the 'right' answers, rather than being honest and giving their own opinion.

Investigator errors

Researchers can accidentally make errors, for example, by entering the data inaccurately. This type of recording error can easily happen when inexperienced researchers are not trained thoroughly.

Administrative errors

Responses to questionnaires often vary according to the day of week and the weather. For example, on a rainy or oppressively hot day, more hotel guests remain in the property. On a pleasant day, in-hotel surveys will therefore have fewer guests to interview.

In large surveys, statistical software packages are used to process the quantitative research data. Optical scanners can also be used to read completed questionnaires and provide detailed data analysis.

There is a variety of survey methods used in quantitative marketing research. The methods commonly used in hospitality organizations include exit surveys, mystery customer audits, telephone (including mobile phone) surveys, and omnibus surveys.

Exit surveys are used by virtually all the major hotel chains and many independent hotels. A common method is to leave questionnaires (often in the bedrooms) for residents to complete prior to checkout or to email a questionnaire to the customer on the next day. Questions typically seek customer feedback on the quality of accommodation, food and service and value for money. These customer satisfaction surveys are important tools for evaluating how a unit is performing, but they suffer from a low response rate and normally attract either the extremely dissatisfied or the highly delighted customer. The example in Figure 2.2 shows the Le Meridien Hotels' exit survey, which has both closed and open questions asking customers to comment in detail on every department in the hotel. Companies such as Malmaison do not ask any questions but simply allow customers to write what they feel (see Fig. 2.3).

Mystery customer audits are used by multiple-unit branded operators to assess how individual units are performing. Researchers posing as customers check whether a unit is conforming to the brand standards and evaluate the operation from a customer perspective. Each aspect of the operation is marked, and an overall 'score' is recorded. Unit managers and employees do not know who the 'mystery customer' is, but later receive a copy of the report, which highlights brand and operational compliance and deficiencies.

Telephone and mobile surveys have been used in consumer research since telephone ownership levels reached saturation point in Western economies. Telephone research is a cost-effective tool to investigate specific segments (e.g., the conference market). Key accounts and conference placement agencies can be contacted to ascertain changes in customer needs and wants. The marketing manager can then introduce adaptations to improve the offer to the customer.

Omnibus surveys are a marketing research method where several companies share the costs of the research. The survey is carried out by an independent marketing research agency that collects data from a common sample for a number of clients. The clients may either come from different industries (e.g. a car manufacturer, an insurance company and a tour operator) or be competitors in the same industry sector. The UK Hotel Brands omnibus survey is carried out each year by BDRC Continental (see the Marketing Insight on pages 126–127 in Chapter 4 Competitive Strategies). Each company participating in the survey can add their own specific questions, for an additional fee. An omnibus survey, which is a form of syndicated research, is a major research exercise. Syndicated research is a research conducted by market research companies and sold to a number (syndicate) of

Le MERIDIEN
GROSVENOR HOUSE

MOMENT
OF TRUTH

L'INSTANT
DE VERITE

Dear Guest

Thank you for staying with us at Le Meridien Grosvenor House.

In order to ensure our products and services are of the highest standards available, and that we are best able to meet your requirements, we would be very grateful if you would take a few minutes to let us know how we are doing. We would also greatly appreciate any suggestions you may have to make a stay at Le Meridien Grosvenor House more enjoyable.

Please leave this card with our Front Office Reception upon check-out.

Thank you for your valuable assistance and we look forward to welcoming you back in the near future.

Gregoire Salamin
Hotel Manager

ART + TECH
by Le MERIDIEN

YOUR ARRIVAL

	Unacceptable				Average				Outstanding	
	1	2	3	4	5	6	7	8	9	10
Accuracy of reservation	1	2	3	4	5	6	7	8	9	10
Appearance of hotel	1	2	3	4	5	6	7	8	9	10
Appearance of lobby	1	2	3	4	5	6	7	8	9	10
Speed of check-in process	1	2	3	4	5	6	7	8	9	10
Helpfulness of front-desk staff at check-in	1	2	3	4	5	6	7	8	9	10
Helpfulness of doorman and bell staff at check-in	1	2	3	4	5	6	7	8	9	10
Overall Rating of Arrival	1	2	3	4	5	6	7	8	9	10

GUEST ROOM

	Unacceptable				Average				Outstanding	
Cleanliness of guest room	1	2	3	4	5	6	7	8	9	10
Decor/furnishing/style of guest room	1	2	3	4	5	6	7	8	9	10
Comfort of bed (include mattress, linens..)	1	2	3	4	5	6	7	8	9	10
Quietness of guest room	1	2	3	4	5	6	7	8	9	10
Availability of amenities (hair dryer, iron etc)	1	2	3	4	5	6	7	8	9	10
Ability to work in room	1	2	3	4	5	6	7	8	9	10
Lighting for reading or working	1	2	3	4	5	6	7	8	9	10
Connection/speed of internet	1	2	3	4	5	6	7	8	9	10
Variety of In-room video/TV/music/entertainment	1	2	3	4	5	6	7	8	9	10
Cleanliness of bathroom	1	2	3	4	5	6	7	8	9	10
Bath/shower water pressure	1	2	3	4	5	6	7	8	9	10
Quality of bathroom amenities (soap, shampoo, etc)	1	2	3	4	5	6	7	8	9	10
Room Smell	1	2	3	4	5	6	7	8	9	10
Overall Rating of Guest Room	1	2	3	4	5	6	7	8	9	10

FOOD & BEVERAGE

	Unacceptable				Average				Outstanding		N/A
Menu choices available in restaurant/bar	1	2	3	4	5	6	7	8	9	10	
Ambience/atmosphere in restaurant/bar	1	2	3	4	5	6	7	8	9	10	
Accuracy of restaurant/bar service	1	2	3	4	5	6	7	8	9	10	
Quality of food and beverage in restaurant/bar	1	2	3	4	5	6	7	8	9	10	
Helpfulness of restaurant/bar staff	1	2	3	4	5	6	7	8	9	10	
Timeliness of room service	1	2	3	4	5	6	7	8	9	10	
Quality of room service food and beverage	1	2	3	4	5	6	7	8	9	10	
Quality of breakfast (taste, variety)	1	2	3	4	5	6	7	8	9	10	
Overall Rating of Food & Beverage	1	2	3	4	5	6	7	8	9	10	

HOTEL SERVICES

	Unacceptable				Average				Outstanding		N/A
Availability of business facilities/services	1	2	3	4	5	6	7	8	9	10	
Fitness/Recreation facilities (pool, fitness centre)	1	2	3	4	5	6	7	8	9	10	
Timeliness of voice mail/message/fax	1	2	3	4	5	6	7	8	9	10	
Helpfulness of front desk staff or concierge staff	1	2	3	4	5	6	7	8	9	10	
Hotel security/safety	1	2	3	4	5	6	7	8	9	10	
Overall Rating of Hotel Services	1	2	3	4	5	6	7	8	9	10	

Figure 2.2 Le Meridien customer questionnaire

DEPARTURE/CHECKOUT

	Unacceptable				Average				Outstanding			N/A
Speed of check-out process at front desk	1	2	3	4	5	6	7	8	9	10		
Accuracy of billing	1	2	3	4	5	6	7	8	9	10		
Helpfulness of front desk staff at departure	1	2	3	4	5	6	7	8	9	10		
Helpfulness of doorman and bell staff at departure	1	2	3	4	5	6	7	8	9	10		
Overall Rating of Departure/Check-out	1	2	3	4	5	6	7	8	9	10		

Did you experience any significant problems with this hotel   Yes ☐   No ☐

What type of problem was encountered? Mark all that apply.
☐ Billing   ☐ Hotel/Room maintenance   ☐ Room cleanliness   ☐ Staff attitude
☐ Check-in   ☐ Noise   ☐ Room location/type   ☐ Staff service
☐ Check-out   ☐ Reservation accuracy   ☐ Room Service   ☐ Other
☐ Heating, Ventilation, and/or Air Conditioning   ☐ Restaurant/Bar   ☐ Small room

Did you report the problem to hotel staff?   Yes ☐   No ☐

If you reported the problem, how would you rate the hotel's resolution of the problem?

Unacceptable				Average				Outstanding	
1	2	3	4	5	6	7	8	9	10

Problem was never solved ☐

Please rate your OVERALL guest experience?

Unacceptable				Average				Outstanding	
1	2	3	4	5	6	7	8	9	10

Considering your entire guest experience, how would you rate the value for money?

Unacceptable				Average				Outstanding	
1	2	3	4	5	6	7	8	9	10

How likely would you be to return to this hotel if in the same area again?

Definitely Will not	Probably Will not	Probably Will	Definitely Will
☐	☐	☐	☐

How likely would you be to recommend this hotel to a friend or colleague?

Definitely Will not	Probably Will not	Probably Will	Definitely Will
☐	☐	☐	☐

How likely would you be to stay at a Le Méridien property again?

Definitely Will not	Probably Will not	Probably Will	Definitely Will
☐	☐	☐	☐

If the hotel you stayed at had NOT been available, which ONE other hotel would you have chosen instead?
☐ Crowne Plaza   ☐ Sofitel   ☐ Hilton   ☐ Ritz Carlton   ☐ Sheraton   ☐ Four Seasons
☐ Intercontinental Hotels   ☐ Other   ☐ Hyatt   ☐ W   ☐ Marriott   ☐ Westin

Which of the following best describes the reason for your stay:
☐ Business   ☐ Leisure   ☐ Both   ☐ Conference

How was the reservation made?   ☐ Directly through the hotel   ☐ Le Méridien reservation centre   ☐ Travel Agent
☐ Corporate travel department   ☐ Internet   ☐ Other

Are you a member of the Le Méridien Moments guest reward programme?   Yes ☐   No ☐

Additional Comments and Suggestions

....

....

....

....

....

Thank you for your time and suggestions, please return this questionnaire to front desk.

Mr / Mrs / Ms   Last Name .... First Name ....

Company .... Position ....

Address ....

City .... Postcode .... Country ....

Your Room No .... Dates of stay ....

Figure 2.2 Cont'd

Malmaison

COMMENT CARD

Name: .... Date of Stay: .... Room No: ....

Comments

Figure 2.3 Malmaison open-ended customer questionnaire

clients. Omnibus surveys are relatively expensive to carry out because of the large sample size, but can be very cost-effective for each individual client. The cost of participation varies according to the number of questions and types of analysis required.

Activity 2.2

Compare the questionnaires in Figs 2.2 and 2.3.

- What is the main difference between Le Meridien and Malmaison's approach to soliciting customer feedback?
- What types of question are used?
- How will the research findings be analysed?

MARKETING RESEARCH PROCESS

A company can either carry out its own marketing research (this is called in-house) or contract out the marketing research to a specialist agency. Although marketing research agencies can be more expensive, as specialists in their field they will have the expertise, experience, qualified staff, connections and appropriate technologies to carry out the research professionally.

The decision to use an agency or do the work in-house will depend on the type of research undertaken and the budget available. Observation, customer satisfaction and exit questionnaires, and competitor surveys are normally handled in-house. Focus groups, in-depth interviewing, mystery customer, telephone and omnibus surveys are more often conducted by specialist marketing research agencies.

Effective marketing research follows a number of logical stages described below.

1 *Formulation of research objectives*. The aims, scope and limitations of the research project need to be established at the beginning. Clearly identifying the research problem, deciding the desired research outcomes and defining the research objectives at the beginning saves time and money later. Establishing the available budget is essential, since budget constraints will determine what type of marketing research is undertaken and whether the activity is carried out in-house or by an agency.

Research objectives are largely determined by the marketing decisions that are to be made. In order to limit the scope of the research, it is helpful to construct pro-forma tables. These are tables in which the data will be entered once the research is completed. This discipline forces managers to decide precisely what information is needed.

2 *Development of a research plan*. Each stage of the research process needs to be carefully planned, with provisional actions, costs, people, planning and deadlines set out. An evaluation of which research methods are most appropriate needs to be based on the research objectives and budget.

3 *Data collection*. There are two major components to this phase of the process: first, identifying sources of information (who has the information and where is it?) and second, deciding how to collect the information from those sources (using primary or secondary research methods). Data collection usually starts with a review of secondary sources. This desk research enables the researcher to understand what has been collected in the past and the data collection methods that have already been used. A good understanding of secondary sources provides the researcher with a solid foundation before embarking on any primary research. Indeed, some research projects can be completed with secondary data alone. If primary research is required, a pilot study to test the research instrument (or method) is essential. Changes can then be made to the research instrument, before the marketing research study is rolled out.

4 *Data analysis*. There is a wide range of statistical tools available to aid marketing data analysis, including

- univariate techniques, which present analyses of single variables such as the value of restaurant receipts or the number of complaints per month.
- bivariate techniques, which analyse two variables simultaneously and establish whether there is a strong, weak or non-existent relationship or correlation between them – for example, the correlation between foreign tourist arrivals and movements in exchange rates
- multivariate techniques, which analyse three or more variables simultaneously to establish what, if any, link exists between them – an example might be all the complex factors that influence customer satisfaction on a foreign holiday.

5 *Assess the reliability and validity of data.* Responsible researchers recognize that marketing research has limitations and that it is important to identify any possible error or bias in the data prior to interpretation. Professional marketing researchers are particularly concerned with the issues of reliability and validity of data. Measures are valid when they measure what they are supposed to measure. If you want to measure customer satisfaction, it would be invalid to use an instrument (questionnaire) designed to measure service quality perceptions. Valid measures are free from the sources of error described earlier: respondent error, investigator error, sampling error and administrative error. A reliable measure is one that is consistent and does not vary over time. Remember that some organizations deliberately manipulate or distort information. In particular, the data from research have to be placed within the context of the PESTE environment at the time of the research, since research findings in the hospitality industry are influenced by different periods of economic prosperity and recession.

6 *Presentation of findings.* Finally, the researcher has to present the findings. Normally, there will be large amounts of data and analysis, which need to be presented in an accessible manner. Key findings should be provided in an executive summary. The main report should contain an explanation of the methodology and detailed discussion of the findings. Any research limitations and source of error or bias should be explained. The raw data can be presented either in the appendices or in a separate document.

INTERNET RESEARCH

Online marketing research is a relatively recent phenomenon, which is growing in popularity. The advantages include significant cost savings in the design and administration of questionnaires and discussion groups, and the ability to accurately target surveys to current, former or potential customers. Hospitality companies can generate a sample for a research project by inviting potential customers to register their contact details on a web-form with a view to being sent product information, or by encouraging guests to hand over their business cards with their email address during the service encounter. Often, customers are incentivized to participate in online surveys by inclusion in free prize draws with attractive rewards. Post-consumption e-surveys provide customers with a convenient tool to give feedback on service quality and customer satisfaction. Some companies are using blogs to entice customers to comment on their customer experiences, or employ technologies that scour social networking sites such as Facebook for customer-generated comment. The Internet is available to all sizes of hospitality companies. Indeed many market research firms provide generic and bespoke online surveys, which can easily be bought on the Internet and enables smaller hospitality companies to conduct their own online research.

CONCLUSION

You now know that marketing research is based on scientific principles and provides hospitality companies with essential information to help decision-making. Managers use marketing research to confirm or reject their own intuitions about a project. Marketing research is a tool that managers use in developing, implementing and controlling marketing plans, but no amount of marketing research can actually make decisions for the hospitality manager. It is the manager's task to make decisions based on the information available.

In this chapter, we have explained

- The purpose of marketing research
- The role of a marketing information system
- How hospitality organizations can utilize internal information for marketing research purposes
- Where to find external sources of information
- Secondary and primary research techniques
- The difference between qualitative and quantitative data
- The marketing research process
- How hospitality organizations conduct research on the Internet.

REVIEW QUESTIONS

Carry out Activity 2.1 again and compare your answers:
- Do you know why hospitality companies carry out research?
- Do you understand what is researched in the hospitality sector?

- List the marketing research activities you have learnt in this chapter.

Now check your understanding of this chapter by answering the following questions:

1 Discuss the components and the role of a marketing information system for a major hospitality organization.
2 Evaluate the relevance of secondary and primary research methods for
   - an owner-managed hospitality unit
   - a branded retail hospitality unit
   - an international branded hotel chain.
3 Describe the differences between qualitative and quantitative data in hospitality marketing.

References and Further Reading

Altinay, L., & Paraskevas, A. (2008). *Planning research in hospitality and tourism*. Oxford, UK: Butterworth-Heinemann.

Brown, S. (2001). *Marketing: The retro revolution*. Sage.

Chaffey, D., Ellis-Chadwick, F., Johnston, K., & Mayer, R. (2009). *Internet marketing: strategy, implementation and practice* (4th ed.). Pearson Education.

Daymon, C., & Holloway, I. (2002). *Qualitative research methods in public relations and marketing communications*. Routledge.

Saunders, M. K., Thornhill, A., & Lewis, P. (2009). *Research methods for business students* (5th ed.). Financial Times/Prentice Hall.

Usunier, J. C., & Lee, J. (2009). *Marketing across cultures* (5th ed.). Financial Times/Prentice Hall.

C H A P T E R **3**

Understanding and segmenting customers

Chapter objectives

After going through this chapter, you should be able to

- Understand a number of core concepts that explain hospitality consumer and organizational customers' behaviour
- Discuss the role of customer expectations
- Identify the factors that influence the hospitality consumer, buyer and organizational customer decision-making process
- Explain the principles of segmenting demand in hospitality markets
- Describe hospitality segmentation variables
- Evaluate the characteristics of hospitality target markets.

INTRODUCTION

In this chapter, we review the complex topics of consumer behaviour and customer expectations and then explore the principles and practice of market segmentation and target marketing. Segmentation and targeting are fundamental marketing disciplines that underpin all marketing practice. Segmentation recognizes that hospitality customers, including both organizations and consumers, are enormously varied, but they can nonetheless be clustered into groups with similar needs, wants, expectations and requirements. Targeting is based on the premise that hospitality organizations cannot hope to satisfy all potential customers, but must choose to focus their efforts on particular clusters that share broadly similar needs and wants. In doing so, they are much better placed to design, brand and deliver their services in a way that delivers enhanced customer satisfaction to the targeted customers, and compete more effectively against other providers.

Activity 3.1. Before reading the rest of the chapter, think about how you make buying decisions

- What influences (or would influence) your decision to purchase a

  - ○ drink in a local cafe?
  - ○ short holiday in your own country?
  - ○ long holiday in a country on the other side of the world?

When you have completed the chapter, carry out this activity again and then compare your answers.

CONSUMER BEHAVIOUR

In Chapter 1, we established that marketers manage demand. Demand is a form of behaviour. So marketers study consumer's behaviour to try to understand and predict what customers will buy, how and why. Marketers need to understand the *processes* consumers go through in buying and consuming hospitality products. If we can understand who buys which hospitality products where, when and why, then we are much more likely to be successful in our efforts to influence demand. By understanding and meeting customer expectations, companies can better deliver customer satisfaction. Research in this subject area is broadly termed *consumer behaviour* research. Extensive research has been conducted in consumer behaviour in a wide range of social science disciplines, including psychology, social psychology, sociology, anthropology, philosophy, economics and marketing. Each discipline takes a different perspective in seeking to understand consumer behaviour. We will now discuss the influences on consumer behaviour and the hospitality buyer decision-making process from a marketing perspective.

Influences on consumer buyer behaviour

The amount of disposable income consumers have to spend varies according to environmental conditions. When economies are growing and there are many employment opportunities, consumers are more optimistic about the future. These factors create the conditions where consumers can enjoy real increases in disposable income. Consumer confidence is higher, and they are likely to spend more on hospitality products. When the reverse happens and the economies slow or go into recession, unemployment increases; consumers become concerned about the future and disposable income falls. Consumer confidence is lower, and they are less likely to spend on hospitality products. In developed countries, consumer confidence is tracked on a regular basis to measure this 'feel-good' factor. In market economies, consumers have choice – they can choose to spend their disposable income as they want. In this sense, hospitality competes against other product categories such as automobiles or clothing for the consumers' disposable income. A young, newly married couple may have to choose between buying items for their home and going on holiday.

Naturally, individual consumers choose to buy different products for different reasons at different times. Research is carried out to identify what influences consumer's purchase behaviour. The major influences on individual consumer buyer behaviour can be categorized into three broad headings: socio-cultural influences, individual differences and contextual circumstances. Socio-cultural influences include culture, reference groups, family and social class. Individual differences include personality, lifestyle, gender, age, income and education. Contextual circumstances include perception of risk and involvement (see Fig. 3.1).

Socio-cultural influences

We now discuss how culture, family, reference groups and social class influence consumer behaviour.

Culture

All of us are born into a culture. Culture can be thought of as the shared values and beliefs that help individuals to understand how society functions. These values and beliefs provide individuals with guidelines for behaviour. Our culture is expressed in and reinforced by learnt behaviours. Culture is passed from generation to generation as a part of the socialization process we undergo when growing up.

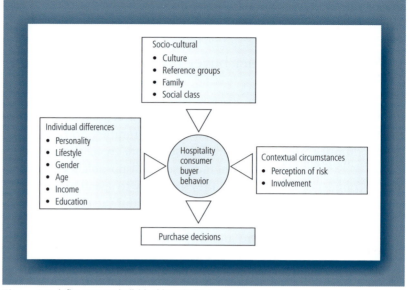

Figure 3.1 Influences on individual hospitality consumers

Some of the factors that are influenced by our shared values are given below.

Human needs	Social organization	Family relationships
Food preferences	Language	Religious beliefs
Education	Political systems	Customs and habits
Economics	Attitudes	Art

People from different cultures behave differently. When hospitality employees look after foreign customers, whether they are from Australia, Brazil, Britain, China, France, India, Italy, Japan, Russia, South Africa or the United States, they notice significant differences in consumer behaviour that can clearly be attributed to culture.

However, although culture is deeply rooted, it can and does change slowly. You should be aware of the debate about 'globalization' in today's international marketplace and how globalization influences consumer behaviour. Levitt (1983), a famous American academic, wrote a seminal article in 1983 suggesting that cultural differences are being eroded as consumer markets become more global. Advocates of this 'convergence' theory propose that the combination of powerful multinational corporations, new distribution channels that transport goods/services efficiently, and new information and media technology that enables companies to communicate messages worldwide, drive the homogenization of global consumer needs and wants. Convergence theory is predicated on the *similarities* that international consumers share. The rapid growth of international business and leisure travel means that hospitality organizations cater for an increasing number of visitors from all parts of the world. If global hospitality consumers have similar needs and wants, then companies can provide a more standardized marketing offer, which is also more cost-effective.

However, critics of convergence theory suggest that post-modern consumers have diverse consumption patterns mixing local and global products and services. Usunier and Lee (2009) emphasize the importance of local culture in understanding consumer choice. This recognition of the importance of culture in marketing focuses on the *differences* between consumers from different cultural traditions and their buying preferences. If hospitality consumers in different country markets have different needs and wants, then companies should adapt their global products and services to local cultural requirements. This local adaptation of the hospitality offer should provide enhanced customer satisfaction, but may not be as cost-effective as standardizing the marketing offer.

Family

Families have a significant influence on consumer behaviour. Adult preferences for food, beverage and leisure activities are largely products of childhood influences. The stereotypical Western family unit of a working father, stay-at-home mother and two children is no longer dominant. Today, Western families comprise a wide range of different combinations, including dual-earning couples with no children, single working parents, same sex partners, extended families and traditional nuclear family groups. An important trend in Western societies is the growing number of people who live by themselves and whose hospitality requirements differ from those of couples or families. In African, Arabic and Asian countries, the extended family plays a much greater role, and many consumer decisions are discussed collectively. The composition of a household affects the amount of disposable income – and, typically, higher disposable income leads to higher household expenditure on hospitality and tourism services.

Reference groups

Individual consumer behaviour is also influenced by identification with or membership of groups. A distinction is made between primary and secondary groups. Primary groups are those in which we interact face-to-face with other members – for example, family, friends and classmates. Secondary groups, being larger or dispersed, do not experience that face-to-face interaction. They include cultural and nationality groupings, business associations and alumni. Reference groups can be classified into three useful ways:

1 *Membership groups*: These are groups to which you belong. Your choice of holiday destination may be influenced by membership groups such as family and friends or by the online social networks of which you are member – Facebook and Myspace.

2 *Aspirational groups*: An aspirational group is a group to which you do not belong, but with which you aspire to be associated. If you want to be thought of as a high adrenaline risk taker, you might read brochures of adventure sports holiday operators and even leave them around, so others can see!

3 *Disassociative groups*: We do not want to be (or seen to be) associated with disassociative groups. In contemporary culture, there are a variety of fashions and fads that appeal to different sub-sets of young people. Although some fashionable groups might appeal to you, there are probably some groups you really want to avoid being associated with and you, therefore, do not wear 'their' clothes, listen to 'their' music or holiday in 'their' resorts.

Reference groups perform two functions: they set and enforce standards, and they act as points of reference for individuals to compare their behaviours. Within peer groups and communities, individuals whose opinions are most respected influence others. These people are described as 'opinion leaders'. In hospitality and tourism, travel writers and food critics are critical opinion leaders, whose positive or negative comments in local and national media can boost or destroy demand for destinations, events, hotels and restaurants. There will be opinion leaders within your own social networks too; these will be friends or family members whose opinion you value and who you turn to for advice.

Socio-economic class

All countries have social class systems (also known as social grading or socio-economic classifications), although some are more formal than others. Class systems are important influences on consumer behaviour. Social class is linked to education, occupation and income, and provides a widely adopted customer classification system for market segmentation. In the United Kingdom, the socio-economic classification system created by the Joint Industry Committee for National Readership Surveys (JICNARS; see Table 3.1), is widely used as a descriptor of consumer groups by marketing researchers, by hospitality managers working on new product development and by media owners who are profiling their audiences for advertisers. The descriptors of social structure in Anglo-American countries (Australia, Canada, New Zealand and the United States) are broadly similar. In some countries like India, the caste system provides a highly formalized social classification system. In other countries, like Norway and Sweden, social class is regarded as less important. However, social class is not a perfect predictor of consumer decisions because social strata are not strictly homogeneous and there are wide differences in the attitudes, interests, opinions and, therefore, purchase behaviour of individuals within the same stratum.

Social grade	Social class status	Characteristics
A	Upper and upper middle	Higher managerial, administrative or professional
B	Middle	Intermediate managerial, administrative or professional
C1	Lower middle	Supervisory or clerical and junior managerial, administrative or professional
C2	Skilled working	Skilled manual workers
D	Working	Semi-skilled and unskilled manual workers
E	Subsistence	State pensioners, widows, casual and lowest grade workers

Table 3.1 Social class classifications in Britain

Source: JICNARS.

Individual differences

Individual differences that influence buyer behaviour are discussed under the headings of age and gender, education and income, personality and lifestyle.

Age and gender

A person's age clearly influences needs and wants. Young adults have very different interests, tastes and income levels compared with their parents and their grandparents. Older people tend to think of a 'good meal' as meat and vegetables eaten as a formal dining occasion, whereas younger people tend to be much more experimental in their food tastes and look for a more informal dining experience. However, many people aged between 40 and 60 tend to think and act much younger than previous older generations. Marketers realize that there is a difference between chronological age (reflected in the passage of years) and cognitive age (what we think and how we act).

Women and men can have different needs and wants and gender can, therefore, influence an individual's purchase behaviour. Often, women feel less safe and secure than men when travelling and staying in hotels, whereas men have a different approach to consuming food and beverages (in terms of taste and portion size) compared with women.

Education and income

Education influences employment opportunities and income, and also shapes our values, beliefs, attitudes, interests, activities and lifestyle. Students who go to university meet a variety of different people, often from foreign countries. They develop their analytical and intellectual competences and learn a wide range of transferable skills, as well as studying a subject in greater depth. Their education also provides them with enhanced employment prospects. This enables graduates eventually to earn higher salaries in their workplace. Normally, but not always, people with lower education have fewer career opportunities and earn lower salaries.

The level of income helps to determine the amount of consumer disposable income available for discretionary purchases. People with higher income levels spend proportionately less on household necessities and, therefore, have more disposable income. This has considerable influence on holiday and dining out expenditure patterns.

Personality

An individual's personality can influence behaviour and the type of products purchased. Personality research categorizes five key dimensions of personality: neuroticism, extraversion, openness to experience, agreeableness and conscientiousness (Judge, Higgins, Thoresen, & Barrick, 1999). Each of these broad categories comprises several subcategories that can be used to research consumer behaviour. People in the same family can, because of their different personalities, have different purchase and consumption habits – especially in more individualistic societies.

Lifestyle

An individual's lifestyle is a powerful influence on the purchase of discretionary products like travel and dining out. Lifestyle is a reflection of an individual's personality and social influences. Researchers claim that lifestyle can be described in terms of a person's activities, interests and opinions (AIO). These can be summarized as follows:

- Activities include work, shopping, sport and entertainment, hobbies and travel;
- Interests include family, the home and garden, watching TV, food and fashion;
- Opinions about our own culture, other cultures, ourselves (and self-belief), social and political issues, business and economics and even about the future – inform our lifestyle.

AIO cross-cultural, social and demographic divides – for example, there are supporters of Manchester United Football Club of both sexes, from every continent, socio-economic class and age group throughout the world. A person's passion for sport, music or bird watching will influence how that person spends his or her time and money. Lifestyle has become an increasingly important concept in understanding consumer behaviour and predicting consumer purchase and consumption activity.

Marketing insight 3.1 Changing consumer behaviour in the restaurant industry

In the 1980s and 1990s, 'TBL' business lunches were popular and provided city restaurants with a strong, predictable income stream. A TBL is a 'two-bottle lunch' – in other words business people used to enjoy long, alcoholic lunches as a recognized way of conducting business. Today, business executives need to be much more productive in the work day and need to demonstrate more responsible behaviour. So the market for TBL lunches has diminished. However, a newer trend has emerged – the business breakfast – that enables city restaurants to partially compensate for the lost TBL revenue. The business breakfast market has different needs and wants; business people expect fast service during their breakfast meetings. Cecconi Restaurant, Mayfair, London, needed to reorganize the kitchen production system with new rotas for the chefs, earlier fresh food deliveries from suppliers and pre-breakfast chef/waiter team briefings at 6.45 AM in the morning to ensure a more efficient service. The breakfast menu was redesigned on a single page with drinks at the top and a maximum of 20 breakfast dishes – starting with complimentary freshly squeezed fruit juice, coffee/tea served within 2/3 min and the breakfast grill within 6/7 min.

Source: Lander, N. (2010). Early adopters. Page 4, Life and Arts, FT Weekend 24/25 April 2010.

Contextual circumstances

Sometimes, contextual circumstances are more important than socio-cultural stimuli and individual differences in influencing our behaviour. Two concepts that are helpful for understanding the role of context are perception of risk and involvement.

Perceived risk

A consumers' perception of the risk associated with buying a hospitality product influences the purchase decision. Perceived risk exists when the consumer is uncertain about the consequences of a purchase or about the decision itself. The perceived risk is higher when a consumer has little experience or knowledge about the product, has low self-confidence about making a purchase decision or faces significant long-term consequences as a result of buying the product. There are different types of perceived risk, including financial, social and psychological risk:

- *Financial risk* occurs when there is a large amount of money at stake. It is linked to major hospitality purchases – organizing a wedding day or planning the worldwide travel arrangements for a gap year. The larger the amount of money involved, the greater is the perceived financial risk.
- *Social risk* is linked to product symbolism and relates to hospitality products that have a social significance for the consumer.

The choice of where to have dinner sends social signals to the other diner(s).

- *Psychological risk* occurs when consumers perceive a threat to their self-image and self-esteem. In Asian societies, the concept of 'face' is very important, so consumers are very concerned about making the correct hospitality purchase decisions to avoid losing face in front of their family and friends.

Involvement

Consumers vary regarding the level of involvement they have in purchasing decisions. A high-involvement purchase decision is one that is personally significant and relevant for a consumer. Older married couples choosing the venue for a landmark wedding anniversary are making a high-involvement decision, whereas the choice of a coffee shop when shopping with friends is a low-involvement decision. Involvement tends to vary between individuals (some people are highly involved in many decisions), products (some products are more involving than others) and context (the level of involvement can vary across purchasing context); for example, the choice of a restaurant for a lunch break may be low involvement, but when a business guest is invited – then it becomes a high-involvement decision.

Involvement is an important idea to understand, because the buying process varies according to whether the decision is high or low involvement. High-involvement decisions (planning a honeymoon – Table 3.2 – or organizing a conference) are more complex than low-involvement decisions (planning where to meet friends at the

Table 3.2 Hospitality consumer decision-making process for a high-involvement or high-perceived risk product	
Process	**Example**
Perception of need	Engaged couple planning a honeymoon
Information search	Search travel agents and Internet, ask family and friends for advice on alternative honeymoon holidays in various destinations
Evaluation of alternatives	Agree 'decision criteria' – these include the budget, number of days on the honeymoon, where to go (domestic, short-haul, long-haul), what type of holiday (sun and sea or culture; all inclusive or go-as-you-please), which destinations
Purchase	Make the decision and buy the honeymoon
Post-purchase evaluation	On returning home, evaluate the consumption experience, which will inform future anniversary holiday decisions and whether to recommend the destination and accommodation to family and friends

weekend). A high-involvement decision will involve much more pre-purchase search for information about alternatives and a post-purchase evaluation of whether the decision was successful.

Buyer decision-making process

If marketers are to influence customer demand, they need to understand how customers make buying decisions.

The starting point for decision-making is when a consumer recognizes that he or she has a need that is not currently being satisfied. The need may be caused by internal conditions (feeling hungry) or motivated by external stimuli (seeing an advertisement). If the decision involves a low-involvement product, the consumer's response is more likely to be a routinized buying decision: feeling hungry at lunchtime and visiting the local sandwich shop. If the decision involves a high-involvement product, the consumer will have to search for a solution. This search process can be internal or external. An internal search uses our memory to recall previous experiences (or information) to provide a satisfactory solution. If the internal search does not provide a solution, then the consumer has to engage in an external search.

Consumers evaluate alternative ways of solving the problem, weighing the alternatives against their own set of criteria. In hospitality, some of the criteria used by consumers include location, quality, convenience, reputation, price and availability. The advent of online and mobile searching for consumer solutions has developed a new online search industry that is both an opportunity and a threat for hospitality providers. The opportunity to reach more significant volumes of potential customers via the Internet is offset by the threat of keener, transparent, price competition plus higher distribution costs through virtual intermediaries.

After evaluating options, the consumer makes a buying decision – assuming that the price is affordable, and the time to purchase and consume the hospitality product is available. After the transaction has been completed, the consumer assesses whether the product actually satisfied their relevant needs and this post-purchase evaluation influences the consumer's propensity to repeat purchase and to recommend positively (or negatively) the hospitality product. If a customer who is not satisfied complains and the company is able to recover the situation and retain the customer, the customer will be more likely to repeat purchase and speak positively about their experience. However, if the complaint is not handled effectively, the unhappy customer is likely to tell many more people about a bad experience than a good experience (see Chapter 13). Unfortunately, most unhappy customers do not complain, so the hospitality company has no chance to recover the situation.

UNDERSTANDING CUSTOMER EXPECTATIONS

An important concept for marketers is *customer expectation*. Customers have expectations of hospitality encounters, which marketers must meet if customers are to be satisfied.

Customer beliefs

Customers form beliefs about what a hospitality experience will be like. Customers' beliefs are formed by a combination of different influences, including culture, reference groups, word of mouth, previous experience, marketing communication, various media including the Internet, and individual personal characteristics. Although individual customer beliefs can be idiosyncratic (such customers are often called eccentric because of their unusual behaviour), different national cultures have a strong influence on customers' belief systems, which in turn influence customer expectations. For example, international tourists who come from high service cultures (such as Japan and Taiwan) have higher expectations when travelling abroad and staying in hotels, while the expectations of travellers from countries with a limited service culture (like some of the East European countries) have lower expectations.

Zone of tolerance

There have been a number of attempts to understand and classify expectations. One scheme suggests that there are four different types of expectation:

1 The ideal level – 'what can be'
2 The desired level – 'what should be' (this is the level that customers think is appropriate given what they have invested in finding and buying the product)
3 The predicted level – 'what will be'
4 The minimum tolerable – 'what must be'.

In seminal research, Zeithaml, Berry and Parasuraman (1993) suggested that the customer expectations lie within a *zone of tolerance* ranging from 'what must be' (minimum tolerable) to 'what can be' (desired level). It is also suggested that customers are willing to accept a level of performance that falls within a *zone of indifference*. This zone ranges around the customer's judgment of what is a reasonable expectation of the supplier.

During and after service performance, customers compare their expectations with their perceptions of the service they have received. However, the special characteristics of service in the hospitality industry mean that the quality of service delivery fluctuates. Customers who are knowledgeable about the variability in hospitality service can have greater tolerance for the variations in a service performance (i.e. a wider zone of tolerance); on the other hand, there are customers who are much less sympathetic and, therefore, have a lower tolerance to service fluctuations. This range of tolerance represents a customer's propensity to accept variable service standards and still accept the service offered.

A number of factors influence the customer's zone of tolerance, including the customer's personality and current circumstances, the importance of the purchase occasion and the characteristics of the product and the price paid. The levels of perceived risk and involvement can explain variations in the zone of tolerance. Clearly, customers have different zones of tolerance at different times. As individuals, we can all have mood swings and hence sometimes we feel more tolerant and relaxed about service quality whilst on other occasions (for reasons we do not always understand) we can be less tolerant and become more easily upset by service quality failings. Customers who have a time constraint are less tolerant of service failure.

ORGANIZATIONAL MARKETS

Although individual consumers represent a significant proportion of hospitality customers, especially for smaller hospitality companies, the larger hospitality organizations cater for the needs of organizational markets. These include business organizations generating corporate travel and corporate meetings; professional and trade associations; convention, exhibitions and trade fairs; tour groups; aircrew; and other miscellaneous types of volume bookings. In tourism and hospitality, some of these activities are clustered into a category known as the Meetings, Incentives, Conference and Exhibitions (MICE) market.

Organizations have a different approach to the buying process compared with individual consumers. These differences include the following:

- The number of participants involved in the organization's purchase decisions tends to be greater
- The users are not always the buyers
- The complexity of the arrangements (coordinating hundreds or thousands of people's travel, accommodation, catering and entertainment needs is not a simple task)
- The technical requirements, involving conference and banqueting arrangements, audiovisual and stage facilities, major event planning, and exhibition stand details, are complex.

Organizational buyer behaviour researchers have identified several roles in group purchase decisions: users, influencers, deciders, buyers and gatekeepers. These roles are collectively known as the 'decision-making unit' (DMU):

- *Users* are the customers who consume hospitality products
- *Influencers* are people who influence any part of the decision, such as the location or venue
- *Deciders* are the people who actually make the purchase decisions – the manager, executive or director
- *Buyers* are the people who make and pay for the booking
- *Gatekeepers* are people who control the flow of information to other members of the DMU – administrators or personal assistants often play a key role as gatekeepers in their organizations.

The buying process in organizations is more formalized, with varying degrees of bureaucratic and/or committee reporting structures. A professional approach is required when discussing or negotiating bookings with these types of organizations. The value and volume of organizational bookings vary, but for many of the major hospitality companies, the MICE market represents a key element in their business – see pages 95–97.

MARKET SEGMENTATION

Understanding individual consumer behaviour and organizational market behaviour helps hospitality organizations to understand customer expectations. Marketers use this information to identify potential customers who have similar needs and wants and describe these customers as *target markets*. This process of identifying subsets of consumers who have distinct, homogenous demand characteristics is called market segmentation. There is a broad consensus that segmentation is the starting point for developing effective marketing strategies because

- Trying to target all consumers is not cost-effective (remember, some consumers may never want to buy your hospitality product)
- Identifying the characteristics of target markets enables a company to design and develop the hospitality offer to satisfy customers more effectively
- Concentrating a company's limited marketing resources on key target markets leads to a more focused and cost-effective marketing strategy
- Segmentation improves profitability by maximizing customer satisfaction, and generating repeat and recommended sales.

However, there are difficulties for hospitality firms trying to establish effective segmentation strategies due to

- The costs of carrying out marketing research
- The complexity of constantly changing consumer behaviour
- The lack of flexibility in many hospitality products

- The additional costs of developing and communicating separate offers for different target markets
- The problem of targeting different and often incompatible target markets who use the premises at the same time.

The key point is that market segments are inherently unstable. Their membership, size and value change in response to changes in the PESTE environment.

The segmentation process

There is a logical sequence that can be followed during market segmentation. The stages of the segmentation process outlined in Table 3.3 are discussed here in more detail.

1 *Specification*: The market to be researched and segmented needs to be clearly identified; taking a broad definition of consumers' needs and wants in the sector.
2 *Establish segmentation criteria*: A set of criteria needs to be developed against which the various segmentation opportunities can be evaluated for market attractiveness. Segmented markets should be:

- discrete – can the segment be described as having a unique set of shared requirements and expectations requiring a specific marketing program?
- measurable – can the market size be measured in terms of value and/or volume, growth rates and market share of current players?
- profitable – does the segment have sufficient profit potential to justify the investment? By careful analysis, companies can often identify smaller, more profitable 'niche' markets within larger market segments. For single-unit hospitality companies, the market will primarily be focused on the company's micro-environment and depends on the local characteristics of demand and existing/potential competitors.
- accessible – can the segment be reached via distribution and marketing communication channels? There is no point in targeting a segment if the company cannot communicate cost-effectively with potential consumers.

Table 3.3 The segmentation process	
1.	Specify the market
2.	Establish segmentation criteria
3.	Generate segmentation variables
4.	Develop and evaluate market segment profiles
5.	Evaluate company's competences to serve selected segments effectively

- compatible – marketers should ensure that any new target markets are compatible with existing target markets.

3 *Generate segmentation variables*: Segmentation variables provide the basis for classifying consumers into different market segments. Hospitality segmentation variables include purpose of visit; geo-demographics; buyer, user and lifestyle characteristics; price and time. In hospitality, a wide number of variables are used to build a more detailed profile of the target markets. The more detailed the segmentation data, the deeper the understanding of potential customers.

4 *Develop market segment profiles based on segmentation variables*: Specific market segment profiles include the size of the market in terms of value and volume, customer purchase details (frequency of visit, customer spend and number in party), consumer characteristics (benefits sought, price sensitivity) and accessibility/responsiveness to marketing programs.

5 *Evaluate the company's competences*: The company needs to ensure that it has the competences and resources to serve and satisfy the segment's needs and wants profitably.

This approach suggests that there is a precision in the analysis of market segments, which is not strictly true. Many hospitality markets are fragmented, and it is difficult to calculate the volume and value of a market segment accurately. Market share can be even more difficult to ascertain accurately. However, an important benefit of using segmentation analysis in hospitality operations is to identify consumer trends to establish which market segments will become attractive in the future and which market segments are becoming less attractive now.

Hospitality segmentation variables

Segmentation variables are the basis for classifying consumers into different market segments. Some of these segmentation variables have already been discussed in the consumer behaviour and customer expectations sections of this chapter. The segmentation variables form the building blocks in developing target market profiles of customer expectations.

The primary segmentation variable used virtually by all hospitality companies is *purpose of travel*. The three main categories are business, non-business (variously defined as leisure, holiday, personal or social) and visiting friends and relatives (VFR). Each of these main categories can be further subdivided into several distinct market segments, but a key point to remember is that the *same person* can have different customer needs and wants depending on whether the purpose of travel is business, non-business or VFR. Each micro-segment has its own market demand factors and individual characteristics with implications for hospitality providers (see Fig. 3.2 for a summary of accommodation market segments).

Hospitality market segments

Tourist accommodation market		Purpose of visit	Segments	Price	Geographic		Demographic & family unit	Party size	User status
Business		FIT Corporate Local company Meeting Conference Exhibition	[Management [Sales [Training [Recruitment [Professional advisors [Board	Luxury Mid-market Budget	Domestic International	Cities Counties States Regions American British Chinese Japanese	Age: 18–24 25–34 35–54 55–65	Single 2–4 Small group Large group	Non-user Potential First-time Light Medium Heavy Lapsed
Leisure		Overnight stopover Family holiday Honeymoon Package holiday Leisure break Exotic holiday Go-as-you-please Fly-drive Incentive	[Destination [Activity [Cultural [Event [Relaxation [Sight-seeing [Sand, sea, sun	Luxury Mid-market Budget	Domestic International	Cities Countries States Regions American British Chinese Japanese	Age: Under 18 18–24 25–34 35–54 55–70 70+ Family cycle: Young single Young couple Couple & children Older couple Old single	Single Couple 2–6 Small group Large group	Non-user Potential First-time Light Medium Heavy Lapsed

Figure 3.2 Hospitality market segments

Business

Accommodation business customers tend to:

* Be less price sensitive, since the employer generally meets hospitality and travel expenses;
* Be more likely to stay for one night, or only a few, on each trip;
* Be more frequent, or regular, users of hotel accommodation;
* Stay at establishments that are within a reasonable (5–30 min) travel time of their place of work – hence, the higher demand for business accommodation close to commercial, industrial and retail areas;
* Be less seasonal – business travel patterns are less dependent on weather and holiday schedules.

The business travel segment includes business trips that are unavoidable, like sales meetings with customers and technical visits to factories by engineers. Other trips are more discretionary, for example attending a conference or exhibition.

Leisure

Accommodation leisure customers tend to:

* Be much more price sensitive than business travellers, since they are paying for the accommodation out of their own after-tax income
* Be more likely to stay longer on each trip – short breaks are normally at least a couple of days, 2-week holidays are common and longer holiday periods are usual
* Be less-frequent users of hotel accommodation (unless they are also business travellers)
* Stay at establishments that are close to leisure amenities and tourist attractions – hence, the demand for cultural, rural and beach resort hotels
* Be much more seasonal, both in terms of climate and the time of year.

There are some business and leisure travel markets that overlap. For example, international conferences and exhibitions often include an element of free time to be enjoyed as a leisure period. The incentive travel sector uses the appeal of free, and often luxurious or adventurous, leisure travel to motivate and reward performance in business markets.

Visiting friends and relatives

From an accommodation demand perspective, this segment does not generate significant volumes of business for hotels, because people tend to stay in the homes of their friends and relatives. This market is more important to tourism establishments in the day-visitor attraction sectors, and to restaurants and bars.

Geographic

A simple segmentation variable is identifiable from a customer's home address, post code and/or country of origin. National governments often require hotels to collect passport details from international visitors, and these data provide important marketing information about the types of international markets being served. Geographic segmentation variables within a country's domestic market include cities, counties, states and regions.

The benefits of segmenting consumers using geographic variables include the following:

- Nationality is a universally recognized method of categorizing visitors in international tourism marketing
- The special needs and wants of consumers from particular regions can be researched and products can be specifically developed to satisfy those needs and wants
- Media channels, which depend on advertising revenues, provide audience statistics and demographic data that profile potential consumers within their catchment area. These data can be used to target marketing communications campaigns cost-effectively;
- Customer registration data make it easy to identify customers' addresses.

A Classification Of Residential Neighborhoods (ACORN) is an example of a geo-demographic (mix of geography and demography) segmentation tool, commercially available in the United Kingdom from the company CACI. All UK homes are allocated a postcode (or zip code), and there are approximately 30 homes in each postcode. Each UK postcode has been classified, in conjunction with the government's census data, according to the type and status of the housing and area. Having identified the clusters of housing, representative samples are regularly interviewed with in-depth personal face-to-face interviews. The research provides a wealth of data about the purchasing habits of people who are representative of their area. CACI has classified British consumers into five broad categories, 17 groups and 56 types based on this research. The broad categories are Wealthy Achievers, Urban Prosperity, Comfortably Off, Moderate Means and Hard Pressed.

Activity 3.2

- Log on to the CACI website at www.caci.co.uk;
- Explore the site and review the research in customer profiling and ACORN – how can this information help hospitality marketers?

Demographic

Demographics is the study of population characteristics and to a large extent rely on data collected by governments during censuses. Market research companies in developed countries use the census data to develop consumer profiles. One of the key influences in changing the demand for tourism products is the change in birth and survival rates, which alters the age structure of populations. Marketers are keenly interested in the growth of the ratio of older people living in Western populations. This 'grey' market creates new leisure and tourism opportunities for hospitality companies.

Demographic variables include age, gender, family size and structure, ethnic origin, religion, nationality and socio-economic class.

Age

Hospitality companies use age as a critical segmentation variable when planning product concepts, especially in the activity, dining and leisure markets. There are considerable differences in consumer needs and wants between, and within, age groups. In the eating out market, the needs of young families with babies (special dietary requirements and changing facilities) are different from the needs of unmarried teenagers. The senior citizen market is often described as the 'grey' market and includes people in the following age groups:

- Older people aged between 55 and 64 years
- Elderly people aged between 65 and 74 years
- Aged people between 74 and 85 years
- Very old people aged over 85 years.

Although this division is somewhat arbitrary, it does help when evaluating the different needs and wants of the sub-segments of the grey market. For example, people older than 75 years are less interested in participating in leisure and sporting activities, whereas people aged between 55 and 70 years are still relatively active and interested in participating in leisure and sporting activities. The disposable income of the people older than 55 years is higher than that of the general population, because they have fewer financial outgoings on expenses like raising a family or paying the mortgage. This provides older people with more money to spend on leisure purchases. We have already identified that one of the characteristics of well-off Western older people is that they are more educated, sophisticated and well travelled than previous generations, and they, therefore, have higher expectations when staying in hotels and dining out. The special needs and wants of older people staying in hotels include quieter rooms with safety features like bath rails and non-slip shower mats, good porterage facilities to help with luggage, early evening dining options and smaller food portions.

Gender

Some hospitality products may be specifically geared to the needs of men or women. Hotel companies have responded to the expectations of women travellers by providing greater security measures in bedrooms, feminizing the bedroom decor and offering healthier menu options in restaurants. However, gender segmentation is not always precise – men can notice and prefer greater security measures, more feminine decor and healthy menus. Gay and lesbian markets, often described as the 'pink market,' are regarded as affluent and mobile consumers – because they do not normally have the expenses of rearing children.

Family size and structure

In Western cultures, the average number of children in a family is just below 2; in China, the one child per couple rule restricts the size of the family; however, in African and Arabic countries, large families are the norm. The size of the family influences the disposable income available for hospitality and leisure purposes. Family size also influences the design of hospitality products such as family accommodation and dining units. The hotel facilities that individuals and couples without children find acceptable are often not suitable for families with several children, and vice versa. The growth in the number of people living alone, especially through divorce, has created a market for singles clubs and organizations that provide opportunities for single people to meet travel and socialize.

Ethnic origin, religion and nationality

Ethnic origin, religion and nationality are important demographic variables that are closely linked to each other and to culture. One consequence of these cultural influences is our very different attitudes to food and what constitutes acceptable food items. Kosher cuisine is one of the well-known religious food disciplines for orthodox Jews, whilst fasting during Ramadan is equally important for Muslims. The differences between Eastern and Western style of cooking are recognized by international hotels in the Far East, who provide both styles of cooking at breakfast, lunch and dinner. Restaurants are typically segmented according to their ethnicity: American (fast food), Chinese, English, French, Indian, Italian, Japanese or Thai.

0175 ## Socio-economic class

Hospitality companies may not state explicitly which socio-economic class they target, but this is implicit in their marketing strategies. The low-cost family holiday camp market clearly targets socio-economic groups C1, C2 and D. The product offer varies but typically includes relatively basic accommodation, with a choice of half-board or self-catering options; a range of bar and food outlets (often with popular fast-food franchises such as Burger King and Pizza Hut), various activities, swimming, live entertainment and a nightclub. This offer caters for the needs of the parents and children of lower income families.

Buyer needs and benefits

The idea of segmenting markets according to the benefits sought from products is well established. Examples of benefits that buyers look for in hospitality products include the following:

- Convenience – this is often linked to location and speed of service
- Luxury – this is naturally associated with high levels of service and high prices
- Child-friendly accommodation – families travelling have specific needs (like informal, low-cost dining facilities)
- Health facilities – spa resorts offer exercise and dietary regimens for the benefit of their health-oriented patrons.

A number of different 'benefits' can be combined together to provide the total solution to a customer's set of problems. All-inclusive holiday resort hotels not only provide the accommodation and food elements of holiday but also all the sporting activities, excursions, leisure and entertainment facilities, and even alcoholic drinks, in a safe environment. This process of creating product/price benefit bundles should be based on a deep understanding of customer needs.

Price/product segmentation

Price sensitivity is a crucial segmentation variable in hospitality markets. Each hospitality market segment has its own specific pricing dynamics that need to be understood. Research and analysis should determine what consumers can afford to pay and what they are willing to pay. The price consumers are willing to pay plays a key role in determining the design, facilities and amenities, and the standard of décor, fixtures and furniture in planning a new product concept.

In hospitality, the link between price and quality in different product classes is strong. Consumers looking to be pampered in a luxurious environment expect to pay higher prices, while consumers of basic products expect to pay lower prices. Whilst the price/quality difference between product class extremes (e.g. the expensive, gourmet restaurant versus the cheap and cheerful café) is clearly apparent to consumers, the difference between adjacent product classes (e.g. a four-star conference hotel/venue and a three-star conference hotel/venue) can be virtually indistinguishable. This can lead to customer confusion, as the relative value for money between competing offers is not transparent.

Many hospitality chains develop their accommodation options with a particular price point in mind – for example, a US$ 50 per night accommodation price.

Many hotel companies describe their accommodation market segments in terms of product. Examples include conference; convention/exhibition; corporate; Free Independent Traveller (FIT); leisure break; local business; function guest and leisure tour group. The flexing of rates is discussed in Chapter 7 under revenue management.

CURRENT USER CHARACTERISTICS

Identifying the characteristics of customers who use hospitality products provides marketers with a profile of current users. These customer profiles can then be analyzed to identify attractive market segments for targeting purposes. There are a number of user characteristics that are important to hospitality operators and these are described here.

Usage status

This characteristic categorizes consumers into non-users, potential users, first-time users, regular users (who can be light, medium or heavy users) and former users (see Fig. 3.3). Marketing communication campaigns can be developed to target the different user categories, to encourage first-time visits, regular patronage or repeat visits after lapsed patronage. Understanding the different usage patterns enables marketing communication campaigns to be designed to influence the category of user.

Frequency

In accommodation markets, frequent business travellers – people who stay away from home on business travel for 15 or more trips per annum – are a highly attractive segment, because their lifetime value is high. Hotels strive to encourage regular and repeat customers, and over time hoteliers can build strong, long-lasting, special relationships with their 'regulars'. The importance of repeat and regular business customers has long been recognized by hotel groups. Frequent guest

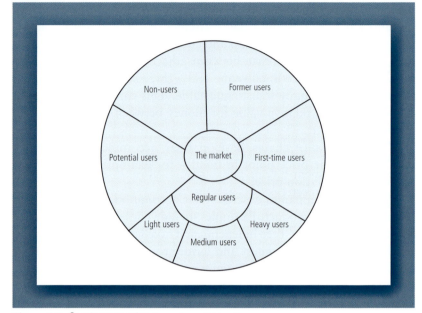

Figure 3.3 Guest usage satus *Source: Osman, 2001, p 41*

promotions, often linked to loyalty programs, are designed to reward frequent guests for their patronage (see Chapter 14).

Given the lower frequency of leisure trips, a regular customer might return to a favourite leisure hotel less frequently. A distinction needs to be drawn here between those hotels catering for long stay, long haul holidays and those catering for short leisure breaks within a couple of hours travelling time of the customer's home. The long haul guest might only return once per year, if that – indeed, a highly satisfied customer may only return once every 5 years – whereas the short break leisure guest might return to a favourite hotel three or four times per year. One consequence of this user profile is that the hotels targeting leisure customers need to allocate a higher promotional spend to attract a wider customer base or distribute their product via tour operators and travel agents.

Brand loyalty

A key objective of frequent guest or visitor programs is to build brand loyalty amongst those business travellers who are heavy users. Consumers' loyalty to hospitality brands varies. There has been considerable research into customers' habits in general and loyalty in particular. Customers have become more promiscuous in their shopping habits; indeed, promiscuous consumers might have several different hotel company reward cards. However, the investment in loyalty programs by airlines, hotels, petrol stations and supermarkets suggests that consumers are influenced especially when several

complementary service offers are included in the same scheme (see Chapter 14).

Purchase occasion

The type of purchase occasion influences the consumers' needs and wants. Many hospitality banqueting, restaurant and event products are aimed at the special family occasions that mark every important event in our lives – birth, coming of age parties, weddings, special birthdays, retirement functions, wedding anniversaries and funerals. The wedding market is often used as an example of a very special occasion.

Size of party

Hospitality managers recognize that party size, which has a considerable influence on the needs and wants of hospitality consumers, can be used as a segmentation variable. Clearly, groups of travellers have different check-in, check-out, dining, drinking, meeting and entertainment requirements compared with individual travellers. Companies that specialize in volume hospitality operations develop the facilities and skills necessary to cater for large-scale events. Sensible smaller outlets should avoid taking bookings from larger parties, which they know that they cannot cater for effectively, to avoid alienating their regular customers.

Lifestyle (or psychographics)

Psychographic segmentation is a behavioural classification of consumers according to their personality traits and lifestyle. It is based on detailed marketing research into the AIO of consumers and is linked to geo-demographic variables to provide consumer profiles. Marketing research analysts combine individual responses to questions about a person's AIO with details about his or her geo-demographic characteristics, and then cluster consumers into groups with similar responses to form psychographic profiles of market segments. The data characterising each psychographic segment provide a detailed picture of where consumers live; what education, occupation and income they enjoy; their AIO; the media they consume and the products they purchase. Proponents believe that psychographic segmentation

- Develops a deeper knowledge and understanding of consumer behaviour
- Is a good predictor of consumer behaviour
- Enables companies to design products better to meet consumer needs

- Provides the opportunity to develop cost-effective marketing campaigns for selected target markets.

Critics contend that psychographic segmentation

- Is unable accurately to define lifestyle variables
- Develops lifestyle segments that are not strictly homogeneous
- Is very expensive – research costs are high because of the detailed face-to-face interviewing techniques
- Is not effective because people change occupation and move homes frequently.

Case study 3.1 **EXTREME hotels' classification of consumer types**

EXTREME is a global brand, predicated on a passion for sports, travel, music and an unconventional way of life. EXTREME offers a range of international experiential products and services including the Extreme Sports TV channel that broadcasts 24/7 in 12 languages to 60 countries and over 40 million homes, TV sports program production, fashion-clothing, on-line mail order and high street retailing, pre-pay credit cards, theme parks, hotels and restaurants, and extreme sports and music events. The brand vision is to 'INSPIRE, EXPLORE, EXPERIENCE'.

EXTREME hotels target two different psychographic profiles – 'discoverers' and 'dreamers'. The discoverers are men and women who spend months travelling and enjoying action sports at a high level. They are hard core sports people and extreme travel junkies who are comfortable in their own skin; own style and with a positive self-image. Discoverers do not conform to mainstream ideals and carry images of their extreme experiences in the form of tattoos, scars, clothing and jewellery.

Dreamers are people who dream of enjoying a discoverer lifestyle, but modern life prevents them living the dream. They might ski once or twice a year; or take a long haul travel experience when they can, but wish they could be travelling for much longer periods of time. Although the dream cannot be delivered, dreamers associate themselves with the aspirational life style of the discoverers. Dreamers want products/services that help them to enjoy extreme experiences in sport and travel for their short holidays.

The majority of the EXTREME customers are dreamers. The target market is ABC1, early adopters who travel extensively (when they can), enjoy partying 24/7, have high adrenalin and are into sport, fashion, music and travel. Age is irrelevant but attitude and a love of the sports is paramount. The target demographic is primarily the 25- to 45-year-old market, but includes 60- and 70-year-old skiers, surfers and bikers. EXTREME hotels also provide family facilities for teen travellers to be *inspired*, to *explore* and *experience* sports.

EXTREME hotels is a management company with operations in Cape Town, South Africa and hotels under construction in Cape Verde, Hungary, Russia (for the winter Olympics, 2014) and Montenegro. The EXTREME concept is delivered in every aspect of the operation with irreverent humour as a key component of the brand essence. There is a flexible ground floor, free-flow area called the HUB, which provides a portable reception (on wheels, so reception can be removed to provide more space during the day and later at night) plus a bar/restaurant. Humour examples include the lift decked out as a shark diving cage; a climbing wall on the outside of the hotel; vertical guest transport using fireman's poles and helter-skelter slides; guest laundry collection bags labelled 'Smelly Stuff', a smoking room furnished with funeral caskets (the Coughin' Room).

Source: EXTREME hotels

Time

There are two aspects concerning the role of time as a market segmentation variable. First, from a seasonality perspective, hospitality operators need to understand why consumers patronize their outlets during quieter periods in order to develop effective marketing campaigns to increase sales during low season periods. Some older people who do not live with children and have flexible holiday arrangements enjoy relaxing in a quiet, peaceful environment, and can be considered a potential target market for holiday/hotel organizations in low season.

In this context, the second aspect of time refers to the advance booking period – the time between the customer booking and then actually consuming the hospitality product. This time period is an important segmentation variable, because the length, whether it is a couple of hours in advance or several years away, influences the design of the marketing program aimed at capturing the customer. The marketing program targeting a convention planner who is booking an international conference to be held in 3 years time will be different to the marketing program targeting an impulse diner who wants to eat out this evening.

Eating out and entertainment

Apart from a small number of high-profile outstanding eating and entertainment establishments (these become known as 'destination' restaurants, because their reputation is so high that customers are prepared to travel a long distance), customer markets for local hospitality units are focused on locally defined areas. Market variations occur according to whether the unit is sited in a city center, the suburbs or a countryside location and are determined by the different geo-demographic characteristics of the neighbourhoods. The characteristics of these target markets are also defined using gender, income and stage in the family life cycle and using benefit segmentation criteria like service/quality, price/value and time/convenience.

Research consistently demonstrates that diners look for quality of food, quality of service, value for money, friendly staff and cleanliness. Different target markets will rate the importance of these criteria according to their own needs. For example, price/value and time/convenience are rated more highly by the family eating-out segment, because of the costs of taking a family out and the need to dine quickly to avoid restless children becoming disruptive. Adults dining out without children can afford the time and money to have a more sophisticated eating out experience. Because the geo-demographic characteristics of an area are the prime influence on potential dining-out target markets, hospitality providers need to choose the sites of their operations with great care to ensure that they target appropriate customer markets.

HOSPITALITY TARGET MARKETS

Companies need to evaluate the potential of market segments using the following criteria:

1 *Market data* – size, growth, accessibility, consumer needs and wants and benefits sought, customer power;
2 *Competitor analysis* – number of competitors, their market share, capabilities, resources, strengths and weaknesses, differentiators and profitability and the potential for new entrants;
3 *Internal company audit* – capability of servicing the market segment, compatibility with existing and future segments and compatibility with the company's resources and values.

Major hospitality firms planning to enter a new geographic market invest in detailed marketing research to evaluate the attractiveness of competing cities or suburbs before deciding which to enter. The smaller operator adopts a much less formal process that is often based more on intuition than marketing research. Once selected, the market segment is defined as a 'target market' for which the company designs an appropriate marketing program. Target markets are groups of consumers, with similar needs and wants, for whom a marketing program is specifically developed to satisfy those needs and wants.

Hospitality companies target several different market segments at the same time, but each target market should have its own marketing mix program. Hospitality operators generally recognize that the 'Pareto Rule' – the principle that about 20 per cent of customers account for about 80 per cent of volume sales and profits – works. Heavy users represent the highest profit potential target market. However, a hospitality company's prime target markets are also going to be the competitor's prime target markets, and the relatively small number of heavy users is, therefore, highly sought after.

There are two broad classes of target markets; consumer markets and organizational markets. Each requires a different marketing approach, because buyer behaviour differs between individuals and organizations.

Consumer target markets

Consumer markets can be defined as travellers and local people who consume hospitality products as individuals, couples, families or small groups of people, for business or leisure purposes. Consumer markets have an influence over their choice of hospitality provider, set their own budget and pay from their own resources. Examples of consumer target markets include the Chinese international market, seniors and the gay/lesbian market.

International outbound market – China

Throughout the Noughties (the decade from 2000), there was significant growth in Chinese outbound tourism – indeed the number of Chinese travelling abroad more than doubled (Euromonitor International, 2010). The drivers for this remarkable change in consumer behaviour are a growth economy and a positive governmental attitude that has increased international outbound business and leisure travel. The growing economy has led to increased disposable income for a small number of very affluent Chinese and crucially a growing proportion of the urban upper/middle classes. Consumption of lifestyle products such as travel and eating out is regarded as an indicator of social esteem and success. Chinese nationals need government permission to travel abroad and the Chinese travel industry is heavily regulated. Only Category A travel agencies are permitted to organize international travel and destination countries have to obtain 'Approved Destination Status'.

The criteria that Chinese use to choose a country to visit include friendly relationship between China and the host country, proximity (e.g. South-East Asian countries like Thailand), the opportunity to visit family and friends and word of mouth recommendation from friends and family. Both business and leisure markets use package tours organized with host-speaking tour guides. The main problems for host countries catering for Chinese travellers are dissatisfaction with accommodation due to different hotel classification systems (e.g. a Chinese hotel star rating is one star higher than that in Australia (Pan & Laws, 2002)); language issues when there is no guide to translate; and disappointment with local restaurants – Chinese restaurants in Western countries adapt their cuisine for indigenous markets, which then disappoints mainland Chinese diners. The number of independent Chinese travellers has also grown and is forecast to continue growth.

Many young, modern, urban Chinese want to delay marriage, and rearing children, to enjoy a contemporary lifestyle – which includes travel abroad. An emerging issue for some popular international tourism destinations is the volume of Chinese visitors, which is forecast to continue exponential growth and might create tensions between mass tourists from one culture, other international visitors and the local host population (Cai, Li, & Knutson, 2007).

Hospitality companies targeting international markets need to adapt their marketing offer to ensure that guests from significant source markets are satisfied. Adaptations include the following:

- Multilingual front desk operatives and food/beverage managers
- Hotel/restaurant information and safety notices written in multiple languages
- International food options (restaurant, in-room service).

The seniors market

SAGA is a well-established company that targets the over-fifties mature market and originally focused on travel, but now also provides complementary health, insurance and financial services. SAGA offers package holiday and travel services to major tourist destinations in every continent. The holiday product, which is carefully designed for people aged over 50, concentrates on safe travelling. Many of the customers' grateful comments stress how the SAGA staff solved minor travel problems. The focus is on companionship, excursions with cultural/historic sightseeing and shopping, educational trips – one holiday is called 'art treasures in Italy' – and good quality, comfortable hotels. Consumer concerns about help for disabled and elderly people travelling (e.g. porters to carry the luggage at airports and hotels) are answered on the frequently asked questions (FAQs) pages on the website. The language in the publicity material and on the Internet is mature and very sympathetic to the needs of older people. Photographs show groups of older people dressed in smart/casual clothes quietly enjoying attractive views of scenic areas. Hotels are selected for comfort and quality and are unlikely to be very noisy late at night. The message clearly conveys confidence that SAGA has great experience in looking after older people when travelling and on holiday.

Gay/lesbian and women-only hotels

There is a distinction between hotels that are gay/lesbian friendly, but primarily target other markets, and hotels that only target gays/lesbians. The five-star designer Hotel Skt Petri, Copenhagen, which targets multiple markets, describes itself as gay-friendly. A women-only hotel such as the Luthan Hotel & Spa in Riyadh, Saudi Arabia,

Enjoy some excellent music breaks with Best Western Hotels

If you love attending concerts and would like to visit some of Britain's leading venues, this will be music to your ears.

Wherever you stay you will enjoy the unique combination that Best Western can offer you. Because every hotel is individually owned and managed each one has its own unique atmosphere and personality. And because they're all Best Western hotels, you are guaranteed the highest standards of hospitality.

So wherever you want to hear some of the finest music in Britain, you can be sure you'll enjoy accommodation to match.

ROYAL OPERA HOUSE, COVENT GARDEN, LONDON

The world-famous home to The Royal Ballet and The Royal Opera has a year round programme of performances.
Ticket office: 0207 304 4000 Website: www.royalopera.org

Stay at • **Best Western Shaftesbury Hotel, Piccadilly, London**
Stay right in the heart of central London in this recently refurbished hotel.

THE GRAND THEATRE, LEEDS

The main Leeds home of the acclaimed Opera North company. Autumn highlights include productions of Tosca and Der Rosenkavalier.
Ticket office: 0113 222 6222 Website: www.leeds.gov.uk/grandtheatre

Stay at • **Best Western Guide Post Hotel, Leeds/Bradford**
A modern hotel in a peaceful village location close to both Leeds and Bradford. The Yorkshire Dales are also just a short drive away.

BIRMINGHAM SYMPHONY HALL, BIRMINGHAM

Right in the heart of Birmingham city centre, this is home to the Birmingham Symphony Orchestra. Since it was opened in 1991 the Hall's superb acoustics have earned it the reputation as one of the world's finest music venues.
Ticket office: 0121 212 3333 Website: www.necgroup.co.uk

Stay at • **Best Western Lea Marston Hotel and Leisure Complex , Birmingham**
A modern, friendly hotel situated in a rural environment, just 15 minutes' drive from Birmingham city centre.

USHER HALL, EDINBURGH

In a city famous for its performance spaces Usher Hall is one of Edinburgh's best known, housing the Royal Scottish National Orchestra and the Scottish Chamber Orchestra.
Ticket office: 0131 228 1155 Website: www.usherhall.co.uk

Stay at • **Best Western Bruntsfield Hotel, Edinburgh**
Its central, yet peaceful, location overlooking an attractive park means you'll enjoy the best of the city with a really relaxing place to stay.

BRIDGEWATER HALL, MANCHESTER

This £42 million concert hall is one of the architectural highlights of the regenerated Manchester city centre and is the home of the famous Hallé orchestra.
Ticket office: 0161 907 9000 Website: www.bridgewater-hall.co.uk

Stay at • **Best Western Willowbank Hotel, Manchester**
Five minutes drive from the city centre, the Willowbank has been recently refurbished throughout to create the perfect base for any visit to Manchester.

There are over 300 individual Best Western hotels throughout the UK.

Call **0845 072 0700** now to arrange your refreshingly different stay quoting MBBC or visit www.bestwestern.co.uk.

Best Western

Figure 3.4 Best Western advert targeting classical music lovers *Source: Best Western Hotels*

is an example of services targeted at straight female travellers. Women-only hotels are obviously staffed only by females. Rainbow Tourism, an Australian-based gay/lesbian travel operator with an international scope, have their own accommodation accreditation scheme (Rainbow Tourism Accredited) and identify gay/lesbian owned and operated hotels in over 20 different countries. However, homosexuality is still a crime in over 70 countries and many countries would not allow a gay/lesbian hotel to operate.

Organizational target markets

Organizational target markets are groups of travellers who consume hospitality products for business and leisure purposes. Individual customers who are travelling as part of a group of travellers have less influence (or none) over the choice of hospitality provider and will sometimes have to pay for the service out of their own resources. If the organization is a corporate business, then the company (not the individual) will pay and will normally set expenditure limits. Examples of hospitality organizational target markets include corporate travel, MICE markets, aircrew, tour groups and a miscellaneous category called SMERFE (social, military, educational, religious, fraternal and ethnic).

Corporate travel

Corporate travel is a major expense item for national and international companies. Corporations regard the purchase of hotel accommodation in the same way as the purchase of any other business necessity. Companies are aware of their own purchasing power and expect discounted rates. Most hotel groups and larger independent hotels offer a standard corporate rate with a minimum 10 per cent discount off the accommodation rack rate and those companies booking larger volumes of nights negotiate higher discounts. However, if the agreed volume of business is not achieved and the contract is not sufficiently specific, there can be problems between hotelier and corporate client.

There is an image of business executives enjoying the most luxurious travel and hotel accommodation, dining out in the finest restaurants and conspicuously consuming the best wines with 'no expense spared'. This might be true for a small number of senior executives, but is certainly not the case for all business travellers. Corporate organizations are hierarchical in design and most companies agree expense limits according to the position of employees within the hierarchy of the company. Business travel allowances depend on the corporate culture of individual organizations, which will vary immensely.

MICE

The MICE market is often discussed in homogenous terms, but in fact each element of the MICE market has its own distinctive needs and wants.

Meetings

The meetings market can be divided into two distinct categories – corporate and association:

Corporate meetings

The corporate meetings market includes company management meetings, planning, recruitment and sales meetings, and training events in locations that are not company-owned. The number of delegates attending a meeting can range from only two to over a hundred. The market is a major source of revenue for hotel operations and includes both day meetings and meetings requiring overnight accommodation. Delegates attending such meetings are obliged to attend. The company organizing (and paying for) the event needs to achieve its own specific organizational goals for the meeting to be success.

Organizers and delegates who attend corporate meetings have professional standards and high expectations of service. Prior to the meeting, the hospitality venue has to work with the meeting organizer to plan the event and ensure that all the details are carefully agreed. In recent years, the major hotel brands have developed guaranteed conference packages to satisfy the needs and wants of meetings organizers and their delegates.

Association meetings

In addition to corporate meetings, there are a large number of professional and trade organizations that hold regular meetings for members. These voluntary meetings are normally held in the evenings, have a variable attendance and do not generate significant amounts of accommodation, food or beverage revenue. However, most associations will hold functions such as annual dinners, and individuals involved with the associations may be important potential users of hospitality outlets in their places of work. Examples of such organizations include the Lions, Masonic Lodges, Rotary Club and Round Table.

Incentive

The incentive market is based on using travel or food and beverage as a sales incentive to improve company performance or as a prize for consumer promotions. The incentive package includes travel to/from the destination, accommodation and a component that is regarded as very special to the organization's employees or customers. With the growth of sophisticated customers, incentive travel often features exotic or extraordinary destinations combined with atypical (adventure) activities or luxurious pampering. Hospitality companies targeting the incentive market need to provide exceptional customer experiences to ensure that the winners of the prize are wowed. Incentive trips are normally short, expensive and unusual. Dedicated incentive travel intermediaries broker destination/hospitality/activity packages to corporate buyers who want to incentivize employees or customers.

Conventions, exhibitions and trade fairs

The lead (or booking) time for major national and international events involving hundreds or thousands of delegates ranges from 2 to more than 10 years. The number of venues capable of hosting these events is limited by the large scale of such events. Major convention and exhibition centers are often built by government initiatives in recognition of the economic value these venues can generate in a region in terms of employment, revenue and prosperity. Cities like Birmingham (UK) and Dallas (USA) and city states like Singapore have provided dedicated facilities that attract major national and international events.

Key issues for event organizers include the following:

- An effective transportation infrastructure (e.g. good airport and road connections)
- Provision of modern convention and exhibition facilities of sufficient size
- The availability of a wide range of quality hospitality facilities
- Resort, leisure and recreational amenities.

For international events, climate factors and the relative cost and travel distances are additional influences in deciding which venue to book. There is considerable international competition between the different venues, which has led to the emergence of convention or visitor bureau linked to tourist information centers and funded by local government and business. The role of the visitor bureau is primarily to promote the area and act as an information provider. Events may last for 7 days and, apart from a main event, include several ancillary minor functions.

Event organizers will be responsible for coordinating the booking of the venue, the dissemination of publicity for the event and possibly some of the catering arrangements. Individual companies and visitors are responsible for making their own travel and hotel arrangements. Individual visitors may see the event as an opportunity to combine work activities with some leisure, relaxation, sporting or sightseeing activities, which explains the appeal of more exotic locations for international events. Examples of organizations booking exhibitions and conferences include professional and trade bodies, and political parties.

Aircrew

A market segment that hotels target in 'gateway' locations is that of airline employees, and specifically airline crew. The high volume of intercontinental, regional and international flights, coupled with the need for aircrew to have proper rest periods between flights has created a demand for group accommodation for hotels within approximately 15–45 minutes travel time of major airports. Aircrew have special needs and wants, including:

- Efficient 24-hour check-in and check-out procedures
- Bedrooms that are available immediately upon arrival and check-in
- Quiet and dark rooms, preferably with blackout blinds, to facilitate sleeping at any time of the day or night
- A 24-hour food and beverage service, at a reasonable charge, since airline crews have limited expense allowances
- Efficient wake-up calls, because the airline crew must meet their flight schedules on time.

Some years ago, aircrew had a glamorous image, appearing to mix well with other guests and upscale hotels regarded them as a compatible and attractive target market. Today, the growth of mass air travel has led to a less glamorous and more workaday image of airline crew, and the more exclusive hotels are less interested in targeting this market. The Arora Group has opened seven UK hotels that primarily target airline crew: three in Heathrow, three in Gatwick and one in Manchester under the Arora, Mercure and Sofitel brands. Facilities in the bedrooms include triple glazing, full blackout curtains, king-sized beds, air conditioning, 24-hour room service and interactive TV with Internet, games and video; this provision enables aircrew to sleep, eat, connect and relax in their room at any time of the day or night.

Tour groups

The growth of global tourism has increased the demand for international group travel that is organized by tour operators. These groups of travellers are provided with inclusive travel and accommodation products and, depending upon the location, food service. This is high-volume business and the hotels interested in this market have to offer low, competitive prices to win the business. Groups need

- Dedicated, efficient group check-in and check-out procedures and concierge/porters' services

- Good-sized lobby/lounge areas, where members of the tour group can conveniently meet
- Efficient food service, because they are often on a strict schedule and do not want to run late.

Sometimes, hotel employees treat tour group customers as the least important of all clients, but in volume terms, tour groups represent a significant market, especially in major tourist attractions.

SMERFE

SMERFE is a North American expression that stands for social, military, educational, religious, fraternal and ethnic, and it is a convenient heading to discuss all the group market segments not already discussed.

This segment is generally very price sensitive. SMERFE organizations are non-profit making and members/family pay for their event out of post-tax income. Consequently, the organizers of SMERFE bookings are inclined to take advantage of low season bargain rates. Although the room rates offered have to be low to attract SMERFE bookings, there can be a significant food and beverage spend linked to the event. An exception to these general comments about the SMERFE market is the special family occasion, like weddings and wedding anniversaries, which can range in price from the very modest budget to the most extreme, extravagant budget.

Intermediaries

The complexity of efficiently arranging group travel has created a role for specialty intermediaries, to act on behalf of organizations in their negotiations with hospitality and travel providers. These intermediaries have become target markets for hospitality companies in their own right. Key intermediaries, who book volume business and expect competitive rates, include

- Conference and meetings planners
- Travel agents
- Wholesalers and tour operators
- Incentive travel houses.

The role of intermediaries is discussed in detail in Chapter 8.

Mixing market segments

A key issue for all hospitality operations is to ensure that the various target markets are compatible. Mixing incompatible market segments leads to customer dissatisfaction and serious customer complaints.

In hotels, the imperative of filling rooms in low and shoulder seasons can motivate reservation managers to accept bookings from customers whose needs and wants are not compatible with prime target markets. Examples of incompatible segments include business and leisure customers, elderly tour groups and families with children, and mixing different levels of employees in the same hotel. Similar problems can arise when hotels cater for banquets, and residents are disturbed by large, noisy, late-night functions with music and dancing. The principle of separating segments with incompatible needs is the answer to this problem. Therefore, accommodation reservation managers need to be aware of the banqueting diary and banqueting sales executives need to be aware of the rooms' situation when they are taking potentially disruptive bookings.

CONCLUSION

Understanding consumer behaviour and customer expectations is essential if hospitality managers are to succeed in delivering customer satisfaction. Segmenting markets is the starting point for effective marketing. Marketers need to identify attractive market segments and then develop appropriate marketing strategies to win and keep customers. We will discuss how to develop the marketing strategies in the later chapters, but the process should always start with the needs and wants of target markets.

   In this chapter, we have explained

- The different factors that influence hospitality consumer behaviour
- Customer expectations and the 'zone of tolerance'
- The hospitality buyer decision-making process
- The importance of segmentation in developing effective marketing strategies
- The market segmentation process
- Key hospitality market segmentation variables
- How to evaluate potential hospitality target markets
- The characteristics of hospitality consumer and organizational target markets.

REVIEW QUESTIONS

Look at your answers to activity 3.1
- What influences (or would influence) your decision to purchase a:
  - drink in a local cafe?
  - short holiday in your own country?
  - long holiday in a country on the other side of the world?
- Can you now explain your decisions using consumer behaviour theory to help you?

Now check your understanding of this chapter by answering the following questions:

1 Discuss the influences that impact on hospitality consumer behaviour. Provide examples to illustrate your answer.
2 Evaluate customer expectations and the concept of the zone of tolerance. How does this model help explain customer behaviour?
3 Discuss the consumer buyer decision-making process for hospitality products.
4 Describe the segmentation variables that hospitality companies can use to categorize potential customers.
5 Evaluate the characteristics of hospitality customer and organizational target markets.

References and Further Reading

Bowen, D., & Clarke, J. (2009). *Contemporary tourist behaviour: Yourself and others as tourists*. CABI Publishing.

Cai, L. A., Li, M., & Knutson, B. J. (2007). Research on China outobund market: A meta-review. *Journal of Hospitality and Leisure Marketing*, *16*, 5–20.

Cooper, C., Fletcher, J., Fryall, A., Gilbert, D., & Wanhill, S. (2008). *Tourism* (4th ed.). Financial Times/Prentice Hall.

Judge, T. A., Higgins, C. A., Thoresen, C. J., & Barrick, M. R. (1999). The big five personality traits, general mental ability, and career success across the life span. *Personnel Psychology*, *52*, 3.

Levitt, T. (1983). The globalization of markets. *Harvard Business Review*, *38*, 45–56.

March, R., & Woodside, A. G. (2005). *Tourism behaviour*. CABI Publishing.

Osman, H. (2001). *Practice of relationship marketing in hotels. PhD Thesis*. Oxford Brookes University.

Pan, G. W., & Laws, E. (2002). Tourism marketing opportunities for Australia in China. *Journal of Vacation Marketing*, *8*, 39–48.

Swarbrooke, J., & Horner, S. (2006). *Consumer behaviour in tourism*. Butterworth-Heinemann.

Usunier, J. C., & Lee, J. (2009). *Marketing across cultures*. Prentice Hall.

Usunier, J. C., & Lee, J. (2009). *Marketing across cultures* (5th ed.). Financial Times/Prentice Hall.

www.euromonitorinternational.co (2010)

Zeithaml, V. A., Berry, L. L., & Parasuraman, A. (1993). The nature and determinants of customer expectations of service. *Journal of the Academy of Marketing*, *21*, 1–12.

CHAPTER **4**

Competitive strategies

Chapter objectives

After going through this chapter, you should be able to:

- Describe how hospitality organizations vary in their segmentation, positioning and differentiation strategies
- Understand the characteristics of hospitality firms that impact on marketing practice
- Carry out a competitive analysis, using Michael Porter's Five Forces model
- Understand the role of branding in hospitality organizations
- Appreciate the international significance of major players in the hotel and restaurant industry.

INTRODUCTION

The hospitality competitive environment is dynamic, intense and turbulent, since there is more supply than demand in most market segments. In this chapter, we examine how companies develop and implement their segmentation, positioning and differentiation strategies as they begin to compete for customers. We then explore the characteristics of hospitality firms – especially the differences between large-scale companies and smaller independent operators. We introduced the 'five forces' model that is widely used to analyse the hospitality industry's competitive environment. Finally, we explain the critical role of branding strategies, especially in the international arena of the hotel and restaurant industry. Competition can be fierce, and knowing your competitors is of crucial importance to hospitality marketers.

Activity 4.1

Before reading the rest of the chapter, think about the major international hotel brands:

- How many hotels and bedrooms do the largest hotel companies manage?
- How many hotel brands can you name?
- Which company owns which hotel brands?

When you have completed the chapter, carry out this activity again and then compare your answers.

SEGMENTATION STRATEGIES

In Chapter 3, we discussed hospitality market segmentation variables and target markets in detail. There are significant differences between the segmentation strategies of large hospitality organizations with multiple sites and those of independent, single-site operators. For larger organizations, there are three alternative strategies: mass marketing, differentiated marketing and focused marketing (see Fig. 4.1).

Mass marketing

Companies that adopt a mass marketing (or undifferentiated) strategy are responding to the *similarities* of consumers' needs and wants in large markets. They develop a single offering to satisfy those customers. The benefits to the company include a standardized product offer and operation, leveraging significant savings in purchasing, production, staffing and promotion via massive economies of scale. The most visible example of mass marketing in hospitality is the fast-food market (McDonald's, Burger King, KFC), where the same offer is

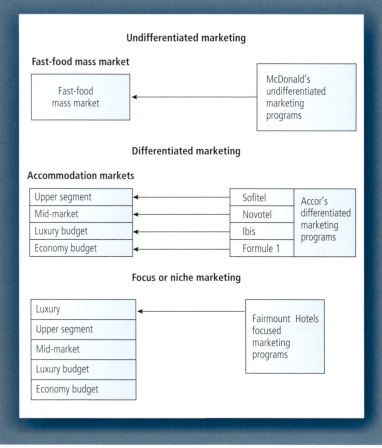

Figure 4.1 Segmentation strategies in hospitality

delivered globally, although even here it is possible to detect marketing responses to segmentation variables. For example, McDonald's has developed special breakfast menus (a time-based market segment) and adapted the ingredients of their burgers in India and Muslim countries (ethnic/religious market segments).

Differentiated marketing

Hospitality organizations adopting a differentiated segmentation strategy identify the *differences* between the needs and wants of various market segments, and develop individual marketing programs to satisfy the needs and wants of each market segment. The advantages of a differentiated approach, compared to mass marketing, include the opportunity to increase sales and market share – by providing more bedrooms in different branded hotels, or more covers/tables in different branded restaurants, in the same locations, with each brand serving different market segments. The development of specific marketing programs for each segment should enable hospitality operators to satisfy customers better than a mass marketing approach, and generate higher repeat and recommended sales.

In the long term, international hospitality organizations with a portfolio of brands serving different segments of the market, and across most continents, are less reliant on any particular segment, thus reducing the financial risk to the group. The disadvantages of a differentiated strategy are mainly cost based. The costs of developing different marketing programs for separate market segments is higher due to separate design and build costs, different purchasing schedules, more specialized staffing and different marketing communication activities. In the international hotel sector, Accor have developed 18 hotel brands whilst in the British eating out market Whitbread has developed five branded restaurant operations: Beefeater, Brewers Fayre, Costa Coffee, Table Table, and Taybarns. Each of these brands targets a different consumer and provides a different marketing offer to deliver the specific needs and wants appropriate for each target market.

Focused, concentrated or niche marketing

Hospitality companies that concentrate their marketing programs on a single-market segment adopt a concentrated or focused segmentation strategy. This strategy can also be called a niche marketing strategy. Hospitality operators can either focus on a specific market segment, for example, the luxury leisure market, or adopt a geographic concentration where all the company's outlets are focused within a specific geographic region. Because of their focus on a single segment, this strategy enables hospitality operators to understand fully the needs and wants of their customers in that market segment. Fairmount, who manage five-star hotels across the world including, the Fairmount in San Francisco, the Plaza in New York and the Savoy in London exclusively focus on the luxury segment. Sandals with four all-inclusive resort brands targeting different markets have a geographic focus on the Caribbean.

Over time, the company builds up greater expertise in serving its customers and in delivering customer satisfaction, as well as enjoying greater operational efficiency and potentially enhanced profitability. The main disadvantage of this strategy is the over-reliance on one-market segment, which can make the company extremely vulnerable to any decline in that segment's purchasing power. Companies that only focus on one market can experience severe trading difficulties during recessions, compared to companies that have adopted a differentiated strategy to spread the risk.

Single-site businesses

The segmentation strategy adopted by individually owned/managed units is inseparable from the property's character, location, catchment area and competition. Most hotel properties within a product class, including chain-owned branded properties, need to target several different market segments to ensure the operation trades profitably. The seasonality of hospitality markets means that operators have to target different segments at different times of the day, week or month. Few hotels can afford to only target one market segment, and even unique, individual leisure destination hotels will normally target several sub-segments of the market. Typically, hotels will target business market segments for midweek occupancy and leisure market segments at the weekends.

TARGETING, POSITIONING AND DIFFERENTIATION

The selection of target markets provides a focus for the development of positioning and differentiation strategies. It is difficult for companies to compete effectively in today's crowded, over-communicated marketplace, where consumers are bombarded by thousands of messages from hundreds of commercial, non-commercial and government organizations on a daily basis. This intense competitive environment forces hospitality firms to try and create a distinctive marketing offer that will help the company to stand out and be noticed by its target markets. The dilemma for hospitality operators is that there are virtually no significant differences between the core products offered by rivals in the same product class. Generic products, which do not have any real differences, are described as commodity products. The original commodity products were items such as table salt and drinking water. In hospitality, the tangible elements of a hospitality experience – a bed, a meal, a drink – are so similar that they can be considered as commodity products, and this means that it can be extremely difficult to provide an offer that is genuinely different from that of your competitors. An innovation or improvement that one company introduces is often quickly copied or imitated by the competitors.

However, hospitality consumers do recognize that some products and companies have very distinct images compared to their rivals, and those companies have worked hard to cultivate that image. This process, the design and maintenance of a distinctive position in the minds of target markets, is the focus of a positioning strategy. *Positioning strategy* is the process whereby hospitality companies try to develop a distinctive and favourable position in the minds of target markets, compared to competitors. The purpose of positioning is to ensure that target markets clearly understand what the product, service or brand stands for in the marketplace. Figure 4.2 demonstrates the link among segmentation, targeting and positioning.

Marketing research and analysis of the market segments should lead to an understanding of what consumers really want. An internal audit should identify the company's strengths that can be developed into

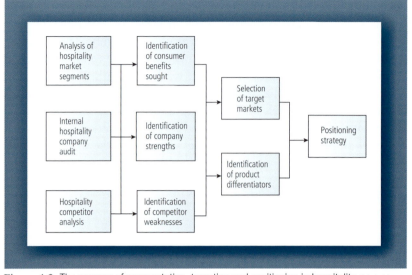

Figure 4.2 The process of segmentation, targeting and positioning in hospitality *Adapted from Lovelock, 2002*

product or service differentiators. An analysis of competitors should identify competitors' strengths and weaknesses, and thereby identify possibilities for effective product or service differentiation. The marketer then evaluates the three separate analyses, with the aim of establishing a match among the benefits sought by consumers, the strengths of the company and the weaknesses of competitors. The process culminates in the articulation of the company's desired position in the marketplace, which is designed to produce a competitive advantage.

Product or service differentiators are attributes used by hospitality marketers as part of the positioning process. Product or service differentiation helps to distinguish between the tangible (and/or intangible) product characteristics of the service offer from competitors in the same market segment. Again, the purpose is to create a competitive advantage attractive to selected target markets. The attributes that hospitality companies seek in order to differentiate themselves from competitors include location, quality (especially service quality), price, range of facilities and services, parking, safety/security and, for frequent travellers, reward programs. The product or service differentiators may only be minor in nature – they may not even be real – but when articulated effectively over a period of time, they help the brand to stand out from competitors in the mind of the target markets. One key differentiator that is more difficult for competitors to imitate is the brand and company history. Well-established hospitality brands increasingly use their history as a way to demonstrate their traditions of service quality over time. The 3 year refurbishment of the Savoy Hotel by Fairmount Hotels from 2007 to 2010 used the Hotel's 100-year-old archive to inform the re-design and décor throughout the refit; the Savoy's brand history was also used as a key differentiator in the communications campaign to re-launch the Hotel.

Activity 4.2

Visit the Savoy Hotel website and explore the brand history in the 'about us' web pages at www.fairmount.com/savoy

There are two different approaches to positioning: objective and subjective (Ries & Trout, 1986).

Objective positioning

Objective positioning refers to the tangible, physical, attributes that a hotel or restaurant offers customers. Attributes like the size of a budget motel bedroom, the facilities in a luxury hotel bathroom and the menu items on a fast-food restaurant menu are objective. The purpose of objective positioning is to use a tangible attribute as the main differentiator to distinguish your offer from competitors. Looking at the examples of attributes – the bedroom, the bathroom facilities and the menu items – you can see that any positioning based on these commodity product attributes can be easily imitated by competitors in the same product class. For this reason, objective positioning is not considered an effective long-term differentiator.

However, surveys of hospitality advertising reveal that all sectors of the industry, from international luxury hotel chains to local independent restaurants, use objective positioning in their promotional campaigns. Unfortunately, managers fail to understand that pictures of their bedrooms and restaurants look the same as thousands of other hotel bedrooms and restaurants.

Subjective positioning

Subjective positioning focuses on the intangible aspects of the offer or customer experience. It is important to note that the perceived image of a hospitality company may not necessarily reflect the true or real state of the product or service offered. What matters is *the customer's perception* of the offer. If the customer believes that a company's hospitality offer is high quality, with exceptional value, then the customer is right – and the offer is high quality, with exceptional value to that target market. Subjective positioning offers hospitality operators more opportunity to position their company effectively because the basis of the positioning strategy is linked to intangible attributes that are more difficult for competitors to imitate.

There are two approaches to subjective positioning, and the approach selected depends on whether the offer is more tangible-dominant or intangible-dominant. When hospitality offerings are tangible-dominant (e.g., the hotel bedroom) and there is little if any difference between the competitors' offers, marketers aim to differentiate their product by stressing intangible attributes. This is not an easy task.

The second approach to subjective positioning focuses on intangible-dominant products. The intangible attributes of hospitality are the service, the atmosphere, the reputation, the history, the impressions and the image. Given that these attributes are abstract, how can hospitality marketers position their intangible products positively in the minds of consumers? One answer is to 'tangibilize the intangible' – in other words, to provide tangible evidence that gives physical substantiation of the intangible attribute and thereby reinforces the position the company is aiming to attain. Hyatt's subjective positioning strategy aims to create an exotic, grand, majestic and distinctive image for its hotels by focusing on innovative modern architecture in the building of their atrium-style hotel lobbies. This relatively minor product differentiator was consistently used in Hyatt's promotional campaigns and succeeded in positioning Hyatt, in the minds of consumers, as a more exotic hotel than its competitors. Today, many hotels in the Hyatt's product class now provide spacious atrium-style lobbies, but Hyatt still maintains its original and distinctive image.

Positioning strategies

Positioning strategies are designed from answers to two basic questions:

1 Against whom should you position? These are usually other brands in the same competitive group – for example, Burger King positions against McDonald's – against whom you can demonstrate a competitive advantage.

2 How should you position? This provides the basis for your competitive efforts. Burger King, for example, positions itself as a healthier burger option because its burgers are flame broiled and not fried.

Reviews of the hospitality industry have identified a number of common positioning strategies:

- *Product feature or special attributes*. This strategy focuses on a tangible-dominant feature – for example, the largest function suite in the area might position a company in terms of space, grandeur and style.
- *Price/quality*. This positioning strategy for a luxury property might focus on the high service quality, high price and exclusive image; for a budget property, the focus might be a standard quality at a lower price, implying better value for money in the economy product class.
- *Customer benefit*. This type of positioning proposes solutions to solve customers' problems – in the events market a customer might

want their special occasion to be a 'night to remember;' and a company might provide a solution by delivering a creative, contemporary entertainment theme that provides the customer with a unique, memorable experience.

- *Use or usage.* This is a positioning strategy that focuses on the reasons why consumers use a product and is often targeted at specific markets – for example, a resort hotel with championship golf course targets executives who enjoy mixing business with sport.
- *User.* This positioning strategy focuses on the class of user – for example, families, younger people, religious people, wealthier older people – and emphasizes the product's appeal to the class of users; it will often feature endorsements by celebrities pertinent to the target market.

Positioning new hospitality ventures

In new hospitality ventures, there is likely to be a greater focus on the positioning strategy, in part because financial backers will expect the marketing plan to be well formulated before advancing any loans. A new venture provides the hospitality company with the opportunity to plan the new concept on the basis of sound marketing research and then to position the offer more effectively.

Positioning existing properties

In hospitality, there is a key difference between developing positioning strategies for existing properties and those for new ventures. In existing hotel and restaurant operations, a number of factors are fixed. These include the location, the geo-demographics of the catchment area, the property's current facilities, size and standards, the customer mix and the property's historic image. These fixed factors are not easily changed, and management must consider these in determining the positioning strategy that best fits the needs of the business and potential markets.

Repositioning

It is not unusual for hospitality operations to re-examine their current position in the marketplace and decide to reposition their property. The reason for repositioning may be:

- Falling sales (often a symptom of customer dissatisfaction)
- An opportunity to service an emerging market segment
- The threat of competition eroding market share.

The process for developing a repositioning strategy is similar to that of developing a positioning strategy for a start-up operation, with one caveat. In trying to reposition a hospitality property, there is the danger of sending out confusing signals to existing and potential target markets. This can damage the business by alienating those existing customers who do not like the changes. They might even abandon the operation. If the lost customers are not replaced with new customers quickly enough, the business can rapidly lose sales and profitability. Repositioning can involve the company in significant capital expenditure to alter the physical product, and may require changes in the personnel to implement the new strategy. For these reasons, repositioning can be a risky strategy, but the alternatives are either to continue trading in a deteriorating, downward spiral or to dispose of the property.

Case study 4.1 Repositioning at The Breakers, Palm Beach, Florida, USA

Property profile: The Breakers was originally constructed in 1896 by Henry Morrison Flagler, a Standard Oil Company magnate who also opened up Florida's East coast for tourism by building railroads and several hotels in the late nineteenth and early twentieth centuries. The Breakers, completely rebuilt in 1926 following a hotel fire, is a luxury oceanfront resort hotel created in the Italian Renaissance architectural style. The AAA Five Diamond Hotel comprises 540 rooms and suites; extensive dining, leisure and sports facilities including two 18-hole championship golf courses and a luxury spa; elegant ballrooms; and highly professional conference and meeting services. The Breakers is still privately owned by Flagler's heirs, and more than US$ 250 million has been invested in capital expenditure since 1990 to ensure that the property matches the needs of contemporary customers. The owners plan to continue investing between US$ 15 and US$ 25 million each year to ensure that The Breakers maintains its high standards.

The positioning challenge: As an iconic hotel with more than 100 years of brand history and its roots in American high society, research identified not only many positive attributes in The Breakers current position but also some consumer perceptions that the feel of the Hotel was too formal and the customer experience overly predictable. The Hotel's management team needed to redefine the market position of The Breakers, to match contemporary needs whilst retaining its high quality and quintessentially American heritage.

The key idea: To embed the concept of 'New American Glamour' as the foundation for the new positioning strategy. Although the phrase 'New American Glamour' is not mentioned in any promotional material to customers or employees, the idea underpins three core components in The Hotel's operations: The physical refurbishment, the service delivery and the organizational culture which is the intangible, critical element of The Breakers – its 'DNA'. Each of these core operational areas developed a range of initiatives to implement the 'New American Glamour' concept and create a feeling of informal elegance, connecting with customers emotionally, and delivering 'delightful surprises'. This repositioning provides a coherent sustainable brand strategy, which has enabled The Breakers to continually evolve and enhance the customer experience whilst retaining its historic roots.

Positioning maps

Positioning maps (Dev, Morgan & Shoemaker, 1995), also called perceptual maps, are tools used by marketers to plot consumer evaluations of competing hospitality products using two or more attributes. The attributes used to map competitors are variables that are important to consumers, and can include price, quality, location, reputation and value for money, quality of food and service, conference and banqueting facilities and availability of car parking. Quantitative research using websites, guidebooks, hotel tariffs and brochures provides useful competitor information. Qualitative consumer research can be undertaken using focus groups of hotel users to evaluate the quality of food, personnel and service items amongst competitors.

Sophisticated statistical packages analyse the data and draw up a series of perceptual maps using two or more dimensions as the axes. Positioning maps are used to identify the strengths and weaknesses of hotels and their competitors over a series of measures. Figure 4.3 provides an illustration of a positioning map using hotels' quality and price points from budget to luxury. Note the relationship between quality and price, where luxurious hotels charge higher prices and budget hotels charge lower prices. Normally, a unit must stay within its price/quality product class, which is indicated by the dotted lines on the map. If a hotel is charging more than the price/quality norm it could be accused of 'ripping-off' customers, unless there is another factor, for example, a convenient location that compensates for the higher price. If a hotel is offering genuinely higher quality at a lower

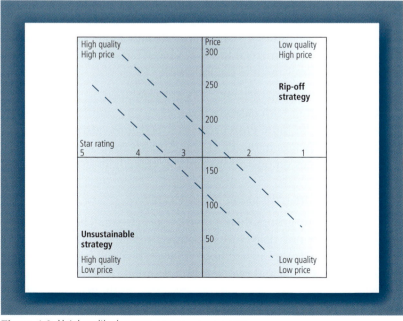

Figure 4.3 Hotel positioning map *Adapted from Lovelock, 2002*

price (five-star quality at three-star prices), this strategy is not sustainable in the long run.

Activity 4.3

Identify five hotels in your local area that represent luxury, upscale, mid-market (full service), mid-market (rooms only) and budget offers
- Research each hotel's prices for accommodation from their websites.
- Draw a positioning map and plot each hotel's price and product quality on your perceptual map.
- Evaluate your findings

Positioning maps can be used to track changing competitive positions over time. This is useful, because the marketing environment does not remain static and consumers' perceptions will change in response to competitors' actions. Hotels constantly battling for competitive advantage continue to adapt their positioning strategies.

CHARACTERISTICS OF HOSPITALITY FIRMS

We now discuss a number of characteristics of hospitality firms that impact on marketing practice. These include ownership and size, ownership and affiliation and hotel classification schemes.

Ownership and size

Many hospitality firms started as single-unit enterprises – often termed 'Mom and Pop operations' – and most remain single-unit businesses throughout their commercial life. The characteristics of small, single-site hospitality firms include the following:

- The owner and management roles are combined
- Owners interact with customers
- Owners can be more entrepreneurial and innovative, responding quickly to changes in the PESTE and micro-environments
- There is a focus on operations and the immediate issues facing the business
- There is a short-term planning timeframe.

The major hotel groups do not own or operate small hotels, because small hotels do not deliver the required revenue and profitability expected from a group-owned hotel. Hence, bed and breakfast, guest houses and small one and two-star budget hotels tend to be privately owned. The three-star market incorporates both privately owned hotels and mid-market chains, whilst larger upscale and luxury units tend to be owned by larger organizations.

Firms that grow are said to have a life cycle, as they develop from a single-site owner/management business operating in a simple environment to multi-site business units with hierarchical corporate organizations, operating in a complex environment. As organizations grow, decision-making often becomes more remote from the customer and frontline staff. The characteristics of larger hospitality firms include the following:

- The separation of ownership and management – typically the general managers and directors of a hospitality corporation will only own a token share holding or share option
- Ownership is normally diffused across a large number of shareholders, although institutions such as pension funds and banks may hold larger stakes in the business
- Multiple-site operations – the largest hospitality corporations comprise thousands of geographically dispersed units, across dozens of countries on all continents, using a complex combination of different brands, targeting a variety of markets, using a range of business formats (ownership, franchising and management contract) and employing hundreds of thousands of employees
- Employment of professionals to manage at both the unit level and at head office – these professionals have developed considerable expertise in hospitality operations management, as well as the functional disciplines of finance, human resources and marketing management.

Large firms enjoy significant advantages in terms of:

- Economies of scale, giving cost savings in purchasing
- Economies of experience (this comprises the accumulated managerial experience that large companies enjoy)
- Access to financial markets, which provide significant financial resources for investment
- Managing powerful and popular brands
- Powerful computerized distribution systems
- Access to specialist resources such as financial consultants, design consultants and advertising and public relations agencies
- Focus on long-term strategic planning.

But

- Management procedures are more formalized and bureaucratic
- Management is much more remote from the customer.

Although smaller, single-site, owner-managed hospitality units can give regular customers a much more personalized service, it is more difficult to attract visiting tourists to stay in an unknown property, especially when consumers do not have the assurance of good service quality. Powerful hospitality brands do provide the reassurance that customers are looking for when travelling and these brands dominate the marketplace and the competitive environment.

Ownership and affiliation

There are at least six forms of hospitality ownership and affiliation.

Owned

A company, partnership or individual can own the business and its freehold property. Ownership enables the organization to develop the property without constraints (subject to planning controls and permissions). The organization may borrow funds from lenders to purchase or develop the business. Ownership of freehold property ties up capital within the business.

Leased

Many small single-unit hospitality firms – bars, cafes and restaurants – do not have the capital to own their own properties, so leasing the premises is a realistic route to start their business. A company, partnership or individual can lease a property from a landlord and pay commercial rent. The landlord has to approve structural alterations, and lease contract details can be complex. In recent years, major hotel companies have sold their freehold properties – often to banks or pension funds – and then leased them back to continue to operate the business. This has released funds to help fuel the expansion of hotel corporations.

Management contract, with an equity stake

Specialist hotel management companies take an equity stake in the property, which demonstrates a long-term commitment to the landlord and the business. This type of management contract enables the management company to share the profits of any property inflation.

Equity-free management contract

Specialist hotel management companies can be responsible for the entire operation of a hotel property on behalf of the owners. This type of management contract is less complex than an equity-stake contract.

Franchise

In franchise operations, the franchisor (the company who owns the franchise) will offer a branded concept to a franchisee, which operates the business according to the standards set by the franchisor. The franchisee buys the franchise and pays a commission on turnover to the franchisor for continued marketing and organizational support. Franchising has been an extremely successful concept for companies such as McDonald's and Wyndham. It enables the franchisor to grow the business without needing too much capital, since the franchisee pays to buy a franchise and also for the business start-up costs. The rapid increase in the number of outlets in a country or region enables the franchisor to gain a critical mass, which funds heavy investment in advertising and promoting the brands. A frequent cause of tension in franchising is the relationship between the franchisee and franchisor. The franchisor needs to have consistent brand standards and will monitor each unit to check conformance. Franchisees often expect more investment in advertising and product development from the franchisor, and this can also become a source of conflict. One way by which an international hospitality brand owner can expand more quickly into foreign countries is by working with master franchisee companies. Occasionally, a master franchisee and a brand owner sign long-term country exclusive contracts that can be beneficial in delivering rapid brand unit growth, but can also be problematic if the partners have different long-term goals. An example of a successful East European master franchisee is the Romanian company Trend Hospitality Consulting and Management, which manages the assets of property owners and operates hotels under franchise. They are a strategic developer for the Wyndham Hotel Group franchising brands in Romania, Bulgaria and Moldavia (Moldova), and with an exclusive contract for Wyndham brands in Romania.

Activity 4.4

Wyndham – the world's largest hotel franchisor

Wyndham claims to be the world's largest franchisor of hotels. It owns the following hotel brands – Baymont Inn, Days Inn, Howard Johnson, Knights Inn, Microtel, Ramada, Super 8, Travelodge, Wingate Inns by Wyndham and Wyndham Hotels – with approximately 7000 hotels and nearly 590,000 rooms in more than 65 countries.

- Log onto the Wyndham Hotel Group website, www.wyndhamworldwide. com and read about its hotel brand franchising opportunities.
- Log on to Trend Hospitality at www.trendhospitality.com and read about the company's hotel operations.

Source: Wyndham Hotel Group

Consortium

Independent hotels seeking the benefits that group-owned chains enjoy can affiliate to a hotel consortium. Membership of a hotel consortium enables independent hoteliers to retain their entrepreneurial freedom and to

- Link to global computerized reservation systems
- Buy into an international or domestic brand

- Participate in the consortium's national and international marketing communication campaigns
- Extend their distribution channels
- Enjoy discounted prices when purchasing, due to the consortium's bulk purchasing power
- Belong to a group of similar independent hoteliers, and share management and marketing information.

Activity 4.5

Best Western Hotels – the largest consortium in the world

Best Western International is the largest hotel company operating under a single brand name, with more than 4000 independently owned and operated hotels. Based in Phoenix, Arizona, Best Western offers over 300,000 bedrooms in 80 countries. Best Western Hotels is primarily a membership organization that gives hoteliers the opportunity to remain independent whilst also providing the benefits of a full-service, international hotel group with a global reservations system, marketing, advertising, purchasing, training and quality standards.

- Log onto the Best Western Hotels website, www.bestwestern.com, and read the benefits of becoming a Best Western member

Source: Best Western Hotels

Implications of ownership/affiliation

Independent operators typically own or lease their property. Although many have joined consortia to maximize their marketing efforts, most independent hotel owners remain unaffiliated apart from in the United States. Some branded hotel chains, like Marriott, utilize all forms of ownership; however, companies like InterContinental Hotels Group (IHG) sold almost all their freehold hotel properties to reduce their debt, improve their balance sheet and return assets to shareholders. IHG now focuses on lease, management contract and franchising to operate properties throughout the world. The fast-food chains like Burger King and McDonald's primarily use franchising as a marketing tool to grow their business.

Hotel operating companies

There are many mid-sized, entrepreneurial hotel management companies that own or lease hotels and operate the properties on behalf of themselves and owners. When appropriate, these hotel operators also work with established high-profile brands. Pandox, a Swedish hotel operator, manages 46 hotels in Northern Europe under the following

brand names: Hilton, InterContinental, Hyatt, Scandic, Radisson Blu, Holiday Inn and Clarion – as well as managing some hotels independently. In Brussels, Pandox manages a Crowne Plaza, a Hilton, a Holiday Inn and the independent Hotel BLOOM!

Hotel classification schemes

The World Tourist Organization and most national tourist boards use the internationally recognized star rating system to classify hotels. The scheme is as follows:

One star	A budget hotel with limited facilities, offering bed, breakfast and possibly an evening meal and characterized by informal standards of service to residents
Two star	An economy hotel with limited facilities, normally offering more extensive dining facilities, and characterized by informal standards of service to residents
Three star	A mid-market hotel with more extensive facilities, offering a full range of dining and bar services, with professional standards of service, to residents and non-residents
Four star	An upscale hotel offering formal standards of service, with extensive facilities and services to residents and non-residents
Five star	A luxury hotel offering 'flawless' service standards, with professional multilingual staff and a full range of facilities of the highest quality

Many motoring organizations also use the star rating system but add their own awards, such as the American Automobile Association, the Automobile Association in the United Kingdom and the *Michelin Guide* from France. Consumer groups have also developed a variety of classification schemes for hotels and restaurants using their own criteria. From a marketing perspective, schemes, such as the AA Red Star Hotel and Michelin Restaurant Stars provide quality standards, which discerning customers understand. These endorsements reinforce the quality image projected in websites, letterheads and brochures, and these can be used in public relations campaigns to generate publicity.

UNDERSTANDING THE COMPETITION

Although some hoteliers and restaurateurs claim their product is so unique that they 'do not have any competitors', the reality is that all hospitality businesses operate against a variety of different types of competition. A broad distinction can be made between macro-competition and micro-competition.

Macro-competition

Macro-competition comprises all those industries that are competing for the consumers' disposable income, including hospitality. Examples of these indirect competitors include the following:

- Major household purchases – for example, a new bathroom or motorcar – compete with luxury holidays in exotic hotels and on cruise ships
- Shopping for clothes and accessories competes with visits to health and sports clubs
- Supermarket outlets, with their pre-prepared, easy-to-cook meals, compete with restaurants and takeaway shops
- Shops that sell alcohol for consumption at home compete against bars and pubs.

The influence of Michael Porter on both practitioners and academics has been significant. Porter proposed that firms can benefit from understanding the forces that drive competition and profitability in their industry and that firms should explicitly formulate a competitor strategy. To understand the competition, a competitive analysis needs to be undertaken. Porter's model is often referred to as the *Five Forces Competitive Analysis*.

The five forces driving industry profitability

Investors and entrepreneurs want to make a return that reflects the risks they are taking and the cost of the money they are using in their investments. Therefore, they need to understand the environmental dynamics that may have a significant impact on those returns. Porter identified five such factors that influence industry profitability (Porter, 1980):

1 *The bargaining power of customers (buyers).* This force reflects the strength of buyers' bargaining position, particularly regarding price, which customers have over suppliers. Customers who purchase larger volumes of bed-nights and who have low switching costs (i.e., it is easy and economical to change supplier) leverage a strong bargaining force in the competitive environment. For example, tour operators, who book thousands of customers in to hotels, have a strong bargaining position and can demand lower prices from hotels. Individual customers have a weaker bargaining position if demand is high and capacity is low, but when demand is variable and capacity is high, the customers have a stronger bargaining position.

2 *The bargaining power of suppliers (including employees).* Suppliers, including employees, can negatively influence the attractiveness and profitability of a sector by increasing their prices

(or wages) and thereby increasing industry costs and reducing profit margins. Powerful suppliers are those organizations that control the supply of goods and services to the hospitality industry. This varies from country to country. Examples include monopoly suppliers controlling electricity, gas or water supplies; oligopoly suppliers, which are concentrations of only a few major suppliers (as in the UK brewing industry); owners of computerized reservation systems; and powerful trade unions, which can negotiate improved pay and conditions on behalf of the workforce.

3 *The threat of new entrants*. The threat of new entrants is dependent on the barriers to enter into an industry. These include the ability to generate economies of scale and experience, the opportunities for product differentiation, the amount of capital required to buy into the industry and access to the distribution channels. In hospitality, there are low barriers to entry in many sectors.

4 *The threat of substitutes*. Substitute industries provide competing offerings that satisfy the same generic needs, or perform the same function. An example is the convenience eating-out market that competes against substitute convenient eat-at-home products marketed by supermarkets. Continual developments in technology keep changing the potential threat from substitute products. The rapid development of mobile communications, personal communications and video-conferencing has presented a substitute product for the hotel meetings market.

5 *The intensity of rivalry between competitors*. Rivalry varies between industries and sectors. The character of rivalry varies, and includes conflict (efforts to destroy competitors), competition (to provide better solutions to customer problems), coexistence (rivals allow each other to operate in different segments), cooperation (rivals cooperate in some activities such as purchasing) or collusion (illegal cooperation to fix prices and produce a managed market). Rivalry is dependent on the number of dominant players, levels of demand and capacity, and the personalities of competitors.

Porter concluded that when these five forces are at high levels of intensity, industry profitability is low. In hospitality markets, whilst competition is intense, most people working in the industry have good personal relationships with rivals working for competitors.

The first step, when conducting a competitive analysis is to agree a relevant definition of the market sector, which sets the parameters for analysis – for example, the fast-food market in central London, the budget hotel market in Germany, the luxury incentive market in South East Asia. The five forces analysis will provide an insight into whether

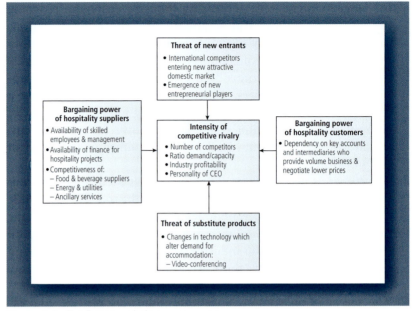

Figure 4.4 Five Forces analysis *Source: Porter, 1980*

the sector can provide a satisfactory rate of return. For example, if buyer power is high and there is an intense price-based rivalry between current players, the prospects for a new venture may not be good. This, plus the information collected in the PESTE analysis, enables management to assess the potential for a hospitality offering. Figure 4.4 illustrates Porter's Five Forces using a full-service hotel example.

Competitive environments analysis

Porter also developed a classification scheme that identifies four different types of competitive environment: fragmented, niche, volume and stalemate. Each of these competitive environments (except stalemate) is common in hospitality, and this language is regularly used to describe the characteristics of hospitality sectors.

Fragmented

In a fragmented competitive environment, no firm has a significant market share. The industry has low-entry barriers, with high product differentiation and low economies of scale. Profitability is unrelated to size; this means that large firms are not more profitable than small firms. A fragmented market comprises a large number of small and medium-sized businesses. In hospitality, examples of a fragmented market include the Italian hotel market (which is dominated by small privately owned family run hotels) and British ethnic restaurants and take-away units (such as fish and chip shops, Indian and Chinese restaurants).

Specialized or niche

In a specialized or niche competitive environment, there are many ways of achieving competitive advantage. Companies focus on serving specific market segments and become specialized businesses. Often, the marketing goal is to be best in class, and a price premium is charged. Image, quality and service are important factors in serving customers in a niche market. There are many examples in the hospitality industry – Gleneagles Hotel in Scotland has a niche market in the leisure golfing market; and Seabourn yachts in the luxury cruise market.

Volume

The volume competitive environment is characterized by mass players serving mass markets. There is a limited number of ways to achieve competitive advantage, and control of costs is a key factor for success. Economies of scale, experience and technology are used to reduce the cost base. The marketing objective is to be the cost and volume leader. Examples of volume businesses in hospitality include brewing, contract catering and tour operators. In Norway, only three companies SAGA, Star Tour (a TUI brand) and Ving (a Thomas Cook brand) dominate 90 per cent of the travel industry.

Stalemate

The stalemate competitive environment is characteristic of industries in the mature or declining stages of the life cycle (e.g., the European steel industry) with a commodity product and limited opportunities for differentiation. This type of competitive environment is characterized by a small number of very large players, which dominate their industry. There are few competitive advantages, so the focus is on large-scale production and improving productivity. Stalemate industries suffer from excess capacity, limited innovation and high barriers to entry. There are no examples of a stalemate industry in hospitality, at the moment.

HORIZONTAL INTEGRATION

Today's major hospitality organizations have evolved by taking over or merging with competitors in the same sector (horizontal integration), and/or by taking over or merging with customers and suppliers (vertical integration – see Chapter 8).

The largest hotel companies have all grown the number of hotels they operate worldwide by horizontal integration using the acquisition of competitor brands to expand more rapidly. Companies such as Accor, Four Seasons, Hilton, IHG, Marriott, Rezidor, Sol Melia, Starwood and Wyndham have all bought brands to grow the business and sold brands to focus in key strategic areas. There are many examples. Companies, such as IHG have their roots in the UK brewing industry and date back to 1777. In the 1980s Bass (as IHG was originally called) acquired Holiday Inn and in the 1990s InterContinental Hotels. Since 2000, Bass sold its brewing interests to become a hotel operator, changed its corporate name twice and is now known as IHG. Hilton's rapid expansion in the United Kingdom was based on the acquisition of competitor hotel chains, such as Stakis. Their international expansion included the purchase of the Scandinavian hotel chain Scandic, which was later divested. Marriott acquired Residence Inn and Fairfield Inn in 1987, Ritz-Carlton in 1995, Renaissance in 1997 and ExecuStay in 1999 and then sold Ramada to Cendant (now Wyndham) in 2005. Accor bought the Motel 6 and Red Roof American budget brands to gain access to the North American market.

When a major player buys a brand, a decision has to be made whether to integrate the acquired hotels into one of their existing brands or to retain the newly acquired brand. Acquired hotels are carefully evaluated to see whether their property profile fits with the requirements of an existing brand's standards. Hotels that conform to brand standards are re-badged and hotels that do not are sold. If the newly acquired brand is retained then existing hotels in the acquirer's portfolio may be re-branded under the new brand name.

Larger organizations enjoy economies of scale, which contribute to improved profit margins. Examples include the following:

- The ability to negotiate better terms with suppliers, through bulk purchasing
- The opportunity to leverage higher brand awareness and drive volume sales, by owning more retail outlets and spending more on marketing communications
- The opportunity to expand operations more efficiently and quickly, by gaining access to capital markets
- The development of managerial economies of experience.

These mega-corporations are continuously evolving and will continue to expand, or they will be acquired by a competitor, or new entrant to the international hotel market. The process of horizontal integration leads to consolidation – this means a smaller number of larger players. However, the dynamic characteristics of the hotel industry means that there are always new entrepreneurs developing new businesses and, just like Charles Forte, Conrad Hilton and Bill Marriott, will grow their companies by acquisition and horizontal integration.

Micro-competition

Micro-competition comprises the branded and independent hospitality units that compete directly with a similar product and similar price, and target the same customer in the same location. This type of direct competition, which is normally local depending on the product category, is also described as *product form* competition. First, a company needs to identify the brands/establishments in its competitor set.

Criteria that can be used to define a competitor set include competitors who are

- Patronized by your target customers
- In the same product class
- Within a specified geographic area
- In a similar price category.

An effective marketing research technique adopted by the Marriott County Hall Hotel, London, is to ask residents where they would be staying tonight if the Marriott were full. The customers' replies help to establish which hotels are in the competitor set. Desk research and local knowledge can establish which businesses compete in the same product, geographic and price set. Examples of direct competition include the following:

- Corporate event companies in San Francisco
- Five-star international hotels in Shanghai
- Pubs and bars on West Street in Sheffield

Once the competitor set has been established, marketers need to carry out research by visiting their competitors and evaluating their marketing offer. One of the best ways to analyse competitors is actually to use their facilities as a paying customer, staying in the bedrooms, having a drink in the bar and dining in the restaurant. The desk and primary research should include assessment of the following:

- The size, quality, décor and facilities of the bedrooms, public areas
- Food and beverage facilities
- The staff and their approach to customer service
- The price and value offered
- The marketing communications and the service promise in print and advertising
- The image projected by the brand signage and physical appearance.

Although managers should be aware of any competitor developments on an ongoing basis, the preparation of an annual marketing plan provides a regular opportunity to re-visit competitors and monitor their activity.

Sustainable competitive advantage

Companies are constantly striving to compete more effectively. However, not all factors are equally influential, and some can be regarded as more important in achieving competitor advantage than others. These *critical success factors* (CSF's) – also called *key factors for success* – need to be identified so that a company can ensure that it delivers value that meets and exceeds the expectations of its targeted customers better than competitors. The process of analysing critical success factors includes

- Researching customer expectations (e.g., consistent service quality)
- Identifying the key components of the offer that create value for customers (this is often an intangible ingredient linked to creating memorable customer experiences)
- Identifying four to six potential CSF's that impact on satisfying these expectations (e.g., recruiting and retaining empathetic, enthusiastic and skilled employees; close relationships with suppliers of fresh produce)
- Analysing company competences that underpin the key factors identified (often linked to inspiring leadership and effective financial/human resource and marketing expertise)
- Scrutinizing the list of CSFs to ensure that superior performance will deliver a competitive advantage
- Identifying the performance standards that need to be achieved to outperform competitors
- Assessing the ability, competences and resources of the company to achieve the required performance standards
- Assessing the ability of competitors to imitate improved performance on the same CSFs.

International hospitality companies, initially start developing their own unique competences in their domestic market as a response to consumer needs, competitor activities and the environmental situation.

Defining the CSFs in a market enables a company to understand its market position *vis-à-vis* competitors, and helps to build competitive advantages. CSFs need to be identified that deliver the experiences and attributes most valued by customers. Examples of CSF's in the hospitality sector include the following:

- Lowest cost base and extensive geographic coverage for chain budget hotels
- High service quality for exclusive hospitality events
- Highly regarded brand reputation and high brand awareness for international hotel chains
- Technical superiority in food production processes for fast-food chain restaurants
- Consistent standards of service in standardized hospitality branded concepts
- Easy to find locations and secure parking facilities for provincial business hotels competing in urban locations
- Superior service, provided by well-trained and highly motivated personnel, in luxury country house hotels

Although the most successful hospitality companies have clearly defined competences and understand the CSFs in their competitive environment, many hotels and restaurants are not so aware. These companies often fail to understand their own competitive strengths and do not analyse their competitors for weaknesses, and thus they lose an opportunity to develop a competitive advantage.

Competitive advantages that are easily copied have limited value. 'Amenity creep' can become a serious problem for hospitality competitors when striving to gain a competitive advantage. When a company starts to offer additional product enhancements to customers in an attempt to gain competitive advantage, this is called amenity creep. For example, if a hotel chain starts to offer customers additional complimentary in-room amenities (chocolates on the pillow, turning the bed down, providing more luxurious bathroom products, increasing the reward benefits on a frequent guest program) to try and increase customer loyalty and repeat business, this is called amenity creep. Since each added amenity is easily copied by competitors, and also significantly increases room costs and prices, chains using this tactic are unable to develop a genuine sustainable competitive advantage. Amenity creep can also inadvertently alter the positioning of the brand and lead to inappropriate pricing policies that erode the original market position.

For hospitality companies, the reputation and image of a business is built up over many years, and a distinctive brand can become a focus for sustainable competitive advantage. Hotels, such as Claridges in London, the Marriott chain of international hotels, and McDonald's fast-food restaurants have all developed strong and sustainable competitive advantages, based on a deep understanding of key factors for success in their market segments. Success factors change over time. New competitors can seize a sustainable competitive advantage by recognizing – earlier than their established competitors – environmental factors that alter the structural dimensions of the market.

Measuring competitive success

Key measures of competitive success include operating statistics such as sales revenue, profit margin, room occupancy, achieved room rate, RevPAR and return on investment. Market share is another important criterion. The success of publicly quoted companies is reflected in financial measures, such as share price performance. A rising share price is good news, since the value of the business is increasing whilst a falling share price – especially if it is company specific and not linked to market forces – is clearly bad news. One marketing metric that is linked to financial performance is called brand value; however, calculating brand value is not a simple task.

Hotel and restaurant chains track the performance of their advertising campaigns using specialist media agencies, such as Nielsen to monitor media expenditure analysis by all leading companies in their sector. If there is heavy investment in advertising between market leaders then each company needs to know what competitors are spending on communications – this is called 'share of voice.' McDonald's and Burger King's advertising campaigns across the world are carefully monitored to measure the share of voice. Comparative brand performance measures for the hotel chains include brand awareness, brand image and attributes. Consultancies and marketing research agencies provide hospitality organizations with these benchmarking services that compare their own brand's performance on a wide range of indicators against their competitor set and best practice in the industry. BDRC Continental provides the leading hotel companies in Europe with confidential, customized research, benchmarking each brand's performance on key attributes relevant to customers in their market sector and in different countries. If a hotel corporate manages several brands in many different countries in a region then the performance across their different brands will vary according to the length of time, number of units and reputation of each brand in each country. So a corporate will manage the marketing of its mature brands in one country in a different way to a newer brand in a different country.

Hotel and brand managers track their hotel's statistics month by month and aim to improve their hotel's performance compared to competitors. Hotels in the same local competitor set (branded chains and independents) sometimes exchange room occupancy and achieved room rates to enable each hotel to benchmark its performance against competitors. When all the hotels in the competitor set experience an increase or fall in business the change can be attributed to factors in the external environment, but if one hotel's performance is consistently better (or worse) than its competitors', this indicates that competitor factors (as opposed to the external environmental factors) are responsible for the difference in performance. Thus, performance needs to be placed within the context of the micro- and macro-environments, and reasons for inferior or superior performance need to be identified. The benchmarking process enables the marketing team to identify and correct important weaknesses compared with the competitor set, and ultimately to improve customer satisfaction.

Marketing insight 4.1

BDRC Continental hotel brands survey

BDRC Continental is a marketing research agency founded by Dr Crispian Tarrant specializing in the service sector. Most of the leading hotel companies, including Accor, Best Western, Copthorne-Millennium, Hilton,

InterContinental, Marriott, Premier Inn, De Vere and Rezidor participate in the company's syndicated research. The research benchmarks each hotel brand's performance against competitor brands and is carried out in a total of 39 different countries across the world.

BDRC Continental has carried out quantitative research in hotel guest behaviour for over 20 years, contacting large samples of business and leisure hotel customers. This longitudinal research allows each brand to monitor its own performance year-on-year. Key performance measures include brand awareness, preference and brand image. BDRC Continental also surveys the meetings, training and conference market by researching the views of corporate event organizers and venue finding agencies, and by extensive mystery shopping to evaluate how enquiries are handled. Although elements of the syndicated research are published, each company also receives a confidential report regarding its individual competitive position.

Source: BDRC Continental

BRANDING

Although the segmentation, targeting and positioning (STP) process identifies target markets, differentiates the product and positions the company or offer in the minds of consumers, it is the brand that is the most overt manifestation of STP strategy. A hospitality brand immediately distinguishes one company's offering from competitors'. Branding is a core concept in hospitality marketing. Crucially, brands help customers to identify what the product or company stands for. There is a considerable evidence to support the view that successful brands enhance company profits. When consumers perceive that one brand offers superior value to competing brands, they not only purchase that brand but may also be prepared to pay more for it. Successful brands not only differentiate themselves from competitors but also add value by meeting consumer's psychological needs, as well as physiological needs. Even though most of the discussion and research into hospitality branding relates to multi-unit chain operations, many of the principles of brand management apply equally to individual properties. In this sense, individual hospitality outlets can be perceived as brands.

Defining the brand

At its simplest, a brand is a specific name, term, sign, symbol, design or a combination of these characteristics applied to a product or organization. Brands function in a number of ways including (de Chernatony & Dall'Olmo Riley, 1998):

- As a legal instrument – companies' value the ownership of the brand name, logo and design, and protection of the brand from imitators leads to the prosecution of companies infringing on the trademark (this happened to an economy lodging chain, branded McSleep)

- As a logo, which differentiates the offer with a visual identity and name, providing customers with quality assurance
- As an integral part of a company image, reflecting the culture, people, personality and reputation of the company
- As a shorthand symbol that is easily recognized by consumers
- As a risk reducer, giving consumers confidence that their expectations will be fulfilled – the brand as an unwritten contract
- By adding value to the customer's subjective experience.

Over time, the marketing investment in brands is rewarded by consumer goodwill and loyalty. This investment is sometimes, but not always, reflected in a company's balance sheet.

Brand concepts

Developing a brand concept involves considerable competitor and consumer research, brainstorming ideas that may – or may not – be further researched, and finally the development of a brand proposition that is presented for corporate and financial approval. In hospitality, there are four fundamental brand concepts (Park, Jaworski & MacInnis, 1986):

- Functional: A functional brand concept focuses on delivering the core benefits of a hospitality service with efficient, well-designed, processes and without any attempts to engage the customer in an emotional relationship. Although functional brands operate in most hospitality market segments, the most appropriate examples are no-frills hotel budget brand concepts, such as Formule 1, Motel 6 and Premier Inn.
- Symbolic: A symbolic brand concept addresses consumers' ego needs and the desire to be associated with higher-status groups. In hospitality, there are many brand concepts catering for consumers wanting to enjoy 'conspicuous consumption' in exclusive settings. Examples include iconic hotels, such as the Savoy Hotel, London and Burj Al Arab, Dubai; and iconic restaurants, such as the Ivy, London and El Bulli, on the Costa Brava, Spain.
- Experiential: An experiential brand concept focuses on sensory pleasures which stimulate consumers. The sensory stimulus could be at one with nature in an ecological environment (Heritance Hotel, Kandalama, Sri Lanka), extreme physical excitement (Extreme Hotels), taste sensations in a gastronomic temple (Heston Blumenthal's Fat Duck Restaurant, Bray, England) and ultimate relaxation (Six Senses Resorts).
- 'Me–Too:' A Me-Too brand concept simply imitates an existing competitor brand. Although some Me-Too brands are not usually as successful as the original brand, occasionally an imitation brand can

be very successful. Jollibee, the leading fast-food chain in the Philippines with 600 stores, borrowed many of its ideas from McDonald's and has been so successful that it now also operates in five countries, including the United States (Frambacha, Prabhub & Verhallence, 2003).

Case study 4.2 **A focused functional brand concept: Chateauform**

Chateauform is a French hospitality brand concept that provides exclusive business conference venues in castles and chateaux in low-cost rural locations within one hour's drive of airports. The venue is hired to one company only – so there are no other customers on the premises. This ensures there are no incompatible groups of customers which reduces the possibility of conflict. The customers remain within the property confines of the relatively remote venues, which helps to ensure social bonding. There are limited in-room facilities. For example, there are no plasma TVs and no in-room mini-bars, again to encourage delegates to mingle with their colleagues instead of staying in their bedrooms. However, there is leading edge conference and meetings technology in the seminar rooms. The residential conferences have all-inclusive price packages; and the management couple is incentivized by a share in profits to deliver a highly personal service. Chateauform has grown in 10 years from one property to approximately 20 units in five adjacent European countries.

Source: http://www.chateauform.co.uk

Brand name

Once the brand concept has been agreed, a key decision is deciding the brand name. A brand name should convey the essence of a brand to its target audience in memorable words or a short phrase. The W in the 'W' brand created by Starwood represents the 'whatever, whenever' service philosophy underpinning the brand values. International brands need to ensure their name translates, and sounds, appropriate in other languages and that the logo is inoffensive. Probably, one of the most innovative and memorable brand names is TGIF (Thank God It's Friday). Alan Stillman, the restaurant entrepreneur who created TGIF and sold the chain when there were only nine outlets, recognized the importance of choosing novel and memorable names for his restaurants more than 35 years ago. He told Nick Lander, the *Financial Times* restaurant correspondent,

> *I thought of TGIF as a way of meeting the young, attractive women who lived on the block. There was a dismal bar which I took over without any experience. The thing about the names of restaurants is that they can be awkward and even weird but they have to be lots of fun as, above all, they must be memorable.*

> *(Lander, 2006)*

Table 4.1 provides a typology of hotel brand names.

Table 4.1 A typology of hotel brand names	
Brand type	**Examples**
Founder	Hilton; Marriott
Geographic description	Best Western; Intercontinental; Scandik
Price	Budget Inns, Econolodge
Functional	Sleep Inn; Travel Inn
Symbolic	Burj Al Arab
Experiential	Extreme
Acronym	IHG; AC; HE1
Lifestyle	Arcadian; Romantik
Market Segment	Budget; Grand; Luxury Collection
Architectural/heritage	National Trust Historic Hotels of America: Artotel
Animals, birds, insects, flowers	Red Lion, Swallow, Butterfly, White Rose
Colours	Green Tree, Orange
Letters	W; M-Hotels
Numbers	Motel 6; H10
Location + brand name	New York Marriott Downtown; New York Marriott East Side
Wacky!	YOTEL

Brand congruence

A critical issue for hospitality brands is to ensure that all the different elements of the marketing mix contribute to the overall customer experience in a brand-congruent manner. Brand standards provide the guidelines for individual units to deliver the operational and communication strategies, and they are set out on the company intranet and in brand manuals. Brand standards are checked and enforced by a range of tools including formal property/service audits and mystery shopper visits. Indeed, in some hospitality companies, the corporate executives enforcing brand standards are called the brand police. Units that consistently underperform on brand standards are vulnerable – managers may be replaced, franchisees may have their franchise removed and ultimately a property may be disposed of, if senior management recognizes that the unit will never be able to deliver the required brand standards.

Harder or softer hospitality brands

Multi-unit hospitality operations have considerable difficulty in delivering a uniform, consistent standard of product and service because:

- Inconsistent service personnel and erratic customer behaviour changes the customer experience
- Refurbishment schedules mean the product varies enormously between the most recently redecorated unit and the most tired unit
- There are differences in the seasonality of demand and in the different locations of the units in the chain
- There are differences in local and regional, planning and building legislative requirements.

Hospitality chains have responded to the inherent inconsistencies in hospitality operations by developing different approaches depending on the product class, and the age, design and style of properties in the portfolio. One approach is to formulate a harder or softer branding strategy, which recognizes the composition of the portfolio of properties within the brand.

A hospitality brand seeking to establish a standardized product/price formula, in similar locations and with a consistent customer experience throughout the chain, is described as a 'harder' brand. A collection of hospitality units being marketed under the same brand name but with limited emphasis on standardization is described as a 'softer' brand. There is no absolute hard or soft brand, since all chains incorporate elements of standardization and elements of adaptation, and there is nothing inherently better about a harder or a softer brand. However, it is essential that softer brands are not promoted as harder brands, since they will not be able to deliver the standardized offer that customers expect from harder brands. Table 4.2 provides details of 'harder and softer' marketing strategies.

Examples of harder hospitality brands include Burger King and Hampton Inns. They have purpose-built properties, using standardized

Table 4.2 Harder and softer hotel brands		
Factor/strategy	**Harder**	**Softer**
Use of same brand name across hotels	Yes	Yes
Level of physical product consistency	Higher	Lower
Level of service range consistency	Higher	Lower
Consistency in pricing	Higher	Lower
Level of national coverage	Higher	Lower

(Continued)

Table 4.2 Harder and softer hotel brands—cont'd

Factor/strategy	Harder	Softer
Consistency in type of locations	Higher	Lower
Emphasis on national advertising and promotion	Higher	Lower
Reliance on growth through acquisition	Higher	Lower
Emphasis on product planning and development	Higher	Lower
Markets targeted	National/specific segments	Local/range of segments

Adapted from Connell 1992.

design, décor and food offers. Examples of softer hotel brands or collections of hotels, which have been individually built in different styles during different historical periods and offer an eclectic choice of dining, include Best Western and Relais et Château.

Activity 4.6

Comparison of harder and softer brands

Research two Best Western Hotels and two Novotels in two different countries of your choice. You should compare the hotels using the following criteria:

- location,
- architectural style,
- number of rooms,
- restaurant/banqueting facilities,
- business and leisure facilities,
- prices.

Which brand provides a more consistent marketing offer and should be marketed as a harder brand?

What marketing strategy should the softer brand adopt?

Brand awareness and brand image

Two key measures are used to monitor the effectiveness of brands: brand awareness and brand image. Public and target-market awareness of a brand can be measured using marketing research techniques. In brand awareness surveys, respondents are asked to name any brands they know. This is called unprompted awareness. Respondents

Business travellers: prompted awareness of UK hotel brands

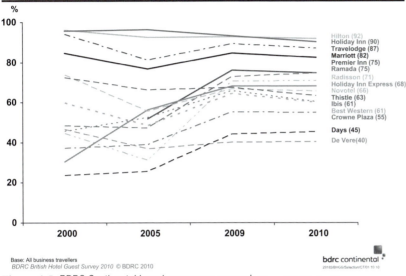

Figure 4.5 BDRC Continental brand awareness research *Source: BDRC Continental*

are then asked if they know the names of specific named brands; this is called prompted awareness. High-brand awareness means that the brand is well known and enjoys a high profile; low-brand awareness means that consumers do not know the brand (see Fig. 4.5 the BDRC Continental hotel brand awareness research). Brand image is a measure of the brand's reputation – a high-brand image means that the brand has a very good reputation and a low-brand image means that the brand has a poor reputation.

In Figure 4.6, brand awareness and brand image are plotted against each other. A brand's position in this matrix is indicative of its future fortune:

- Brands that have low awareness and a poor image are fortunate that their reputation is not well known. They have time to improve their performance. However, if no action is taken then the brand will gradually lose sales and become unprofitable
- Brands with low awareness and a good image have the potential to grow, if brand awareness is increased
- Brands with high awareness and good image are successful brands that need to be protected and nurtured
- Brands with poor image and high awareness are in a difficult situation. If action is not taken quickly to improve the brand image, then the brand will lose value and die quickly.

Benefits and disadvantages of branding

It takes a long time to develop a positive brand image in the minds of consumers. Many of the most well-known hospitality brands have

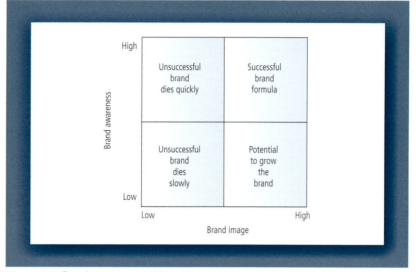

Figure 4.6 Brand awareness and brand image

been operating since the end of the Second World War, and some of the exclusive, grand old American, Asian and European hotels date back more than 100 years. Brands provide consumers with quality assurance. Once consumers have experienced and liked a hospitality brand, they will be more likely to use the other outlets in the chain, since the brand promises to reduce the risks for the customer when travelling away from home.

There are both financial and operational disadvantages associated with branding. Consistency in delivering service is the principle problem in hospitality. Customers develop quality expectations based on previous experience and the brand's reputation, regardless of where the outlet is in the world. Companies have to set and monitor operational standards to ensure consistent brand performance, but enforcement is not easy and can be costly. Delivering brand conformance in service operations and marketing programs requires costly administration procedures, quality assurance programs and inspections. Most brands operate in franchised and management contract formats, making control and consistency even more problematic than for owner-operated properties. The cost of maintaining and further developing a brand is high. It cost one hotel company the equivalent of building a new 100-bedroom full service, mid-market hotel to introduce a new corporate identity, with the design costs, exterior and interior brand signage and publicity material.

Multiple branding

The history of many hospitality companies reveals a typical development process based on a founding entrepreneur who gave his name to the company – Hilton and Marriott. It is interesting to note just how many new chains still use the founder's family name when choosing their brand name. Starting with one or a few properties, the founder grows the business, often focusing on a specific market segment and offering his or her single 'branded product'. The commercial pressure to continue growth and to protect the company from relying on a single market segment eventually leads to the development of multiple branded hospitality companies targeting a wide range of market segments. Multiple branding has become the preferred development strategy for the major hotel groups.

The way in which the hospitality corporations have introduced branding has varied. Some have retained the original name and added brand extensions to distinguish the various branded concepts. Of 16 Marriott International hotel brands, 10 retain the 'Marriott' brand name in the brand title. Other hotel groups have ensured that each brand name is completely distinct from the other brands in the group – for example, Accor with their Formule 1, Motel 6, Ibis, Etap, Mercure, Novotel and Sofitel brands.

The advantages of multiple branding include

- Increased market share
- Less dependency on the volatility of a single-market segment
- Reduction in financial risk.

The main danger of multiple branding is the potential to 'cannibalize' the company's sales by encouraging the company's existing customers to trade down and stay at a cheaper brand of lodging facilities also owned by the same company. This criticism is particularly directed at corporations who have retained one family name for the entire range of lodging brands. This strategy gives lower graded accommodation the badge of approval from a higher graded brand.

International hotel and restaurant chain expansion

International hospitality companies expanded at an exceptional rate in the 1990s and 2000s. The major hospitality companies already have a presence in most countries, where it is politically possible to operate. The characteristics of a hospitality company's home country play a central role in determining how successful its international expansion is. In particular, the nature of demand and competition in their domestic market shapes the culture of the management team – indeed, the core competences and competitive advantages of international firms are first developed in the home environment. For example, Accor's French origins and Marriott's North American origins clearly influence their different approaches to managing hospitality operations in other parts of the world. Perlmutter (1969) developed a typology using four categories – ethnocentric, polycentric, regio-centric and geocentric – to explain the different approaches which firms can choose to manage their international operations. Each category is discussed below:

Ethnocentric

Companies taking an ethnocentric approach to their international hospitality operations are adopting a *home country orientation*. Home country operating systems and procedures are set up in their international subsidiaries (the host countries), and a home country 'knows best' culture is implied. This approach is suitable if the domestic marketing strategies are applicable in the foreign countries, or if the company is targeting home country customers. An all-inclusive holiday operated by a British home country tour operator (such as Ski Olympic) in a host country such as France, and targeting British customers, could adopt an ethnocentric approach. However, because host country cultures can be very different from the domestic country culture, the ethnocentric approach is not suitable if the target markets comprise large numbers of host country residents. When Asian hotel companies entered North America, they tried to replicate the high levels of attentive service offered in their home countries, but this led to very high payroll costs, and the strategy was rescinded.

Polycentric

Companies taking a polycentric approach to their international hospitality operations are adopting a *host country orientation*. The home country management recognizes that managers in the host country know their own culture better than the home country managers, and the local operating systems and procedures are retained in foreign markets. This approach is suitable if the host country marketing strategies are targeting the host country customers. It is based on the premise that there are fundamental differences between domestic and foreign marketing, and that local managers understand their customers better than does the international head office. The marketing of Best Western Hotels is typically polycentric; each country has considerable autonomy in devising its own marketing campaigns, which are developed for host country consumers.

Regiocentric

Some hotel operations are geared towards a particular continental region, which has a similar culture and is at a similar stage of economic development. The Scandinavian countries of Denmark,

Finland, Norway and Sweden have a strong regional identity. A similar marketing offer can be developed for a hospitality brand operating in Scandinavia, which is culturally suitable for all Scandinavian consumers; and Scandic Hotels does operate on this basis. One advantage of a regiocentric approach is the cost and marketing benefits of standardizing the offer.

Geocentric

A geocentric approach implies a worldwide orientation that does not favour either the home or the host country. This is often called a global approach to management. The company adopts a positive attitude towards other cultures, and borrows what is best from many countries. 'Global consumers', who have similar consumption patterns regardless of where they live, are an attractive target market for companies seeking to adopt a geocentric approach. However, many of the international hospitality companies who claim to be 'global' still retain strong elements of their ethnocentric origins.

None of the international hospitality firms operates purely in one of these four forms, but firms do exhibit ethnocentric, polycentric, regiocentric and geocentric management tendencies. Some hotel brands strive to combine the advantages of a polycentric and geocentric approach to international management by adopting a 'glocal' strategy and mixing the global/local to achieve a more appropriate balance to manage their worldwide hotel operations.

International hotel competitor sets

There is strong competition between the major international hotel brands (see Table 4.3). IHG, Wyndham, Marriott, Hilton, Accor, Choice and Starwood are global competitors with multiple brands targeting most market sectors. There are a small number of hotel companies that operate on a global scale with a single brand, typically in niche markets. Four Seasons is a luxury niche operation, whilst Best Western is a mid-market niche operator. Other key European and North American competitors include Rezidor, Hyatt and Sol Melia. Rapidly growing Asian hotel operators include Jin Jiang, Shangri-La, Prince and Taj. In individual countries, domestic competitors can provide strong local based competition to the global brands.

Companies choose the markets in which they want to compete, and in that sense we can say that they choose their competition. Equally, if companies find that they are not competing effectively in a marketplace, they can choose to exit and sell their units and/or brands. Whitbread exited the United Kingdom mid- and deluxe hotel market in 2005 by selling their franchises in the Marriott Hotels and

Table 4.3 Major international hotel corporations and their lodging brands

Corporate brands	Product brands	Number of hotels	Number of bedrooms '000	Number of countries
IHG	Intercontinental Hotels and Resorts, Crowne Plaza, Hotel Indigo, Holiday Inn Hotels and Resorts, Holiday Inn Express, Staybridge Suites, Candlewood Suites	4500	650	100+
Wyndham	Baymount, Days Inn, Hawthorne, Howard Johnson, Knights Inn, Microtel, Ramada, Super 8 Motel, Travelodge, Wingate, Wyndham	7090	593	66
Hilton	Waldorf Astoria, Conrad, Hilton, Doubletree, Embassy Suites, Hilton Garden Inn, Hampton Inn & Suites, Homewood Suites by Hilton, Home Suites by Hilton and Hilton Grand Vacations.	3500	NA	81
Marriott	Marriott Hotels & Resorts, JW Marriott Hotels & Resorts, Renaissance Hotels & Resorts, Edition, Autograph, Courtyard by Marriott, Residence Inn by Marriott, Marriott Conference Centers, TownePlace Suites by Marriott, Springhill Suites by Marriott, Marriott Vacation Club, The Ritz-Carlton Hotel Company, L.L.C., The Ritz-Carlton Club, Marriott ExecuStay, Marriott ExecuStay Apartments, Grand Residences by Marriott	3000+	NA	67
Accor	Sofitel, Pullman, MGallery, Novotel, Grand Mercure, Mercure, Suitehotel, Adagio, All Seasons, Ibis, Etap, Formule 1, HotelF1, Motel 6, Studio 6, Thalassa, Lucien Barriere, Orbis	4100	Approximately 500	90
Choice	Comfort Inn, Comfort Suites, Quality, Sleep Inn, Clarion, Cambria Suites, MainStay Suites, Suburban, Econo Lodge, Rodeway Inn, Ascend	5570 TO DO	452	40
Starwood	St. Regis Hotels & Resorts, The Luxury Collection, W Hotels, Westin Hotels & Resorts, Le Meridien, Sheraton Hotels & Resorts, Four Points by Sheraton, Aloft, element by Westin	897 TO DO	275	95

Source: Individual hotel company websites, October 2010.

Note: These data are constantly changing – you should check the company's website for current data.

Courtyard by Marriott to focus on the growing budget market with their Premier Inn brand.

The scale and size of these companies are truly global and represent 'big business!' However, at any one moment, the mega hotel corporations will be signing deals for new hotel openings around the world, whilst at the same time unhappy franchisees and property owners will be switching 'flags' to a competitor brand. The rate of churn (hotel properties moving from one brand to another) is high. Also individual branded properties may close some rooms for refurbishment or open new-build room extensions and therefore decrease/increase the brand's worldwide hotel bedroom stock. So, for these reasons, major companies may not be able to say precisely how many hotels and how many bedrooms they are operating at any one time.

CONCLUSION

Segmenting markets to identify profitable target markets, developing a differentiated offer to deliver enhanced customer satisfaction and positioning the hospitality brand against competitors are essential components in the development of marketing strategies to compete effectively.

In this chapter, we have explained:

- Three segmentation strategies – undifferentiated, differentiated and niche
- The difficulties of differentiating the hospitality product
- The criteria for successfully positioning a hospitality offer
- The Five Forces Competitive analysis
- The four industry competitive environments – fragmented, niche, volume and stalemate
- Different forms of ownership and affiliation, including ownership, lease, management contract, franchising and consortia
- The benefits and forms of branding in hospitality
- International competition in the hotel industry.

REVIEW QUESTIONS

Carry out Activity 4.1 again and compare your answers:
- How many hotels and bedrooms do the largest hotel companies manage?
- How many hotel brands can you name?
- Which company owns which hotel brands?

Now check your understanding of this chapter by answering the following questions:

1 Analyse a hospitality industry competitive environment using Porter's Five Forces model

2 Discuss differentiation and positioning strategies in the hospitality industry
3 Discuss the advantages and disadvantages of branding in hospitality:
  • from a customer's perspective
  • from a company's perspective.

References and Further Reading

Connell, J. (1992). Branding hotel portfolios. *International Journal of Contemporary Hospitality Management, 4,* 26–32.

de Chernatony, L., & Dall'Olmo Riley, F. (1998). Defining a brand: Beyond the literature with expert's interpretations. *Journal of Marketing Management, 14,* 417–444.

Dev, C. S., Morgan, M. S., & Shoemaker, S. (1995). A positioning analysis of hotel brands. *Cornell Hotel & Restaurant Quarterly, 36,* 48–55.

Frambacha, R. T., Prabhub, J., & Verhallence, T. M. M. (2003). The influence of business strategy on new product activity: The role of market orientation. *Journal of International Research in Marketing, 20,* 377–397.

Jones, P. (1999). Multiunit management in the hospitality industry: a late C20 phenomenon. *Journal of Contemporary Hospitality Management. 11,* 155–164.

Lander, N. (2006). Steak and the city. *Financial Times Weekend,* life and arts, 9/10 December 9 2006.

Lovelock, C. and Wirtz, J. (2007). Services Marketing: people, technology, strategy, 6th edition, Pearson Prentice Hall.

Morrison, A., & Thomas, R. (1999). The future of small firms in the hospitality industry. *International Journal of Contemporary Hospitality Management, 11,* 148–154

Park, C. W., Jaworski, B. J., & MacInnis, D. J. (1986). Strategic Brand Concept-Image Management. *Journal of Marketing, 50,* 135–145.

Perlmutter, H. V. (1969). The tortuous evolution of the multi-national corporation. *Columbia Journal of World Business, 4,* 9–18.

Porter, M. E. (1980). *Competitive strategy: Techniques for analyzing industries and competitors.* The Free Press.

Ries, A., & Trout, J. (1986). *Marketing warfare:* McGraw-Hill.

C H A P T E R **5**

Developing the offer

INTRODUCTION

Although experts think about the hospitality product offer from a number of different perspectives, all agree that the product is a complex combination of tangible and intangible elements. The product is the starting point in the development of the marketing offer. Without a product there is nothing to sell. All hospitality products deliver basic functional solutions to consumers' needs and wants. However, to succeed in the marketplace, products must be configured as a marketing offer that is designed to deliver customer satisfaction to specified target markets. In Chapter 4, we discussed commodity products and branding in detail and explained that successful brands add value for consumers. In this chapter, we will explore the components of the hospitality product, product/benefit bundles, the standardization versus adaptation debate and the product life cycle (PLC).

We can consider the product from two perspectives – first from the customer's perspective as a bundle of benefits that will solve their problems, and second from the firm's perspective in terms of what we create for and offer to the customer. It is important to note that the hospitality product that marketers strive to create and deliver may be quite different from the hospitality actually experienced by the customer. Especially in service situations, unplanned elements can dramatically distort and disrupt the customers' experience, leading to unplanned customer dissatisfaction, or, on the contrary, customer delight.

Activity 5.1

Access the following websites and explore details of the hospitality product offer:

- http://www.jumeirah.com/Hotels-and-Resorts/ – Jumeirah manage the Burj Al Arab Hotel and several other hotels in Dubai
- www.visitlasvegas.com – the tourist destination website of the Las Vegas Convention and Visitors Authority
- http://www.malmaison.com – Malmaison Hotels
- http://www.yotel.com – YOTEL
- http://www.accorhotels.com – Access the Formule 1 brand by logging on to the main Accor Hotels website

---

DEFINING THE PRODUCT

An important distinction can be drawn between the core product, the tangible product and the augmented or extended product (Kotler & Armstrong, 2010). Figure 5.1 provides an example of each component of the product for a budget hotel.

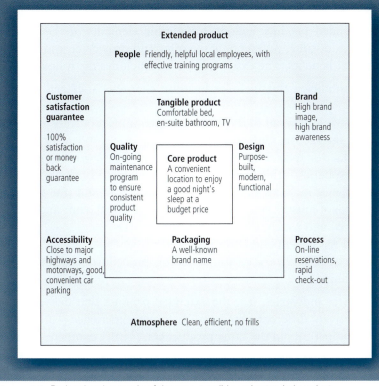

Figure 5.1 Budget hotel example of the core, tangible and extended product

Core product

The core product delivers the functional benefits that the customer is seeking. In hospitality, a hotel offers a place to sleep; a restaurant offers a place to eat; an event provides a venue and service for an occasion. It is the customer, not the company that defines the core product. If a customer wants convenience, low cost and a good night's sleep, then, that is the core product for that customer. Normally, hospitality organizations do not compete at the core product level; however, companies should ensure that the requisite capabilities and competences are in place to deliver the core product effectively.

Tangible product

The tangible product is composed of the physical elements that are necessary for the core product (benefits) to be delivered. The tangible product includes product features (the size and range of facilities) and design components (external and internal). In hospitality, companies can differentiate their offer in the form of the tangible product, for example, the size and comfort of a mattress and the quality of the sheet on the bed or the use of fresh organic ingredients to enhance food quality.

Extended product

The extended product includes intangible elements of the product that can add value, differentiate the offer and provide customers with additional benefits. The extended product includes the following:

- Accessibility – this includes location characteristics and opening times
- The people element of the offer – staff training, courtesy and quality of interaction with customers
- Ancillary or special facilities – for example, the spa in resort hotels
- Atmospherics – this important sensory element of the hospitality experience includes sight (the visual design), sound (the style and volume of music), smell (the aroma), taste (the flavour and texture of food) and touch (the feel of quality fabrics)
- Brand reputation and corporate ethics
- After sales service – customer billing procedures and complaint handling.

In service industries, it is the extended product that delivers what is distinctively different about the customer experience – and this is where competitors in the same product class really compete. Delivering a memorable hospitality experience consistently is a major challenge for hospitality organizations.

Tables 5.1 and 5.2 provide examples of hospitality product concepts.

Table 5.1 Hotel product concepts	
Concept	**Examples**
Exclusive luxury hotels	Dubai's Burj Al Arab Hotel claims to be the world's first 'seven-star hotel'. Built in the shape of a giant sail and taller than the Eiffel Tower, it combines modern architecture, extravagant décor and furniture, with state-of-the-art technology, and provides superior service with a six-to-one staff-to-guest ratio.
Boutique hotels	These are exclusive hotels that focus on contemporary design as the key factor in delivering customer satisfaction – examples include Ian Schrager's hotel, The Morgan, New York; London's Hempel Hotel and the W Hotel in Sydney.
Eco hotels	The concept underpinning an eco hotel development is sustainability in both construction and operations. Eco hotels range from those offering ultimate sheik-luxury (Al Maha Desert Resort, Dubai); to more affordable eco luxury (Scarlet Hotel, Cornwal, England); to the remote and more simple rainforest lodges (Laguna del Lagarto Eco-Lodge in Northern Costa Rica). See the Marketing Insight about the Heritance Hotel at Kandalama, Sri Lanka.

Table 5.1	Hotel product concepts—cont'd
Concept	**Examples**
Large convention, entertainment and gambling complexes	15 of the largest hotels in the world are located within a 2-mile radius of Las Vegas. Vegas hotels combine a wide range of hospitality offers and entertainment on a grand-scale plus gambling. At the time of writing, the largest hotel in Vegas is the MGM Grand with over 5000 rooms.
Mid-market classic contemporary hotels	The Malmaison concept focuses on individually designed, stylish bedrooms complete with modern sound systems, state-of-the-art interconnectivity and French brasserie cooking at mid-market prices.
Capsule hotels	Capsule hotels originated in Japan and comprise pre-fabricated plastic or fibreglass capsules, stacked in rows with one unit on top of another, and designed for solo occupancy. There are no en-suite facilities. Some Japanese capsule hotels are mixed, but with separate areas for males and females; others are men- or women-only. Examples include the Capsule Hotel Askausa River Side, Tokyo and the Nine Hours Kyoto Teramachi. A Western adaption of the capsule concept is YOTEL. Its design copies the space limitations from luxury airline travel to provide cabin style accommodation for one or two people with en-suite (rainforest showers), free Wifi, wired Internet access and a techno wall entertainment system in a 3.045 m by 2.747 m space. The design, with no external windows and limited food service, is cost-driven and enables YOTELs to be located in basement or roof locations that are usually unsuitable for more traditional hotels. The first YOTELs have been located in airports and range in size from 32 to 700 cabins.
No-frills budget hotels	Formule 1, Accor's budget European product, focuses on functionality, with small bedrooms (a double bed and upper bunk bed), and minimal service levels. There is, however, a high use of technology, with self-cleaning showers and toilets, and automatic computer terminals to provide check-in and billing services when reception is closed.

Table 5.2	Restaurant product concepts
Restaurant	**Concept**
The Fat Duck	Heston Blumenthal, a controversial television chef, uses molecular gastronomy – a low temperature, ultra-slow cooking technique – to create innovative food which tastes extraordinary in his three-Michelin star Restaurant in Bray, England.
Conran	Conran's fashionable restaurants combine innovative and stylish design with fine dining on a mass-market scale in London, Paris and New York.

(Continued)

Table 5.2	Restaurant product concepts—cont'd
Restaurant	**Concept**
Rainforest Café	An environmental concept café based on the rainforest, with special effects including mist, regular thunderstorms with thunder and lightning and a Magic Mushroom Bar, operating in North America, Asia-Pacific and Europe.
Dans le Noir	A Parisian restaurant concept where diners eat in the dark, the waiting employees are blind (but the kitchen brigade is sighted) and now operating in Paris, Barcelona, London and New York. Eating in the dark changes our sensory understanding by removing our vision and enhancing other senses to create an unusual dining out experience. See www.danslenoir.com for more details.
Meatball Shop	A single-food concept offering a variety of meatballs (beef, chicken, pork and vegetarian) with a choice of sauces (classic, mushroom, parmesan, spicy and tomato) in Manhattan, New York. There are several examples of single food restaurant concepts including burgers, fried chicken, fish and pizzerias.
Otarian	Otarian is an ethical vegetarian restaurant chain launched in 2010 which strives to create a low-carbon restaurant concept in New York and London (Williams, 2010). The strapline is 'Love food; Love Life; and Love the Planet'. See http://www.otarian.com

Product benefit bundles

Consumers rarely purchase a single hospitality product in isolation. Customers generally look for a combination of features or benefits to satisfy their needs and wants, and hospitality businesses can provide these benefits either independently or in partnership with other organizations. We call these combinations 'product benefit bundles'. The benefit for customers is that buying bundles makes the purchase decision more convenient. Instead of making many separate decisions about travel, accommodation and food and beverage, the customer makes a simple, single decision about a package. For the hospitality business, the benefits are that we can brand 'bundles' as marketable offers, enjoy economies in selling (for example, sell one package rather than three separate components) and increase the value of a sale. Within hospitality examples include:

- Bed and breakfast; Dinner, bed and breakfast; Full board (accommodation with breakfast, lunch and dinner)
- Themed accommodation packages with (or without) meals – like murder mystery weekends
- Restaurant, function and wedding menus with drink packages (inclusive of starter, main course, desert, coffee and relevant taxes)

- 24-hour conference packages including accommodation, all meals, tea and coffee and hire of meeting room
- Exotic themed party events with inclusive menus, live entertainment, dancing and activities.

In addition, hospitality businesses can work with external organizations – for example, local leisure and sporting attractions – to offer inclusive product benefit bundles, like theatre weekends or tickets for popular sporting events.

Activity 5.2

Access details of a conference or wedding package from a conference venue, event company or hotel website and review the different product combinations and prices. What are the benefits of product bundles for

- The customer?
- The hotel?

The accommodation, food and drink products offered by hospitality businesses form part of the larger tourism product, either formally through a tour operator or informally when the customer independently visits tourist destinations. External factors, which are outside the control of hospitality operators, can affect the customers' experience of a trip. Typically, the weather influences our holiday experience, as well as the service provided by other retail and tourism outlets. Tour operators combine all the essential elements, such as flights, transfers, rooms and food, excursions and offer a combined product in one inclusive package. Tourists buying a package holiday regard the hospitality product simply as one component of the entire package, not as an independent product, and customer satisfaction with the hospitality product cannot easily be separated from satisfaction with the other elements of the travel package.

This means that hospitality businesses need to work in collaboration with other organizations to create an effective marketing strategy and to ensure repeat and referral business. This collaboration can take different forms:

- Individual hospitality operations formulate, develop, promote and deliver their product as a part of the total tourist offer of the destination
- At the destination, hospitality operators work with official tourist organizations who formulate and develop tourism products based on the destination attributes and promote them to target markets
- Tour operators co-ordinate the products offered by hospitality operators and other suppliers, and then formulate them into a single offer (package) which is promoted to target markets.

SERVICE DELIVERY CONCEPTS AND THE PRODUCT

Any consideration of the product in hospitality must be based on a thorough knowledge and understanding of the needs and wants of target markets. Understanding customer needs, within a given price band, is fundamental in providing successful products that match customer expectations. One of the most important product decisions facing multiple-unit organizations is, how much of the product should be standardized and how much should be adapted? When hospitality organizations aim to standardize a product, the objective is to provide a standard experience for all customers in every unit. An adapted hospitality product deliberately offers a modified product, which can, in desired, be different in each unit.

Standardized products

The international fast-food restaurant chains provide many examples of standardized hospitality products. They offer the following features in their restaurants:

- The same menu at the same price
- The same kitchen production process
- The same service delivery process
- The same staff recruitment, training and service standards
- The same layout, seating and internal décor
- The same external frontage, signage and brand logo.

There are advantages to both the consumer and the organization from a standardized product. Customers receive a consistent, reliable product that fulfils their brand expectations. Companies gain significant economies of scale and experience through fully pre-configured design concepts, volume purchasing, reduction in stock levels, lower employee skills requirements and easier staff training procedures. Service processes can also be blueprinted (see pages 311–313). Essentially, a blueprint is a flowchart that sets out the various tasks that have to be performed for a service to be delivered to a customer. Blueprints can also identify who is to perform the task and the required performance standards. There are also opportunities to maximize brand awareness through marketing communication campaigns based on promoting the same, standardized product formula.

A precondition for developing a genuinely consistent standardized product in hospitality operations is to build new developments instead of adapting existing buildings and structures. The budget hotel chains are more likely to have a standardized product because the accommodation is factory built, with prefabricated bedroom units erected on the building site. As we saw in Chapter 4, hospitality brands offering a standardized product can be described as 'harder' brands. However, trying to adapt older buildings to a standardized brand formula inevitably creates brand inconsistencies.

Companies with successful standardized offers can expand more easily – every time a new unit is proposed, all the product decisions have already been tried, tested and agreed. This has enabled a small number of standardized hospitality branded products to grow rapidly throughout the world. The standardized product concept is either loved or loathed by consumers!

Adapted products

The alternative approach to standardization for a branded chain operation is to adapt the product according to local consumer needs, niche market segments or deliberately to provide less-standardized products. Examples of adapted products in branded hospitality chains include the following:

- Individually designed hotels in different sites, often built-in different historical periods, offering a different range of services and facilities in different locations
- Restaurants with different menu concepts, different menus reflecting local ingredients and different cultures of cuisine
- Different décor and different types of furniture
- Staff who are trained to unit standards of operation, instead of group standards of operation.

Advantages of an adapted approach include providing consumers with different experiences in different unit locations – this approach appeals to customers who are bored with standardized product offers. Other advantages include the possibility of lower costs by sourcing locally; and the opportunity to enable managers to respond to local consumer/competitor requirements. Disadvantages of an adapted approach include higher hospitality product development costs, since there are fewer opportunities for economies of scale. Hospitality brands offering an adapted product must retain some core brand standards, and can be described as 'softer' brands.

International product decisions

The level of standardization or adaptation is a major product decision for international hospitality brands. The international hospitality product needs to take into account local country cultural differences and make suitable adaptations to gain local consumer acceptance (Usunier & Lee, 2009). Identifying target markets is crucial when developing the international product.

If the target market is primarily from the home country then the product can be standardized using the home country culture. The British-based tour operator, Ski Olympic provides a British skiing holiday product for British customers in the French Alps. The product includes British-style food (porridge and cooked English breakfast, Tetley tea bags, evening meals using British recipes), British beers, British television (especially sport and TV soap operas), British and Commonwealth staff and management and even British ski instructors. This British product in France delivers customer satisfaction because the customers are all British.

If the target market is primarily people from the host country, the product should be adapted to take into account local cultural values. McDonald's makes many local adaptations, including adapting the meat in its burger products to conform to the cultural expectations of customers in Muslim countries, and providing rice as an alternative to fries for Asian markets.

If the target market has regional or global characteristics, then a standardized product should be developed. Scandic Hotels provide a relatively standardized regional hotel product in Scandinavian countries and other countries in Northern Europe. Scandic Hotels incorporate a distinctive Scandinavian atmosphere, décor and design in its product offer, which is strongly influenced by environmentally friendly policies.

In reality, most international hospitality groups have varying degrees of standardization and adaptation. For hotel companies, accommodation, the range of facilities offered and service standards tend to be easier to standardize, whilst décor, design, staff uniforms and some elements of the food and beverage offer tend to be adapted to reflect local country culture and cuisine. Even the most standardized concepts, like McDonald's, adapt elements of their product offer when necessary. Whilst Best Western Hotels – which operates the most heterogeneous brand of hotels on the international arena – strives to standardize the product offer through its quality audit for each property. The concept of providing international product standards with local adaptations – sometimes called glocalization – combines the best of both approaches effectively.

PRODUCT LIFE CYCLE

All products experience a life cycle, which charts their sales and profit behaviour from birth, through various stages, to decline and extinction (see Fig. 5.2). The product life cycle (PLC) is one of the most well-known concepts in marketing theory, and hospitality managers should be aware of its importance when developing marketing strategies for their businesses. PLC concepts can be applied to an item on the menu or in the bar, a sales outlet within a hotel (the accommodation,

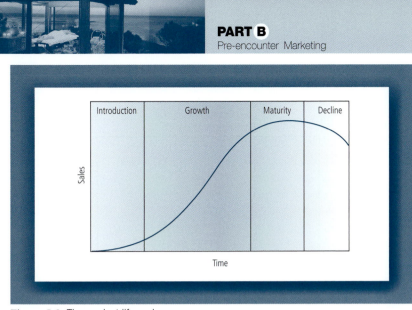

Figure 5.2 The product life cycle

the restaurant and the banqueting), an individual property or unit, a brand or chain of outlets or even a destination. The global hospitality industry comprises hundreds of thousands of 'products', all at different stages of their life cycle.

The PLC includes the following stages, but note that the timescale can vary from a very short period of only a few months to a very long period lasting several generations and even hundreds of years (see Fig. 5.3):

- *Product development*. During this period, the new product concept is conceived, researched, assessed and, in some cases, test-marketed prior to launch in the market place. Most new product concepts fail to deliver a strong business case, and at this stage they are never actually brought to market.
- *Introduction*. This is the launch period, when the new hospitality product is introduced to the market – for example, the opening of a new restaurant. Some new products never really take-off, but if they do, they enter the next stage.
- *Growth*. This is the period when the new product becomes more widely accepted by consumers and sales grow as the concept becomes better established
- *Maturity*. At this stage, the product has reached its potential and growth slows
- *Decline*. Eventually, the product no longer satisfies the needs and wants of its customers, as alternative products/competitors provide better benefits to consumers. Sales fall as the product goes into decline, and the management has to decide whether to retain or dispose of the declining product. However, a product that is in decline for one company can still be highly profitable for a different company. There are many products in declining markets that are still highly profitable – for example, bed and breakfast houses in British seaside resorts.

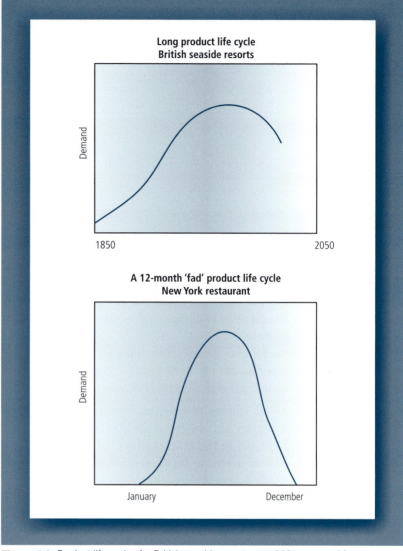

Figure 5.3 Product life cycles for British seaside resorts over 200 years, and for a New York fad restaurant opening and closing in 12 months

There are a number of criticisms of the PLC. First, it is not always clear where a product is precisely located on the PLC. Second, the PLC is not an accurate forecasting tool, and sales may fall due to an economic downturn or other external cause, rather than a change in customer preferences that typically underlies movements from stage to stage of the PLC. So, if a manager makes a marketing decision based on a faulty analysis of the PLC then the marketing strategies adopted might be incorrect and damage the business. Whilst accepting these valid criticisms, the simplicity and terminology of the PLC helps us to understand important product management issues, which we will now explore.

New product development concepts

Effective hospitality managers constantly seek to improve customer satisfaction by reviewing their offer. As a result of managers' observations, business performance and customer/staff feedback, product improvements can be introduced. These can range from minor low-cost enhancements to multi-million pound new-build developments. IHG have developed a new design concept for their Holiday Inn brand that uses 20 per cent less space and is consequently much more energy efficient. Clearly, many product developments are successful, but the rate of new product failure in hospitality is high – especially in food service. Unfortunately, many independently owned restaurants open in a blaze of publicity, only to close within 12 months. The reasons for the high failure rate of new products in hospitality include the following:

- Undercapitalization – this means not having sufficient funds to open and operate the business; many new hospitality businesses borrow too much and cannot afford to pay the interest and consequently fail
- Inexperienced and over-optimistic entrepreneurs
- Poor marketing research
- A flawed product concept
- An inappropriate location
- Competitors' responses
- Inconsistent service delivery
- Negative publicity from dissatisfied customers and journalists
- Poor interior and/or exterior design
- Limited market potential
- Higher development costs than planned
- Poor timing (e.g. opening during the decline or recession phase of the business cycle).

Innovation

Major hospitality organizations have a large number of products at different stages of the PLC. Since all products decline, there is a constant requirement to research and find successful new product concepts to ensure continuous profits. Companies use two different methods to find new concepts: they can either *acquire* products that have been developed by others; or they can *develop* their own new products.

Acquisition

The bureaucracy of larger organizations can inhibit creativity whilst entrepreneurs, who are often closer to customers, can innovate with much more freedom. In hospitality, there are many examples of people who develop successful new product concepts based on their 'gut' feeling, their intuitive understanding of customer needs and their entrepreneurial flair. Simon Woodroffe founder of YOTEL explains how that eureka moment arrived. He was thinking how to adapt the Japanese capsule hotel concept for the western market when he was upgraded on a flight by British Airways to first class; when he woke he realized the solution was all around him – all he needed was the designer of the British Airway cabin who could create the YOTEL product. Once a successful entrepreneur has proved the viability of the new product concept, larger hospitality organizations can either imitate the concept or buy out the entrepreneur's company.

Development

The alternative route for new product development in larger organizations is to set up an in-house new product development team to generate and evaluate new product concepts formally. The team may be an established part of the organization structure or an ad hoc cross-functional group. New product teams need marketing input to ensure that the customer's voice is heard. Most so-called new products are actually product modifications, cost reductions or product line extensions, as opposed to original product concepts.

Marketing insight 5.1

The Kandalama Eco Hotel

Heritance Hotels, Sri Lanka, derives its name from combining heritage and inheritance and this green philosophy is central to the Heritance Hotels brand. During the construction of the Kandalama Hotel, the local eco system was protected by building the hotel on a raised platform between two rock formations. This minimized the impact on wildlife – indeed no trees were damaged during construction. State-of-the-art technology was incorporated to ensure efficient use of energy and resources. The innovative design means that no lights are required during daytime, due to natural light throughout the property – thus making substantial savings in energy. A comprehensive energy and water conservation policy reduces operating costs and minimizes consumption with power cut-off switches, energy efficient lighting (CFL bulbs), photo-active garden lights and solar power hot water systems. To avoid using surface water, wells with 200-ft deep tubes and recycled rainwater provide for all the hotel's water needs. The philosophy of sustainable development includes air quality protection, noise control and waste management (all paper and polythene are removed from the hotel's environs to preserve the natural eco system); and close involvement with local villagers to assist with the local community's social and economic well-being. Indeed guests are not allowed to walk alone in the nearby forest to ensure that they do no harm to the ecosystem!

Source: www.heritancehotels.com

New product development process

Many companies have a formal new product development process that features some or all the following stages:

- *Idea generation*. There are several sources for new product ideas, including managers, employees, customers, suppliers, intermediaries and competitors.
- *Idea screening*. Ideas need to be screened to ensure that they can be developed further; some ideas lack potential and are immediately discarded; other ideas might be desirable but do not fit the competences of the company. Screening aims to eliminate bad ideas quickly so that the costlier stages of new product development (such as concept development) are not required.
- *Concept development and testing*. In this stage, the idea is more fully developed into a new product concept with a detailed, workable proposal. Companies then need to test consumers' reaction to the new concept, using marketing research techniques such as focus groups.
- *Marketing strategy*. A marketing strategy is developed that describes the innovation's target market, market positioning and marketing mix. Initial costs, sales and profit projections can then be formulated.
- *Business analysis*. In this stage, the new product is evaluated against company investment and return hurdles. Investment in new product development is a board-level decision when significant capital sums are involved.
- *Product development*. Finally, the idea starts to become a reality. Large companies sometimes develop a prototype for test marketing. A test market is a limited-scale launch of the product concept to establish the potential for the innovation and the marketing necessary to make it a success. New brand concepts can be experimented in a single unit to gauge customer reactions before rolling out the concept, but smaller businesses cannot afford to test market the concept.
- *Commercialization*. The final decision to proceed is based on the results of the test marketing or the business analysis. Depending on consumer response and the capital investment/profit return calculations, a final decision will be given to proceed or halt the new product development.

Whilst larger companies have a more structured approach to new product development, smaller hospitality companies are generally more entrepreneurial. A restaurant proprietor can introduce new menu items for a trial period before making the add-or-drop decision. Failed ideas can be dropped without serious cost consequences.

Adoption theory

Some new products become popular very quickly, whilst it can be years before others takeoff. Some never become viable. Researchers have identified a number of different categories of new product adopters, according to which the customer is amongst the first or later groups to buy. This classification of consumers is described as adoption theory. These categories are as follows:

- *Innovators*. These are the first people to buy a product once it appears. In hospitality, they are the first customers to visit a new restaurant when it opens. They are prepared to experiment and take risks and are an important influence on the next category.
- *Early adopters*. These people respond to good reports from innovators and media commentators, and form the next category to try a new product. Many are opinion leaders, whose judgment about a product can determine whether it will succeed or fail. If the early adopters endorse the product, it will become more established.
- *Early majority*. These people follow the early adopters, whose opinion matters to them. This group consists of people who tend to conform to social trends, are well-integrated socially and accept change.
- *Late majority*. This group is very slow to purchase new products. They are less responsive to change, are more sceptical, and prefer products they know rather than experimenting.
- *Laggards*. These people are aversive to change and reluctant to alter their purchase patterns. They tend to be older, more cautious and conservative, and continue to buy products even when they are no longer fashionable.

New product launch strategies

The introduction stage for new hospitality products includes new-build openings for hotels, restaurants and bars, new brand launches, and relaunches of tired products that have been refurbished and repositioned in the marketplace. For hotels, the time involved in planning, gaining permissions, constructing and finishing a new-build project can take several years and substantial capital investment. For restaurant and bar concepts, the lead-time will be shorter and investment costs lower. A common problem is that hospitality new-build and refurbishment program are not always completed on time, and often the new hospitality product has to be opened incomplete. Customers experience a distressingly long list of minor problems, such as incomplete décor finishes, that can take several months to complete.

A typical launch strategy will include a 'soft opening', where invited guests stay and/or dine on a complimentary basis. This provides an opportunity to train staff on the job, and test the service process and the equipment before paying customers arrive. Feedback from invited customers and staff helps to identify problems, which can then be resolved. If problems are not identified and resolved in the soft opening, then (especially with new restaurants) a poor reputation can quickly spread – which is often fatal. The marketing communications challenge during the launch period is to establish the market position and create awareness and interest in the new hospitality product concept in order to generate trial purchases.

During the launch period, sales are low and there can be major fluctuations in demand, causing service problems at crucial times. Start-up costs are high owing to the uncertain patterns of demand, staff training and recruitment costs, and the promotional spend to raise awareness. The unit is unlikely to be profitable during the introduction stage. However, the launch period is vital for the new hospitality product because the business needs to generate

- satisfied customers,
- positive word of mouth and
- repeat sales.

Smaller companies may never recover from a poor launch, because they may not be able to repair the damage from negative word of mouth publicity quickly enough. A successful opening means that sales will increase, leading to the growth stage of the PLC.

Growth product strategies

In the growth stage, the hospitality product should be earning a good word of mouth reputation, the early adopters return and recommend the product to their social networks, who patronize the establishment in growing numbers. Sales grow, but despite this healthy trend there are pitfalls associated with growth. Successful hospitality products are dependent on a consistent product/service offer, and as the business grows there can be over-demand at peak periods, resulting in either excessive waiting times or having to turn customers away. Hospitality customers are notoriously fickle, and once they have found another hospitality product that suits them, they may never return. Management can also inadvertently create problems by raising prices on ancillary products to boost profitability (e.g. on drinks and wines), which might deter repeat customers. Arrogant management, thinking that the business is now a success, may start to overlook customers' special requests and even ignore customer complaints.

Marketing strategies that hospitality companies adopt in the growth stage include the following:

- Relationship marketing to build long-term relationships with customers
- Enhancing the product and service delivery by continuous feedback from customers and staff
- Setting prices to gradually grow the market; this means not raising prices quickly simply because the establishment is becoming popular, and in some cases might involve making price adjustments downwards
- Targeting new market segments to grow demand, possibly with minor product modification
- Continuing investment in marketing communications activity to maintain awareness and build loyalty based on product preference
- Encouraging word of mouth recommendation by inviting satisfied customers to refer friends
- Opening additional units in similar geographic and demographic catchment areas
- Building partnerships with other organizations that can generate a stream of customers, such as theaters or hospitals.

The growth stage should be increasingly profitable, because fixed costs are spread over a greater number of customers and, as trading patterns become more established, the management become more experienced at controlling staff rotas to enhance customer satisfaction and reduce wage costs.

Mature product strategies

The majority of hospitality product concepts operate in the mature stage of the life cycle, which can last for a very long period of time. The market for the product is well established, and the product itself is clearly positioned against its competitors. Sales level off, as the business has consistent demand from a loyal customer base. Growth is limited and is largely dependent on gaining market share from competitors. The mature hospitality product can suffer from a number of problems, including

- A dated product concept
- A tired product in need of refurbishment
- Management and staff working in a routine way and no longer 'wowing' the customers
- More intense competition from newer product concepts, which cater better for customer needs and wants
- Increased segmentation of the market, ultimately with the risk of market fragmentation.

Aware managers will recognize these symptoms and take action to avoid the product entering the decline stage prematurely. Mature product strategies in hospitality include the following:

- Relationship marketing to nurture and sustain loyal customer segments
- Continued investment to maintain and enhance service and product quality.
- Product modifications – for example, introducing new menus/new recipes – which can revitalize a tired hospitality product
- Reformulation of the product concept and/or refurbishment of the premises to relaunch the product
- Adaptation of other marketing mix elements – for example, lower prices, increased promotional activity – and targeting new intermediaries to generate additional sales.

By careful management of the marketing mix, the mature stage can remain profitable for a very long time. Gradually, profits will begin to decline as increased investment, with heavier promotional costs to maintain market share, coincides with lower prices, driven down by competitors. Even major international brands suffer from many competitors eroding their market share. Eventually, the mature stage will enter decline, unless the product has been reformulated and relaunched to start another cycle.

Case study 5.1 provides an illustration of the PLC.

Case study 5.1 **Little Chef**

Little Chef is a roadside diner chain in the United Kingdom, normally open from 7 in the morning until 10 in the evening. Since its opening in 1958, to its peak in the 1990s and its subsequent decline in to administration (bankruptcy) and possible rejuvenation, Little Chef has travelled through all the stages of the PLC.

The first unit was opened in Reading in 1958 with 11 covers and was a British adaptation of an American restaurant diner concept. In the introduction stage, growth was modest and the chain increased to 25 units in the first 10 years. In the late 1960s, the British catering sector underwent a period of consolidation and Little Chef became part of the Trust House Forte group, which at that time was one of Britain's largest hotel companies. During the 1970s, 1980s and early 1990s, there was considerable growth in British tourism and as a brand leader Little Chef expanded rapidly. Indeed, there was little serious competition apart from the Happy Eater brand. Trust House Forte acquired this main rival in 1987 and for 10 years the two brands retained their independent identity under the same ownership.

In 1996, there was a hostile takeover of Trust House Forte by Granada – the broadcasting and catering conglomerate. Granada merged Happy Eater in to the Little Chef brand and bought another competitor, AJ's Family Restaurants, which was also badged with the Little Chef brand. About this time, Little Chef reached its peak with 435 units and the brand was valued at several hundred million pounds.

Granada's mantra was to return value to shareholders and earn the senior management very high bonuses. To deliver this strategy other stakeholders suffered. So product quality was reduced, prices increased, and there was very little meaningful investment in the brand. Gradually, customers drifted away, employees became less motivated and demonstrably unhappy, and Little Chef's reputation declined. From 2000, the brand changed hands in corporate deals a number of times – but new owners failed to invest in Little Chef. Indeed, the 2005 new owners immediately sold or closed 130 of the underperforming restaurants. Unfortunately, these new owners soon went in to administration 2 years later and the value of the brand collapsed.

In 2007, a private equity company bought the brand and approximately 200 Little Chefs for less than £ 10 million. There was a serious attempt to rejuvenate Little Chef, including a much-publicized initiative with one of the Britain's celebrity chefs Heston Blumenthal. However the Chief Executive suddenly left in April 2010 and the prospects for this well-known brand remain uncertain.

Declining product strategies

There is no precise moment when a product or brand enters the decline stage, and the decline period can take place over a long period of time or be extremely rapid. Once decline really sets in, then the rate of decline accelerates. The decline stage can be caused by changes in consumer tastes, changes in technology, increased competition causing overcapacity, changes in management personnel, or changes in ownership. As sales begin to fall, the typical hospitality operator will

* Aim to cut costs in every facet of the business
* Reduce staffing levels
* Only invest in essential repairs (there will be limited, if any, investment in redecorating or refurbishment)
* Reduce overall product quality by purchasing cheaper food ingredients, bar and housekeeping products
* Take a longer time to pay suppliers.

Disappointed customers, overworked employees and dissatisfied local suppliers can combine to generate powerful negative word of mouth publicity. Returning customers will notice the poorer standards of product quality (e.g. tired décor and furniture, chipped and faded crockery and cheaper quality in-room amenities) and stop patronizing the hotel or restaurant. Customer complaints increase and there is little prospect of management being able to encourage the unhappy customers to return. The spiral of decline increases in a deadly no-win situation for all concerned. As sales deteriorate faster, more desperate cost-cutting measures are introduced to try and stem the losses which in turn reduce customer satisfaction.

For larger firms with several hospitality outlets or brands, the problem of a unit in decline is exacerbated by the negative publicity, which can damage the overall brand image of successful units in other stages of the life cycle. In addition, the costs of managing a declining brand are disproportionate to the benefits generated. Owners and managers need to decide whether to keep a declining product and harvest it to maximize profits or to dispose it. If the product is retained, costs have to be reduced and unprofitable segments eliminated, which further reduces sales.

Disposal or rejuvenation

At any one time, there are thousands of hospitality businesses that have reached the end of their PLCs. If staff and customers know that the business is for sale, the spiral of decline accelerates even more quickly. Indeed, if a hotel or restaurant is not sold quickly, the business can go bankrupt. The key point to remember is that when a hospitality product is sold, it often remains in the sector. The new owners can reformulate the product offer and invest in the relaunch of the business and a new PLC starts. In destinations that are in decline, the hospitality product might be bought and converted into other uses – for example, housing and retail outlets.

Alternatively, the existing owners might decide to rejuvenate the product by closing the existing business, investing in a new product concept and starting the PLC again.

CONCLUSION

Throughout this chapter, we have explored different perspectives of the hospitality product and emphasized the importance of matching the product to the needs of target markets. Given the intense competition in the hospitality business, marketers need to ensure that the product concept is designed to deliver customer satisfaction.

In this chapter, we have explained:

*   The complex combination of tangible and intangible elements that comprises the hospitality product
*   How products should be designed to cater for the needs and wants of target markets and to deliver customer satisfaction
*   That the hospitality product comprises a core product, a tangible component and an extended element
*   How hospitality businesses design product–benefit bundles to satisfy a combination of consumer needs and wants
*   That multiple-chain operations need to decide the degree of standardization and the degree of adaptation in their branded product
*   The PLC, which charts the sales and profits during the lifetime of every product

- The five stages in the PLC – product development, introduction, growth, maturity and decline
- The high failure rate of new products in hospitality
- The different marketing strategies at each stage of the PLC
- That when a product reaches the decline stage of the PLC, management needs to decide whether to dispose of, or rejuvenate, the product.

REVIEW QUESTIONS

Now check your understanding of this chapter by answering the following questions:

1 Discuss the tangible and intangible elements of the hospitality product

2 Discuss the advantages and disadvantages of standardizing the product offer for a branded hospitality chain

3 Evaluate the effectiveness of the PLC in marketing decision-making. Illustrate your answer by providing examples from the hospitality industry.

References and Further Reading

Bateson, J. E. G., & Hoffman, K. D. (1999). *Managing services marketing: Text and readings*. Dryden Press.

Horner, S., & Swarbrooke, J. (1996). *Marketing tourism, hospitality and leisure in Europe*. International Thomson Business Press.

Kotler, P., & Armstrong, G. (2010). *Principles of marketing*. Pearson-Education.

Lewis, R. C., & Chambers, R. E. (2000). *Marketing leadership in hospitality: Foundations and practice*. John Wiley.

McDonald, M. (2008). Malcolm McDonald on Marketing Planing: Understanding Marketing Plans and Strategy. Kogan Page.

Roper, A. J., & Brookes, M. E. A. (1996). *To standardise or not to standardise?*. CHME Annual Research Conference, Nottingham: Marketing International Hotel Groups.

Usunier, J. C., & Lee, J. (2009). *Marketing across cultures*. Prentice Hall.

Williams, M. (12 April, 2010). Ogilvy launches ad campaign for world's first low-carbon restaurant, Campaign.

www.yotel.com

CHAPTER 6

Locating the offer

Chapter objectives

After going through this chapter, you should be able to

- Understand the importance of location as a prerequisite for developing a successful hospitality business
- Identify the main classes of hospitality locations
- Research the characteristics of potential sites using relevant criteria
- Argue a case for the complexity of the destination product
- Evaluate the components of a destination's image
- Understand how hospitality companies work with destination marketing organizations.

INTRODUCTION

When the target markets have been defined and the product concept has been agreed, the next crucial marketing decision is to find the appropriate location(s) for the development of the hospitality business. Location has a critical influence on the selection of target markets and has a major influence upon potential demand. Finding and occupying suitable locations is a prerequisite for managing a profitable hospitality company. The famous quotation attributed to Conrad Hilton, who defined the three most important factors for success in the hotel business as 'location, location, location', remains valid today.

We now discuss in detail why location is important for both a single-site business and multiple-unit operators and examine the marketing research task of finding and evaluating appropriate locations. Finally, we will review destination marketing from the hospitality operators' perspective.

IMPORTANCE OF LOCATION

For owners, location choices have major capital investment and long-term consequences. When the agreement to buy a site or rent premises is finalized, it is difficult and costly to change the decision – the location is fixed. So the initial selection of the site is most important. An appropriate site will have the necessary characteristics to ensure strong demand for the business. Although there are many examples of poorly managed hospitality outlets that trade successfully because of an outstanding location, even very good marketing cannot really compensate for a poor location. Clearly, thorough research needs to be undertaken to establish the patterns of demand in potential locations. Companies need to know whether there is a sufficient level of demand from target markets for the product concept to justify the investment in a specific location. The major hospitality brands recognize the importance of location and may research a potential location for up to 3 or 4 years in advance. This ensures that a thorough evaluation of the area's future growth and economic potential is undertaken before investing in the acquisition of a site.

For the single-site operator, the choice of location is even more important, because the costs of a poor decision cannot be spread among a chain of outlets. Unfortunately, too many individual operators have overly optimistic demand projections and underestimate how long it can take to establish a new hospitality business. This is one of the reasons why so many small hospitality businesses fail in the start-up period. There are, of course, a small number of examples where successful hospitality businesses are located in difficult sites, but this is because of the extraordinary skills of the entrepreneurs involved.

Developing a network of hospitality units

Multiple-site operators, and in particular the leading branded hospitality chains, have dramatically expanded their network of outlets in the recent past and plan to continue to expand. This expansion is driven by the need to

- Grow the business (sales and profits) to satisfy shareholders' expectations
- Locate where customers need to stay or dine
- Be where competitors are located.

If your brand is not located where your customer wants to stay or dine, then you might lose that customer forever to one of your competitors.

The theory of location strategy has primarily been developed for multiple retail shopping outlets; however, the principles are equally applicable to hospitality operations. Academic modelling of location decisions has generally taken the form of spatial interaction models that focus on the flows between countries, regions or cities. Each hospitality unit's location possesses a bundle of attraction and deterrence factors, which determines the flow of customers to the property. Attraction factors might include a large number of business and retails facilities in the area; deterrence factors might include travel times and inadequate local transportation. The balance of attraction and deterrence factors accounts for variance in customer flows to different hospitality sites. The hospitality brands with multiple units and growth strategies use computerized attraction/deterrence models to aid location decisions.

MAIN CLASSES OF HOSPITALITY LOCATIONS

Hospitality locations can be categorized in several ways, and these are described here.

Capital city

Capital cities usually generate strong demand from business, government and leisure markets. Capital cities, such as Beijing, London, Moscow and Washington attract both domestic and international visitors and often have the highest room occupancy, achieved room rate and revenue per available room (RevPAR) in a country.

Provincial city

Provincial cities are more likely to generate good domestic business demand, with a proportion of international business customers, and limited leisure demand. Provincial cities such as Leicester, Lyons and Stuttgart fall into this category.

Gateway locations

Gateway locations are locations based at convenient destination access points, such as major airport terminals, key shipping ports and railway termini. These sites handle large volumes of travellers, although not all travellers actually stay in the gateway location. For example, Zurich is a major gateway for visitors taking a skiing holiday in the Alps, but few skiers actually stay in Zurich. However, Heathrow, as a major international airport and gateway to London, England, the United Kingdom and Europe, generates one of the highest levels of demand for hotels in any location in the United Kingdom.

Highway locations

Highway locations are found on motorways and roads and serve the driving public, whether on business or leisure. Highway stops are normally associated with budget accommodation, and travellers typically stay for only one night. The famous Route 66 from Chicago to Los Angeles has many highway hotels such as the Vega Motel in Vega, Texas.

Resort locations

Resorts primarily focus on leisure markets but often include conference facilities to attract the corporate business market in shoulder months and low seasons. Many resorts have been developed at coastal and country locations. Resorts offer accommodation with a wide range of leisure and sporting activities, often but not always on an all-inclusive basis. The One&Only in Cape Town, South Africa, is a Resort and Spa hotel with non-package pricing, whereas the Club Mediterranean at Port Saint Lucia, Florida, offers couples and families all-inclusive prices.

Rural locations

Country locations also focus on the leisure market and frequently target niche markets, for example, walkers in the English Lakes District or climbers in the Swiss Alps.

Honey-pot destinations

Major tourist destinations are also described as 'honey-pots' because of the large volume of visitors. Examples include Dubai, Las Vegas, Venice and York.

RESEARCHING HOSPITALITY LOCATIONS

Researching suitable sites for a hospitality operation is time-consuming. The experience of one British hotelier who inspected 50 locations over 6 months before buying a hotel is not uncommon. For international hospitality groups, there is the added complication of deciding which countries to enter.

There are three levels of spatial analysis in researching locations (Ghosh & McLafferty, 1987). The research starts with geographic market selection and then focuses on area analysis within the chosen geographic market, and finally, the most attractive sites are identified from the area:

- *Market selection* decisions analyse the geo-demographic and socio-economic characteristics of a geographic region or country; this includes looking at the current situation, examining trends and projecting future conditions.
- The *area analysis* focuses on the characteristics of specific local areas within a region.
- *Site evaluation* examines local demographics, traffic flow and accessibility, individual competitors and the attractiveness of specific sites.

We will now review the criteria used by hospitality companies in country, regional and site selection.

Country selection

We have already mentioned the rapid growth of international hotel companies. This growth has been driven by the globalization of travel markets and intense competition by the major players. As one competitor develops an operation in a new country, other competitors may feel obliged to follow. A PESTE analysis identifying the advantages and disadvantages of specific countries provides the basis for country analysis. Key criteria for evaluating the attractiveness of a country market include political stability, planning risk, development route and market attractiveness.

Political stability

High political stability creates a favourable investment climate. Most Western countries have stable political systems, whereas countries that have considerable political turmoil, such as Columbia, Nigeria and Pakistan, are more risky and therefore less attractive to international investors. Countries with high *political stability* generally offer opportunities to purchase freehold properties or negotiate long leasehold agreements. In countries with high *political instability*, the preferred entry option is to franchise the brand to a local company because local organizations understand how to manage their own political environment better than foreigners, or negotiate an equity-free management contract. The United States and British governments provide information for companies planning international investment and advice about political stability in websites such as the American Central Intelligence Agency (www.cia.gov).

Planning risk

Regardless of the stability of a political regime, countries have different approaches to planning control. This can mean that there are difficulties in obtaining planning consent for building new developments, converting existing properties into hospitality outlets or carrying out major refurbishment program. Knowledge of the local culture and business/governmental regulations and customs is essential when negotiating planning permissions. A key goal of international marketing is to understand the influence of culture on the way of doing business in a foreign country, but it is much easier to conduct business in a familiar cultural climate.

Development route

There are three options for network expansion:

1 *Acquisition* – companies buy a group of hotels (or restaurants), and/or an independent hotel, and re-brand these properties. This is the most convenient, proven and popular approach, especially if a brand wants to grow rapidly. However, there often are issues of ensuring brand conformity between the newly acquired properties and the company's international brand standards.
2 *Conversion* – companies buy an existing property (e.g. an office block, high-rise flats or warehouse) and convert the property into hotel (or restaurant) premises. This is much more time-consuming and expensive. Softer hotel and restaurant brands with more flexible approaches to brand standards can convert premises more easily than harder hospitality brands.
3 *New-build development* – companies purchase land and build their own property to their own design specifications or to the design brief of the designated brand (subject to planning controls). For hotels, this can be more time-consuming than acquisition, but the advantage is that the brand standards are delivered from the moment the property opens. For fast-food operations, a common option is to acquire a site and erect a purpose-built unit constructed from modular components.

The major international hospitality companies have used a combination of all three development routes. Which route is preferred depends on the target location, the flexibility/rigidity of brand standards, the form of ownership and regulatory planning constraints.

Market attractiveness

The evaluation of market attractiveness uses demand analysis and competition analysis. The essential hard data, which help companies to forecast operating performance in a new country, include the following:

- Visitor arrivals, visitor mix (by country) and visitor spend
- Host population and demographic statistics
- Economic statistics
- Hospitality industry operating performance benchmarks.

The attractiveness of a country market will depend on the potential demand from the selected target markets and the intensity of competitor rivalry. An important consideration for ethnocentric companies is the number of home market visitors travelling to target countries. One North American hotel company uses the ratio of American visitors to a city as a key criterion for European site selection, because American tourists are likely to stay at the American brands they know and trust.

Country evaluation

When all the data have been collated, companies input the data on to computerized modelling software packages (either developed in-house or bought in) to evaluate the attractiveness of different countries and locations. Figure 6.1 provides a typical example of the data used in a European development strategy for a major international hotel group. Each criterion is assessed using an internal company grading system. For example, a gateway location might be awarded between 30 and 50 points, whereas a secondary location might be awarded between 10 and 20 points. In the example, London, Paris and Berlin are major capital cities and the airports Heathrow and Charles de Gaulle are all gateway locations, so each might score very highly, whereas Manchester and Strasbourg are clearly secondary locations, with lower scores. When all the criteria for all the destinations have been assessed, the accumulated scores for each location are computed and a ranking scheme provides a prioritization of the locations. A refinement of this scoring process is to weigh some criteria as more important than others. For example, a company may develop a business rule that says they will not invest in a country that has a political stability score of less than 8 on a 10-point scale.

Geographic			Location		Timing	Development route			Attractiveness of market segments		Risk		Mix home tourists	Score	Ranking
Country	City	Population	Gateway	Secondary	Urgency	1	2	3	Business	Leisure	Political	Planning			
UK	London														
	Heathrow														
	Birmingham														
	Manchester														
	Edinburgh														
France	Paris														
	Charles de Gaulle														
	Lyons														
	Bordeaux														
	Strasbourg														
Gemany	Berlin														
	Hamburg														
	Munich														

Figure 6.1   A typical example of the data used in a European development strategy for a major international hotel group

Region selection

Having selected the country, the next decision is to choose which region, area or city to locate in within the country. Many hospitality organizations are domestic companies that only operate in their own country. Compared with international companies, local hospitality operators have one major advantage: they understand the local environment, the culture and markets and how to conduct business in their own country.

Case study 6.1 **Premier Inn site selection strategy**

Premier Inn, Britain's largest hotel brand increased its portfolio from 250 units in 2001 to 580 units with 42,800 rooms in 2010. The target number of bedrooms for 2015 is 55,000 rooms, an increase of 30%. This will require an additional 150/175 units, approximately 30/35 per year. To achieve this rapid growth, Premier Inn have developed a sophisticated approach to site selection using an in-house computer model with an extensive database of 1600 cities and towns in the United Kingdom. Demographics, including key data on businesses, the employment profile, tourism visitor statistics, road network and traffic densities, and other relevant hotel demand drivers, have been compiled for each location. These data are then analysed to identify the characteristics of each UK city/town according to Premier Inn criteria. Similar cities and towns are clustered into one of the 19 categories, for example, Capital (London), Airport, High Volume Motorway, Major City, Small Town and Seaside Town. Premier's existing property portfolio provides extensive current occupancy and RevPAR data across the United Kingdom, and the combination of all these data enables the marketing team to identify suitable target locations. This desk-based research is then discussed with the Premier Inn acquisition managers to confirm or challenge the findings, before discussions are entered into with potential site owners. The data also enable Premier Inn to evaluate the most appropriate size of property (number of bedrooms) and the most suitable restaurant brand to install. Premier Inn has mapped the entire United Kingdom using these data to help the company to achieve its ambitious property network expansion plan.

Source: Premier Inn

Regional location decisions include the criteria discussed in Fig. 6.1, as well as the following factors:

- Micro-climate – a detailed examination of regional climates, the hours of sunshine, level of rainfall (or snow), temperature and seasonal variations is important for leisure resort operations
- Infrastructure – establishes access for target markets via air, road, rail and sea connections
- Regional demographic characteristics – within a country there are wide differences between regions in terms of employment

opportunities, disposable income distribution, cost of living and living standards, which impact on domestic and local levels of demand
- Competitors – an evaluation of the locations of major competitors is essential; indeed, locating where your competitors are based is often a sensible entry strategy.

Expanding hospitality companies need to identify the location gaps with their regional network of units to complete their portfolio of properties. Case study 6.1 illustrates the importance of site selection.

Site selection

This decision refers to the process of identifying individual sites that are suitable for purchase, rent and development. Hospitality outlets in good areas can fail because of poor site selection. Sites can be categorized as follows:

- *Prime*. These sites are the best locations. They are in high demand and can be difficult to acquire (because most are already in the hands of existing operators), and expensive to maintain. An example is the famous Dorchester Hotel on Park Lane, London.
- *Secondary*. These sites are not prominent but are still reasonably accessible. Most hospitality units are in this category.
- *Tertiary*. These sites are less accessible and may have other deterrence factors, for example, being close to a truck stop or an industrial estate. An example of a hospitality company having successfully developed a low-cost product concept using tertiary sites is Accor, with its Formule 1.

Factors influencing individual site selection include the following:

- Local demographics and the characteristics of neighbourhoods. Village Hotels, part of the Alternative Hotel Group who also manages Liberty of London, Malmaison, Hotel Du Vin and Greens Health and Fitness, has explicit site selection criteria for the Village Hotels brand to ensure high hotel occupancies and achieve target membership levels for their health and fitness clubs. These clubs target affluent consumers, not families, aged 25–55. To generate a club membership of between 4000 and 5000, Village Hotels look for sites with more than 100,000 ABC1 consumers within drive time of 20 min.
- Accessibility, pedestrian and vehicle traffic flows and car parking.
- Competitors. The number, size, quality, prices and occupancy of branded and local competitors provide an insight into the local marketplace. Restaurant operators targeting local consumers often cluster together in prime sites, which is an indicator of the attractiveness of the location. Food courts in city centers are an example.
- Individual site characteristics, which include the size, landscape, adjacent buildings, aspect (south or north facing) and further development potential.

Case study 6.2 illustrates the importance of site selection.

Case study 6.2 Sophie's Steak House and Bar, Fulham Road and Covent Garden, London

Sophie Bathgate had always wanted to open her own restaurant, and her friend Rupert Power had always wanted to own his own bar. Both already had very good restaurant and bar operational experience. Sophie worked for the Mezzanine Group, owners of Smolensky's Restaurants, and had been involved in opening one of their new restaurants. Rupert had worked at Browns and at Quaglino's – a Conran Restaurant. On holiday in New York, they ate out in a different type of steak house, which really caught their imagination; and the concept of Sophie's Steak House was born, but both knew that getting the right site was crucial if they were going to launch a successful restaurant business.

The search took 18 months; they looked at hundreds of sales brochures for restaurants on the market. They visited more than 50 sites and actually asked their architect to draw up plans on five sites that were really promising. Originally, they looked at the West End of London, but the property prices were too high; however, they eventually found a site in Fulham that fulfilled their criteria. They needed a minimum 90 covers to make the business viable. Rupert wanted a separate bar area, with its own license to attract non-diners and seating for another 20 customers; and they both thought that the production kitchen should be visible to diners. This meant that they needed approximately 2000 square feet of floor space.

Why was the Fulham Road such a good site for Sophie's? Rupert says that the restaurant, which had been part of a chain, was situated in the middle of an affluent cosmopolitan neighbourhood where house prices are high and the socio-economic profile of residents indicates high disposable income. The Fulham Road has a wide range of quality shopping, professional offices, is close to fashionable Knightsbridge, and has lots of passing traffic. It is a busy place, with several other bars and restaurants in the area. The premises are located opposite a cinema and supermarket and only half a mile from a major hospital. Sophie and Rupert believed all these factors would generate strong demand for their mid-market restaurant.

After 18 months of searching, Sophie and Rupert finally agreed to buy the leasehold, and as soon as they took possession in October, they closed for a 3-month refurbishment. The kitchen was re-equipped, the ceiling levels altered, the décor and external signage were improved and finally, 2 years after starting their search, Sophie's restaurant was opened for business at the end of January. After 12 months had passed, Sophie's 90-cover restaurant was serving 2000 meals each week. They are open from midday to midnight and can re-lay tables three times on a Saturday night, with a good spend. The cinema, hospital staff and visitors generate demand at normally low season periods, like early Saturday evening.

As the Fulham Road Steak House became a success, Sophie and Rupert looked for another London site. Rupert was still keen to open a restaurant in the West End because his work experience in this part of London convinced him that the dining out market was strong. However, they did not want to simply replicate the Fulham Road formula in a similar-sized unit; they wanted a much larger space to be able to drive more significant volumes of sales. Rupert remained in touch with the specialist restaurant estate agents, and one day an agent suggested that the owner of a suitable site close to Covent Garden might be interested in selling. The secret negotiations took 18 months, but Rupert was always concerned that another operator might learn about the opportunity and close the deal before they could. However, they finally secured the site, closed the premises for 6 months to refurbish and opened in October 2008 – just as the financial world collapsed and Britain went into recession.

Although this was a difficult time to open from a demand perspective, Sophie and Rupert were able to secure the funding just before going into the recession and the price to buy a restaurant in such a premium location was right. Covent Garden is in the heart of London's business center; it is a shopping destination, has many tourist attractions and is surrounded by theatre land. There is a strong demand throughout the year from local business people, domestic and international tourists and theatre goers. The new Sophie's Steakhouse and Bar has seating for 60 customers in the bar, 220 restaurant covers and is open from midday to midnight. On a busy day, tables can be turned over between four and five times, and a record 1200 customers were served on the busiest day to date.

The long search for the right sites has paid off, and both of Sophie's Steakhouses have become very popular eating houses.

Source: Rupert Power and http://www.sophiessteakhouse.com

Location decisions

Clearly, a considerable amount of research is invested in the location decision, and making a correct decision is fundamental to the success of any hospitality business. However, location decisions involve a trade-off between the different characteristics of potential sites and the capital available for investment. Although La Quinta Inns, a brand with 750 North American hotels, uses 35 independent variables to predict the profitability of a site, there are four key factors: the purchase price of the site, median income levels for the catchment area, the state population per inn and the location of nearby colleges. Indeed, 51 per cent of the profit projection can be calculated using this formula (Heizer & Render, 2008). From a marketing perspective, the crucial factor is the potential demand of a site, but sites with greater demand potential have more expensive site acquisition costs. Location decision theory assumes a high element of rational decision-making, but historically, hospitality companies have expanded opportunistically. So, despite all the research, many location decisions are based on 'gut feelings' and instinct. As Rupert Powell, of Sophie's Steak House, says: 'You walk into a property and you just know, that gut feeling is really important!'

Activity 6.1

Identify three hospitality units, one in a prime site, one in a secondary site and one in a tertiary site. Carry out some marketing research, both desk research and a site visit if you can, to evaluate the demand characteristics of each site using the following criteria:

- Local demographics and neighbourhood characteristics
- Accessibility
- Competition
- Individual site characteristics.

DESTINATION MARKETING FROM THE HOSPITALITY PERSPECTIVE

We have discussed the importance of location, and the criteria that hospitality companies use to evaluate the attractiveness of a location. Although chain hospitality operators do have the advantage of access to their own branded distribution systems, the effectiveness of the destination's marketing activities does impact on most units located in that destination. However, destinations are complex products (Middleton & Clark, 2001):

- Destinations exist across a wide spectrum of different geographic levels – continents, countries, regions, cities and rural areas
- Destinations have layers of administrative bodies responsible for the development and promotion of tourism, and roles and responsibilities can be confused, diffused and, in some cases, duplicated
- Destinations comprise physical characteristics (the natural landscape and climate), which obviously cannot be changed and the built environment
- Destinations present deep-rooted cultural and historical heritages, which influence the character of local peoples and the visitor experience
- Destinations incorporate all the components of the tourism product – hospitality operations, transport, travel, intermediaries, attractions
- There is no single owner of the tourism product in a destination.

The proliferation of geographic and administrative layers is illustrated by the example of Castleton, a village in the Hope Valley, Derbyshire, which is in the United Kingdom's Peak District National Park. Table 6.1 details the eight layers of administration in Castleton, from the local parish council to the European Commission. Each administrative body has an interest in tourism. However, there is often a conflict within and between the different administrative organizations.

Table 6.1 Layers of tourism administration, Castleton, Derbyshire

Boundary	Destination	Administrative responsibility
Village/town	Castleton	Parish/Town Council
District	High Peak	District Council
County	Derbyshire	County Council
National Park	Peak District	National Park Authority
Region	East Midlands	East Midlands Development Agency
Country	England	VisitEngland
Country	United Kingdom	VisitBritain
Continent	Europe	European Commission

This reflects the conflicting perspectives of different stakeholders: local companies will want to develop tourism further and grow visitor numbers, but local residents and conservationists will want to control and inhibit tourism development.

Clearly, destinations have a multitude of public and private stakeholders, including the following:

- National tourist organizations, local tourist organizations and public–private partnerships between government and private sectors
- Tourism companies (mainly small and a few larger businesses), their owners, management and employees
- Pro- and anti-tourism lobbies
- Local inhabitants and visitors.

No single organization has total control over the tourism product and the destination image. This has implications for tourism development, quality control and marketing.

Destination image

The image of a destination is a crucial component in today's competitive tourism market. A destination's image is a mixture of the following:

- Inherited physical attributes
- The built environment
- The cultural and historical heritage
- Myth
- The people.

When we discussed brand image in Chapter 4, we explained that image is a perception in the minds of consumers. We all have images of a tourism destination, regardless of whether we have visited the place or not. Images that are formed from indirect sources, through the media (online material, news reports, television travel program, newspapers and advertising) and by word of mouth from friends and/ or relatives, are *induced images*.

Organic images are formed by actually visiting the destination in person. Our organic perceptions are based on the actual experiences, enjoyable or otherwise, of visiting the destination. The organic image that we form is more fixed and less likely to be influenced by destination-marketing activity. When we tell family and friends about our impressions of a destination, we are projecting an induced image.

Activity 6.2

- Identify two tourism destinations, one which you have visited and one that you have not.
- Analyse the 'induced' image you have formed about the destination you have not visited.
- Analyse the 'organic' image of the destination you have visited.
- Compare the image of the destinations – can you identify any differences between an induced and an organic image?

The problem with an induced image is that it may be completely inaccurate, depending on the reliability of the source. For American and British tourists, the induced image of a country such as Iran is largely negative, because the popular media portray Iran in an entirely negative tone. Interestingly, the organic image of Iran formed by Western tourists visiting the country is largely positive and strongly infuenced by the friendliness of the local population.

The world's major tourist cities have powerful images, which in tourism terms are represented by one or a series of iconic images easily recognizable by international tourists. The iconic images of a red double-decker bus, the Eiffel Tower, the Golden Gate Bridge and the Opera House immediately suggest London, Paris, San Francisco and Sydney. Iconic images can be manufactured; the Big Apple and 'I Love New York' campaign is a successful example of a manufactured iconic image supported by an effective marketing communications campaign.

Image and personal safety

The overwhelming majority of tourists are concerned about their personal safety when travelling. Political instability, the threat of war, war itself, terrorist incidents and crime have a major negative impact on the tourist destination image and on visitor arrivals. Throughout the first decade of the twenty-first century, numerous terrorism incidents and wars have damaged tourist consumer confidence in certain country destinations (Afghanistan, Bali, Egypt, Israel, Kenya and

Pakistan) and cities (London, Madrid and New York), and this has created a negative impact on the tourism images of these destinations.

Destination marketing organizations

Destination marketing organizations (DMOs) can be government funded, a private company or a combination of the public and private sectors. Their primary role is to

- Carry out marketing research and provide market intelligence for stakeholders
- Monitor visitor statistics and trends
- Coordinate marketing campaigns and in particular promotional activity
- Build and maintain destination websites
- Liaise with intermediaries
- Provide tourist information for visitors before and during visits (this may include booking services)
- Manage the brand image of the destination.

Case study 6.3 illustrates a successful DMO.

Case study 6.3 **Destination marketing at work – New Zealand**

In the late nineteenth century, many famous authors and scientists had visited New Zealand to explore the natural scenery, wildlife and Maori culture; and in 1901, New Zealand was the first country to establish a national tourism organization. By 1903, the country was attracting 5000 international visitors per year. Today Tourism New Zealand is a government-funded tourism marketing organization that advises, coordinates and manages a variety of marketing activities – including extensive research – to support hospitality and tourism in New Zealand. In 1999, the '100% Pure New Zealand' campaign was launched to promote a single message that focused on the country as a unique destination for the natural environment (hence the 100% 'pure' theme). New Zealand attracts a significant number of adventure tourists who enjoy a wide range of physical outdoor activities. Given the importance of nature to the country's product, Tourism New Zealand also encourages hospitality operators to practise sustainable tourism. The Tourism New Zealand website provides helpful marketing information about their focus, mission and values; the consumer research they conduct; the collation of in-depth international visitor arrival statistics; the advertising campaigns they manage; the crucial role of channel management; training and support for in-country tourism operators and responsible tourism in New Zealand. At the time of writing, New Zealand attracts approximately 1.5 million international visitors per annum.

We noted earlier that organizations responsible for marketing a destination suffer from limited control of the product and have to resolve the conflicting demands of several stakeholders. Limited resources

> **Activity 6.3:**
>
> Log on to: www.tourismnewzealand.com. Click on 'About Us' and explore what services the tourist board provides for New Zealand hospitality and tourism organizations. Click on Market and Stats, Campaigns and Delivering the Promise to read about how one country delivers destination marketing to its various stakeholders.
>
> *Source: Tourism New Zealand and www.tourismnewzealand.com*

and unrealistic stakeholder expectations compound these problems. Hospitality companies within a destination work with DMOs in the following ways:

- Companies join the DMO, which normally involves paying a membership fee
- Companies provide detailed information for the website listings and printed guide entries; sometimes companies will pay for advertising in destination tourist brochures
- Companies participate in tourist information and accommodation booking services
- Companies provide hospitality for familiarization (FAM) visits by travel journalists, conference/exhibition organizers and other key intermediaries visiting the destination.

Proactive hospitality managers join the committees of DMOs and can leverage a degree of competitive advantage by developing good personal relationships with the personnel and management of the DMO.

CONCLUSION

Location decisions involve considerable research, and the consequences are significant. Attractive sites with good demand characteristics have to be balanced with the capital available. Once the location decision has been made, hospitality companies work with DMOs to market the destination.

In this chapter, we have explained the following:

- Why the location decision is a major investment with long-term consequences
- The thorough research that needs to be undertaken to evaluate the potential demand and competition in a location
- Major hospitality companies will use computerized models to evaluate site selection decisions, whereas entrepreneurs may use their 'gut instinct' to choose an appropriate site
- The three levels of spatial analysis in researching locations – geographic market selection, area analysis and site evaluation
- The wide range of criteria used by hospitality companies to evaluate the market potential of locations

- Tourism destinations can be categorized under the headings capital city, provincial city, gateway, highway, resort, rural and honey-pot
- Destinations are complex products with a host of public and private stakeholders
- Destination image has a major impact on tourist destination selection
- Hospitality organizations work with DMOs to market the destination effectively.

REVIEW QUESTIONS

Now check your understanding of this chapter by answering the following questions:

1 Why is the location decision an important element of the marketing mix?
2 What are the differences between single-site owners and multiple-unit hospitality operations when making location decisions?
3 Discuss the site selection criteria for locating a hospitality product.
4 Explain the characteristics and relevance of destination image in hospitality marketing.
5 How can hospitality managers work with DMOs?

References and Further Reading

Butler, R. W. (1980). The concept of a tourist area cycle of evolution: implications for the management of resources. *Canadian Geographer*, *24*, 5–12.

Ghosh, A., & McLafferty, F. L. (1987). *Location strategies for retail and service firms*. Lexington Books.

Heizer, J., & Render, B. (2008). *Operations management*. Pearson Prentice Hall.

Jones, P. (1999). Multi-unit management in the hospitality industry: a late twentieth century phenomenon. *International Journal of Contemporary Hospitality Management*, *11*(4), 155–164.

Middleton, V. T. C., & Clark, J. (2001). *Marketing in travel & tourism*. Butterworth-Heinemann.

CHAPTER **7**

Pricing the offer

Chapter objectives

After going through this chapter, you should be able to

- Understand the significance of pricing in the pre-encounter marketing mix
- Identify external and internal factors that influence pricing decisions
- Appreciate how online search and transparency influences contemporary pricing strategies
- Explain quality/pricing strategies in a hospitality context
- Understand how hospitality organizations set price
- Describe the practice of dynamic pricing and its role in optimizing revenue
- Describe the role of price promotions to increase revenue in low-demand periods
- Recognize the complexity of pricing in an international context.

INTRODUCTION

In this chapter, we review the significance of pricing in the pre-encounter marketing mix and examine how companies set prices. We then look at the external and internal factors that influence pricing decisions, including the role of the Internet, and explain the pricing techniques that are especially relevant to hospitality organizations.

Pricing is the tool that matches supply and demand. Price influences the demand for a product, which in turn determines volume sales. Therefore, setting an appropriate price is one of the most important factors in demand management and in generating revenue. Revenue management (RM) is the tool used to manage demand through flexing prices in medium- and large-sized accommodation businesses. Price is the only element of the marketing mix that does not generate costs, but price is also the only element of the marketing mix to generate revenue. Pricing decisions contribute to product and brand image, and product/pricing decisions are therefore inseparable. However, the influence of the Internet and online technologies has challenged conventional approaches to pricing and introduced more complexity to price decisions.

Throughout this discussion of pricing, you need to recognize that different types of hospitality products and different sizes of businesses have different approaches to the pricing decision. The cruise sector, large conference, event and hotel companies, tour operators with volume travel/accommodation packages and many large independent hotels use dynamic pricing and complex revenue management systems (RMSs), with sophisticated databases and online booking to manage real-time availability and pricing decisions. Smaller accommodation businesses and bar, café and restaurant operations use more traditional *fixed-price* menus and tariffs. In this chapter, we discuss pricing from both perspectives.

SIGNIFICANCE OF PRICING IN THE PRE-ENCOUNTER MARKETING MIX

There is a clear link between the price a customer pays and the customer's quality expectations. The higher the price, the greater the expectations of a high-quality hospitality experience. Price is an indicator and a measure of quality, particularly in the absence of other cues. If a high-quality gourmet restaurant routinely offers cheap menus, or a five-star hotel continually promoted budget holidays, customers would become confused and might suspect that the product quality offered was not genuine. Price plays an important part in establishing customers' perceptions of a product and of a company's or brand's position in the marketplace. Over time, brands often become associated with particular price points, which become fixed in the consumers' perception of that brand.

Although price is the easiest variable to change in the marketing mix, traditionally it is considered to be the most complex and the least understood variable. However, recent research and the development of computerized and online RMSs have improved our understanding of pricing.

Price is defined as 'the summation of all sacrifices made by a consumer in order to experience the benefits of a product'.

This definition includes both financial and other sacrifices, such as time and effort. It is a broad definition, because monetary price is not the only consideration consumers have to think about when making purchase decisions. In many countries, some consumers are described as 'money rich and time poor'. These affluent consumers typically have busy lifestyles with limited time to enjoy discretionary purchases. 'Time is money' is an appropriate expression for these important target markets.

One of the first questions customers ask before booking a hotel or restaurant is 'how much is a room?' or 'how much is the price of a meal?' Although the reply will be given in money terms (and customers quite sensibly want to know if the room or meal is affordable), what they are really interested in is value and not price. Customer value is found in the relationship between costs incurred (money, time and effort) and the benefits enjoyed (food, beverage, service, entertainment, atmosphere and experience). If costs increase without enhanced benefits for the customer then the value decreases. If additional benefits can be included for the customer, without increasing price, then the customer enjoys better value.

An important distinction to recognize is that consumers' perception of the value/price of a product is strongly linked to their perception of the product concept. Product concepts are targeted at selected market segments with different needs and wants. Two very different product concepts are those that cater for special occasions and those that provide convenient solutions to consumers' everyday needs.

The price band for dinner at a luxury gourmet restaurant, a special occasion, is at the top end of most consumers' affordability, whilst the price band for a self-service meal, often a convenience purchase, is at a much lower price point. Consumers form expectations of what they will have to pay for a gourmet meal and compare competing gourmet restaurant price/product offers. Equally, consumers choosing a self-service restaurant have price expectations of what to pay for a self-service meal and compare competing self-service price/product offers.

Consumers tend not to compare the value/price offer between *different* product concepts; whereas they do compare the value/price offer within the *same and adjacent* product classes. In most cases, branded hospitality products are able to charge a higher price than non-branded products.

Activity 7.1

Compare the online prices of two different product concepts in the same hospitality sector, for example, compare either

- Dining out – a self-service restaurant and a luxury restaurant or
- Accommodation – a backpacker hostel and a luxury hotel.

Evaluate from your own perspective as a consumer, the value/price offer between *different* product classes in the same hospitality sector.

Then compare the online prices of two competing hospitality offers in the same product class, for example, compare

- Two self-service restaurants
- Two luxury restaurants
- Two backpacker hostels or
- Two luxury hotels

Evaluate from your own perspective as a consumer, the value/price offer for direct competitors in the *same* product class.

FACTORS INFLUENCING PRICING DECISIONS

Factors that influence price decisions can be sorted into two major categories (Kotler, Keller, Brady, Goodman & Hansen, 2009):

1 External environmental factors, over which companies have little (if any) control

2 Internal factors, over which companies have a considerable amount of control.

These factors have major influences on pricing decisions.

External factors

The outer circle of Fig. 7.1 illustrates five of the environmental variables that impact pricing decisions – demand, inflation, industry structure, competition and legal/regulatory factors.

Demand

We discussed the drivers of demand in Chapter 3. In this section, we review price elasticity, business and consumer confidence, exchange rates and the influence of the micro-environment on pricing.

Price elasticity of demand

Understanding the price elasticity of demand is essential to making good pricing decisions. The sales volume of a product that has *inelastic* price demand does not vary significantly when price changes.

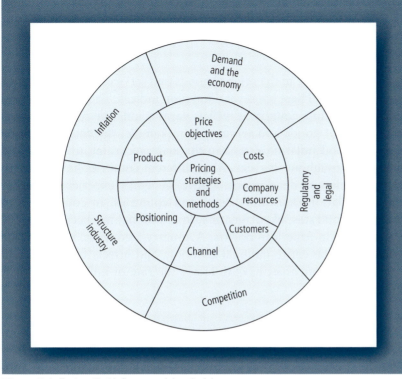

Figure 7.1 Factors that influence pricing decisions

In hospitality, demand from the business market for accommodation is traditionally considered to be more price-inelastic. Conversely, the sales volume of a product that has an *elastic* price demand varies significantly when prices change. Traditionally, demand for leisure products is considered to be more price-elastic because they are discretionary purchases. A simple way to understand the price elasticity of demand is to consider *essential* purchases as being price inelastic and *non-essential* purchases as being more price elastic. The price elasticity for generic products can change over the long term, as products that were originally considered to be 'non-essential' become an 'essential' part of consumers' lifestyle. For example, many consumers now regard leisure breaks and holidays abroad as an essential purchase, whilst during recent recessions, demand from the business market for meetings and events has declined like a more price-elastic product.

Business and consumer confidence

We have already discussed the business cycle and its impact on business and consumer confidence. During periods of economic growth, there is rising confidence and less price sensitivity from business and consumers. This means that there is less resistance to price increases. However, during a recession, the loss of business and consumer confidence significantly reduces demand. Both corporate and individual consumers become much more price sensitive and there is resistance to price increases – indeed, customers will expect price discounts.

Inflation

Inflation is the rise in the price of goods and services, measured over a period of time. There are several inflation indices. There is the overall inflation rate in a country as well as various inflation rates for different classes of goods and services. For example, the energy inflation rate and food inflation rates can fluctuate according to supply and demand throughout the year. Also, different countries have different rates of inflation; developing countries generally experience a higher rate of inflation than more developed countries. In countries with high inflation rates, like Argentina, international markets are quoted room prices in American dollars. A country's domestic inflation rate impacts on the entire national economy and affects businesses and consumers. Companies have to factor the rate of inflation into their pricing strategies.

Exchange rates

Exchange rate fluctuations present unique pricing difficulties for hospitality operators catering for international group markets, as contracts between hotels and tour operators can be negotiated 18 months in advance of customers actually taking a package holiday. Factoring exchange rate movements into the pricing contract, with possible surcharges if the rate moves unfavourably against the hospitality offer, is essential – but unpopular with customers.

Micro-environment

Micro-demand is dependent on the local characteristics of the area – the number, scale and buoyancy of local manufacturing and service industries; the image and appeal of local tourism amenities; and the density, wealth and purchasing characteristics of the local population. All these factors will influence both group-owned and independent units within the area. Typically, most of the businesses in an area with buoyant demand will be prospering, although all businesses in an area suffering from poor demand will generally struggle. Popular destinations can charge higher prices and less popular destinations use lower pricing strategies to attract price-sensitive markets.

Type and structure of industry

Structural factors that influence the pricing dynamics in hospitality sectors include the cost structure, number of players and capacity of the industry.

Cost structure

Different hospitality sectors have different cost structures, which impact pricing strategies. A five-star luxury hotel requires a high investment in the building, décor, facilities and staffing ratios compared with budget hotels which are constructed with pre-fabricated standardized bedrooms, in secondary locations, offering minimal staffing levels and no ancillary facilities. The pricing strategies of the five-star hotel sector must reflect the higher investment and operating costs, whereas the pricing strategies of the budget sector should reflect the lower investment and operating costs. The luxury sector has more potential for price flexibility given the relatively high, published, rack rate – this is the normal room price printed in tariffs. The budget sector has limited ability to flex prices due to the relatively low rack rate. The sourcing of produce in remote destinations increases the cost structure – for example, hotels in the Seychelles have to air-freight food produce that is not available locally, increasing food costs significantly.

Number of players

If the sector is highly concentrated and dominated by a small number of very large players, the sector's overall profitability is dependent on players *not* adopting price competition to gain market share. The impact of genuine price competition results in all players cutting their prices to prevent a loss of market share, thus leading to erosion of the sector's profitability. In this case, competition is normally based on product differentiation rather than price. The rivalry between McDonald's and Burger King in the fast-food sector is primarily based on product differentiation and not on price. When there are a large number of players, and no firms are dominant, the opportunity for players to adopt different pricing strategies is greater.

Capacity

Given sufficient demand at a given point in time, limited capacity will enable firms to charge higher prices; while sectors with lower demand and 'over-capacity' will suffer from intense price competition. Because of the relatively low start-up costs, the restaurant market suffers from excess capacity and remains intensely price competitive.

Competition

In Chapter 4, we discussed the 'five forces' model driving industry profitability. If the competitive environment is benign and the rivalry between competitors is restrained, industry pricing strategies should enhance profitability. However, if the competitive environment is fierce and the intensity of rivalry bitter, industry pricing strategies can adversely affect profitability.

Legal/regulatory

National government taxation strategies, like Value Added Tax (VAT), airline passenger taxes, tourist taxes levied in the form of charges on occupied bedrooms and excise duties imposed on alcoholic beverages, impact on the prices charged by the hospitality industry and influence consumer behaviour. Since each country sets its own taxation strategies, companies operating in countries with lower taxation regimes can gain a considerable competitive advantage over companies operating in higher-taxed countries.

Governments can impose regulations on companies, which increase the costs of running a business. For example, the European Commission directives on minimum wages and health and safety force hospitality companies to comply with new work practices and equipment/maintenance schedules. This means that companies have to increase prices to recover the costs of complying with these regulations. In recent years, Turkish hospitality operators have had significant price advantages over operators in European Union Mediterranean countries due to the European Commission legislation and the Euro exchange rate.

Internal factors

The inner circle in Fig. 7.1 shows seven internal factors that affect the pricing decision: pricing objectives, costs, company resources, positioning, customers, product and channel.

Pricing objectives

Price objectives are dependent on marketing objectives, which in turn are dependent on corporate objectives. Organizations often have long-term strategic price objectives and short-term tactical price objectives; crucially, pricing objectives need to be consistent with the objectives of the other elements of the marketing mix. Pricing objectives should be SMART – Specific, Measurable, Achievable, Realistic, and within a set Timetable (see pages 413–414).

In some instances, corporate objectives very clearly dictate pricing objectives. A corporate objective for a company with trading difficulties might be to maximize cash flow in the short term. This would lead to a marketing objective of setting prices designed to maximize revenue, regardless of the type or suitability of the sales generated and the fact that profit may not be optimized.

Pricing objectives can be classified into the following categories: marketing orientated, financial orientated and competitor orientated.

Marketing-orientated pricing objectives

Marketing-orientated organizations try to understand how price influences customers' perception of their product offer, and consequently develop pricing objectives using a customer's perspective.

Market leaders in high-quality hospitality markets, such as luxury hotels, gourmet restaurants, first-class travel providers and luxury cruise ships, adopt a 'prestige' or premium pricing objective (i.e. to charge high prices for the top-quality service) and must ensure that the customer perception of their service matches the premium prices charged.

Hospitality operators adopting the 'best value for money' objective in a given product class monitor customers' perception of their hospitality offer, scanning competitors' prices and ensuring that their offer delivers the best perceived value for money.

Another marketing-orientated pricing objective is to encourage trial or repeat purchases. When launching a new hospitality concept, marketers need to generate interest in the new venture and one of the tools used is a free sample or discounted trial purchase. Repeat visits can be encouraged using price promotions.

Financial-orientated pricing objectives

The majority of for-profit hospitality organizations focus on financial objectives rather than marketing-orientated objectives.

Profit-orientated pricing objectives are effective for setting management performance targets, but typically fail to take into account the external environment, competitor and customer factors. A typical profit-orientated pricing objective would be 'to set prices to achieve a 15 per cent return on investment, per annum, over a 5-year period'. Profit-orientated pricing objectives focus on the company's profit requirements and include survival, target return on investment (ROI), skimming, optimal current profit and harvesting.

- *Survival*: A company fighting for survival, for example during a recession, adopts short-term low prices, designed to attract value-sensitive customers. These prices are justified on the grounds that even a small contribution to fixed costs is better than none. Generating cash flow is critical to service high finance and labour costs. This pricing objective could have serious consequences for competitors who not only lose market share but could also be forced into financial difficulties as a result of the price competition.
- *Target ROI*: The selected ROI depends on the type, scale and risk of the investment; the weighted average cost of capital; the forecast rate of inflation and the company's internal minimum ROI strategy. Prices are calculated to ensure that the ROI is achieved.
- *Skimming*: The objective of a price skimming is to maximize the contribution from price-insensitive customers. This involves charging a high price at the launch of a new product. Price skimming is only occasionally used by hospitality companies as they tend to operate in markets with well-established price bands. However, in corporate hospitality and the exclusive events market (like prestigious

sporting events in iconic venues) a high-price skimming strategy is feasible.

- *Optimal current profit*: Leading players in mature markets generally seek to optimize their profit by setting prices that are consistent with maintaining market share. In mature markets, it is difficult to lift prices, not only because customers have well-established price expectations but also because competitors may fail to follow, thereby trying to secure a price advantage.

- *Harvesting*: In the late maturity or decline stage of the life cycle, corporations can 'milk' the remaining revenue stream from a product by strategically reducing marketing support, thereby increasing profit margins, with a view to investing the cash generated in a newer product that has greater growth potential. This requires a business to maintain prices in less price-sensitive market segments and to exit price-sensitive segments. The goal is to maintain demand as long as possible whilst reducing marketing expense.

Sales-orientated pricing objectives focus on achieving sales, market share or volume targets. A typical sales-orientated pricing objective would be 'to set prices to achieve a 20 per cent market share within 2 years'.

- *Maximizing sales revenues*: Firms with well-defined, highly differentiated market positions may be able to maximize sales revenue by managing prices upwards over time. For this to be possible, the business must have strong and price-insensitive demand. Firms that are not market leaders and suffer from inconsistent demand may flex prices with a view to increase sales revenues.

- *Penetration pricing strategy*: Hotels, resorts and newly opened restaurants/bars urgently need to develop sales. Unless the location and offer is unique, this is normally achieved by attracting competitors' customers. Pricing objectives to build sales quickly, a strategy known as penetration pricing, may require a business to develop special offers to encourage potential customers to trial purchase.

- *Volume*: Some hospitality managers agree prices that enable them to achieve high-volume sales. Key intermediaries, such as major tour companies, booking agents and high-volume customers, are able to negotiate large discounts from larger hotel companies for a guaranteed sales volume. This negotiation can be one of the most crucial pricing decisions affecting the hotel's profitability for that period.

- *Tactical pricing*: Because many hospitality operators have low or shoulder seasons, there is a need for tactical product/price promotions to generate sales during quieter trading periods.

Cost-orientated pricing objectives involve setting a target cost percentage or value, and calculating selling price so that the target is achieved. This pricing method is typically used in catering operations, where the management will set target food/bar cost percentages or profit margins. A typical cost-orientated pricing objective would be 'to set restaurant prices to achieve a food operating cost of 30 per cent during the financial period from April to September'. Although cost-orientated objectives are widely used in hospitality operations, they fail to take into account external competitor and customer factors.

Competitor-orientated pricing objectives

It is easy for hospitality companies to find out competitors' published online prices, and many do. Competitors' prices establish a benchmark and range for players in the same and in neighbouring product classes. When market leaders' prices change, market followers will simply move their prices up or down in line with them to maintain the same price differential as before. The problem with this 'me-too', follow-the-leader strategy is that the cost base of competitors might be very different, and the strategy does not take into account what customers might be prepared to pay.

Costs

A major input into the pricing decision is the cost of producing and marketing the product. Marketers need to understand the nature of the costs in delivering the hospitality offer. *Fixed costs* do not vary with sales volume – examples include rent, property taxes, salaries of permanent staff, insurance and depreciation. In some companies, bank interest and loan repayments are considered to be fixed costs. The key feature of fixed costs, given the seasonality of hospitality products, is that they do not vary and must be paid on a regular monthly or quarterly basis.

Variable costs vary in proportion to sales – examples include food and beverage purchases, and laundry services. *Semi-fixed costs* vary in sympathy with, but not in proportion to, sales volume – examples include energy costs (light, heat, air-conditioning) and part-time wages.

In hospitality businesses, a high proportion of costs are fixed or semifixed. This is partly due to the high level of capital invested in buildings, equipment and refurbishment. Although the total capital investment is usually smaller in catering establishments, the predominance of fixed costs is similar.

There are several difficulties associated with the incorporation of cost considerations into pricing decisions. Cost-based pricing techniques are essentially retrospective – that is, prices tend to be based on costs that are known because they have already been incurred.

Yet, companies need to recover future costs, which may be quite different.

Whatever prices are set, they must eventually recover the long-term total costs of being in business. In the short term, however, companies can use marginal costs to set prices. The *marginal cost* is the variable cost to the company of making the last sale – for example, letting the last room. If a room is unoccupied, there is no contribution margin earned; if the room is occupied at any rate above the marginal cost, there is a contribution to fixed costs.

There is a critical relationship between costs, volume (the number of customers) and profit. Typically, but not always, lower cost operations are driven by higher volumes at lower prices and higher cost operations are driven by lower volumes at higher prices. Marketers need to be aware of the cost structure of their business and products, and the volume of customers required to achieve target profits.

Company resources

The size and financial assets of a company also influence the pricing decision. International hospitality companies operating with strong brands in many countries have easy access to a variety of capital markets and develop a strong resource base. They enjoy economies of scale and better purchasing, which reduces operating costs and improves profitability. Larger companies have more business experience and can afford to experiment with different pricing strategies in selected outlets. They can also tolerate short-term losses during the launch of a new product concept and, if the product concept fails, they can afford to write the investment off and learn from the experience. Single-unit, privately owned operations do not have significant financial resources, and a single pricing error can seriously (perhaps even fatally) damage a small business.

Positioning

Prices must accurately reflect the business's desired market position, be consistent across the range of products offered and match the target market's expectation of quality and value. There is a close relationship between price and customer-perceived quality. Experienced customers are quick to note a mismatch. Price not only has to cover costs and generate profits but also reflects the quality position that the brand wishes to occupy. In planning new hospitality concepts, the price target markets are prepared to pay is a key determinant in the sales volume/cost/profit relationship and helps to shape the product format. New hospitality offerings are often designed to match a pre-conceived price point.

Distribution channel

When setting prices, hospitality operators must understand their channels of distribution and factor in the costs of their online and/ or offline intermediaries. There are two main distribution models in tourism: the 'agency' model and the 'merchant' model. In the agency model, the hospitality company pays a travel agent or online intermediary a fixed commission for each booking. The minimum commission paid to travel agents is 8 per cent and the norm varies between 10 and 15 per cent, though on certain products (e.g. weekend leisure breaks), the commission can increase to more than 25 per cent.

In the merchant (or wholesaler) model, the intermediary negotiates an allocation of inventory (cabins, rooms, seats) at an agreed rate from the hospitality operator. The discounts for a contract rate can vary from 15 to 65 per cent off the rack rates. Within the contract, there will be a rate parity agreement that prevents the wholesaler from selling the hotel rooms below the same price as the hotel. Rate parity is designed to ensure that all the hotel's distribution channels offer potential customers the same rate for the same product and can offer a 'best rate guarantee'. The merchant/wholesaler then charges customers whatever price they can achieve. If the merchant/wholesaler bundles several components of a holiday/activity into one 'package' then the actual hospitality rate is not public – this is often called opaque pricing and enables the wholesaler to bypass the rate parity agreement. When the merchant is left with unwanted inventory, then the distressed inventory can be offloaded via the Internet at very low prices using opaque pricing techniques, which might then damage the image and credibility of the hospitality company. The transaction charges of computerized reservation systems and credit card payments incur additional costs, which the business has to cover. Credit card commissions can vary from less than 1 per cent for major international companies to over 5 per cent for smaller operators. From a strategic pricing perspective, marketers must understand their distribution costs to ensure that the rates are profitable or at least generate a contribution to fixed costs.

Customers

In Chapter 4, we discussed how hospitality companies segment consumers into target markets and that many operations target several different segments at the same time. Each of the different segments has different price points – for example, the conference segment normally commands a significantly higher price than tour groups. Managing the pricing and volume mix between various segments is critical to achieving target revenue and profits (see Activity 7.2).

Activity 7.2

The table below presents the hypothetical operating statistics for a 200-bedroom downtown hotel for June (30 days) using segment, volume mix and rate. The hotel achieved 80 per cent occupancy (4800 rooms nights sold of a possible 6000 rooms), with variable average daily room rates (ADR) for each segment. What actions should the hotel take to improve sales revenue?

Segment	Rooms sold	Mix %	ADR	Total revenue
Free independent travellers	480	10	240	115,200
Local business	960	20	190	182,400
Corporate negotiated	960	20	180	172,800
Conference	480	10	180	86,400
Leisure break couples/ individuals	480	10	160	76,800
Leisure tour group	1440	30	80	115,200
Total	4800	100%	175.50	748,800

Another issue in pricing from a consumer perspective is consideration of customers' response to pricing and value. Customers not only judge the total bill in determining whether they have enjoyed value for money but may also focus on its component parts. High-individual drink prices can generate dissatisfaction, even when the overall bill is regarded favourably. As part of an effective positioning strategy, business must be aware of the dangers of mixing incompatible market segments. In attempting to maximize sales, hospitality marketers' use of discounted prices can attract and encourage the 'wrong' type of customers. This is especially evident when luxury hotels offer low accommodation prices via online merchants' websites like lastminute.com and attract customers who might not 'fit' with other customers. From a financial perspective, since these customers do not spend in the bars and restaurants, their total spend is low and their contribution is poor; but during low-demand periods, any contribution to fixed costs reduces profit erosion.

Product

Characteristics of the hospitality product that influence pricing strategy include the product class, the stage in the product life cycle, the production process and the level of people-skills involved in

Table 7.1 Examples of hospitality price objectives, strategies and tactics

Price objective category	Hospitality product	Price objective	Price strategy	Price method and pricing tactics
Customer; prestige	Five-star international luxury hotel	To charge the premium price for the highest product quality in order to maintain a prestige price positioning offer for the next 5 years	Monitor customers' perceptions of the luxury product offer	Carry out regular customer and consumer marketing research via focus groups to establish whether the luxury product offer justifies the premium price position
			Monitor local and international competitors' product/service/price offer	Check online non-promotional prices for luxury competitor set
			Introduce innovations and improvements to maintain the product quality, whilst always charging premium prices	Visit new-build and recently refurbished competitors; evaluate innovations and develop detailed plans to improve product/service constantly
Customer: trial purchase	Health and leisure club	To set a special offer price that will encourage 100 trial purchases of club membership in March	Research existing and potential club members' attitudes to price-sensitivity towards health and leisure clubs to identify price points	Identify most cost-effective method of reaching members
				Draft online questionnaire and run pilot study; adapt questionnaire and carry out main study
				Analyze results and set special price offer; test price offer and promotional material with focus groups
				Fix price of special offer and launch promotion
				Monitor results of promotion

(Continued)

Table 7.1 Examples of hospitality price objectives, strategies and tactics—cont'd

Price objective category	Hospitality product	Price objective	Price strategy	Price method and pricing tactics
Financial: volume	International 500-bedroom four-star gateway hotel	To win a 60 rooms per night contract for 6 months from October to March, from a major airline company, at a rate of $100 per room per night	Research current and potential demand for aircrew room-nights	Identify major airline operators and the number of flights requiring overnight stopovers for crew, number of crew per flight, length of stopover
			Research existing and potential hotel supply to major airlines	Visit competitor hotels to establish which competitors are catering for which airlines
			Evaluate contract aircrew room rates	Establish competitor rates and estimate discount offered to airline companies
			Develop a good rapport with airline	Prepare discount rate and confirm with general manager
				Contact airline purchasing departments and request opportunity to quote for business
				Negotiate competitive market-orientated rates
Financial: sales target	60-bedroom provincial mid-market city hotel	To increase room sales revenue by 2% above inflation for the 12-month period from October to September	Scan online and offline environment for potential increases in inflation, consumer demand and hotel room supply during the next 18 months	Carry out detailed research in local and national economy to evaluate forecast industry and general inflation

	Review historic and current trading performance Set price increases	Identify potential market demand during period, including seasonal variations Research competitor prices and any additional accommodation supply Identify volume (number of bed-nights) and value (achieved room rate) of each market segment Set room rates to guarantee 2% plus inflation increase across total room revenue
Financial: cost-led	To achieve a bar cost of 35% for the next financial year To achieve a food cost of 30% for the next financial year	Utilize a computerized stock-control system to set and monitor bar and food costs and prices to ensure that the target is achieved	Carry out a monthly bar and food computerized stock check on all items purchased and selling prices Monitor the sales mix and ensure that high-volume food and drink products are achieving their required target profit margin
Competitor: price followership	To undercut the mid-market price leader by 10% on all bedroom rack rates during the high season	Monitor competitor price movements and adjust room prices accordingly	Scan competitor hotels online offers on a daily basis to check on current room rates Adapt own hotel's prices accordingly

producing the product. Different classes of hospitality products are sold within different price bands, which determine the boundaries for setting prices.

PRICING STRATEGIES

Having established the price objectives, hospitality companies need to consider pricing strategies, which should be linked to the quality standards offered by the operation. The examples below refer to the hotel sector, but the principles are applicable to all hospitality sectors. In hotels, consumers often associate quality standards with star ratings and there are strong linkages between perceptions of quality and price. Alternative pricing strategies include the market leader and market follower options, but there are also unsustainable pricing strategies that are ultimately self-defeating.

Market leader strategies

Well-established hotel companies with a loyal customer base, a strong brand image and high levels of repeat business can adopt *market leader strategies*, where the prices are aligned with the brand's quality positioning. These strategies are suitable for

- The most exclusive, luxurious, five-star hotels in the world; they deliver the highest quality customer experience and can justify charging premium or prestige prices (prestige pricing appeals to status conscious customers who are normally affluent and enjoy conspicuous consumption)
- Traditional three-star, well-maintained hotels in good locations offering appropriate value for money and competing effectively with a mid-market pricing strategy
- Budget hotels and motels charging relatively low prices for a product offering fewer facilities and delivering value for money.

Market follower strategies

New entrants and less-established hotel brands, seeking to build market share by penetration pricing, adopt a *market follower strategy*. A market follower strategy offers similar quality but pitches prices lower than the market leader in order to be more competitive, attract customers and grow market share. These strategies are suitable for:

- High-quality four-/five-star properties, seeking to grow market share by exceptional value pricing

- Mid-market hotels competing against more established properties; or aggressive chains, and individual properties, seeking to increase room occupancy and build market share by offering exceptional value pricing.

Unsustainable pricing strategies

Unfortunately, some hotels implement *over-priced* strategies compared with their competitor sets and market conditions, which are unsustainable as a long-term proposition. These companies charge rates higher than the quality can justify. Some of these hotels might have myopic management who unknowingly have allowed their offering to become over-priced. As customers recognize the poor value for money, the reputation of the business will rightly suffer. Either the company will have to adopt a more appropriate balanced strategy or be forced into either selling or liquidating the business. Examples include the following:

- Old-established, grand three-/four-star hotels that are no longer as luxurious as they used to be and whose facilities no longer match the price charged; these properties are trading on an historic image as they gradually decline; owners will eventually either have to re-invest in their facilities or reduce their prices
- Once glorious now shabby hotels, possibly in good locations, which only generate passing trade but charge high prices; this rip-off value will lead to a poor reputation, and limited – if any – repeat and recommended business
- Mid-market hotels with falling standards but still maintaining a medium pricing strategy, which does not represent value for money
- Budget operations, which have gradually increased prices to pay for 'amenity creep' items and are no longer competitively priced.

Finally, some hotels can adopt an unsustainable price/quality strategy, where the price offered is too low to support the product/quality offer indefinitely.

- High-quality four-/five-star properties charging unsustainable, relatively low, year round prices due to a decline in the destination's popularity; hotels in this situation should reposition the property as a mid-market hotel and accordingly reduce the product/quality, the cost structure and set a more profitable pricing strategy
- Mid-market hotels operating in highly competitive environments and offering budget hotel prices without reducing product/service quality standards
- Hotels do not manage their cost base effectively and do not respond quickly enough to inflationary changes in the external environment.

Companies need to adopt pricing strategies that take into account demand patterns and their relative quality compared with competition. There are several companies such as Rate Tiger and RateVIEW who provide competitor price benchmarking services for hotels and enable room rates and availability to be updated across online multiple distribution channels quickly. Table 7.1 provides several examples of hospitality products combined with price objectives, strategies and tactics.

PRICING METHODS

The next aspect of pricing is to review how prices are calculated in the hospitality industry. A generic pricing model consisting of eight sequential stages has been proposed (Kotler et al., 2009):

1 Select pricing objectives
2 Assess the target market's ability to afford the purchase price and consumers' perception of the price/product offer
3 Determine the potential demand
4 Analyze the demand, cost, volume, price and profit relationships; businesses need to understand their fixed and variable costs
5 Research competitors' price/product offer
6 Select a pricing strategy
7 Select appropriate pricing methods
8 Set specific prices for rooms, food, beverages, conference and leisure products, and for special product-price bundles.

Clearly, this approach requires a considerable amount of consumer, competitor and internal company research. The managers of smaller hospitality companies adopt a much simpler approach to setting prices, based on a combination of historical factors and the current economic situation. Their approach to setting prices might be as follows:

1 Review last season/year's prices and business performance
2 Review current and potential cost increases
3 Take into account current and forecast inflation
4 Take into account the general economic situation and factors likely to influence customers' attitudes to prices
5 Check competitors' current prices
6 Set prices by adding a percentage (e.g. 5 per cent on the tariff of each room price) or a fixed amount (add $ 1 to each *à la carte* menu item) onto the current prices
7 Flex prices on the website according to current demand.

Although this process is flawed, managers of smaller businesses set prices using the historic price, plus or minus a sum, because it is simple and easy to adopt.

Pricing methods can be classified under similar headings to pricing objectives: cost-led, profit-led, competition-led and marketing-led. Here is a summary of the main features of each pricing method.

- *Market-led* – the highest price that customers are willing to pay; considers the competition, demand and profitability, and sets the ceiling for prices
- *Competitor-led* – prices simply follow competitors; fails to take into account customers' willingness to pay, return on investment goals and company costs
- *Profit-led* – return on investment target provides internal goals to motivate managers, fails to take into account customers and competitors
- *Cost-led* – cost-based pricing sets the floor for prices, fails to take into account customers' willingness to pay and return on investment goals, is sometimes used to establish the lowest pricing level that a company can charge to remain viable.

DYNAMIC PRICING AND REVENUE MANAGEMENT

Hospitality companies have adopted the computerized yield management systems first developed by the airline industry to maximize their potential revenue by controlling inventory and using price as a demand management tool. Known as revenue management (RM), this is a complex form of price discrimination primarily used in the accommodation market (bedrooms, cabins and suites) to help maximize revenue (in hotels, this is called revenue per available room). Dynamic pricing flexes prices to match forecast demand with current available capacity. Prices change according to the probability of selling the last rooms in a given period and are influenced by the length of time between the date of booking and the date of arrival, customer demand and different customer segments' willingness to pay. Revenue Management Systems (RMS) are normally found in hotels with at least 50 bedrooms, although some smaller properties with only 16 rooms can effectively adopt a revenue management system. A minimum 1 year's historic data including daily occupancy and achieved room rates is needed – but new hotels, especially chain managed units, can utilize RMSs by aggregating representative data from similar properties. A 200-bedroom hotel might have 2000 different prices for different room categories and products inputted into the RMS with a price range from $ 60 to $ 600 for the next year.

Although smaller accommodation properties and other hospitality sectors retain fixed prices, the emergence of transparent pricing and convenient online comparative shopping, coupled with the development of sophisticated databases and data management techniques, has changed the pricing strategies of the medium and larger accommodation businesses. They flex their online prices using the *Best Available Rate* (BAR). The BAR is the best rate a customer can book at the *time of booking* and is determined by the estimated value of the last rooms to sell. The BAR fluctuates as the RMS recalculates forecast demand and changes the BAR on a periodic basis (e.g. every 12 hours). This raises an interesting issue for customers staying several nights when each night has a different BAR (Noone & Mattila, 2009). One approach is to give the customer a blended rate that averages the rates for each night of the stay into one single nightly price. For a two-night stay with one night quoted at $ 200 and the second night quoted at $ 220, then the average nightly rate using a blended approach would be $ 210. The alternative approach is to provide non-blended rates: the rate for each night of the guest's stay is given to the customer separately. In the above example, the first night is quoted at $ 200 and the second night quoted at $ 220. Although the overall price of $ 420 is the same, customers naturally respond to the different approaches in different ways. At the moment, there is no accepted hotel industry practice about blended and non-blended rates, so different companies adopt their own strategies (see Activity 7.3).

Activity 7.3

- Log on to the following hotel websites and check the room/price availability for a three-night stay – Sunday, Monday and Tuesday – at one of the branded hotels. Look for the 'Best Available Rate' and see whether the rates are blended or nonblended:

- Marriott Hotels

- Starwood

Now check the rates for the same days, at the same Marriott and Starwood hotels, using Expedia.

Compare the different approaches to presenting room price information to customers.

Since rates fluctuate over time, save a copy of these rates and then check the same hotels over a Sunday, Monday and Tuesday in 2/3 weeks time. Compare the rate fluctuations over time.

Companies using RM no longer publish fixed prices; instead rate bands from high to low indicate the likely range of prices to potential customers. Contract corporate, aircrew and group negotiated rates can either be fixed rates or are discounted from the BAR and fluctuate with the BAR. Hence, if the BAR for a bedroom tonight is $ 200 and the agreed corporate rate is a 10% discount, then the rate would be $ 180.

One of the consequences of an RMS is the requirement to over-book, this means during busy periods selling more rooms than the hotel actually operates. In other words, a 100-bedroom hotel will book 105 rooms because some customers will cancel at the last moment or not arrive. From a customer satisfaction perspective and from a front desk employee perspective, overbooking creates problems when the hotel is full and very angry guests are 'walked' (booked into a nearby hotel); a situation that frontline employees do not enjoy having to manage.

Traditionally, hotels have always used seasonal pricing strategies to stimulate demand in low or shoulder demand periods – these price variations can, for example, be based on different mid-week/weekend rates or on early booking discounts. Hotels also set length of stay restrictions on the booking to prevent customers obtaining a lower price during a higher period – for example, to prevent a customer from enjoying a lower weekend rate during the higher priced mid-week. These restrictions are an example of rate fences because they act as a barrier and protect revenues in higher yielding periods. Hotels use the RMS to set restrictions. However, customers must perceive that the pricing strategy as fair and any fences are considered reasonable. Hotels can experience problems at check out when customers book at one price and then become aware of different rates being offered to other customers – due to different booking conditions.

Dynamic pricing is a pricing mechanism designed to tackle the problems caused by the special characteristics of service industries. Hoteliers have always recognized that it is better to sell a room at a low price tonight rather than have an empty room, because of the low marginal cost to service another room. Each room sold above marginal cost, even at lower prices, helps to contribute towards the fixed costs of operating a hotel property. An RMS can prevent reservation agents from making critical decisions for themselves, because prices available in the property management system are usually controlled via an interface within the RMS. Although there is an over-ride facility to allow some discretion by the reservations manager, any excessive use of the over-ride facility has to be justified. In some chain-owned hotels, the management of properties that use the over-ride facility more than three times per month will be asked to explain why.

In the restaurant sector, RM is used as a tool to manage duration control (how long customers actually spend eating at the table) to optimize table turnover rather than flexing prices. Duration management (Kimes, 2008) focuses on the period between arrival at the restaurant, being seated, ordering and consuming the meal, paying and leaving the restaurant. Restaurants can increase their revenues and profitability by reducing service inconsistencies within the service process, making the service more efficient by upselling and serving more customers during busy periods.

PRICE PROMOTIONS

The impact of price promotions needs to be carefully evaluated in the planning stage to protect revenue streams from the core business and brand image. City hotels offering low demand price promotions to leisure travellers' rate-fence the promotion to prevent business travellers from taking advantage of it, by insisting on pre-booking conditions (see rate restrictions in previous section). Price led promotions must also make a realistic contribution towards the overheads and justify the cost that goes into their development and promotion.

One tactic is to use loss leaders to attract customers. Bars typically have a special drinks offer – perhaps half-price on quiet evenings or 'doubles' at a single price during a happy hour promotion. Joint marketing initiatives between hotel chains and media outlets make use of other promotions – one example is 'free accommodation' at selected hotels, which is offered exclusively to the readers of a newspaper providing the customer pays a minimum price for meals whilst staying in the hotel. 'Two for the price of one' or BOGOF (buy one, get one free) promotions are popular and effective in promoting hotel and restaurant products.

These price-led promotions help to boost sales in quiet periods, but they do have limitations and drawbacks. In principle, the promotion should attract new customers who, having enjoyed the hospitality experience, will be expected to return at other times and pay the normal prices. In practice, many (even most) of the customers who enjoy a promotional price do not return and book at the 'normal' price once the promotion has finished. There is also the danger of cannibalizing customers. This means that loyal customers may take advantage of the price promotion, changing their booking and purchasing habits, and consequently the hotel or restaurant loses prime rate business and suffers a reduction in sales and profits.

Product price bundles

All sectors of the industry bundle a package of benefits at an all-inclusive price (see Chapter 5). Examples include foreign package holidays, activity leisure breaks, 24 hour conference delegate packages, wedding receptions and fast-food and drink combinations. The advantages of product bundling for the consumer include the perception of added value (indeed, really effective packages *do* provide customers with added value) and the ease of booking all the components of the bundle at one price in one transaction.

Price cuts

There is considerable research into the effects on company and industry profitability of price/rate cuts and price wars. Although individual companies who initiate price cuts may gain market share, eventually competitors are forced to respond. If a price war ensues, customers begin to expect a lower price point, reacting unfavourably when companies attempt to increase prices later. The evidence suggests that all companies in an industry involved in a price war lose profitability. Price cuts in hospitality can be a natural reaction to excess capacity, but the consequences can be damaging if maintained for a long period. The introduction of RMS, dynamic pricing and online transparent transactions mean that consumers and hospitality operators both recognize that prices constantly change – both downwards and upwards.

INTERNATIONAL PRICING

The difficulties in setting a pricing strategy for companies operating in more than one country are compounded by:

- The different currency and cost structures between countries
- The different types of competitors – global, regional, national branded chains and local independents
- The different stages of the market/product life cycle in each country
- Different inflation rates and exchange rates
- The ability to repatriate profits, which again varies significantly from country to country.

For companies aiming to promote and protect their hospitality brands by standardizing the product offer, a uniform price position presents particular problems. Whilst the pricing strategy can be consistent, for example to adopt a market leader strategy and charge the highest prices in the competitor set, the actual price charged will vary between different countries. In Western countries, all customers regardless of their nationality are charged the same price; but in some cultures, like Egypt and India, it is acceptable to charge a lower price for domestic customers and a higher price for international customers in local hotels.

CONCLUSION

In the final analysis, customers decide whether the company is charging the right price. Although pricing decisions are the easiest element of the marketing mix to change, they remain a complex phenomenon. In this chapter, we have explained:

- That pricing is the tool that matches supply and demand
- That price is the only element of marketing mix that does not generate cost; price generates revenue
- That price, in the absence of other cues, is an indicator of quality and sets customer expectations

- That price is the summation of all sacrifices made by a consumer in order to experience the benefits of the product
- Why companies have little control over the *external* factors that influence pricing decisions, but considerable control over the *internal* factors that influence pricing decisions
- How the Internet has transformed consumer awareness of comparative hospitality products and transparent prices
- Why pricing decisions should reflect market positioning
- That medium and larger accommodation based businesses use dynamic pricing strategies and RMSs to drive revenue
- Price promotions, linked to product benefit bundles, are extensively used to grow revenue in low-demand periods
- International pricing decisions are subject to local country environmental factors.

REVIEW QUESTIONS

Now check your understanding of this chapter by answering the following questions:

1 Why is pricing significant in the pre-encounter hospitality marketing mix?
2 Discuss the external and internal factors that influence pricing decisions. Provide examples from the hospitality industry to illustrate your answer.
3 Evaluate pricing and product quality strategies in three hotel markets.
4 Explain the role of RM in larger hotel properties.
5 Evaluate the role of price promotions in the hospitality industry.
6 Discuss the pricing issues for a standardized international hotel brand.

References and Further Reading

Burgess, C. (2010). *Essential financial techniques for hospitality managers – A practical manual*. Oxford. Goodfellow Publishers.

Cross, R. (1997). *RM: Hard-core tactics for market domination*. New York: Broadway Books.

Harris, P. J., & James, P. (1999). *Profit planning*. Butterworth-Heinemann.

Ingold, A., McMahon-Beattie, U., & Yeoman, I. (2000). Yield management: Strategies for the service industries, Cassell (2nd ed.). ISBN 0-7506-5250-0.

Kimes, S. E. (2008). The role of technology in restaurant revenue management. *Cornell Hospitality Quarterly*, *49*, 297–309.

Kotler, P., Keller, K., Brady, M., Goodman, M., & Hansen, T. (2009). *Marketing management*. Pearson Prentice Hall.

Noone, B. M., & Mattila, A. S. (2009). Hotel revenue management and the Internet: The effect of price presentation strategies and customers' willingness to book. *International Journal of Hospitality Management*, *28*, 272–279.

Talluri, K. T., & Van Ryzin Garrett (2005). *The theory and practice of revenue management*. Springer.

Tranter, K. A., Stuart-Hill, T., & Parker, Juston (2008). *An introduction to revenue management for the hospitality industry*. Prentice Hall.

Varini, K., Englemann, R., Claessen, B., & Schleusenier (2003). Evaluation of the price-value perception of customers in Swiss hotels. *Journal of Revenue and Pricing Management*, *2*(1), 47–60.

Yeoman, I., & MacMahon-Beattie, U. (2004). *Revenue management and pricing: Case studies and applications*. Thomson Learning.

CHAPTER **8**

Distributing the offer

Chapter objectives

After going through this chapter, you should be able to

- Define the role of distribution in the hospitality and tourism industries
- Explain the functions of travel and tourism intermediaries from a hospitality perspective
- Understand the role of traditional distribution channels in hospitality markets
- Understand the role of online distribution channels in hospitality markets
- Explain how Internet technology, computer reservation systems (CRS), global distribution systems (GDS) and mobile technology impact on hospitality distribution
- Evaluate channel relationships between principals and intermediaries.

INTRODUCTION

In this chapter, we define distribution, describe the role of intermediaries, review how Internet and mobile technology is constantly changing hospitality and tourism distribution systems and explain the channel options available to hospitality operators. Most of the discussion in this chapter refers to accommodation providers since several hospitality sectors, for example, bars and cafes, do not need to use intermediaries to reach their customers.

The concept of a distribution channel is relatively simple, but the management of distribution in practice can be extremely complicated, especially for large organizations. Since hospitality products are perishable, it is crucial to generate advance bookings. Major hotel companies with thousands of bedrooms to fill in hundreds of locations need to use a wide range of distribution channels to reach their targeted customers.

Distribution provides two key utilities or benefits to customers. Distribution makes hospitality products and services available when and where customers want them; these are known as time and place utilities, respectively. Online and traditional intermediaries, for example, travel agents and tour operators, help customers to find and choose hospitality and travel products. Intermediaries (also called channel partners) are normally paid by charging a commission to the hospitality company that receives the booking or by using the merchant model (see page 193). The relationship between hospitality organizations and their channel partners can be complex.

The Internet has enabled organizations to perform both distribution and marketing communication activities online. Websites that have e-commerce functionality allow customers to book and pay online, as well as enabling bi-lateral communication between the organization and its customers. However, to help you to develop a better understanding of the different roles that distribution and marketing communication play in the marketing mix, we discuss them in separate chapters. Remember, distribution provides time and place utilities or benefits to customers, whilst the role of marketing communication is to influence customer demand by informing and persuading target audiences.

Before the development of the Internet, the emergence of conventional distribution channels was pioneered by entrepreneurs, such as Thomas Cook who created tourism packages for individuals and groups of customers by combining elements of travel, accommodation and other components of a holiday. From the mid-nineteenth century to today, the travel and tourism industry has evolved in to a mass, complex system of interdependent organizations varying in size and scope. However, although the Internet has increased the accessibility to tourism information, speeded up transactions and triggered the emergence of innovative online businesses, the basic principles of distribution are the same as the pre-Internet era. Airlines, hospitality organizations, car hire firms and leisure attractions are normally described as principals. These principals provide the core tourism product that customers consume. Without principals there is no product. Hospitality principals, especially larger companies, need intermediaries to distribute their product either solely or combined with other travel products in a package. Intermediaries sell the principals' products to customers and are normally paid by the principals.

We now explain the role of different categories of intermediary in hospitality and tourism; discuss conventional and online distribution channels from multiple hospitality perspectives; and explain horizontal and vertical integration in the hospitality and tourism industry.

Marketing insight 8.1

TUI

The origins of TUI are in a German industrial company, called Preussag, that shifted its focus to travel and developed an acquisition strategy originally based on buying German, British and French tourism companies. TUI has three divisions: TUI Travel, TUI Hotels & Resorts, and TUI Cruises. TUI Travel has more than 200 brands including travel agents, such as Lunn Poly, Thomson the tour operator, Britannia Airways and online booking agencies, such as Hotelopia. There are nearly 250 TUI Hotels with brands such as Riu, Grecotel, Grupotel, Iberotel, Dorfhotel, Robinson and Magic Life. Like its main competitor Thomas Cook, the growth of TUI was based on both horizontal integration and vertical integration. Indeed from a hospitality perspective Thomas Cook and TUI have become major owner–operators of hotels, especially across the Mediterranean.

Sources: www.tui-group.com and www.thomascook.com

Activity 8.1

Before reading the rest of the chapter

- Visit the TUI Group (corporate) website at www.tui-group.com; at the top of the page, click on 'About Us;' read about the TUI Group profile, sectors and heritage, which provides the history of TUI.
- Visit the Thomas Cook website at www.thomascook.com; scroll down to the bottom of the home page and click on 'About Us;' read about the history and development of Thomas Cook and their different brands.

INTERMEDIARIES

The structure of the travel and tourism industry is continually evolving. There are different structures in different countries depending on the historical development of tourism. Although the vast majority of tourism intermediaries are small, independent organizations, a few major international companies have emerged with dominant market positions. From a hospitality perspective, intermediaries can be categorized under the following broad headings:

- Search engine
- Travel agent
- Tour operator
- Conference and meeting planner
- Corporate business travel agent
- Incentive travel house
- Representative agent
- Specialist online travel retailer
- Affiliate marketing agency
- Tourist Board
- Airline

You should be aware that, although these distinct categories of tourism intermediaries help you to define and understand the roles of different types of distributor, the boundaries between the categories are not precise. For example, many firms combine travel agent and tour operations within their range of business activities. Companies are continually evolving as the environmental and technological landscape changes. Indeed, the boundaries between major principals and distributors is becoming more indistinct, as some airlines that normally act as principals have also created an intermediary business to help their passengers book hotels and car hire. This of course aims to improve those airlines' profitability.

Small-scale intermediaries usually focus on a specific leisure or business sector, whereas the large-scale organizations can provide both leisure and business services. Almost all hospitality intermediaries have their own website. However, some intermediaries provide retail travel shops for customers as well as providing an online distribution presence; these are called bricks-and-clicks companies, such as Thomas Cook. Other intermediaries, such as Expedia only have an online presence and are called 'clicks-only' or 'dot.com' companies. In certain countries, travel consultants working for specific companies, or independently on commission, visit the homes of customers to help them choose holidays and hospitality products using laptop computers to demonstrate the competing offers.

We now discuss the main categories of intermediary from a hospitality perspective.

Search engines

A search engine is a software program that searches the Internet for files containing keywords specified by the search engine user. Dominant search engines are Google, Yahoo! and MSN search.

Search engines use robotic, spider or web crawler software to search for files that match the query (keywords). Search engines use complex proprietary algorithms (Google's algorithm considers over 200 variables) to identify files that match the keywords and provide a list of results (hits). The results can be listed on many pages, so organizations often advertise to ensure that their offer appears at or close to the top of the list. On Google pages, these sponsored links appear on the right of the screen. The majority of links listed on the left of the screen occur organically as a result of their conformance to the search engine's algorithm. For companies that do not want to spend on advertising, Search Engine Optimization (SEO) provides a way of appearing towards the top of the organic listing.

One aspect of the ICT revolution is the significant role played by search engines in providing consumers with information about hospitality and travel products, prices and availability. Indeed, at the moment search engines have become the first and critical channel for hospitality operators. We discuss the role of search engine marketing in more detail later in the chapter.

Travel agents

Travel agents are retail businesses that provide information, advice and booking for individual and group travel in both business and leisure markets. They are also known as infomediaries. The concept of a travel agency is well established in the travel market. They act as an intermediary between customers and principals such as airlines, hotels, car rental companies, attractions, entertainment, event and sporting venues. The agency business model is based on the principals paying commission. Agents prefer prompt payment. The lowest commission paid is eight per cent and the norm is between 10 and 15 per cent. However, up to 25 per cent commission can be paid on specific products, especially during the low season. Hotel groups use the following tactics to target travel agents:

- Regular email, ezine (electronic magazines), print newsletters and direct mail promotions
- Sales visits to head office and individual retail outlets
- Incentive promotions, with rewards for the most successful staff
- Familiarization trips to the group's hotels.

The sales team of the hotel chain negotiates with the head office of the retail travel agent chain on a regular basis. They review sales figures, discuss customers' complaints and guest satisfaction surveys, and negotiate commission rates. Individual hotels rarely target travel agents, since their product offer is too narrow and localized to be of interest.

Tour operators

Tour operators are tourism industry wholesalers. They package inclusive holidays by combining the travel and accommodation elements with varying elements of food, beverage, activities, entertainment and sightseeing. They are sometimes described as aggregators because they create new travel products by packaging the principals' existing products. Some tour operators specialize in particular products (ski packages) or destinations (South-East Asia); others offer a wide range of tours. Tour operators generally work on volume sales, offering attractive, all-inclusive prices to generate high sales, with low margins. This formula implies a high break-even point, which makes tour operators financially vulnerable. Hotels wanting to target tour operators must be prepared to offer low rates and accept that the additional spend in the bar and other areas can be low. To protect themselves, hospitality operators need to transact business with tour operators who are covered by recognized trade indemnity policies and make sure that they are paid on a regular basis.

Often, the tour operator has representatives working in the resort or a tour guide accompanies the tourists on their holiday. These front-line employees play a key role in supporting the relationship between tour customers and the hotel. Much tour operator business is booked in hotels for a set of nights – in any combination from 1 to 14 nights – to coincide with working consumers' leisure time and holiday patterns. However, the senior citizens' market can book for longer during the low season in large holiday hotels.

Marketing insight 8.2

Distribution Strategy at Harmony Hotels, Austria

The Thaler family own and manage three Alpine resort hotels, all located close to each other in Niderau, Austria. Although there is a basic website, the number of direct bookings is limited. The business relies entirely on tour operators to fill approximately 350 bedrooms in the hotels. In the winter season, specialist European ski tour operators feature the Harfenwirt and Sonnschein hotels in online and printed brochures. Jill and Herbert Thaler negotiate low-contract rates with dozens of distributors such as Crystal, Directski, Igluski, J2ski, lastminute.com, Ski Austria, Thomson and Trip Advisor for skiing holidays. In the summer season, tour operators, such as Inghams, ThomsonLakes and Voyages Jules Verne as well as coach companies from Britain, France, Germany and Holland, bring older people for Alpine touring and walking holidays. The Thalers do not invest in any other marketing activities – for example, there is no budget for advertising. They accept the lower margin from tour operators because their distribution network fills the hotels.

Conference, event and meeting planners

These specialist agencies provide venue search and expert advice to customers who want to run conferences, events and meetings. Specialist planners do not normally charge the client a venue-finding fee; instead, the venue will pay the planner a commission on the business booked. Planners justify their role by:

- Providing impartial advice as to the suitability of the venue
- Negotiating the contract between the client and the venue
- Ensuring that the venue delivers what the organizer is looking for.

Planners adopt a professional approach to their businesses, especially since their customers can be high-spend, frequent users. They will often personally inspect alternative venues, and they develop considerable expertise in this competitive market. The major hotel groups regard conference and meeting planners as a priority target market. The Association for Conference and Events brings together a wider range of organizers and suppliers and provides useful information on its website: www.aceinternational.org.

Corporate or business travel agents

Business travel agents focus on service quality, in addition to price, in dealings with corporate customers. They arrange air travel and car hire as well as hotel bookings. The globalization of business has increased the demand for corporate travel, but at the same time the cost of travelling and staying in hotels has become a significant cost item. An American Express survey revealed that travel-for-business is the third highest item of controllable costs for companies.

Although smaller business travel agents still rely on commission payments, the largest have reinvented themselves to provide blue-chip clients with cost-effective travel advice. These business travel agents are not interested in collecting commission from hotels; instead, they charge their clients a management fee for providing a travel management service – just like any other professional organization charges for a service. Business travel agents are keenly interested in negotiating competitive rates with the hotels that their clients want to use, to demonstrate that they are delivering better value to their clients. American Express is one of the leading corporate travel agents in North America and Europe.

Incentive travel houses

Companies often use travel as a reward to motivate customers, dealers, distributors, salespeople, staff and managers. This idea has developed into a major sub-sector of the tourism business, and is called 'incentive travel'. The demand for incentive travel has increased dramatically during the past 20 years, and specialist incentive houses have developed expertise in this market. To be a successful motivator and 'incentivize' the target audience, the reward should be highly desirable. Many of the most attractive incentive destinations are foreign, unusual and even exotic. This specialized market is not suitable for all hotels; however, exotic hotels in idyllic or unusual locations can seriously target the incentive travel market.

Incentive houses carefully check the facilities and quality of service of hotels in appropriate destinations. Since the promoters of incentive schemes are always looking for unusual themes, venues can help incentive travel houses by packaging distinctive, interesting programs that are suitable for well-travelled, sophisticated consumers. Some incentive packages involve large numbers of winners all travelling in one party at the same time; others are designed for couples, and can be booked on an individual basis as and when it suits the winners. The magazine *Incentive Travel and Corporate Meetings* (ITCM) provides international coverage of hotel developments and initiatives targeting this market. ITCM gave Gleneagles Hotel, Scotland, the Gold Award for 'Best Hotel of the Year (UK)' and the Fairmount Hotel in Monte Carlo the Gold Award for 'Best International Hotel of the Year'. Visit the ITCM website to gain a better understanding of the incentive market. http://www.incentivetravel.co.uk/.

Representative agents

Representative agents are another type of intermediary who link hotels, travel agencies and customers. These are independent companies with their own sales teams. The largest representative agency in the world is Utell, which books millions of room nights each year into the hotels they represent. Utell connects 1000s of hotels, including many of the leading brands and independents, to travel agencies using the Global Distribution System (GDS). Utell also has its own sales force, which negotiates competitive rates for corporate clients and provides incentives to travel agents to book via Utell.

Marketing insight 8.3

Honourway, an independent representation agency

Honourway was founded by Honour Schram de Jong as a representative agency for luxury lodges in southern Africa. Honourway is the public relations, sales and marketing agent for small, exclusive lodges in Botswana, Malawi, Uganda and Zambia. Clients include Jaci's Safari Lodge, Tongabezi Lodge and Sausage Tree Camp. Each of the lodges is characterized by their remote rural locations set in the African bush, proximity to wildlife, high-quality facilities and service, and a passion for responsible tourism. The source markets are primarily from the United Kingdom, United States, Germany, France and Australia. Honourway carries out eight sales visits on behalf of clients to existing and potential tour operators in the United Kingdom each month and conducts regular sales visits to Europe and the United States. The clients are represented at annual events, such as the International Tourism Exchange (known as ITB) in Berlin, Cannes International Luxury Travel Market, World Travel Market in London, the South African INDABA tourism event, and the Asian Luxury Travel Market in Shanghai. Each of the clients pays an annual fee to be represented by Honourway. Honourway is an effective agency – one client increased their annual occupancy from 34% to 69% in 3 years.

Source: Honour Schram de Jong and www.honourway.com

Specialist online travel retailers

There is a wide range of specialist online retailers in the travel business. Many of these online retailers were originally used by hotel companies to sell distressed inventory. As the popularity of online distributors like Lastminute.com increased, principals have come to regard them as key intermediaries. Lastminute.com operates the merchant model for hotels by contracting to sell an allocation of inventory for the hotel. Many travel intermediaries, such as Lastminute.com, offer a wide range of tourism products. A smaller number, for example, Booking.com (which operates on a commission-based model), focus only on hotel bookings. Sites, such as Travelzoo and Cheapflights, are media websites operating on a sophisticated classified advertising model. Travelsupermarket.com is a comparison shopping site with a revenue model that combines both advertising and commission. KAYAK, a dedicated American-based travel search site that has strategic partnerships with distributors such as Ryan Air and Lastminute.com, is a meta search engine using technology to crawl and search other travel websites and derives its revenue from advertising. Some online sites allow potential customers to name their price for staying at a destination, and then match the customer with those hotels interested in accepting that price. Priceline is the American pioneer of this model with operations in 34 languages and 94 countries in America, Africa, Asia, Europe and the Middle East. TripAdvisor, the social networking site, is based on user-generated content-driven consumer reviews; and enables customers to search and compare a range of travel/hospitality products either separately or in packages.

Marketing insight 8.4

TripAdvisor

TripAdvisor, founded in the United States in 2000 and now a subsidiary of Expedia, provides an online travel advice and booking service to millions of travellers. TripAdvisor's original differentiator was to provide travellers and hotel guests the opportunity to critique their hospitality and tourism experiences and rank the principals' service. TripAdvisor operates 15 brands in the Americas, Europe and Asia, including www.cruisecritic.com, www.smartertravel.com, www.virtualtourist.com and the Chinese brands daodao.com (http://www.daodao.com) and Kuxun.cn (http://www.kuxun.cn). At the time of writing, there are one million businesses listed on the various websites; 15 million registered members; 35 million reviews; and collectively 46 million monthly visitors . . . and TripAdvisor continues to grow.

Source: www.tripadvisor.com

Online affiliate marketing agency

In the online world, there is a mass of formal/informal and official/unofficial information sources, including companies, consumer groups, governments, media, individuals, infomediaries, and social networks. Although companies clearly want to control product-related information, bloggers and tweeters are growing in influence. Much of the content from these information sources contains hyperlinks that take a browser either directly to the principal or to an intermediary where they can obtain more information and make a booking. In return for generating potential customers, the source is paid either a fee or a standard commission. The principal can pay on a pay-per-click (PPC) or a cost-per-thousand impressions (CPM) basis; or the principal pays on results basis using a pay-for-performance (PPP) model.

Affiliates who want to provide an 'own' branded booking service for visitors to their sites can partner with larger online companies who provide all the necessary off-the-shelf technology. For example, the Expedia Affiliate Network provide an easy to set up template, which enables an affiliate's potential customers to directly book 100,000 hotels and 500 airlines using the Expedia booking engine – without the customer even realizing that they are using Expedia. This is called a 'white label' service. The benefit to the affiliate is low-cost access to Expedia's network and the benefit to Expedia is additional revenue from the booking transaction fees.

The affiliate marketing model has grown exponentially and there are thousands and thousands of potential affiliates for hospitality principals. This has spawned the growth of affiliate marketing agencies who manage affiliate networks on behalf of major distributors and principals by linking principals and affiliates, organizing contracts, measuring traffic and performance, and collecting payments. Commission Junction, based in California, is one of the global leaders in affiliate marketing – have a look at their website: http://www.cj.com for more information.

Tourist board

Local and national tourist boards are often described as destination marketing organizations (DMO – see pages 178–179) and have an important role as an infomediary in tourism distribution channels. Most online tourist board sites provide hospitality product information with links and contact telephone numbers for visitors to make their own booking arrangements. The provision of online booking services has been inhibited due to the complexity of managing a large number of small tourism stakeholders who are unwilling to enter in to costly online distribution transactions. Some countries have legislation to prevent their tourist board from providing a booking service (e.g., Australia), although they can still provide very good information about hospitality products: see www.australia.com.

Airline

Although airlines are traditionally considered to be principals, some have developed a distribution business selling hospitality and other travel-related products through their online booking systems. Providing this online service to the airline's passengers helps the airline to give their passengers a one-stop shop for booking all their travel needs and reduces the need for customers to visit competitor sites. Indeed, for budget airlines, such as Southwest Airlines and Ryan Air, the revenue derived from commissions on the sale of hospitality products is a significant component of the airline's business model.

VERTICAL INTEGRATED MARKETING CHANNEL

A small number of international companies have become dominant players in both hospitality and travel by taking over or merging with competitors in the same sector (we discussed horizontal integration on pages 121–122), and/or by taking over or merging with customers and suppliers (vertical integration). The two largest global travel organizations are TUI and Thomas Cook. They effectively control all customer touch points in their proprietary distribution chain by owning the travel agent, tour operator, airline and hotel – this is called a vertically integrated marketing channel (VIMC). The advantages of a VIMC include the following:

- Coordination of all operational and marketing activity across all channel members
- Improved communication between channel members
- Reduction of channel conflict between the channel members, who are all working for the same company

- Cost savings through economies of scale
- Potentially superior customer service
- The opportunity to respond quickly to changes in the PESTE environment.

The main disadvantage for a dominant travel conglomerate is the threat from regulatory authorities (e.g., the European Commission and the UK Mergers and Monopolies Commission) over possible monopoly concerns and the lack of consumer choice. For customers, there are potential benefits in terms of a better coordinated holiday experience. Although the travel conglomerates own a range of travel agents, tour operators, charter airlines and hotel operations, customers are not always aware of this common ownership.

GLOBAL DISTRIBUTION SYSTEMS AND ONLINE DISTRIBUTION TECHNOLOGY

The origins of electronic distribution are the airlines' internal inventory systems developed in the 1950s and 1960s. The airline companies recognized that the installation of booking terminals in travel agents, with instant access, real-time availability, prices and reservations, would give their customers a better service. The system was cost-effective and efficient, and gradually more and more bookings for the airlines were sourced through travel agents. In the late 1970s, airlines developed GDS and encouraged travel agents to cross-sell complementary travel products such as hotels and car hire. Originally, there were four competing systems called Amadeus, Galileo, Sabre, and Worldspan. Today, the Galileo and Worldspan brands are both owned by Travelport, whereas Sabre is owned by Travelocity.

The GDS in hospitality and tourism are a network of large-scale computer reservation systems, which link principals to travel agents anywhere in the world. The GDS is described as a 'global travel supermarket', and provides travel agents with rapid search, booking and confirmation facilities for airline, hotel and car-hire products. In hospitality, links to the GDS is dependent on hotel property management systems (PMS) that provide computerized reservation systems (CRS) with full details of properties, locations, room types, availability, prices and booking conditions. To resolve the problem of connecting several different hotel companies' CRS to the original four GDS, a 'switch' mechanism was developed by two competitors – Thisco and Wizcom. The 'switch' mechanisms enabled each hotel CRS to connect with each of the GDS providers using a single interface, which enables all the travel agent intermediaries who are linked into the GDS to book hotels in seconds. In 2010, Pegasus who developed the Thisco switch bought Wizcom to become the only switch provider in the GDS. CRS and GDS technology works in conjunction with online and Internet networks to deliver search, booking and payment systems for hotel organizations. However, GDS are closed networks and the information is only available to the users – the principals and the travel agents. Many non-travel agent distributors and all end-user customers do not have access to the GDS. Also, intermediaries are very aware of their cost base and strive to reduce costs like GDS transaction charges when possible. So some companies prefer to use the Internet or extranets to provide connectivity between the various databases instead of GDS.

Although the Internet is an open network, which anyone can access, an intranet is a closed network for people working within the company. Extranets, which use Internet technology, provide a dedicated link between suppliers and customers. Hotel chains provide corporate account customers with access to their websites via a password-protected, dedicated extranet link. This allows a hotel group to give key account clients the opportunity to book online using privately negotiated, confidential prices.

Increasingly, hospitality distribution is conducted via mobile networks and applications that do not use GDS. Consumers download free applications to access hotel and restaurant booking services provided by either principals or intermediaries via General Packet Radio Services (GPRS) or Wi-Fi. InterContinental Hotels developed an app to enable Priority Club members to manage bookings for all their seven brands in partnership with Apple's iPhone. Michael Menis, vice president, Global Interactive Marketing, IHG stated:

> It's important to have a holistic view of a customer's needs when creating a mobile strategy and supporting applications. Customers want access to information whenever and wherever they want and mobile provides that capability. With this in mind we developed our iPhone app to complement our mobile strategy which includes our optimized mobile websites. These websites allow customers to reach us through various mobile devices giving them greater accessibility. This is particularly important as different regions of the world have different customer needs and smartphone adoption rates
>
> *(IHG Press Release 2010).*

CHANNELS OF DISTRIBUTION

By now, you should have an understanding of the many different categories of intermediaries in the hospitality and tourism industry. Our next task is to discuss how the channels of distribution link customers, travel and tourism intermediaries, and hospitality principals work and to explain the advantages and disadvantages to hospitality organizations of using distribution channels. Figure 8.1 provides a *simple* diagram of traditional hospitality distribution channels; each channel is described below.

Channel	Distribution system				Number of intermediaries
1. Direct marketing	Hospitality unit	→		Customer	0
2. Referral network	Individual hospitality unit	→	Branded outlets and C.R.S →	Customer	0
3. Retail networks	Individual hospitality units	→	Travel agent →	Customer	1
4. Wholesale network	Individual hospitality unit	→	Tour operator →	Customer	1
5. Wholesale network with travel agent as retailer	Individual hospitality unit →	Tour operator →	Travel agent →	Customer	2

Figure 8.1 Traditional hospitality and tourism distribution channels

Channel 1: Direct-to-customer

In the first channel, hospitality organizations and customers communicate directly with no intermediaries. This is called direct marketing. Principals use a combination of direct distribution methods, but primarily online reservations, to reach potential customers. Direct marketing is particularly effective when targeting repeat customers. Because there are no intermediaries taking a commission and no wholesalers managing the principal's inventory, this channel can be the most cost-effective and profitable distribution strategy.

Channel 2: Referral network

Hospitality chains and individual units, whether corporate-owned, franchised or members of a destination organization use every retail outlet to market the other properties in the network. No intermediaries are involved and, providing customers are satisfied with the hospitality offer, the 'referral network' is another cost-effective distribution channel. Hospitality chains also use their websites to promote and cross-sell units in the referral network. Customers can book directly for themselves online, at the unit (PMS), via the network's CRS, or by telephone.

Channel 3: Travel agent as intermediary

In tourism distribution, travel agents perform the role of a retailer stocking a range of hospitality and travel products online and/or in brochures. The travel agent advises customers, makes bookings, collects payments, and provides tickets and accommodation vouchers. The travel agent works on the customers' behalf and will take up customer complaints with the principals. In leisure and most business markets, the travel agent does not charge the customer for this service; instead, the principal pays commission to the travel agent. Over time the travel agent can develop a very close relationship with their regular customers on either a face-to-face or virtual basis.

Channel 4: Tour operator as intermediary

Tour operators are wholesalers. A tour operator negotiates bulk allocations of seats from charter airlines and bulk accommodation from hotels, and then develops a packaged product, which is marketed to consumers directly. The tour operator does not charge principals a commission; instead the tour operator agrees discounted prices with the principals and makes a profit by charging the customer an inclusive price for the package holiday.

Channel 5: Tour operator and travel agent as intermediaries

This channel is similar to channel 4, with one major exception: tour operators also use travel agents to promote and sell their all-inclusive travel products. In this situation, the tour operator has to pay the travel agent a commission for any bookings. When there are more intermediaries in the distribution channel there is a problem for the principals, because each intermediary needs to make a profit for the service they provide. This means that there are greater pressures on the principal to keep prices low.

Benefits and disadvantages of distribution channels

From a hospitality perspective, the benefits of using distribution channels include the following:

- Convenient global/local access points for customers away from the hospitality location
- The provision of relevant information and guidance to potential customers by knowledgeable travel experts
- The bundling of hospitality products into combined travel packages
- An advance reservation and payments system
- The opportunity to work with specialist intermediaries who understand the dynamics of their own markets.

The disadvantages for hospitality organizations using intermediaries include the following:

- The loss of margin paid to agents through commission;
- The loss of margin caused by adopting the merchant model of distribution – charging wholesalers (tour operators) low accommodation rates for volume business – and losing control of inventory at low rates;
- Losing control of a key element in the marketing mix (distribution), which can lead to an unhealthy dependence on intermediaries – for example, dominant tour operators can dictate pricing decisions to individually owned hotels in Mediterranean destinations

- Lack of trust between the managers of hospitality units and distributors, often caused by cultural differences that leads to non-disclosure of inventory information and inappropriate over-booking practices
- Intermediaries taking 'ownership of the customer' away from the hospitality organization

Online distribution from a hospitality perspective

The principles of distribution are largely the same whether the trans-action takes place in a travel agent's retail outlet, over the telephone or online. However, the online environment presents differences because:

- Consumers have access to information 24 hours each day, 7 days a week and every week of the year
- Consumers have fast, mobile interconnectivity to access online data either at home, in the office or on the move
- The speed of search and multiple sources of hospitality and tour-ism information from principals and a host of intermediaries give consumers a wide variety of instantaneous choices
- This means that there is a real-time product/price transparency between competing hospitality offers
- The transparency of prices and comparative shopping sites makes the online competitive environment more intense
- There is the potential to create confusion for consumers when the same hospitality offer is priced differently on the principal's site and different distributors' sites
- From the hospitality principal's perspective, the online environ-ment creates difficulties in maintaining product/rate hurdles to protect margins and yield (see Chapter 7)
- Fast, relatively safe booking and payment transactions facilitate online channel bookings
- Hospitality operators have the opportunity to move distressed inventory quickly via specialist online distributors.

The proliferation of online travel information and booking chan-nels means that a diagram similar to Fig. 8.1 that explains the mul-tiple networks linking customers, intermediaries and principals in the distribution system is complex and would look very messy. However, Fig. 8.2 tries to capture the picture of a fragmented online distribution system in hospitality and tourism using brands already mentioned in this chapter as examples of different categories of intermediary. As always, the most cost-effective distribution channel is direct from the customer to the hotel.

Three important issues about online hospitality distribution need further discussion: disintermediation/reintermediation, transparent pricing and search engine marketing.

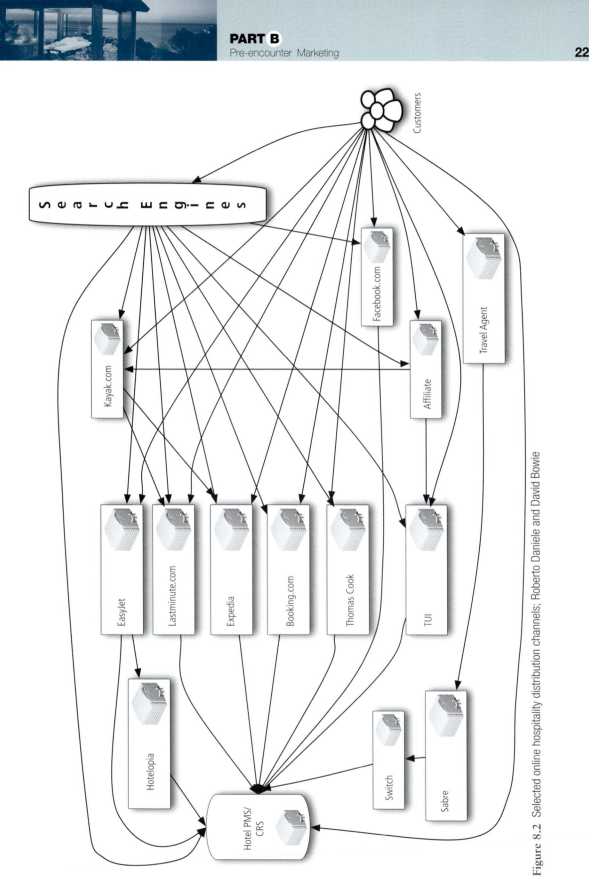

Figure 8.2 Selected online hospitality distribution channels; Roberto Daniele and David Bowie

Disintermediation and reintermediation

Originally, hospitality companies thought that the emergence of the Internet would eliminate the need for intermediaries, because end-user customers would book directly with principals via their websites. This process, which is described as disintermediation, would also eliminate the high commissions paid to intermediaries and other distribution costs. However, the Internet created opportunities for new travel e-intermediaries to emerge (such as Expedia and Lastminute.com) and existing players (such as Thomas Cook and TUI) quickly adopted the new technologies. The process of intermediaries re-establishing their influence in the online environment is called reintermediation. Today intermediaries continue to dominate hospitality and tourism distribution channels. However, both principals and distributors are continually looking for ways to manage their cost structures better, so the process of disintermediation and reintermediation is constantly evolving.

Transparent pricing

Consumers searching for hospitality offers online can easily compare products and prices, and this makes the prices *transparent*. The transparency of online prices presents hotels with multiple online distribution channels with a dilemma. Consumers can and do compare prices listed on a hotel website with prices for the same hotel on the websites of intermediaries. The intermediaries' prices can sometimes be lower than those published by the hotel on its own website. This creates confusion for consumers as well as a loss of revenue for the hotel company, because most consumers will choose to book a lower, commissionable price via an intermediary. The hotel companies have responded to this dilemma by offering 'Best Available Rates' (BAR) and guarantee that customers cannot find the same price, *with the same conditions*, offered on other websites (see pages 201–203). However, the conditions impose many restrictions such as 'blackout' dates (days when the BAR rates are not available); exclusions for negotiated rates for frequent guests, corporate, government and group rates; and rates available through online auction sites. Unfortunately, due to the large number of intermediaries and the complexity and number of rate deals, many hotels have difficulty in giving customers a genuine best available rate.

Search engine optimization

From an accommodation provider's perspective, effective online marketing is based on an understanding of how search engines work, recognizing the importance of destination links, developing accessible and easy-to-use websites and mobile applications, developing effective booking engines and controlling BAR through the distribution network. Numerous surveys confirm that users depend on search engines and directories when looking for information on the Internet. To capture the widest possible online audience, a site needs to ensure that the domain name, destination, text copy, page titles, description tag and Meta tags are designed to ensure that search engines and directories find the web pages. In general, the earlier (or higher on the page) and more frequently a site appears in the search results list, the more visitors it will receive from the search engine. Google is currently the dominant search engine and hospitality companies need to ensure that their website is ranked highly – preferably on the first page of the search results. For many hospitality operations, the location is a primary search item for potential customers, so links to destination sites, local and national tourist organizations, and local attractions are important.

Ensuring easy accessibility for Internet searchers is clearly important for the hospitality brand. It is interesting to note that smaller affiliates who provide significant volumes of bookings to hospitality operators either directly or via other channels are also reliant on optimizing their search engine effectiveness – this activity is known as search engine optimization (SEO). SEO is a specialist area of online marketing and companies, such as TravelCLICK, which provide consultancy services to help hotels. The website of the 41-bedroom three-star hotel Le Senat in Paris had been delisted from several major search engines and was underperforming. TravelCLICK diagnosed the problem, developed a new hotel website strategy, which regained the confidence of the search engines, and resulted in a 475 per cent increase in website traffic in one quarter. (http://www.travelclick-ims.com/seo/case-en.html, downloaded on 16 July 2010).

The costs of distribution

Each organization involved in the distribution channel needs to cover its costs and make a profit. A typical distribution channel for a hotel might include one or several of the following organizations:

- Search engine
- Affiliate
- Booking agent
- Travel agent
- Tour operator
- Travel search site
- GDS
- Switch company
- Hotel chain CRS
- Credit card company (since most reservations are confirmed using credit cards)

From a hotel property's perspective, fees or commission paid to intermediaries are deducted from the rate charged to the customer who is actually staying in the hotel. Independent and smaller hospitality companies pay higher commissions, GDS, Switch and credit card charges. The largest hotel companies can negotiate better deals from intermediaries due to the greater volume of booking transactions. It has been argued that distribution is the highest marketing cost for hotels but effective channel management should control distribution costs. Although the airlines have capped commission payments to travel agents and managed to significantly reduce commission rates, few hotel companies have successfully managed to challenge the payment systems to intermediaries – apart from some budget chains who are able to generate high occupancy without needing intermediaries. For hospitality providers, there is a constant imperative to drive down distribution costs. The online distribution system continues to evolve and hospitality companies have to constantly monitor the costs, volume and effectiveness of bookings generated through each channel. Hospitality companies do see the online environment as a means of reducing distribution costs and enabling direct communication with consumers and customers. However, as we have seen, the role of the intermediary is well established; the major tour operators and travel agents organize travel and accommodation for millions of tourists every year.

CONCLUSION

Innovations in ICT continue to drive the development of distribution channels in hospitality and tourism. The continual evolution of the online world – including the rapid development of social networking sites such as Facebook – will create new distribution channels in the future. Depending on the size of the business and the market segment targeted, accommodation providers need to use intermediaries to obtain advance bookings to generate occupancy, but the high cost of distribution forces hospitality companies to look for alternatives. The online environment is an important facilitator of hospitality distribution and can help hotels to reduce their distribution costs via direct booking. However, online search engines and intermediaries, well-known travel agents, and popular tour operators have a critical role as intermediaries for most hotels.

In this chapter, we have explained

- Various definitions of distribution in hospitality and travel
- The role of conventional and online travel and tourism intermediaries
- The role of the GDS, Switch, CRS, PMS and mobile technology in facilitating online accommodation bookings

- The benefits and disadvantages of distribution channels from a hospitality perspective
- The high cost of intermediary fees and booking charges for hotel companies.

Activity 8.2

The Hotel Electronic Distribution Network Association (HEDNA) is a not-for-profit association for international hotel executives and managers, many of whom work for the leading hotel companies. Browse to the HEDNA website and explore what is has to say about hotel distribution. http://www.hedna.org/

REVIEW QUESTIONS

Now check your understanding of this chapter by answering the following questions:

1 Discuss the role of distribution in the offline and online hospitality and tourism industry from a hotel company's perspective
2 Evaluate the relationship between hotel organizations and intermediaries
3 Who, if anyone, owns the customer – the hotel where the customer stays or the intermediary who makes the booking for the customer?

References and Further Reading

Buhalis, D., & Laws, E. (2001). *Tourism distribution channels: Practices, issues and transformations*. London, UK: Continuum.

Buhalis, D., & Law, R. (2008). Progress in information technology and tourism management: 20 years on and 10 years after the Internet – the state of eTourism research. *Tourism Management*, *29*(4), 609–623.

Cunill, O. M. (2006). *The growth strategies of hotel chains: Best business practices by leading companies*. New York, NY: Haworth Hospitality Press.

Daniele, R., & Frew, A. (2004). From intermediaries to market-makers: An analysis of the evolution of e-mediaries. In A. J. Frew (Ed.). *Proceedings of the Information and Communication Technologies in Tourism 2004* (pp. 546–557). New York, NY: Springer Wien.

Duffy, D. L. (2005). Affiliate marketing and its impact on e-commerce. *Journal of Consumer Marketing*, *22*, 161–613.

Duffey, D., Ellis-Chadwick, F., Johnston, K., & Mayer, R. (2006). *Internet marketing, strategy, implementation and practice* (3rd ed.). London, UK: Financial Times/Prentice Hall.

IHG Press Release. (*IHG Launches New Priority Club Rewards iPhone App; Complements Broader Global Mobile Strategy Currently Generating Over $1 Million per Month*. www.ihgplc.com2010, April 27, Retrieved from.

Middleton, V. T. C., & Clarke, J. (2001). *Marketing in travel and tourism*. Oxford, USA: Butterworth-Heinemann.

O'Connor, P., & Galvin, E. (2001). *Marketing in the digital age*. London, UK: Financial Times/Prentice Hall.

O'Connor, P., & Frew, A. J. (2002). The future of hotel e-distribution: Expert and industry perspectives. *Cornell Hotel & Restaurant Administration Quarterly*, *43*, 33–45.

Porter, M. E. (2001). Strategy and the Internet. *Harvard Business Review*, *79*, 62–79.

Reichheld, F. F., & Schefer, P. (2000). E-loyalty: Your secret weapon on the web. *Harvard Business Review*, *78*, 105–113.

Ryan, D., & Jones, C. (2009). *Understanding digital marketing: Marketing strategies for engaging the digital generation*. London, UK: Kogan Page.

Strauss, J., El-Ansary, A. J., & Frost, R. (2003). *E-Marketing* (3rd ed.). London, UK: Financial Times/Prentice Hall.

CHAPTER

9

Communicating the offer

Chapter objectives

After going through this chapter, you should be able to:

- Understand the primary role of marketing communication in communicating the hospitality offer
- Explain the marketing communication process
- Evaluate each element of the hospitality communication mix
- Understand the role of offline and online promotion
- Plan a marketing communication campaign.

INTRODUCTION

In the marketing mix, communicating the offer is variously known as promotion, the promotional mix, communication, the communication mix, customer communication or marketing communication. The public simply thinks of it – wrongly – as advertising and selling. As we made it clear in Chapter 1, there is much more to marketing than advertising and selling; it is also true that marketing communication encompasses more than advertising and selling. By now, you should be aware of the importance of each of the other elements of the marketing mix, and that effective marketing is dependent on marketing research, segmenting markets, understanding customers, designing hospitality products at the right price for appropriate target markets, finding the most suitable location(s) and using the distribution network to reach target markets.

Providing the pre-encounter marketing mix has been designed to provide an attractive offer, then communicating that offer should raise awareness, influence expectations and ultimately – through its influence on customer or consumer behaviour – increase sales and profits. However, sometimes companies think that marketing communication campaigns can compensate for deficiencies in other elements of the marketing mix. If the offer does not satisfy customers, then investing in marketing communications is a waste of resources, which can lead to serious problems with unhappy customers and negative word of mouth.

We stated in Chapter 8 that companies use the Internet to perform both marketing communication and distribution. Websites have dual purposes – they are both a vehicle for communications and a distribution tool. To help you develop a better understanding of the different roles that marketing communication and distribution play in the marketing mix, we discuss them in separate chapters. Remember the role of marketing communication is to influence demand, by communicating with target audiences and persuading potential customers to buy your company's hospitality offer, whereas distribution focuses on helping customers to find information about products and to make purchasing easy.

In the past, companies aimed to control what was said about their products and brands by dominating communication channels with carefully planned messaging. Companies now realize that messaging control is impossible to achieve due to the sophistication of contemporary consumers and customers ability to access information from multiple sources including the online world. Today, customer communication takes the form of bilateral dialogue. In online communications business-to-customer or business-to-consumer communication is known as b2c. Customers also communicate with companies, this is known as c2b communication. Customers communicate face-to-face, by phone, email, text, webform and in other ways. We have also seen the emergence of powerful consumer-to-consumer (c2c) communication, which is particularly evident online in blogs, discussion forums, comparison travel shopping websites and social network communities such as Facebook and Twitter. It is clear that companies no longer control product, brand and corporate messaging, and this creates challenges in promoting a product, or protecting a marketing asset (such as a brand) from negative sentiment.

We now discuss the role of marketing communication and review the different elements of the marketing communication mix.

Activity 9.1

Before reading the rest of the chapter, think of how you first heard about a tourism destination or hospitality product which you have already experienced or want to experience:

- Was it a word of mouth recommendation from family and friends?
- Was it reading an advert either online or in a newspaper/ magazine?
- Was it listening/viewing an advert on the radio or television?
- Was it hearing/reading/viewing a news item?

When you have finished the chapter, we will explore these questions again.

THE ROLE OF MARKETING COMMUNICATION

The goal of most marketing communications, both online and offline, is to influence customer demand. To do so, marketing communications need to raise the target audience's awareness of the hospitality brand and help form their expectations of the hospitality experience. Marketing communications' end goal can be achieved in different ways, depending on the characteristics of the target audience and their knowledge of hospitality companies' brands and products. There are three main communication strategies – to inform, to persuade and to build relationships with target audiences.

Inform communication strategies

Companies need to ensure that potential customers are aware of their marketing offer. This is partly about building brand awareness and partly about developing product knowledge – both of these help the prospective customer to form expectations. Awareness of the major hospitality brands is continually researched in company marketing research and omnibus surveys. For companies with low brand awareness, a typical marketing communication objective is to raise brand awareness so that more potential customers will learn and recognize the brand name. Companies also need to ensure that target audiences understand what the marketing offer represents. Companies that have successfully communicated their marketing offer to target audiences develop more positive, strategically desirable, reputations. A company with a poorer reputation may not have conveyed an appropriate message in its marketing communication activities. However, trying to change consumers' beliefs about, and attitudes towards, a brand is a very complex task, particularly when these beliefs and attitudes are deeply held.

Persuade communication strategies

Consumers who are brand aware and have a favourable perception of the brand still need to be persuaded to buy the company's hospitality product. We have already discussed how consumers have choice and that there are many types of different competitors vying for consumers' disposable income. Hospitality marketers, therefore, need to persuade target audiences to buy their product instead of the competitors' offer. Marketers strive to stimulate buyer behaviour by offering attractive inducements and incentives to book now – often using telephone (fixed or mobile), email and website – rather than later, or never at all.

Relationship communication strategies

We have emphasized that most hospitality companies want to build long-term relationships with targeted customers. Generating repeat and referral sales is crucial in most hospitality markets. Major hospitality companies use a combination of online and offline communication strategies to communicate with members of their loyalty club and recent guests. Customer databases hold useful, relevant, customer information (club membership details, email and postal addresses and frequency of stay), which enable companies with the right sort of technology to run automated marketing communications. The right sort of technology is a customer relationship management (CRM) application called *campaign management*. Smaller hospitality companies also compile lists of their customers to send out emails and direct mail by post. Both approaches can be effective in building closer relationships with customers.

Throughout this discussion, we have been using the expression 'target audience'. The starting point for any communications activity is to establish who the target audience is. In hospitality, the target audience is typically end-users, intermediaries or other key people in the decision-making unit. Each of these different target audiences has different characteristics, different information needs, is exposed to different media, and therefore different communication channels and messaging strategies need to be used to reach each audience.

For end-users, marketing communications might be used to raise awareness about the recruitment of a new celebrity chef or promote a low season product/price offer; for intermediaries, marketing communications might be used to promote a brand relaunch following refurbishment or to encourge travel agents to book a familiarization visit.

Much end-user communication is intended to create awareness or stimulate demand, and in doing so, it influences customer expectations. This creates a dilemma for campaign managers. Companies' marketing communication activity must attract the target audiences' attention, stimulate interest and, most importantly, move them towards purchase, without over-promising what can really be delivered. Unfortunately, because of competitive pressures some hospitality marketing communication campaigns exaggerate the quality of the promised service and raise customers' expectations beyond what can be delivered. Customers who book in good faith, believing the promise, end up being disappointed when they actually experience the hospitality service. Many ordinary restaurants make exaggerated claims about the quality of their cooking, which then disappoints discerning customers.

THE MARKETING COMMUNICATION PROCESS

Ultimately, the goal of most marketing communications is to move target markets towards purchase of the hospitality product. However, this goal is not as simple as it sounds, because consumers in modern societies are bombarded with thousands of competing messages from hundreds of different sources every day. We call this interference 'noise', and noise disrupts a company's communication with potential customers. Figure 9.1 provides a simple model of the communication process, and features the hospitality organization as the sender. The model comprises the sender, a target audience (or receiver), noise in the communication environment, message, medium and feedback process.

- The *sender* is the hospitality organization that wants to communicate with a target audience
- The *target audience* (receiver) consists of the end-users, influencers, decision-makers, gatekeepers or intermediaries. The target audience must be precisely defined to ensure that the marketing communication reaches the right people cost effectively
- *Noise* comprises all the communications from other sources, including both people and organizations, which compete for the target audience's attention and interfere with the sender's message
- The *message* is the content that the sender wants to communicate to the target audience
- The *media* are the various communication channels that senders can use to communicate with target audiences. Channels include

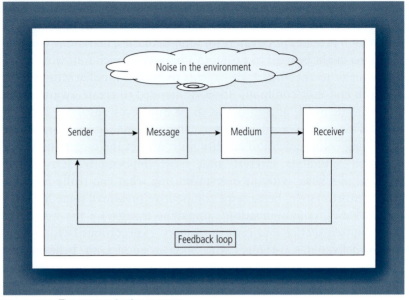

Figure 9.1 The communication process

personal communication (such as sales visits) and non-personal communication (websites, brochures, point-of-sale, advertisements in offline and online media and public relations (PR) activity)

• *Feedback* from the audience tells the sender whether the communication objectives have been achieved.

As noted earlier, the goal of much marketing communication aimed at the end user is to move the receiver (audience) towards purchase. Many marketers have made use of a framework called AIDA to ensure that the messaging decisions do move audiences towards purchase. AIDA stands for:

• Attention – the message should grab the target audience's attention
• Interest – the message should arouse the target audience's interest
• Desire – the message should stimulate desire so that the target audience wants to experience the product
• Action – the message should encourage the target audience actually to take action now, such as call a reservation number, jump on a website or make a booking.

Sometimes marketers try to achieve all four AIDA outcomes in a single communication; often they fail. Moving potential customers down the AIDA pathway may involve a number of different campaigns in different media, over time, employing different messaging strategies for each step on the AIDA pathway. Different communication tools may be needed at each stage of AIDA – for example, advertising might be used to stimulate attention and sales promotions to generate action.

Before constructing messages and choosing communication tools, marketers need to be clear about their communication objectives.

These will be derived from the three core communication strategies we describe above, and may even be informed by the AIDA model. Generally, these can be split into three categories. Communicators want their targeted receivers to learn, feel or do something. Examples include:

- Learn: raise awareness of a new product launch; recall the brand name and recognize the company logo
- Feel: develop a positive attitude to the company; prefer the brand to competitors
- Do: visit the website; telephone the call center and make a booking.

Messages need to be constructed so that they achieve the specified communication objectives. In devising the message, marketers have to decide what to say (message content) and how to say it (message format). This equally applies to the online environment as well as offline.

Message content

The message content depends first on the objectives of the campaign and then on the characteristics of the target audience and their knowledge and understanding of the hospitality product. A campaign for a new brand will most likely stress information that builds awareness and influences expectations – for example, the brand name, location and a description of the customer experience. For an established brand aiming to fill demand in the low season, the focus will be on price and availability. Audiences who are already aware ('Attention' in the AIDA model) are at a more advanced stage of readiness to buy. Message content for them can be more attuned to interest, desire and action outcomes. Different members of the decision-making unit may be at different AIDA stages, and therefore need different messages.

The marketer then needs to decide what type of appeal to use in the message – rational, emotional or moral.

- *Rational messages* appeal to the target audience's practical mind-set. This approach is effective in markets, where the end-user has a set of tangible requirements. A rational message can provide the factual answers, which reassures the audience: 'Just 50 meters from the beach' to reassure holidaymakers; and 'Close to the airport, but quiet' to reassure corporate markets. Online 'great value' price offers often appeal in part to the rational consumer.
- *Emotional messages* are explicitly designed to arouse consumers' passions, interests and activity. This approach is often effective in dining out and leisure markets. Appeals to book a table for two in a restaurant on Valentine's Day, or to take a relaxing weekend leisure break, are popular examples of emotional messages in hospitality.

- *Moral messages* are linked to consumers' belief and value systems. There are a number of religious organizations that arrange holidays for members of their faith, and some faiths have even bought their own properties to cater for their members. These organizations, which provide dedicated facilities for their fellow believers, still need to carry out marketing communication activities, and their moral message is essentially a spiritual one. Restaurants that promote non-genetically modified or organic food appeal to consumers' core values.

Marketing insight 9.1 Creativity in marketing!

Creativity is an essential ingredient for the professional marketer. Creative thinking uses a combination of situation analysis and thinking outside-the-box to create campaign ideas, which capture the imagination of the target audience. The creative element can be copy or design-led; in a creative treatment of a graphic, still photograph, television or video; a phrase or strapline; the use of humour and an unusual treatment of a mundane topic. Sometimes the wackiest ideas work and other times the creativity can badly misfire. It is best to test the more creative ideas with focus groups representing the target audience to ensure that the message works.

Can you think of any really creative adverts that you liked? What did you like about the advert? Did you tell your friends about the advert?

Message format

Messages are received using one or more of our five senses – sight, sound, smell, taste and touch. Message format depends on the choice of communication channels, and refers to the actual design or configuration of the website, advertisement, brochure, press release, sales promotion, PR activity and/or sales visits. Creativity is essential in message formatting in order to create cut-through, that is, to stand out from all competing messages. Website-related considerations include page layout, text, visuals, embedded audio or video files, links to external sites, opportunities for interactivity and visitor engagement; and crucially, ease of navigation and simple-to-use e-commerce functionality so that potential buyers are able to book when they want. For print advertisements and brochures, important considerations are size, shape, layout, copy and illustrations; for publicity, important considerations are the gimmick or storyline that creates interest. Other format considerations include food samples or aromas from the restaurant and the design of the hotel's conference laptop presentation. Attention to detail in designing the appropriate message format is time-consuming, relatively expensive and crucial.

COMMUNICATION CHANNELS

There are two main classes of communication channels: personal and non-personal. Personal communication refers to people who are directly talking to each other, face-to-face in a meeting, or on the telephone or via PC/video-conferencing. It can also include personal interactions by email, text, web collaboration, fax or mail. The advantages of personal communication are primarily the personal interaction that such communication allows. By directly talking with customers and influencers, the hospitality organization creates the opportunity for a dialogue so that the customer can ask questions about the hospitality company's brands and products, and the company can find out more about customer needs and wants.

Non-personal communication channels refer to mediated and publicity events and include all online and offline print, broadcast and display tools. The main differences between using personal and non-personal communication channels is that the latter do not permit personalized interaction, and so they are not guaranteed to capture the attention and respond to the specific concerns of the target audience. The design and production of mediated communications require support from specialist suppliers like design companies, advertising agencies, print companies and PR agencies. These agencies offer creative expertise in copywriting, graphics, photography, radio, television and online advertising and nurture useful contacts in the media for publicity purposes. They provide important advice and a professional service in delivering a marketing communication campaign.

The hospitality communications mix

Figure 9.2 presents the key communication tools used by hospitality companies, and each of these marketing communication tools is discussed here in more detail. In small hospitality businesses, the owner/manager will typically be very involved with the planning and implementation of all marketing communication activity. The owner's control over these activities should ensure that the promotional

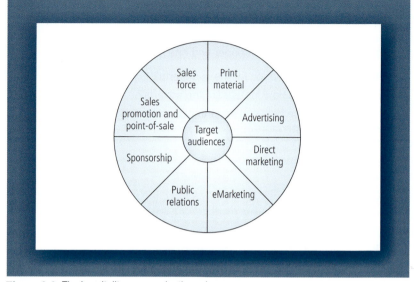

Figure 9.2 The hospitality communication mix

campaigns are coordinated and integrated. This is important, to ensure that a consistent message is always communicated to the target audience. In this sense, smaller hospitality companies do have an advantage over their larger rivals.

Probably, the most critical communication tool for hospitality marketers is not mentioned in Figure 9.2. *Word of mouth recommendation* (WOM) by family and friends is the most cost-effective marketing activity. We do not discuss WOM in this chapter because most companies do not fund and manage WOM in the same way as the other elements of the communications mix. We do however discuss word of mouth recommendation again in Chapter 13.

Integrated marketing communications

The global hospitality giants, such as McDonald's, Burger King, Accor, Hilton, Marriott and IHG, invest billions of dollars, euros, pounds and yen in promoting their products and brands to millions of customers in different target audiences around the world. This creates enormous marketing communication and organizational difficulties. Cultural differences and regulation in different countries are the major barriers to effective marketing communication.

First, there is the issue of language. Some languages need more copy space than other languages – for example, written French and Italian need up to 25 per cent more space than written English, whereas written German and Scandinavian languages need up to 30 per cent more. This creates different page layout requirements from a visual design perspective. Translating an advertising message can present problems, especially if humour is involved. Humour often involves a play on words, which may not convey the same meaning in a second language.

Second, there is the issue of cultural symbolism. Not only words, but colours, gender roles, behaviours, artefacts and symbols vary in meaning between cultures, resulting in consumers making different interpretations of the same communication. Finally, there is the problem of different governmental approaches to regulating marketing communication activity. Not only do voluntary codes vary between countries but so do legislative and regulatory controls. Different legislations impose restrictions on advertising, selling, telemarketing, sales promotion and publicity. Even a relatively simple pan-European sales promotion targeting families with children can be difficult to implement because of the different national government restrictions on promotions to young people.

Major hospitality organizations employ their own marketing specialists working in website and online marketing, sales, sales promotion, PR and advertising in their national, regional and international offices. They also have to work with external advertising, PR and design agencies in several countries. With so many marketing communication specialists working on a range of campaigns, but all involved in delivering the global company's branded message, it is easy to see how difficult it is to maintain consistent message. The concept of integrated marketing communications is the response to this confused approach to organizing the international marketing communication function. Major international advertising agencies like Leo Burnett and WPP provide a global one-stop shop for all the marketing communication services that a global client needs, and provide an integrated service for international campaigns. Whether a hospitality corporation uses a global one-stop shop or continues to use specialist agencies and their own in-house marketing specialists, the important point is that effective international marketing communication campaigns need to be coordinated across all countries, and all elements of the marketing communication mix, to provide a consistent branded message to the target audiences.

Projecting the brand image

The quality and design of all communications material have to reflect and project the desired brand positioning to target audiences. The use of colour, photographs and graphic design, the style of copywriting and the quality of materials used influence consumers' perception of the hospitality brand. Online and offline marketing collateral (collateral is the term used to describe all the print materials designed to support the sales function) need to complement each other to project a consistent brand position.

Intranet technology has enabled the hospitality chains to develop intranet solutions to the problem of delivering brand-consistent marketing communications collateral across all the units in the company. The brand manual and brand standards are provided on the intranet in digital format, with standardized sizes and layouts for logos, brand identities, adverts, print material and signage. Some also include a searchable database of marketing assets including photographs, marketing campaigns and press releases to help support current marketing activity in the online brand library. Links are provided to external suppliers such as advertising agencies, designers and printers like Kall Kwik, which has local printing shops in many key locations. A unit planning to develop a marketing communications campaign can access the intranet and customize the promotional material, inputting the menus, prices, dates and address/contact details. The artwork is sent electronically to the corporate head office for approval, which is much quicker than relying on snail mail. Once approved, the artwork can then be sent to the commercial printers, also online. This use of technology is cost-effective and allows the corporate head office much greater control in delivering consistent brand standards in marketing communications materials.

Case study 9.1 Integrated distribution and marketing communication at IHG

With 4500 hotels badged under seven brands operating in over 100 countries and accommodating 160 million guest nights each year, IHG has developed a global approach to integrating distribution and marketing communications.

Called 'Holidex', the IHG system comprises brand management, channel management, sales and reservations and – *with 50 million members* – the largest hotel loyalty club in the world.

The brands are marketed on a global and regional basis using a US$ 1 billion fund raised by charging each hotel 2% of rooms' revenue. Branding decisions are strategic and set by the IHG head office. For example, the design of the IHG strapline 'Great Hotels Guests Love', which is set in a red heart, was a strategic decision. Each country has its own tactical national marketing and PR, whereas direct guest marketing is driven through the Priority Club Rewards program.

Like all hotel groups, IHG aim to drive reservations direct to their websites (the IHG web presence includes 13 local languages) and via their dedicated call centers. However, IHG recognize that Third Party Internet (TPI) channels cannot be ignored and therefore IHG negotiate better commission rates for their franchisees. There are over 2000 reservation agents working in 12 call centers around the globe providing reservation services in at least 26 different languages.

The sales force comprises 8000 sales professionals operating from local hotels, local market area sales teams, with key account managers and directors working in regional sales centers. Global account directors build relationships with the largest international corporate clients who often work in the banking, finance and IT sectors.

The IHG approach to marketing their seven brands provides an interesting insight to the scale and complexity of international hospitality distribution and communication activities.

Source: IHG

Providing information

Both online and offline marketing communications need to provide accurate, essential and useful information, which helps the customer to easily find out what they want to know. Specialist collateral is required for specific products including:

- Menus and wine lists
- Conference brochures
- Wedding brochures
- Function menus
- Leisure break products (e.g. walking weekends).

Customers interested in these products have specific information needs, for example, the conference organizer requires:

- Accurate location maps
- Information regarding the availability of car parking
- Conference/meeting room layout details, including the number of delegates who can be accommodated in boardroom, horseshoe and theatre-style layout; the width, length and height of meeting rooms; the location of light fittings and power points
- Information regarding air-conditioning facilities
- Details of the number of bedrooms and bedroom types suitable for delegates
- Menus
- Details of leisure and spa facilities
- Examples/testimonials from organizations who have recently used the conference facilities
- 24-hour delegate rates.

Online technology enables hospitality companies to provide high quality, more personalized and less obvious information, which appeals to target markets. The InterContinental Hotels brand was the first to introduce destination-specific concierge websites and videos for Priority Club Members. In these videos, the Head Concierge provides customers with interesting, unusual and vibrant commentary about places to visit, where to have a drink or eat out and what makes the destination special. In the videos, the Head Concierge actually visits the places they are recommending visitors to explore and introduces local characters who add their own comments to enrich the story. By using the Head Concierge in this role, InterContinental have exploited a natural and most appropriate voice to provide Club Members with interesting insights into the destination.

eMarketing

Please note that during most of this discussion we use the phrase online communications instead of eMarketing. The commercialization of the World Wide Web (WWW) in 1993 revolutionized communications for organizations and people. Current and future developments in ICT will continue to radically change the *way* we communicate. However, the theory of communications that we have just explained (the communication process, message content and message format) does remain relevant in eMarketing. The ICT industry has developed a number of communication and data processing devices including PC, laptop, iPad and handheld devices such as Blackberrys and mobile phones, which businesses and consumers use to access destination, travel and hospitality information online. Although most hospitality businesses have websites, the vast majority adopt a passive online marketing strategy due to a lack of financial, technological and human resources. A passive marketing strategy is typically a business follower strategy, where companies wait for market leaders to adopt and popularize an innovation. So at the moment, most hospitality companies provide a relatively basic website possibly linked to a booking engine to facilitate reservations, and an email address or webform to receive inbound enquiries. These websites provide essential information and are primarily a one-way communication tool with limited interactivity.

The larger, more professional hospitality companies and a small number of tech-savvy hospitality entrepreneurs who have access to appropriate resources can experiment with more innovative technological developments, invest in more sophisticated interactive communications and engage in proactive online marketing. Their websites are designed with more imagination, higher specifications, more graphics and better quality digitally enhanced photographs, greater use of video clips and greater interactivity. They can adopt the latest channels to engage with consumers and customers. Recently, social networking sites such as Facebook, Bebo, Twitter, and LinkedIn provide opportunities for companies and customers to interact. Future innovations will no doubt have a similar revolutionary impact and the major hospitality companies will strive to connect with consumers accordingly.

Viral marketing initiatives gain credibility and popularity via acceptance and circulation within social networks (see Marketing insight 9.2). The current use of ICT allows hospitality companies to communicate interactively with customers via email, SMS and applications such as iPhone apps. For example, luxury hotels can send guests a 'guest preference form', which the guest returns before staying: this helps the hotel to better prepare for the guest's stay (see Fig. 9.3). Hotel company directories can link information from satellite navigation systems (sat nav) so that customers can obtain easy-to-follow directions to the hotel they are staying in that night. This communication activity reinforces the brand's messages and helps to enhance service quality.

THE
EGERTON HOUSE
HOTEL

It's so good to know that we will have the pleasure of welcoming you to the Egerton House. If you have a few moments please fill in the form below and return it to us prior to your arrival as this will enable us to ensure your comfort and special requirements are all attended to. Our fax number is + 44 20 7584 6540, our email is bookeg@rchmail.com.

Your stay
Name & Additional Names:
Arrival Date: Arrival Time:

Travel
Could we organise a Bentley or Range Rover transfer from the airport for you?
(Heathrow £123 one way, Gatwick £177 one way)

Alternatively, could we organise a private chauffeured car transfer for you?
(Heathrow £75 one way, Gatwick £106 one way)

Flight Details: Flight Arrival Time: Airport:

May we organise a pre-paid underground & bus Oyster travel card for you?
(Please specify £10/£20/£50)

Would you like us to arrange your luggage to be collected anywhere in the World and delivered to the Hotel prior to your arrival without any hassle or stress *(We use the services of First Luggage www.firstluggage.com, charges apply).*

Your preferences

Foam pillow	yes / no	Neck support pillow	yes / no
A pre programmed iPod in the room	yes / no	Duvet-hypoallergenic filling	yes / no
Additional hangers	yes / no	Yoga Mat	yes / no
Mobile phone hire *(charges apply)*	yes / no	Lap top hire *(charges apply)*	yes / no
Dietary requirements	_____	Preferred fruit	_____
Preferred drink or cocktail	_____	Music/DVDs	_____
Hobbies/Interests	_____	Favourite colours	_____
Newspapers/Magazines	_____	Birthday/anniversary	_____
Special requirements	_____	Special occasion	_____

Spoil yourself

Box of chocolates	from £15.00	Basket of fresh fruit	from £15.00
Birthday or anniversary cake	from £30.00	Bouquet of flowers	from £35.00
Box of Ladurée macaroons	from £25.00	Personalised bathrobes	from £75.00

Bottle of Guy Cadel house Champagne £50.00   Bottle of Joseph Perrier Rose Champagne £75.00

Tasting of South African Bouchard Finlayson Wines served with Canapés   £35 per person
Martini Master-class with Antonio including certificate and Ice cold Martini   £20 per person

Luxury Penhaligon's Basket *(includes 5 200ml luxury essences, 100ml soap and exclusive lip-balm)*   £90.00
Romantic Turndown *(includes Scented Candles, Rose Petals, Strawberries dipped in chocolate and bottle of Champagne)*   £65.00

Please state how you would like to spoil yourself and specify the nights of your preference, A-for arrival, E-for every night of your stay or note the exact date: _____
_____

Figure 9.3 Guest preference form *Source: Red Carnation Hotels (2010)*

THE
EGERTON HOUSE
HOTEL

Wellness
Our clients will enjoy 20% off the prices for services at award winning Paul Edmonds Hair & Beauty on Brompton Road. Or we can arrange for in room hair & beauty treatments, our register includes numerous beauty therapists offering everything from facials to nail treatments:

_____
_____

Personal Trainer at the local LA fitness Platinum Health Club (£65 per hour):_____

Shopping
We can arrange for Personal shoppers with our friends at Burberry's, Missoni, Alfred Dunhill & Thomas Pink:
_____

Culinary Highlights
We would love you to dine with us, either in the luxurious surroundings of our Drawing Room or Dining Room.

Or why not reserve dining experiences at our award winning sister restaurants; Cheneston's, The Old Masters, The Library, Butlers or the Blue Door Bistro. For a more casual but fun and excellent night out, we recommend bbar. Our concierge will also be able to secure the best tables at London's top restaurants.

Date: _____ Time: _____ Number of guests: _____ Restaurant: _____
Date: _____ Time: _____ Number of guests: _____ Restaurant: _____

Would you like us to reserve a table in our Drawing Room for the Egerton's Traditional High tea?
(High Tea is £25.00 per person, Champagne High Tea is £34.50 per person)

Date: _____ Time: _____ Number of guests: _____

If there is anything else that we may be able to assist you with prior to your arrival, from theatre tickets, to fast track sight seeing trips and tours and tickets to London's newest exhibitions, please do contact us on 020 7589 2412 or bookeg@rchmail.com, alternatively you may wish to visit our website www.egertonhousehotel.com for further information.

We look forward to seeing you soon.

Yours sincerely,

Sandra Anido
General Manager

Figure 9.3 Cont'd

Marketing insight 9.2 IHG viral campaign

Two media consultancies, Mischief PR and VisualMedia, created a viral campaign to promote the IHG 'Get a Free Night' website to the media. The core idea was to build 'the world's four biggest beds in four different time zones – Shanghai, London, Paris and New York'. The beds were 45 feet long, 35 feet wide and 10 feet high. Professional trampoline performers started the 'bed jump' and then passers-by were encouraged to participate as well. Within seven days, 830 image and video clips were downloaded from the VisualMedia online image and video library by members of the media, and subsequently used in offline and online articles for their readers and viewers. The viral campaign was part of an integrated offline and online PR exercise, which generated significant media coverage in dozens of countries.

Source: New Media Knowledge (2009). Jumping Ahead: InterContinental Hotels Group's Latest Viral Campaign, NMK, May 19th

Print material

Hospitality units still need a wide range of print material, which is also described as collateral. Print material for individual hospitality units includes:

- Stationery
- Brochures, tariff and price lists
- Menus and wine lists
- Conference brochures
- Wedding brochures
- Function menus
- Promotional material for the sales team
- In-room information (hotel facilities and in-room service menus)
- Special product brochures
- Special price promotional flyers
- Newsletters.

Print material produced for branded chains includes:

- Corporate directory listing all branded units in the country, region or world
- Corporate leisure breaks brochure
- Corporate conference brochure
- Group business brochure targeting tour operators
- Corporate sales teams' sales support material
- Corporate newsletters
- Loyalty club leaflets, application forms and newsletters
- Special promotions.

Different types of print material provide different types of information and have different lengths of shelf life. Shelf life is the period of time for which the collateral material performs its communicative function. The design and production costs of a new full-colour brochure will be relatively high and, with reprints, will be expected to have a shelf life of several years. A leaflet promoting a single event for one day or night has a finite shelf life of a few months, and is relatively cheap to produce. Only general information should be provided in the long-life pieces of print, whereas price details that change more frequently need to be produced separately.

Case study 9.2 The importance of menu design

For restaurants, the most important marketing tool is the menu! Indeed, the menu expresses the brand personality of a restaurant and projects the brand promise. However, many menus fail to entice potential customers because of simple mistakes in menu design. The starting point in creating an effective menu design is to research competitor establishments. There is a logic to the menu design of different categories of restaurant. For example, family restaurants need an element of fun to attract children; gourmet restaurants need to present their menu in an elegant, sophisticated style.

Menus have to be easy to read. If the menu is handwritten, then it should be legible. If the menu is printed, then Mike Dempsey, a graphic design expert, suggests a minimum font size of 12. The menu structure should follow the typical order of drink and food items (appetizers, main meals and deserts) in a natural hierarchy. Effective menu design draws on the principles of newspaper and magazine layouts by using headlines, body text, illustrations and white space to break up the copy and make it easier on the eye. A criticism of many menus is the excess of copy – the descriptions of some menu items are too long and are not always intelligible. Prices need to be clearly labelled.

Dempsey suggests that since 'restaurants are about giving pleasure, menus should also convey the same emotions and work to convey the restaurant's personality'. In the competitive world of dining out, restaurants need to project a distinctive experience to encourage customers to return and tell their family and friends. A distinctive menu that not only conveys the information that the diner needs but also creates a unique talking point that creates a competitive marketing advantage for that restaurant. Figure 9.4 provides an example of a distinctive menu from Langham's Brasserie.

Source: Lander, N. (2009). Beware the Small Print, Financial Times, April 25/26 Arts and Weekend, 4

Linking print material to other elements of the marketing communications mix

Print material is used to support a number of other marketing communication activities. The hotel or corporate sales team need print material when they are discussing potential client needs in sales visits away from the hotel premises. Although the major companies have computerized presentations available on CD-ROMs that are also streamable or downloadable via the Internet, many clients still want to be provided with print collateral to look at when the salesperson has left the meeting. There should be a mutually supportive relationship between print material and hospitality websites. Collateral can promote the website address and direct information seekers to the site, whereas the brochure can be downloaded from the website.

Advertisements in local and national print media are often restricted in space terms and are mainly used to stimulate consumer interest to visit the website and/or make a telephone call for further information (the last 'A' for Action in the AIDA model). The brochure, tariff and accompanying sales letter are designed to convert the inquiry into the booking. Another use of print material is in direct mail campaigns, often to members of the loyalty club and/or guests who have stayed before. The letter, newsletter and special promotion mailing are pieces of print material that form the core of direct mail activity.

Unfortunately, recipients throw a large number of brochures and leaflets away. There is also the problem for companies of the disposal of boxes of dated print material, as removal and disposal can be expensive in terms of freight haulage costs. The combined environmental costs of destroyed trees and waste disposal are significant. Wastage and high costs of producing high quality hospitality brochures, coupled with inaccurate target marketing, means that companies are always searching for more cost-effective solutions. Although the online environment has clearly changed marketing communication techniques, the prediction that online promotion will completely take over from print material is premature for all but a small number of independent operators Figure.

Sales force (personal selling)

Personal selling uses direct communication techniques to present information about the hospitality company to target markets, to move potential clients to action and to maintain relationships with customers. Although personal selling includes correspondence and telesales, the main focus in hospitality is face-to-face contact with potential clients by the sales force. Employing a salesperson is very expensive, with major costs including salary, commission and bonuses; travel and accommodation costs; professional presentation equipment; laptops with intranet access to demonstrate the company's products, locations and prices; CD-ROMs to leave with the client after a presentation and mobile/telephone charges and administrative support. Indeed, personal selling is the most expensive marketing communication activity available to hospitality companies, and for this reason most small hospitality companies do not employ salespeople. However, the outward-looking owner/manager can actually take on the sales role and actively promote the company to prospective clients.

STARTERS

SPINACH SOUFFLE & ANCHOVY SCE (GROUND FLOOR ONLY) 10.00
SOUP OF THE DAY 5.50
CAESAR SALAD 9.00
SMOKED SALMON WITH BROWN BREAD & BUTTER 12.50
LANGAN'S SEAFOOD SALAD 9.50
MEDITERRANEAN PRAWNS 1/2 DOZEN 16.50
CROUSTADE D'OEUFS DE CAILLE 9.50
PARMA HAM WITH MELON 8.50
FIELD MUSHROOMS WITH BACON & LANCASHIRE CHEESE 9.50
AVOCADO & PRAWN SALAD 9.50
TOMATO & MOZZARELLA SALAD 9.50
POTTED CRAB WITH GRANARY BREAD 12.50
* GOAT'S CHEESE TERRINE WITH PICKLED WALNUTS &
                    WATERCRESS SALAD 8.00
DUCK LIVER PATE WITH TOAST 6.00
CHILLED MELON 6.50
POACHED EGGS WITH HADDOCK, CREAM, SCE 9.00
CALVES LIVER SALAD WITH RED ONIONS 8.00
BLACK PUDDING WITH RED CABBAGE, MUSTARD
                            SAUCE 8.00

MAIN COURSES

GRILLED LEMON SOLE WITH PARSLEY BUTTER 17.50
LANGAN'S COD & CHIPS 17.00
GRILLED SCOTCH SIRLOIN STEAK WITH GARLIC BUTTER 21.50
LANGAN'S BANGERS & MASH, WHITE ONION SCE 16.00
STEAK HACHE, FRIED EGG & ONION RINGS 17.00
CALVES LIVER & BACON 19.00
GRILLED SCOTCH RIB OF BEEF WITH PROVENCAL TOMATOES,
    WATERCRESS, SALAD & CHIPS (FOR TWO) 43.00
COLD HAM & POTATO SALAD 15.00
BAKED HALIBUT WITH HERB CRUST, BUTTER SCE 19.00
GRILLED SWORDFISH, ROAST TOMATO, BASIL DRESSING 18.50
ROAST DUCK, SAGE & ONION STUFFING, APPLE SCE 19.00
SALMON & SPINACH FISHCAKE WITH PARSLEY SCE 17.50
TAGLIATELLE WITH MARINATED CHICKEN, SPINACH,
    OYSTER MUSHROOMS & CHERRY TOMATOES 16.50
BAKED WILD SEABASS WITH FRENCH BEANS, POTATOES,
    BLACK OLIVES, TOMATOES, SPRING ONIONS 19.50
ROAST MAIZE FED CHICKEN, THYME & PARSLEY STUFFING,
    BACON & BREAD SCE 18.00
ESCALOPE OF VEAL CORDON BLEU 18.50

SPECIALITIES

POT ROASTED SHANK OF LAMB WITH BUTTER NUT MASH,
                    ROSEMARY GRAVY 16.50
SPICED COUSCOUS & FOREST MUSHROOM, CAKE &
    GRILLED ASPARAGUS, CHILLI DRESSING 15.50
ROAST GROUSE WITH BACON, GAME, CHIPS, BREAD SCE
                    & GRAVY 23.00

VEGETABLES / SALADS

NEW POTATOES 2.50
MASHED POTATOES 2.50
MIXED OR GREEN SALAD 3.00
MUSHY PEAS 3.00
LEAF SPINACH 3.00
FRENCH BEANS 3.00
CARROTS 3.00
PAN FRIED COURGETTES WITH
    ROSEMARY 3.00

DESSERTS (8.50)

SELECTION OF SORBETS OR
    ICE-CREAM 4.50

LEMON POSSET WITH TUILLE
                BISCUITS
PLUM TART WITH SOUR CREAM
* MANCHESTER TART
* CHOCOLATE & HAZELNUT PARFAIT
* GREEK YOGHURT, HONEY &
    ROASTED ALMONDS
TREACLE TART WITH CUSTARD
    OR VANILLA ICE-CREAM
CREME BRULEE
APPLE & MIXED BERRIES CRUMBLE
SPOTTED DICK & CUSTARD
STRAWBERRY PAVLOVA
FRESH FRUIT SALAD & CREAM
CHOCOLATE BROWNIE WITH
    VANILLA ICE-CREAM

* CONTAIN NUTS

CHEESES (8.50)

CROPWELL BISHOP STILTON: MADE
WITH ORGANIC PASTEURISED MILK

TOMME DE SAVOIE: MADE FROM
UN-PASTEURISED COW'S MILK
FROM SAVOIE FRANCE

BRIE DE NANGIS: FRENCH
UN-PASTEURISED MILK
CHEESE

WEST COMBE CHEDDAR: WEST
COUNTRY FARMHOUSE CHEDDAR,
UN-PASTEURISED COW'S MILK

GOLDEN CROSS: UN-PASTEURISED
GOAT'S CHEESE FROM THE
ASHDOWN FOREST

DAILY SPECIALITIES

MONDAY:
PAN FRIED MEDALLIONS OF BEEF,
GREEN PEPPERCORN SCE 21.50

TUESDAY:
GRATIN OF CHICKEN, BACON, MUSHROOM
    & LEEK 16.50

WEDNESDAY:
FILET DE BOEUF EN CROUTE
    SCE MADERE 23.50

THURSDAY:
* ORIENTAL DUCK SALAD (STARTER) 8.50
PAN FRIED MEDALLIONS OF PORK
    WITH SPRING ONIONS, TOMATO, CHEESE
    & MUSTARD SCE 17.50

FRIDAY:
BRAISED BEEF IN BEER & ONIONS,
    SCALLION MASH 17.50

SATURDAY:
ROAST SIRLOIN OF BEEF, ROAST
    POTATOES & YORKSHIRE PUDDING 21.50
GRILLED SCOTCH FILLET STEAK,
    BEARNAISE SCE 23.50

VENETIAN ROOM TROLLEY

ROAST BEST END OF LAMB
WITH PROVENCAL HERBS 19.50

COFFEES

CAPPUCCINO 2.50
ESPRESSO 2.50
FILTER COFFEE 2.50
IRISH COFFEE 9.50
LIQUEUR COFFEE 9.50
TEAS 2.50

ALL PRICES INCLUDE VAT.
AN OPTIONAL 12.5% SERVICE
CHARGE WILL BE ADDED
TO THE BILL & DISTRIBUTED
TO ALL SERVICE STAFF.
ALL CHEQUES ARE ACCEPTED
TO THE LIMIT OF A SUPPORTING
CHEQUE GUARANTEE CARD

COVER CHARGE 1.50

WEEK OF THE 11TH OCTOBER 2010

Langans Brasserie - Stratton Street, Piccadilly. Telephone: 7491 8822

Figure 9.4 Langan's Brasserie menu *Source: Richard Shepherd (2010)*

WHITE WINES

1. HOUSE WHITE LANGAN'S SELECTION   17·50
2. 1/2 LITRE HOUSE 12% 14·00/BY THE GLASS 12% 175ML 7·00
3. MARQUES DE RISCAL RUEDA BLANCO SPAIN '09 21·00
4. PICPOUL DE PINET BEAUVIGNAC '09 23·00
5. PINOT GRIGIO TRENTINO ITALY '09 23·50
6. MUSCADET SEVRE-ET-MAINE SUR LIE
CHATEAU DU CLERAY '08 24·50
7. MACON-VILLAGES DOMAINE CHENEVIERE '08 24·75
8. BUITENVERWACHTING SAUVIGNON BLANC '09 26·50
BY THE GLASS 12·5% 175ML 7·50
9. COOPERS CREEK CHARDONNAY '09 26·50
BY THE GLASS 13·5% 175ML 7·50
10. ST VERAN CUVEE COQ D'OR '08   27·00
11. HUNTER'S MARLBOROUGH SAUVIGNON BLANC '09 N. ZEALAND 27·00
12. TERRA LAZARICA SAUVIGNON BLANC SERBIA '06 27·50
13. GAVI DI GAVI LA MEIRANA '09 ITALY 29·50
14. LANGAN'S CHABLIS LOUIS PETIT '08 32·50
15. SANCERRE LES BOFFANTS CHARLES DUPUY '08 35·50
16. MONTAGNY 1ER CRU ALAIN ROY '07 37·50
17. POUILLY FUME DOM GILLES CHOLLET '09 41·00
CHABLIS 1ER CRU FOURCHAUME '08 44·00
19. MEURSAULT VIEILLES VIGNES VINCENT GIRARDIN '07 65·00

CHAMPAGNES

46. MUMM CORDON ROUGE 55·00
47. PERRIER JOUET NV 55·00
48. TAITTINGER BRUT 55·00
49. MOET & CHANDON NV 60·00
50. BELLEFON CUVEE DES MOINES BRUT ROSE 60·00
BY THE GLASS 12·5% 12·00
51. TAITTINGER ROSE 60·00
52. BOLLINGER NV 65·00
53. LAURENT PERRIER ROSE NV 70·00
54. PERRIER JOUET BELLE EPOQUE '02 110·00
55. DOM PERIGNON '00 125·00

SPARKLING WINES

56. PROSECCO DI VALDOBBIADENE 27·00
57. BLANC DE BLANCS RESERVE FERE FRANCE 27·50
58. BALFOUR BRUT ROSE '04 63·00

A FINE WINE LIST IS AVAILABLE

WINES BY THE GLASS ARE ALSO AVAILABLE IN 125ML MEASURES ON REQUEST

RED WINES

20. HOUSE RED LANGAN'S SELECTION 17·50
21. 1/2 LITRE HOUSE 12% 14·00 /BY THE GLASS 12% 175ML 7·00
22. NORTON CABERNET SAUVIGNON ARGENTINA '09 19·75
BY THE GLASS 13·5% 7·50
23. SANTA RITA MERLOT '09 CHILE 20·50
BY THE GLASS 14% 175ML 7·50
24. VINA TORCIDA RIOJA '09 22·00
25. COTES-DU-RHONE ST ESPRIT DELAS '08 24·50
26. COOPERS CREEK HAWKES BAY MERLOT NEW ZEALAND '07 26·50
27. TERRA LAZARICA CABERNET SAUVIGNON SERBIA '07 27·50
28. FLEURIE CLOS DES QUATRE VENTS '09 29·75
29. HUNTERS MARLBOROUGH PINOT NOIR '08 NEW ZEALAND 30·50
30. RUPERT & ROTHSCHILD CLASSIQUE '08 SOUTH AFRICA 30·50
BY THE GLASS 14% 175ML 8·00
31. BOURGOGNE PINOT NOIR GIRARDIN '08 33·50
32. CHATEAUNEUF DU PAPE DOMAINE DU GRAND TINEL '05 34·50
33. RIOJA RESERVA CONDE DE VALDEMAR '04 35·50
34. CHIANTI PEPPOLI CLASSICO '07 38·00
35. CHATEAU DE GIRONVILLE HAUT MEDOC '03 38·00
36. DOMAINE CARNEROS AVANT GARDE PINOT NOIR '08 38·00
37. CHATEAU D'ANGLES A C LA CLAPE '06 39·00
38. CHATEAU LALANDE DE GRAVET GRAND CRU
ST EMILION '07 40·75
39. CHASSAGNE MONTRACHET LES CHENES COLIN '08 46·00
40. CHATEAU BELLEGRAVE PAUILLAC '06 58·50
41. MOULIN D'ANGLUDET MARGAUX '06 61·00
42. CHATEAU DE SALES POMEROL '02 66·00

ROSE WINES

43. LES QUATRE TOURS COTEAUX D'AIX-EN-PROVENCE '09 18·50
BY THE GLASS 12·5% 175ML 7·00
44. COTES DE PROVENCE '09 LES MAITRES VIGNERONS
DE ST TROPEZ 22·75
45. SANCERRE ROSE GITTON '07 35·50

DESSERT WINES

MUSCAT DE BEAUMES-DE-VENISE '08 ALC 15%
BY THE GLASS 100ML 8·00   BY THE BOTTLE 37·50
CHATEAU LA FLEUR SAUTERNES '06 1/2 BOTTLE 27·50
MISSION HILL RIESLING ICE WINE CANADA '03 1/2 BOTTLE 76·00

PORTS

	GLS 100ML	BOTTLE
VINTAGE PORT RAMOS PINTO ALC 20% '91	12·00	75·00
RUBY PORT RAMOS PINTO ALC 19·5%	7·00	45·00

BRANDIES 50ML

HENNESSY ***	9·50
MARC DE BOURGOGNE JULES BELIN	9·50
CALVADOS BOULARD	10·50
HINE VSOP FINE CHAMPAGNE	11·50
JANNEAU VSOP ARMAGNAC	11·50
MARTELL VSOP	11·50
COURVOISIER VSOP	11·50
MARTELL CORDON BLEU JP MARTELL	16·00
HENNESSY X.O	16·00
DELAMAIN PALE & DRY GRANDE CHAMPAGNE	16·00
REMY MARTIN FINE CHAMPAGNE X.O SPECIAL	16·00

MALT WHISKIES 50ML

CRAGGANMORE	40% 12 YEARS	9·50
GLENFIDDICH	12 YEARS	9·00
GLENKINCHIE	10 YEARS	9·00
GLENLIVET	12 YEARS	9·00
GLENMORANGIE	10 YEARS	9·00
MACALLAN	40% 10 YEARS	9·50
OBAN	43% 14 YEARS	9·50
LAGAVULIN	43% 16 YEARS	9·50
TALISKER	45·8% 10 YEARS	9·50
DALWHINNIE	43% 15 YEARS	9·50
PENDERYN	46% 12 YEARS	10·00

LIQUEURS 50ML

AMARETTO	28%	8·50
BAILEYS	17%	8·50
BENEDICTINE	40%	8·50
COINTREAU	40%	8·50
CREME DE MENTHE	25%	8·50
DRAMBUIE	40%	8·50
KUMMEL	39%	8·50
SAMBUCA	38%	8·50
TIA MARIA	20%	8·50
GRAPPA	40%	8·50
GRAND MARNIER	40%	8·50

GIN, VODKA, RUM & WHISKEY ARE ALSO AVAILABLE IN 25ML MEASURES ON REQUEST

" IF YOU REQUIRE AN ALTERNATIVE PLEASE ASK "

Figure 9.4 Cont'd

From a customer's perspective, low-risk and low involvement hospitality products do not really need a detailed personalized explanation in a face-to-face meeting. Budget hotels are relatively simple product purchases and budget brands do not therefore need to employ a sales force. However, more complicated or high value hospitality products – for example, major conference bookings from key corporate accounts and intermediaries who generate volume bookings – require more detailed discussions in face-to-face meetings. Prospective clients, who are often knowledgeable about the hospitality industry and are aware of the value of their booking, expect a salesperson to pitch for their business; and because of the high sales value, the competition will almost certainly want to talk to prospective clients as well. In sum, face-to-face selling is appropriate when:

- The product is complex or risky and needs detailed explanation
- The product specification can be adapted to suit the needs of the client
- The potential value of the sale is relatively high
- The price is negotiable
- The prospective clients, or intermediaries, can influence or make the decision to book business
- The prospective clients expect a sales visit
- Competitors are likely to pitch for the business.

In larger hospitality companies, responsibility for unit sales can rest with either the corporate sales organization or the unit. In the latter case, proactive general managers will join their hotel sales executives when meeting key accounts. Indeed, most medium and large hotels will employ at least one sales executive, unless this function is entirely managed by the head office.

The corporate sales team

We have frequently mentioned that the hospitality industry is extremely competitive, and all the major hospitality organizations use personal selling as an important competitive tool in servicing clients. Important clients are called 'key accounts', and potential clients are called 'prospects'. Selling is a professional art. Effective sales executives follow systematic procedures when organizing and conducting sales visits. The sales process includes:

- *Prospecting*: This refers to the search for prospective customers. It includes searching for new leads from local organizations and local companies, and finding existing and lapsed customers from the hotel's database. Prospects need to be qualified, which means checking that the contact has the authority and budget to buy. Salespeople can also check that the prospect is a good fit with existing customer segments.

- *Sales calls*: Hotel sales executives will occasionally turn up at a prospect's office unannounced, hoping to arrange a meeting by chance. This tactic is called 'cold calling' and can occasionally be effective. However, the most effective sales approach is to pre-book an appointment by telephone or email. This ensures that both the prospect and the sales executive do not waste valuable time. Often, sales executives will have to make several telephone calls before they can actually book a meeting date in the prospect's diary; and normally dozens of calls need to be made everyday to identify genuine prospects. Sales executives might need to meet a client several times and gradually build up a personal relationship before actually signing any business. Arranging sales meetings with existing clients is also an important function of the sales executive, in order to continue building a close relationship with the customer.

- *Relationship management*: Sales executives not only win new business but are also responsible for maintaining long-term profitable relationships with customers. Sales executives therefore have to have service accounts, deal with queries and complaints and be proactive in relationship maintenance. Keeping accurate records of contacts and sales opportunities are important tasks for salespeople and this is made easier through CRM software applications.

Occasionally, a sales force will organize a 'sales blitz'. This is a coordinated sales campaign using a large number of sales executives who work together to saturate a target geographic area, combining cold calling, telesales and pre-booked meetings with prospects and key accounts. Although a sales blitz is an effective tool, it requires a considerable amount of organization.

Prospective customers who want to book significant volumes of business will contact hotels directly and arrange to visit them. The hotel sales executives, the conference and banqueting manager or the duty manager will host the meeting, show the prospect the hotel's facilities and explain the services available. These visits are key opportunities to impress potential customers.

Personal selling is an important part of the marketing communication mix. The salesperson represents the unit and the brand and can be regarded as the human face of the company.

Advertising

Advertising is any paid-for mass communication in media owned by third parties. Although advertising reaches a wide audience, the proportion of readers, listeners and viewers who are potential customers can be relatively small. For this reason, advertising can be relatively expensive, and it is notoriously difficult to measure its effectiveness.

Although the advertiser does have control over the message content, message format and message source, there are legal, voluntary and social constraints that advertisers need to recognize. Most countries have legal restrictions on advertising, ranging from tight censorship controls in countries like Saudi Arabia to voluntary agreements like the British Code of Advertising Practice. These regulations are designed to ensure that adverts do not mislead consumers with inaccurate or dishonest claims. Advertisers need to recognize that inappropriate adverts that offend people's religious or cultural values can be extremely damaging to their product and company.

Most hospitality advertising is aimed at consumer and customer (business) markets, but occasionally a major company will communicate with other audiences (such as financial and political stakeholders) by advertising in the business and financial media. When there is a contested takeover battle, both companies will invest in advertising to influence the outcome. The following media can be used for advertising campaigns:

- Online media
- Newspapers
- Magazines
- Tourist board publications
- Guide books
- Broadcast media (radio, cinema and television)
- Outdoor media: billboards and posters
- Ambient media (buses, taxis, overground and underground trains, gas and petrol stations).

The decision as to which media are selected depends mainly on the campaign's marketing communication objectives, the audience the medium delivers, and the available budget. We will now discuss the advantages and disadvantages of the main advertising media.

Online advertising

As consumer access to the Internet has grown so has online advertising. All major hospitality companies utilize online advertising as part of their integrated communication strategy. Generalist advertising agencies or hotel specialists like TravelCLICK advise, create and place online adverts for hospitality companies. Campaigns are normally placed across a range of websites, as opposed to a single site to achieve a broader reach. Online advertising is often described as banner advertising, originally because the advert was placed in a box across the top of the web page. Banner adverts (more commonly known as pop-up ads) can be static, animated, interactive or interstitial (Chaffey, Ellis-Chadwick, Johnston, & Mayer, 2006). There are two ways in which the advertiser benefits from banner advertising; firstly, viewers are exposed either consciously or subconsciously to the brand's message and secondly, they can click on the banner advert to obtain more information, which might result in a sale. Each view is described as an impression (not a hit). The ratio of viewers seeking more information by clicking on the banner ad is called the 'clickthrough rate'. The costs of a banner campaign can be calculated on the frequency of impressions – called cost per impression or more often on the basis of cost per thousand impressions (CPM). Alternatively, the costs are based on the number of clickthroughs, which is called a PPC method. The PPC is regarded as a more cost-effective model because the advertiser only pays for the number of viewers who have actually registered an interest in the advert by clicking through for more information.

Newspapers

Newspaper advertising varies in cost according to:

- Circulation and readership – the number of copies sold and the number of readers per copy
- Geographic coverage – local, regional and national
- Audience profile – socio-economic profile, income and lifestyle
- Size of advert – larger adverts cost more; display adverts can use graphics such as line drawings or photographs, whereas classified advertising is copy only
- Colour – these are more expensive than monochrome ads
- Location of advert – where an advert is actually placed in the newspaper (front page, back page and requests for a specific spot are more expensive)
- Timing – Sunday is one of the most popular days to read newspapers, and so it is more expensive
- Number of adverts placed – a series of adverts booked at the same time can qualify for volume discounts.

The key point about newspaper advertising is the short shelf life. This means that yesterday's newspaper has old news; readers quickly throw out old newspapers and the adverts in them.

Magazines

Magazines have similar cost variables to newspapers, with two important differences. First, whilst newspapers have a broad readership, magazines focus on specialist subject areas and attract discrete, distinct readership profiles. Second, magazines have a longer shelf life; this means they can continue to generate responses months after the publication date. Magazines generally use higher quality paper and encourage full-page colour adverts to emphasize lifestyle advertising. Hotels and restaurants located in popular city destinations from Abu Dhabi to Zagreb can advertise in magazines like Time

Out, which target visiting tourists. Country hotels targeting leisure break consumers can advertise in specialist bird, gardening and walking magazines, whereas adverts aimed at the family market use appropriate imagery and text (see the Best Western magazine advert in Figure 9.5).

The international luxury hotel brands create brand image advertising campaigns primarily using colour magazines, such as in-flight airline magazines for business class users and the financial media (e.g. the *Financial Times* weekend edition), to project their brand personality. The Four Seasons Hotels' campaign targeted both business executive travellers and the family market using appropriate models in carefully staged leisure settings with the strap line 'what will you remember?' Park Hyatt adopted a more formal foyer setting with no people in the photograph and the line 'embrace the art of hospitality'. One and Only used a black and white shot of a couple having fun with wrap-around hammocks on a private deck in their Maldives Hotel using the phrase 'live the moment'. Radisson Edwardian adopted a more risqué, cartoon style 1920s pastiche of younger, mainly female customers partying in a bar. Shangri-La, mimicking their brand name's heritage, has photographs of couples in exotic locations sandwiched between the header 'HEAVEN' and the footer 'EARTH' with the strapline 'where will you find your Shangri-La?' Peninsula Hotels use photographs and brief storylines of their employees under the heading 'Portraits of Peninsula', and Mandarin Oriental uses a personality endorsement strategy with the simple strapline – 'He's a fan' or 'She's a fan'.

Activity 9.3

Log on to the Mandarin Oriental website (http://www.mandarinoriental. com). At the bottom of the home page, click on 'our fans' and find out why the different international celebrities have endorsed Mandarin Oriental.

Log on to the Time Out website (http://www.timeout.com/). At the bottom of the page, on the left-hand side, there is a section About Time Out – click on 'advertise with us'. Explore the different options hospitality companies have to advertise in Time Out.

Tourist board publications

Destination marketing organizations produce tourist board publications, which carry advertisements for and listings of accommodation, attractions, bars and restaurants and events taking place in the area. Potential visitors to the area contact the destination marketing organization to request information and are sent these brochures. For

We go to great lengths to make children feel welcome at our hotels

(At the Thornton Hall Hotel, Wirral, you can even read them Aesops fables on the way up to bed)

From the ground floor right up to the first floor, you can read the amazing Aesops fables as you walk up the main staircase of the hotel.

Captured forever on the 24 wooden carvings are the moral tales of one of the world's most renowned storytellers.

This is just one of the many charming stories waiting to be discovered at any of the 350 Best Western hotels across the UK. Every hotel is individually owned and managed and offers its own unique way of welcoming guests, so you can enjoy a truly refreshing stay. The one aspect that all Best Western hotels do have in common is their shared commitment to offering you the highest levels of quality and service. So, if you'd like to enjoy a stay where you're guaranteed a happy ending, why not book yourself into a Best Western hotel?

350 hotels across the UK • enjoy a refreshingly different stay • to find out more call 0845 072 0700

Figure 9.5 Magazine advert targeting the family market *Source: Best Western Hotels*

smaller accommodation businesses, for example, a farmhouse with bed and breakfast, Tourist Board publications provide one of the most effective promotional tools.

Guide books

Country and city guide books provide tourists with information about travel, where to stay, what to do/see, where to eat and local cultural/historical anecdotes in several different languages. They are published by a wide range of organizations and individuals. Popular guides include the motoring organizations (AAA and AA); Baedeker; Dorling Kindersley; Fodor; Lonely Planet; Rough Guide and Wallpaper. Printed guides have a very long shelf life. Some guides, like the motoring ones, will only accept advertising from hospitality organizations, which have been inspected and are listed in the guide; others will accept advertising from any source. Although there is a downward sales trend for many printed guides due to the rise of 'free' online travel, tourism and hospitality information, their brand names remain established. Most printed guides provide online facilities to download information in a variety of modes, and the development of smartphone apps and the iPad is encouraging the development of digital online travel guidebooks. Indeed, real-time mobile technology already provides hospitality businesses in some locations with the opportunity to advertise their offer to visitors; as take up of the technology increases, this type of advertising will become more prevalent.

Marketing insight 9.3 Hip Hotel guides

Herbert Ypma, the creator, copywriter and photographer of 14 Hip Hotel guides has sold over 2 million copies in 10 different languages. Although the hotels are hip in the sense that they are highly fashionable, Ypma also describes them as 'Highly Individual Places' to reflect the character and personality of the hotels he selects to feature in his guides. Ypma carries out extensive secondary online research to vet potential hotels prior to arranging a visit. He then plans to check in mid-afternoon, takes photos of the property and has an early dinner whilst he writes notes. In the morning, he takes more photos, breakfasts and checks out. The hotels provide him with complimentary accommodation, and Ypma's company pays for his food and extras. The entire production of each guide book (all the copy and photos, layout and design) is the work of Ypma.

400 hotels in over 35 different countries are included in the Hip guide books. The hotels do not pay to be listed, but Hip Hotels does provide an online booking service for a 10% commission. For the hotels, to be featured as a 'Hip Hotel' is an accolade. Babington House, Somerset, England stated 'being in Hip Hotels ups our customer base a lot'.

Source: Shoard, C. (2007). I have a lot of curiosity, Financial Times, June 23/24, Life and Arts, 3

Television

Television reaches mass audiences and is consequently the most expensive advertising medium. TV advertising costs include both origination costs (for producing the commercial), which can be significant and media costs for purchasing time. Media costs vary enormously depending on the length of a television commercial, the time it is broadcast and the program in which it is embedded. The norm for a TVC (television commercial) is 30 seconds, though slots vary from 10 seconds to several minutes. A prime spot during the evening news or in the middle of one of the most popular national program costs a significant sum of money, because these program attract peak audiences. An advert running during the 'graveyard shift' in the middle of the night on a local television channel is much cheaper because the audiences are so much smaller. The impact of television advertising can be diminished because viewers channel hop or leave the room during the commercial break. Some networks embed ads in banners that appear at the top, bottom or side of screen during programing to counter this behaviour. Effective television advertising requires significant budgets to afford the slots and frequency to generate brand name or message recall. Television advertising is appropriate for mass marketed products and for this reason the most significant hospitality advertisers on major television channels are the fast-food brands like McDonald's, Burger King, KFC and Wendy's. Although fast-food TV advertising is used to promote product-price offers, hotel companies also use TV for building brand awareness and enhancing brand image. Travel agents such as Thomas Cook have developed their own dedicated interactive television channels, which promote package holidays, cruises and destinations that can be booked by viewers as they watch the program.

Cinema

Cinema advertising has many similarities to TV advertising but is not as expensive. Generally, cinemas tend to attract a younger audience, typically aged between 18 and 30. The main hospitality advertisers on cinema are the fast-food chains and local restaurants. Production costs can be low because local advertisers simply use stock footage and overdub a relevant local soundtrack.

Radio

In recent years, radio has become a more popular advertising medium because the target audiences have become much more tightly defined. Different stations have clearly identified target audiences and formats such as Top 40, Classical Music, Talk, Sport, niche and retro-music.

Because of this, program hold the attention of the audience better than television. Radio advertising is not as expensive as television, and the cost of making radio commercials is considerably lower. Most local radio stations offer simple, low cost advertising production facilities to enable local advertisers to use this popular communication tool.

Sales promotion and point-of-sale

The primary role of sales promotion and point-of-sale material is to stimulate short-term or immediate sales. Virtually all hospitality organizations utilize these tools at new product launches (to attract trial purchase), during low and shoulder periods (to boost demand) or at customer contact points (to promote in-house offers). Effective sales promotions are designed well in advance. However, on occasions, when there is a sudden collapse in demand, the marketing department needs to respond quickly with a sales promotion campaign. Many sales promotions are bundled products offered at attractive prices, which offer enhanced value for the customer. The design and pricing of a hospitality packaged sales promotion must be:

- Carefully targeted and conformed with current marketing objectives – in particular, a sales promotion must be targeted at compatible target markets that will fit in with the existing customer mix
- Competitive, since competitors will probably have a similar demand pattern and will be planning their own sales promotion
- Properly costed – both the level of the discount and the promotional costs (print material, online and offline advertising and email/surface mail) must be calculated during the planning stage of the campaign; bookings from sales promotions are generally stimulated by an attractive discounted price, but the price must cover the costs of the campaign
- Consistent with the current market position and brand image
- Creative! The promotion needs to grab the interest and imagination of the target audience and encourage potential customers to respond quickly, so creativity in designing and publicizing the offer is essential to ensure that the sales promotion stands out from competitors
- Of a fixed time period that is long enough for the target audience to learn about the promotion and have time to book the offer, but not so long that there is little urgency for the customer to book.

Sales promotions that become the principle long-term marketing communication activity eventually become ineffective. Sales promotions lose their vitality, and over a longer period of time repeated price discounting can damage upmarket brands.

There are a number of issues to consider when planning a sales promotion. First, promotional price discounting can be particularly complicated. If two restaurants in the same product class are competing and one restaurant has a sales promotion offering 'Two meals for the price of one' (the equivalent of a 50 per cent discount), then the other restaurant cannot compete effectively with a 25 per cent discount voucher. Second, sales promotions do not necessarily generate customer loyalty. Indeed, bargain hunting customers are unlikely to remain loyal, as they will always be looking to patronize competitors with similar or better deals. Finally, the sales promotion should not be too attractive, because the company has to service the increased demand generated by a creative promotion cost-effectively. Examples of typical sales promotions include:

- Price discounts on accommodation, food, drink and leisure activities
- Added value promotions – bundling a range of hospitality products into a single price and package
- Discount vouchers and coupons.

Marketing insight 9.4 Baldwin's salmon and strawberries summer promotion

Pauline and David Baldwin created Sheffield's most successful banqueting operation at Baldwin's Omega. In the summer season, a 'Salmon and strawberries' sales promotion is publicized in-house and sent out to party organizers to stimulate sales on quiet nights. The literature is designed to make it easy for organizers to book either online or by telephone. This simple, cost-effective promotion has been working successfully for more than 30 years!

Point-of-sale material

Hospitality businesses use a variety of point-of-sale material to promote in-house products. Examples of point-of-sale material include calendars of events (see Figure 9.6), coupons, leaflets, menus and posters at the reception desk, in the lift, bedrooms, bars, restaurants and at leisure outlets. Point-of-sale material is usually a tangible piece of collateral that projects the image of the business and is noticed by customers. Many hospitality brands produce excellent point-of-sale material, but there are also many units with dated, tired collateral, and this sends out negative signals to customers.

Marketing insight 9.5 The Feversham Arms Hotel, North Yorkshire, England

Jill and Simon Rhatigan who own The Feversham Arms Hotel, North Yorkshire, England promote a calendar of events program for each season of the year. These midweek mostly lunchtime and sometimes evening events, target the local, affluent female market. The events include subjects such as health/beauty, fashion, home decorating and art, culture, literary, music topics. The formula is to provide a welcome drink, an interesting speaker who provides an entertaining discussion/ performance and a formal meal at an all-inclusive price. These events, promoted via the website (http://www.fevershamarmshotel.com) and in-house via print material, generate cost-effective publicity and positive word of mouth.

Belmont House Hotel

Dates

for your diary

JANUARY

Jamie's Bar
Champagne treats.
Live up to your New Year's resolutions.
Carpe Diem!! House champagnes at January sale prices! Delicious.

13th Cherry Restaurant
New menus, New prices, Better value.

20th Jamie's Bar
Jamie's new sandwich menu, out with the old and in with the new, except for old favourites of course.

25th Cherry Restaurant
Burns night supper in the Cherry Restaurant, with our own Head Chef, Stewart, adressing the Haggis! £24.95pp

31st Bowies
New monthly music nights start our first evening with local singer Lindsey Cowlishaw singing all her favourite classic pop songs. Book a table for a candlelight dinner and a relaxing evening. Dinner £15.00pp. Entry fee £1.50pp.

FEBRUARY

3rd Bowies
New menu!

Jamie's Bar
Jamies warms up the month with Claret. A selection of very special clarets available from £4 a glass, a real treat.

14th Valentine's Night
(or overnight!)
Choose from a delicious menu for 2 in **Cherry's Restaurant**, or be extravagant and book dinner and one of our lovely rooms. Or go down to **Bowies** and enjoy a romantic candlelight dinner with a hint of blues music playing. And if you can't make the 14th come on the 15th!
Cherrys £24.50pp
Overnight £130.00 including dinner, bed and breakfast for two, half a bottle of champagne and a rose.
Bowies £19.50pp

MARCH

2nd The Belmont Wedding Fair
A must for all brides, or even those just contemplating. A collection of dedicated suppliers there to help you with all those tough decisions. Hopefully you've already made the most important one and booked the Belmont... *(Well, OK, I suppose your partner could also be the most important decision.)*

Jamie's Bar
Jamie's Bar is going Australian, a few little wines from down under (is there such a thing as a little wine from down under!), and we might have a prawn or two off the barbie

21st Cherry Restaurant
Tonight is our FUN wine appreciation night in Cherrys. Come and enjoy a great meal with an intriguing selection of wines, the origins of which will be described to you by our experts...but are they telling the truth? Dinner including wine is all inclusive, really good value at £29.50

Jamie's Bar
Great coffee served from 8am weekday mornings. Coffee & Croissant or Danish £2.95
Choice of Teas and cakes £2.95

28th Bowies
Bowie's Jazz night, come and listen to our singer and the Sax player in the candle light.

> Don't forget Cherrys serves the best breakfast around and is a great way to get through your first meeting of the day.

10th-17th Cherry Restaurant
Lobster week in Cherrys, one or two special dishes of this most delicious of shellfish to titillate the palate.

28th Bowies
Bowie's monthly Music Night! Tonight we have Karaoke! Dinner £15.00pp

30th Cherry Restaurant
30th is a most important date, yes it's Mothering Sunday so book early and make sure you give her a great treat. Cherry's Restaurant will be serving its usual great food. £18.50pp 4 courses, coffee and a gift.

Figure 9.6 Point-of-sale collateral *Source: The Belmont Hotel*

Public relations

The focus of most PR is to generate positive publicity for the company in the media. Such publicity is generally regarded as 'free', because space and time are not bought as in advertising; although the design, effort, creativity and networking required to generate media coverage

are not cheap. Public relations (PR) is a profession with a structured career pathway and specialized education with formal examinations. Many countries have professional bodies representing their PR industry, which can provide useful information about career opportunities and professional development for students.

Marketing insight 9.6 Prêt-à-Portea, The Berkeley Hotel, Maybourne Hotels London

The Berkeley Hotel located in a fashionable part of London created a designer afternoon tea menu, called Prêt-à-Portea, which because of its innovative fun and exquisite cakes has generated over a million pounds of publicity worldwide. Conceived in 2005, the afternoon tea menu is inspired by the themes and colours of the fashion world. A team of leading international designers help the Head chef to select the current season's 'fashionista afternoon tea menu'. The design of the cakes is actually based on fashion apparel (fashionable boots, handbags, hats and shoes) and this stimulates the interest of the media. The cakes, served on Paul Smith china, are stunning and each designer gives her/his name to one of the cake designs. For example, the 'Christian Lacriox dark chocolate dress with soft center and chic golden bow'. Designers include Anya Hindmarch, Paul Smith, Yves Saint Laurent, Christopher Kane, Jean Paul Gaultier, Jason Wu, Sonia Rykiel and Erdem. The unusual feature of this PR campaign is that twice a year, a new 'seasonal' tea menu is presented to the media that still generates significant publicity at minimal costs.

Source: Maybourne Hotels (2010)

The major hospitality corporations employ PR managers in their national and international head offices. The corporate PR role includes managing publicity aimed at financial stakeholders and political bodies, crisis management (e.g. when a case of food poisoning is reported in the media) as well as promoting the parent company image and specific brands. Although the management of media relations at national and international level is clearly a role for the professional PR executive, individual hospitality owners and general managers can become adept at generating publicity for their own properties. The principles of effective PR are the same regardless of the scale of business. PR activity should

- Ensure that the proposition, or the publicity idea, is consistent with the brand's positioning and the current brand image. Some hoteliers are so keen to be in the news that they forget the purpose of PR activity, which is to generate positive publicity for the business. Inappropriate stunts can generate significant amounts of irrelevant or even negative publicity, which undermines the brand's position in the marketplace.
- Develop a creative concept that stimulates the media's imagination. Media journalists and their editors are well informed, very aware and frequently cynical. To capture their imagination, the

publicity concept needs to be different, interesting and, therefore, newsworthy.

- Make sure that press information is professionally presented and made available at the right time. Old news is not interesting. The tools that PR executives use include press releases, a press pack with all the relevant company information, photographs and arranging familiarization visits for journalists.
- PR activity needs 'stories' around which a publicity campaign can be created. Suitable stories include company news (e.g. new hotel/ restaurant openings, new product launches), events, new menus and special offers, winning accolades and awards and human interest stories about customers and employees.

Effective PR activity uses a wide range of different activities, events and human interest stories that generate brand awareness and raise brand image. Success is measured by print column inches and air time minutes, but the level of sales generated by PR is more difficult to calculate.

PR and crisis management

PR is especially important when a company experiences a newsworthy crisis. Unfortunately, events such as terrorism, natural weather disasters, food poisoning incidents, hotel fires and high-profile court cases involving customers or employees generate media interest, even though the company does not want this type of publicity. The role of PR during the crisis is to present the hospitality company's version of events as favourably as possible. Journalists are more likely to portray the crisis sympathetically if their questions are taken seriously. When a senior figure in the company acts as the spokesperson and answers the media's questions with open, honest and helpful information, the media are more likely to be supportive. However, investigative journalists and those working for sensationalist tabloids may be more difficult to handle. The major hospitality organizations develop crisis management protocols that are implemented in the event of a crisis; when an incident occurs it is easy for unit employees and managers to panic in the glare of the publicity and make inappropriate statements. Companies that respond effectively to a crisis can actually improve their image as a result of positive media publicity.

PR and destination marketing

A relatively new dimension in tourism PR activity is the active promotion of destinations, by destination marketing organizations, to film and television companies. The popularity of destinations that have been featured in successful film and television programing has

increased the number of visitors to these locations. The American entertainment industry has been a key attraction for tourists visiting Hollywood, Los Angeles and Orlando in Florida. Films such as the Harry Potter series and the Lord of the Rings have helped to promote tourism in Oxford, England and New Zealand. Today, destinations actively promote themselves as ideal locations for film and television productions in the hope that positive exposure will generate an increase in tourism.

Activity 9.3

Log onto the following websites of hospitality companies and look for media, press, press releases or press room (if you have difficulty finding the media/press pages use the site map):

- www.burgerking.com
- www.hiltonworldwide.com
- www.icehotel.com
- www.shangri-la.com

Review the latest press information – these are real press releases sent out by companies to the media to generate publicity. Evaluate the approach different companies take to creating stories, and the content, interest and writing style.

Sponsorship

Sponsorship is often used in conjunction with PR to obtain publicity. It is a major component in the financing of sports/arts/cultural activities and events. Football teams, tennis stars, golf tournaments, music festivals, art exhibitions and literary events depend on other organizations for financial support. Hospitality companies can either provide financial donations or complimentary services such as accommodation as part of a sponsorship arrangement in return for publicity. Sponsored activities promote the name of the sponsor on clothes, equipment, posters and vehicles during the event. The sponsorship can also become the focus of a marketing communications campaign. Indeed, key customers can be invited to the sponsored event and provided with VIP status and exclusive hospitality.

The cost of sponsorship is closely linked to the amount of media coverage generated. Obviously, the higher the sport's profile and the higher the profile of the celebrities, the more it costs. Major hospitality companies can afford to sponsor popular national and international events. Crowne Plaza has a long-term sponsorship agreement with Andy Priaulx, three times world touring car champion, which generates significant media coverage in a wide range of countries and enhances the brand's positive image. Small hospitality businesses can, with a modest amount of money, sponsor local community activities just as effectively; for example, by sponsoring a local children's football team and buying their strip (sportswear) to generate huge goodwill.

Direct marketing

Direct marketing (DM) is any form of direct-to-consumer communication, such as direct mail, door drops, SMS (text messaging) and email promotions. Usually DM aims to inform and persuade customers to respond to a particular offer. A key benefit of DM is that it cuts out the intermediaries and the commissions paid to them. This type of marketing communication activity remains popular with smaller hospitality businesses. Newsletters and seasonal greeting cards from small hotels, bed-and-breakfast houses and local restaurants are cost effective and help maintain customer relationships. The communications can be highly personalized, if somewhat quirky at times.

We have already mentioned how the cost of computers has fallen whereas the capacity and interconnectivity of computer systems has risen, and the impact of this ICT revolution has enabled major hospitality organizations to capture customer transaction data. The technology enables customer information and geo-demographic details from lifestyle databases to be analysed to improve targeted DM.

The process of DM in hotels involves use of the computer reservation system. Customer details from the front office are linked to customer transactions and accounts in the back office, to provide a database of customer activity. Companies with a sales force will keep records of existing accounts and potential prospects in their CRM system. Hospitality brands with millions of customers enrolled as members of their loyalty club sometimes outsource the management of this service to a specialist service provider, and this database will be located on another site. These different computer systems should be interconnected but for various reasons might not be. The process of computerizing hotels has evolved over a number of years, and different systems have been implemented at different times; even linking front and back offices took a long time for some companies to manage. The hotel groups that have grown through major acquisitions have also inherited different PMS, different CRS and even different technological hardware platforms, such as Internet booking systems. The cost of integrating such disparate systems is high but is essential if the company is going to have an effective DM system capable of drawing on customer-related data held in different databases.

Hotel groups store customer-related information in secure data warehouses, or data marts, away from the operational units. Information typically includes names, contact details, geo-demographic data, number of visits, purpose of visits, time of visits, average spend and personal comments – for example, birthdays, wedding anniversaries or the number and age of children. Data mining tools can search and analyse the data to identify current customer usage patterns and clusters of customer segments. It can then identify customers who are most likely to be interested in booking specific hospitality products, at specific times. This information can then be used as part of a more accurately targeted DM campaign, assuming that the customers have actually given their permission to be contacted.

In hospitality, DM generates better results in leisure markets where the products have low involvement characteristics and prices are relatively modest – for example, leisure weekends. DM is frequently used in hospitality new product launches, such as new restaurants. It can also be used when targeting specific business markets, like the conference market. However, if the products have high involvement characteristics, then DM often needs to include a follow-up by the sales force.

Indeed, DM can work effectively with all the other elements of marketing communication mix in an integrated campaign. DM is a powerful marketing communication tool for the following reasons:

- The company has complete control of the message, medium and timing of its delivery
- Customers and prospective customers are precisely targeted – this solves the traditional criticism of direct mail, which is that many recipients do not want to receive unsolicited mail
- The message can be more easily personalized
- The impact of the DM campaign has immediate results, and the costs and return from a DM campaign can be measured.

Finally, over time people's geo-demographic characteristics alter, and their lifestyle patterns change. The major criticism of DM is that customer-related data become dated. One estimate suggests that on average people move home at least once every 8 years, and many people move much more frequently. This means that databases needed to be 'cleaned' on a regular basis to ensure that people who have died or moved house are removed from them.

The role of marketing agencies

The marketing agency industry is a global one comprising a small number of global players, a large number of regional and national companies and many small local businesses – some with only one employee. Advertising agencies emerged in the mid-nineteenth century as salespeople who worked for the newspapers and magazines on a commission basis turned into professional advisers for their customers by creating, designing and planning campaigns for them. Today there is a wide range of specialist companies working in each of the different elements of online and offline marketing communications. These include specialists in advertising, PR, copywriting, media buying, merchandising, DM, photography and collateral. Online specialist interactive agencies provide web design and development, search engine marketing, search engine optimization, Internet advertising and PR services. There are also agencies that monitor and measure the effectiveness of marketing communication campaigns.

Although specialist agencies focus on one specific service, full service agencies provide:

- *Research* – including research into audience characteristics, campaign effectiveness and new media forms.
- *Creative services* – the design and production of advertising, publicity material, PR concepts and ideas. Creative planning is needed to make sure that the message cuts through and is heard and seen by the target audience. A creative brief summarizes the task, and the creative team will first brainstorm ideas and then develop those ideas into a storyboard that presents a visual interpretation of the message execution. Storyboards can be used to pre-test the effectiveness of the creative concept, by obtaining feedback from focus groups representing the target audience. Their response indicates whether changes in the basic idea or message execution are needed. Although an agency will be responsible for the creative planning, the client needs to be involved and has to give approval at key stages in this process.
- *Media planning* – selecting appropriate offline and online media, negotiating and buying the media space and time. Agencies have experience regarding which media are more effective to accomplish the task and can obtain better prices for clients because of their bulk buying power.

Agencies employ account executives, who are responsible for looking after individual clients and coordinating the agency's services to them. Traditionally, there are three ways in which agencies charge for their work:

1 *Commission*: Here, media owners pay agencies a commission for placing the client's business. The commission is approximately 15 per cent, but this is subject to negotiation. However, the system has been criticized because unscrupulous agents can place business with the media that pay the highest commission, which is not always in the client's best interest or spend more money buying media than is strictly necessary to achieve the campaign's objectives.
2 *Fee basis*: Here, the client pays the agency a fee for the work. This can be on a project basis, or, in the case of PR agencies, clients may pay a regular monthly/annual retainer to ensure that any publicity opportunities are captured as they happen.

3 *Payment by results*: Cost control and a quest for greater cost-effectiveness have produced a third alternative, payment by results. However, this is not as simple as it sounds, because measuring the outcomes of marketing communication campaigns and attributing sales to specific activities is notoriously difficult.

Although all three systems are possible, most agencies use a combination of commission and fee.

PLANNING THE MARKETING COMMUNICATION CAMPAIGN

The steps in developing a marketing communication campaign include setting objectives, setting the budget, defining the target audience, agreeing marketing communication strategies and tactics, implementation and measuring the results of the campaign.

Marketing communication objectives

As mentioned earlier, communication objectives can be classified into 'learn', 'feel' and 'do' categories. Marketing communication campaigns for most small hospitality companies are short-term and tactical. The marketing communication campaigns for the major hospitality companies however are usually part of a long-term, coordinated, planned and professional activity to support the company's marketing objectives. The starting point in planning a marketing communication campaign is setting objectives that support and are consistent with long-term marketing objectives. Most long-term communication objectives focus on the brand, rather than on particular products or experiences. Typically, brand owners want to ensure that the customers understand what the brand means and to develop favourable attitudes towards the brand. These are 'learn' and 'feel' objectives, respectively. We will discuss objectives in more detail in Chapter 15, but all objectives should be specific, measurable, achievable, realistic and set to a timetable. Examples of marketing communications objectives include

- *Learn* – a new product launch objective for a restaurant opening in September could be 'to generate 15 per cent awareness of the restaurant among the target market of ABC1 men and women, within a 15-minute drive-time radius of the site, by the end of October'.
- *Feel* – an objective for a conference hotel in an Adriatic tourism destination could be 'to become the destination's preferred conference hotel for Italian small and medium-sized professional associations within 2 years'.
- *Do* – an objective for a leisure hotel could be 'to generate a 25 per cent increase in domestic leisure break TPI bookings in the next 12-month period'.

Short-term marketing objectives employ tactical activities like sales promotions to drive bookings and sales.

Setting the marketing communication budget

There are four recognized ways of setting a marketing communication budget: affordable, percentage of sales, competitive parity and objective and task. The approach taken really depends on the size and ownership of the hospitality business and which sector a company operates in. Generally speaking, budgeting methods become more systematic as the business grows in complexity.

Affordable

Small hospitality operators, like the independent sandwich shop, the farmhouse with bed and breakfast and the wine bar, make promotional decisions on the basis of what is affordable. These entrepreneurial owners may respond opportunistically to media offers and make judgments on a trial and error basis. Financial forward planning is rarely a strength of such businesses, but prudent calculations and 'gut instinct' should keep the marketing communication budget within the bounds of common sense.

Percentage of sales

Historically, most hospitality businesses set their marketing budgets as a percentage of last year's or future projected sales. Over time, industries establish norms for marketing costs and expenditure patterns. In hospitality, this process is complicated by a lack of consensus about which budget line items count as marketing communications expenses. For example, the sales force can be budgeted as a payroll item or included in the marketing communication budget. Fees paid to a consortium group and ultimately used for marketing purposes might appear as a general administrative item in the budget. However, the major hotel companies, which use the Uniform System of Accounts for the Lodging Industry (USALI), have adopted an accounting standard for marketing that includes payroll costs. TRI Hospitality Consulting conduct an annual financial survey of 600 British hotels that establishes benchmarks for UK hospitality industry operating ratios. The typical investment in marketing communication budgets, stated as a percentage of total sales, are as follows (TRI HotStats, 2010):

Chain hotels	2.5–4 per cent (including marketing payroll costs)
Independent hotels	2–6 per cent, depending on the location and business mix

For example, an independent city hotel with a turnover of £ 1.8 million, using 5 per cent as the percentage of sales method, would allocate £ 90,000 to marketing communication activity (see Table 9.1). Franchised hospitality businesses have developed complex formulae, which include fees to pay for national marketing communications activity as well as local promotions. However, independent restaurants typically spend 2–3 per cent on their marketing communications activity.

Table 9.1 Typical independent hotel's marketing communication budget

A 4-star city center hotel with sales of £ 1,800,000 (accommodation sales of £ 1,000,000) and a marketing communication budget based on 5% of total sales might allocate the £ 90,000 like this:

Salary for sales person	25,000
PR Agency fee	8,000
Local paper and magazine adverts	10,000
Advertising in Directories	4,000
Christmas advertising	5,000
Promotional print including brochures, posters, calendar of events	10,000
Website re-design	10,000
Search engine optimization	6,000
Consortium fee	12,000
TOTAL	90,000

The problem with percentage of sales calculations is that the budget is not linked to the needs of the business. In some years the budget may be too high, because of economic prosperity, whereas during difficult trading periods the budget will probably be too low. It also does not take into account each company's cost/profit structure, different location issues or potential opportunities that might require an investment in additional marketing communication expenditure. However, the percentage of sales method remains the preferred choice of most hospitality organizations.

Competitive parity

Major hospitality brands competing in mature markets fight for market share. These companies already invest heavily in marketing communication activity and are very aware of one another's marketing communication campaigns. The competitive parity budget concept recognizes the importance of investing similar amounts of money on marketing communication activity as competitors. If one competitor tries to increase its share of voice (SOV) in a competitive market by substantially increasing its marketing communication expenditure, then competitors may be forced to match the increase in spending to maintain their SOV. *Share of voice* is a measure of the amount of money invested in promotion, and particularly in advertising, in comparison to competitors. If total sector spend on advertising is US$ 10 million and your company spends US$ 2 million, your SOV is 20 per cent.

Objective and task

The objective and task approach adopts a systematic method to budgeting. Specific objectives are set, and the marketing communication tasks to deliver those objectives are determined. The costs are then calculated and the marketing communication budget is agreed. For smaller companies, this is seen as a complicated and time-consuming approach. For larger organizations, the objective and task method is favoured. This approach can be problematic if the costs are higher than predicted and expected sales do not materialize.

Costs

Although each budgeting approach has advantages and disadvantages, the important point is that setting a budget is essential when planning the offline and online marketing communication campaign. The costs of a campaign include:

- Agency fees for advice and creative design
- Production costs – a black and white leaflet or a local radio station advert is a relatively low-cost item to produce, compared to printing a high quality, full-colour glossy brochure or making a one-minute television commercial on location with celebrities as part of an international campaign
- Media costs – this refers to the cost of buying online advertising, the space in a printed publication or the time on TV or radio stations
- Buying or renting mailing lists.

Budgeting often becomes an iterative process, as the costs of different media are evaluated and campaign decisions are changed to fit the allocated budget.

Above and below the line

When discussing marketing communications, marketers distinguish between 'above' and 'below' the line to describe different types of

activity. *Above the line* is used to describe advertising activities where the space (the online banner advert, the page in print or the time slot in broadcasting) has to be paid for. *Below the line* is used for any other non-personal marketing communication activity. This terminology originates with the agencies and refers to commission-earning activity (above the line) and fee-earning activity (below the line).

Target markets

In marketing communications, the target market is described as the target audience, and the key is to match the audience characteristics of the available media with the hospitality organization's target market profile. There are two alternative strategies in prioritizing target audiences for hospitality companies who use intermediaries: push and pull (see Fig. 9.7).

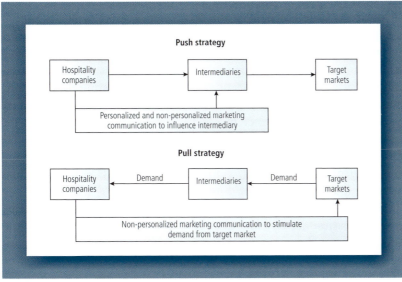

Figure 9.7 Push and pull stratergies

A *push strategy* prioritizes intermediaries as the main target audience. Marketing communication activities focus on intermediaries, who are then expected to influence the end-user to choose the company's products ahead of competitors. Hospitality marketing communication campaigns targeting intermediaries use all the elements of the marketing communication mix, but competitors are also targeting intermediaries – so it is difficult to gain competitive advantage.

A *pull strategy* prioritizes marketing communication activity on the end-user, aiming to make the hospitality product the customer's first choice by direct decision, or when discussing requirements with an intermediary. Because the intermediary should acknowledge the customer's wishes, the intermediary should then make the appropriate booking.

The major hospitality players use both strategies to influence intermediaries and end-users. Accurately, defining and prioritizing the target markets help in the selection of which media to use.

THE MARKETING COMMUNICATION CAMPAIGN

Marketing objectives, marketing communications strategies, tactics and budgets are interlinked. Before the communication campaign is devised, appropriate market research and planning need to be undertaken (this is discussed in detail in Chapter 15). Normally most, if not all, of the various marketing communication tools we have discussed are used to support the annual sales plan. These activities can be either at the brand level or at the unit level, or more typically a combination of both. A monthly planner setting out the key marketing communication/sales activities is drawn up in an annual marketing schedule (see Table 9.2). For each of these activities, a detailed tactical marketing action plan needs to be drawn up, listing the schedule, timing, budget and responsible person. For example, the PR activity to launch a new conference product will require its own brief to the agency and its own budget and implementation plan. However, the PR activity will be coordinated with the sales team, new website copy and images, print collateral, an online and offline DM initiative and in-house launch.

The major hospitality players have continuous marketing communication activity and are adept at managing implementation. Smaller hospitality companies run campaigns during specific periods. During the campaign period, target audience responses must be monitored. Occasionally, a campaign can be adapted to improve the message execution or even 'pulled' if a serious error of judgment has occurred. Regular customers and employees can enjoy the 'buzz' and excitement when an innovative marketing communication campaign generates lots of interest – especially if real employees are actually featured in the campaign.

Measuring the results

Effective measurement of results is based on setting measurable marketing communication objectives in terms of what you want the audience to learn, feel or do and establishing tracking systems to monitor audience responses. There are two main methods of

Table 9.2 Annual marketing communications activities schedule planner

Year Sales	Jan	Feb	Mar	Apr	May	Jun	Jul	Aug	Sep	Oct	Nov	Dec
Sales visits		New York		Paris		Hong Kong, Shanghai					World Trade Market, London	
Conference sales blitz			X	X	X				X	X		
Exhibitions			ITB, Berlin			Tokyo						
Print												
New design and production	X	X	X									
PR		X	X	X	X			X	X	X	X	
Adverts												
Leisure breaks	X	X	X			X	X	X	X	X	X	
Conference	X	X	X	X					X	X	X	
Direct marketing												
Loyalty club newsletter		X			X			X			X	
Sponsorship												
Golf events				X			X	X				

measuring the results of a marketing communication campaign: one is to use marketing research to measure the effectiveness of marketing communication activity and the other is to measure the return on investment (ROI) by calculating the profit generated from the bookings attributed to the campaign.

Marketing research measurement

A company wishing to raise brand awareness and brand image ('learn' objectives) first needs to employ an agency to establish the current levels of awareness and image before the campaign starts. This provides a comparison standard for setting a measurable objective. During and after the campaign, the agency – using the same research methods – can establish whether there have been any changes in the levels of brand awareness and brand image (see Chapter 4). Similar research tracks the target audience's recall of recent advertising heard or seen that is another 'learning' measure of the campaign's effectiveness.

Response measurement and ROI

Most hospitality companies want a measurable behavioural response to their marketing communications campaigns – calls to the contact center, website visitors, coupon redemptions, competition entries, or, more importantly bookings. A number of different people or processes are involved in monitoring and reporting behavioural response. The reservations department, or the telesales bureau, can record the number of bookings received through the website or telephone enquiries generated by each of the different elements of the communications plan. Online promotions and bookings are easily monitored using appropriate technology. Many offline advertisements ask consumers to quote a code when they call for more information, and this allows the responses for each advert to be separately monitored. However, some campaigns stimulate lots of interest and enquiries but little in the way of sales. This is why the conversion ratio of turning enquiries into bookings is important. The conversion ratio allows companies to track the actual number and value of bookings generated by each advert in each medium, which in turn allows the marketing team to evaluate the effectiveness of each medium and of different adverts, to learn what works and to improve the campaign for next time. We have already mentioned vouchers and coupons, which are distributed as part of sales promotions and DM activity – especially in the bar, club and restaurant sectors. The number of customers using the vouchers also provides a simple tracking system to measure the effectiveness of voucher campaigns.

The ROI is calculated by calculating the costs of the campaign and measuring the resulting profit or loss. The costs of the campaign include agency fees, design and production of collateral and online graphics, buying media space/time and monitoring the campaign results. The results can be measured by the profit generated directly by the campaign, expressed as a percentage of the cost of the campaign. This means that the marketer must know and understand the cost/profit drivers of the hospitality product that is being promoted. Calculating the profit can be a complex task; however, there are accounting/marketing software packages that can produce ROI ratios. There is a simple formula that represents the complex task of calculating the ROI:

$$ROI = \frac{\text{Profit generated by campaign} - \text{Marketing campaign investment}}{\text{Marketing campaign investment}}$$

Table 9.3 provides a hypothetical example to illustrate the ROI for a 1000-bedroom downtown hotel.

Table 9.3 Return on investment for a leisure break campaign

ROI for a leisure break campaign

Objective: To generate a ROI of 140% from this year's US$ 50,000 summer city leisure breaks campaign (June to September).
Strategy: To target leisure break guests who have stayed at the hotel at least twice during the past 3 years with a new all-inclusive leisure product package.
Tactics: To promote the new leisure product to repeat guests via a direct mail campaign, including email and an attractive, full colour leisure break brochure and personalized letter from the Hotel's General Manager.
Price: The price of the leisure break must be set to generate profit – in this example the profit per booking is US$ 80.
Costs: Design, copy, photography, print and postal costs for leisure break brochure; redesign of website; email creative copy; database employee costs.

Number of mailings	10,000
Average cost of unit mailing	US$ 5
Total cost of campaign	US$ 50,000
Enquiry response rate	30% (3000 enquiries)
Conversion rate of enquiries to bookings	50% (1500 bookings)
Leisure break price, two people staying for two nights	US$ 200
Profit per booking	40% (US$ 80)

Total profit	US\$ 120,000
Profit after campaign costs	US\$ 120,000 – US\$ 50,000 = US\$ 70,000
ROI	$\dfrac{\text{Profit} - \text{Marketing campaign investment}}{\text{Marketing campaign investment}}$ $= \dfrac{120,000 - 50,000}{50,000} = 140\%$

This is a relatively simple measure that does not take in to account more complex investment appraisal accounting techniques. However, for the purposes of most marketing and sales campaigns this simple ROI provides a reasonably effective marketing measurement.

CONCLUSION

Marketers are primarily responsible for communicating the hospitality offer, and this is the most visible part of marketing. When designing a campaign the hospitality marketer has to choose from a wide range of options, and the decision is dependent on the budget available and the campaign's objectives. It is essential to ensure that a consistent message is delivered across the communication elements of a campaign. Creativity can increase the effectiveness of a campaign. Hospitality marketers work with agencies that provide professional, specialist marketing communication services. All the marketing communication activities should be assessed against whether objectives have been achieved, or the investment in marketing communication may be wasted.

In this chapter, we have explained:

- The strategic role of marketing communication, which is to inform, persuade and build relationships with target audiences
- The communication process that involves a sender, a target audience, noise in the environment, the message, media and feedback
- Personal communication channels in hospitality, which usually involve salespeople directly talking with, or writing to, customers on an individual basis
- Non-personal communication channels, including online, print, broadcast and display tools aimed at target audiences
- The hospitality communication mix that includes eMarketing, print material, the sales force, advertising, sales promotion and point-of-sale material, PR, sponsorship and DM

- That setting marketing communication objectives is a prerequisite for successful marketing communication planning
- Marketing communication campaigns that comprises a budget, prioritization of target audiences, creative planning, media selection, implementation and a mechanism for measuring the results of the campaign.

Activity 9.4

At the beginning of the chapter, you thought about how you first heard about a tourism destination or hospitality product that you have already experienced or want to experience:

- Was it a word of mouth recommendation from family and friends?
- Was it reading an advert either online or in a newspaper/magazine?
- Was it listening/viewing an advert on the radio or television?
- Was it a hearing/reading/viewing a news item?

Review what you wrote and think about these questions again. Can you explain how marketing communications worked for three of the four questions?

REVIEW QUESTIONS

Now check your understanding by answering the following questions:

1 Discuss the role of marketing communications in communicating the hospitality offer.
2 Evaluate the communication process from a hospitality company's perspective.
3 Discuss the hospitality marketing communication mix and explain the role of each tool.
4 Explain the stages in developing, implementing and measuring the effectiveness of a marketing communication campaign for a hospitality product.

References and Further Reading

Chaffey, D., Ellis-Chadwick, F., Johnston, K., & Mayer, R. (2006). *Internet marketing: strategy, implementation and practice* (3rd ed.). Prentice Hall.

Lander, N. (2009). *Beware the Small Print,* Financial Times, April 25/26 Arts and Weekend, 4.

McCabe, S. (2009). *Marketing communications in tourism and hospitality, concepts, strategies and cases.* Butterworth-Heinemann.

Morgan, N., & Pritchard, A. (2000). *Advertising in tourism and leisure*. Butterworth-Heinemann.

New Media Knowledge (2009). *Jumping Ahead: InterContinental Hotels Group's Latest Viral Campaign,* NMK, May 19th.

Reich, A. Z. (1997). *Marketing management for the hospitality industry*. John Wiley.

Shoard, C. (2007). *I have a lot of curiosity,* Financial Times, June 23/24, Life and Arts, 3.

Smith, P. R. (1995). *Marketing communication: An integrated approach*. Kogan Page.

TRI HotStats. (2010). *TRI hospitality consulting*. London: TRI.

Wai-sum Siu, W -S., & Fung M-, Y. (December, 1998). Hotel advertisements in China: a content analysis. *Journal of Professional Services Marketing, now published as: Services Marketing Quarterly, 17*(2), 99–108.

Yeshin, T. (1998). *Integrated marketing communications*. Butterworth-Heinemann, 324.

Zeithaml, V. A., & Bitner, M. J. (2003). *Services marketing* (3rd ed.). McGraw-Hill.

PART C

Encounter Marketing

CHAPTER **10**

Managing the physical environment

Chapter objectives

After going through this chapter, you should be able to:

- Understand the role of the physical environment in marketing a hospitality business
- Have an awareness of design principles used in the development of the hospitality product
- Identify the external and internal elements of the hospitality physical environment
- Recognize the importance of maintenance and refurbishment program for hospitality properties in delivering customer satisfaction.

INTRODUCTION

The physical environment sends important signals to all of the hospitality organization's stakeholders but most importantly to customers. Customers intuitively respond to the signals that the external appearance and internal atmosphere project. If the physical environment is appropriate, then target markets are more likely to find the offer attractive and want to buy; at the same time, potential customers who do not 'fit' into the target market profile can be deterred. In this sense, the physical evidence in the hospitality product helps 'tangibilize the intangible' aspects of hospitality services. At the same time, the physical environment influences customer expectations in the pre-encounter marketing stage, which the customer experiences during the encounter.

In this chapter, we explore how environmental psychology helps hospitality companies to understand consumers' responses to the physical environment. We will then introduce key principles of design and discuss the various elements of the physical environment. Finally, we focus on the crucial issue of maintenance and refurbishment. The physical environment in hospitality is strongly associated with the product, and the product design decisions are interconnected with the physical environment.

ENVIRONMENTAL PSYCHOLOGY AND CUSTOMERS' RESPONSE TO THE PHYSICAL ENVIRONMENT

This discussion is largely based on the research carried out by Zeithaml and Bitner (2003) who put forward a framework for understanding the impact of physical surroundings on customers and employees. Figure 10.1 summarizes these influences and helps us to understand the customers' psychological and social behaviour within the physical environment. There are four elements, which we now discuss – individual behaviour, social interaction, customer responses and the characteristics of the physical environment. Although most of this discussion refers to the 'built environment' that is made up of buildings, furnishings, signage and the like, many of the principles apply equally to the natural environment.

Individual behaviour

Research by environmental psychologists suggests that people respond to the physical environment with one of two diametrically opposed types of behaviour – approach behaviour or avoidance behaviour. People are, to varying degrees, comfortable in a physical environment

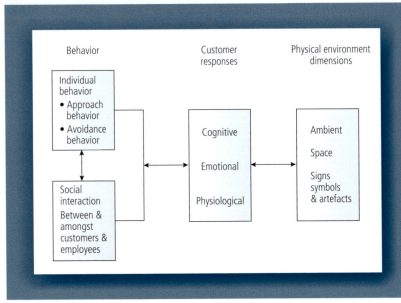

Figure 10.1 Customer behaviour and responses to the physical environment *Source: Zeithaml, Bitner, and Gremler, 2009*

or they are uncomfortable. When people are comfortable, this creates *approach behaviour*. Customers who demonstrate approach behaviour are more likely to enter the hospitality outlet, stay and spend money; they may return and/or recommend the experience to others. When people are uncomfortable with a physical environment, this tends to cause *avoidance behaviour*. Consumers who demonstrate avoidance behaviour will probably walk or drive past the hospitality unit; if they do enter the premises, they may walk out without purchasing anything. Indeed, consumers with an extremely negative response to the physical environment can even become hostile towards that hospitality brand.

When designing the physical environment, it is important both to create positive responses from the target markets to attract them into the premises and to create an environment in which it is appealing to work. At the same time, environments can be designed deliberately to deter people who do not fit the target market profile.

Social interaction

Research also suggests that the physical environment influences how customers and employees interact and relate to each other. The design of the physical environment can encourage or discourage social interactions.

Different types of hospitality product need to generate different types of social interaction. Hospitality business products, for example, meetings and conferences, are designed to create more formal social interactions. Customers who do not know each other will be polite, but they may not engage in any other type of conversation. Customers will also tend to adopt more formal, polite behaviour with employees, and similar behaviour from the employees will be expected. However, many hospitality leisure products are designed to encourage customers to interact with each other, and with employees, in a much more informal manner. Indeed, social interactions form a significant element of most hospitality leisure product concepts and social interaction is the core product that customers consume in sports bars, clubs and many holiday environments. If the social aspect of the hospitality experience in these environments fails to meet expectations, this will adversely influence customer satisfaction. Therefore, the character of social interactions needs to be considered when developing the product concept or writing a design brief. Designers should consider:

- The use of space
- The design of seating arrangements – the distance between the seating can encourage or discourage conversation between customers
- The décor – the choice of colours, fabrics and furniture
- Lighting and background music.

Ultimately, the physical environment sends signals to consumers about how to conduct social interaction, by defining what is acceptable and appropriate behaviour and what is not.

Consumer responses to the physical environment

There are three types of human response to the physical environment: cognitive, emotional and physiological (Bitner, 1992).

The physical environment and cognition: Cognition in this context means knowledge and perception. The physical environment influences people's beliefs about places, which in turn creates preconceptions about the characteristics of the product or brand and the behaviour of people in that environment. Therefore, the physical appearance and layout of hospitality premises, signage, the décor and employees' dress, reinforces or challenges people's prior beliefs about the hospitality offer. Consumers recognize these different combinations of the physical environment which *differentiate* product categories from each other. In this sense, the physical environment acts as a tangible clue for consumers and helps them to categorize the firm's offer accordingly.

The physical environment and emotion: As human beings, we are all aware of our own emotional responses to the physical environment. Research suggests that the physical environment can, subconsciously or overtly, generate two types of emotional response: pleasure and arousal. Arousal refers to a tendency towards being alert, excited and energized. Pleasure refers to a tendency towards

Activity 10.1

Compare the physical environment of two restaurants you know; one can be a fast-food restaurant and the other a fine dining restaurant. What signals does the physical environment send to potential consumers?

Physical evidence	Fast-food branded restaurant	Fine dining restaurant
Surrounding environment		
External building appearance		
Signage		
Décor		
Table setting		
Staff appearance/uniforms		

---

enjoyment, happiness or euphoria. Figure 10.2 illustrates four emotional responses based on the pleasure/arousal continuum. Of course, different consumers respond to the same physical environment in different ways – some people will feel pleasure at the sounds and visual stimuli in a fashionable club, whilst other people will be distressed by them. Research suggests that there is a U-shaped relationship between arousal and pleasure. Too little arousal is unpleasant; too much is also unpleasant. The optimal level of arousal lies between these two extremes and will vary between different types of consumers.

Consumers' emotional responses to the physical environment influence their behaviour, and therefore an understanding of peoples' emotional responses is important when designing the physical environment.

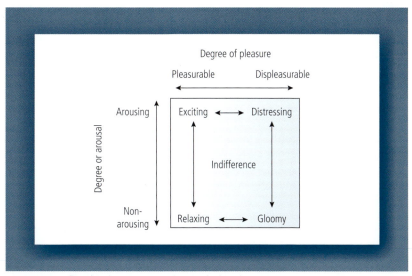

Figure 10.2 Emotional responses to the physical environment *Source: Zeithaml et al., 2009*

The physical environment and physiological response: People have different physiological responses to environmental stimuli. Environmental stimuli can be sensed through one of the following or any combination:

- Visual stimuli (brightness/darkness; colours and shapes)
- Aural stimuli (the volume, cadence or rhythm of sounds)
- Olfactory stimuli (fresh or foul scents and smells)
- Taste stimuli (bitter/sweet/salty/savoury/sour tastes and hot/cold temperatures)
- Tactile stimuli (the texture of food products, the softness in furnishings and the level of comfort with the temperature).

When marketers attempt to manage the sensory environment they are said to be engaged in sensory marketing. Sensory marketing 'engages consumer's senses and affects their . . . emotions, memories, perceptions, preferences, choices and consumption of products' (Krishna, 2010). Sensory marketing is not a new phenomenon and all hospitality brands whether they consciously plan to do so or not engage the customer's senses. Some sectors apply considerable thought to sensory marketing: the more luxurious hotel, spa and restaurant brands recognize that combining sensory elements to create a signature environment can add value to the customer experience.

Extreme stimulation can cause consumers varying degrees of physical discomfort, ranging from the mildly aggravating to the health threatening. Clearly, these types of physiological factors influence both consumers' and employees' response to the physical environment, and the consumers' initial attraction, enjoyment and propensity to return or reject the hospitality offer.

As consumers have become more sophisticated and markets more fragmented, hospitality operators have recognized the importance of physiological response in designing the physical environment to satisfy the needs and wants of the target markets (see Marketing insights 10.1 and 10.2).

Marketing insight 10.1

Hyatt's signature scent

At the opening of the Park Hyatt Vendome, Paris, Blaise Mautin, a celebrated French perfumer created a range of scents for the bed linen, bath gels, interior sprays and massage oils, which 'smell like a wet cement poured over a raw plank of oak, coupled with fresh, ever-so-slightly-cinnamoned pastry dough' (Burr, 2006). This signature scent concept was further developed by the novel idea of blending the scent with taste. Mautin collaborated with Jean-Francois Foucher, the pastry chef, to create pastries imbued with the Hyatt signature scent, which eventually became the hotel's signature dessert. Upon check-in, a tiny, delicate macaroon was delivered to the guest's bedroom to complement the other scents in the room. Today, the Park Hyatt Vendome offers a 'Universe of Senses' leisure break, which incorporates the visual art throughout the hotel, a specially compiled music collection, the sensory touch of Le Spa and of course the aroma and tastes of the signature scent in the bedroom and the cuisine.

Sources: Burr, 2006; www.hyatt.com

Variations in consumer responses to the physical environment

Earlier in this chapter, we mentioned the differences in consumer response to the same physical environment. Consumer behaviour research into personality traits can explain why certain types of personality might respond to certain types of physical environment differently. Also, each of us can also respond to the same physical environment differently according to changes in our own disposition (good mood/bad mood). Variations in peoples' responses can be linked to different lifestyles and different cultural backgrounds. In hospitality markets, we have already discussed how the 'purpose of visit' influences consumers. The same customer may show different responses to the same physical environment, depending on whether the purpose of the visit is business or leisure.

DIMENSIONS IN THE PHYSICAL ENVIRONMENT

Hospitality companies can control the built environment and create atmosphere through design. Three environmental dimensions – ambience, spatial layout and functionality, and signs, symbols and artefacts – influence consumers' cognitive, emotional and physiological responses.

The *ambient dimension* refers to the sensory elements we have just discussed – features such as colour and lighting (which effects pleasure and arousal) and temperature (which impacts physical comfort) can be linked to consumers' zones of tolerance (see Chapter 3). Relatively minor irritations can be a source of amusement for some consumers, whereas more extreme ambient conditions can be a genuinely serious issue and create highly distressed customers.

Spatial layout refers to the way in which space is used and how furniture and equipment are arranged in rooms. The scale and size of a hospitality property influence the spatial layout. For example, in the layout of the public lobby area and front desk: is the lobby a large, formal, spacious area for a grand hotel with high ceilings, chandeliers, many items of furniture and an extensive desk to cater for many customers checking in/out; or is it a smaller, more intimate area for a boutique hotel with low ceilings, darker lighting and a more informal check in/out area. Functionality refers to the effectiveness of the spatial layout to facilitate efficient service and deliver customer satisfaction. Spatial layout achieves an optimal balance between operational requirements and customer expectations. Employees such as kitchen crew and customer service staff need to be able to perform their jobs effectively and efficiently, but the needs of the customer must also be considered.

Signs, symbols and artefacts refer to the range of tools that companies can use to communicate with consumers via the physical environment. For example, contemporary hotels can use modern art to convey a fashionable image to customers; historic hotels can use antique furniture to convey the unique heritage of the property.

Each of these three dimensions needs to be coordinated effectively to ensure that a consistent and appealing physical environment is achieved.

Design and the physical environment

During the development stage of a new hospitality product, factors such as ownership, the site's characteristics and planning permissions/conditions will influence the type of development built. Multi-brand operators will evaluate the market potential for their different branded concepts before selecting the most appropriate brand for a specific site. Hospitality brands vary from the formulaic, standardized concepts, where the design component is replicated in each unit, to eclectic collections of units that have no common design theme at all. Ownership attributes can also influence design features. Occasionally, wealthy individuals can afford to be extravagant when investing in an ancillary interest like a hospitality development, but usually the independent sector is characterized by restricted funds. However, the major operators have access to more significant financial resources and have more opportunities to invest in innovative design.

When the product concept and funding has been agreed, the architects, interior designers and management team need to draw up detailed plans for the site. Architects are not hoteliers or restaurateurs, and many new-build hospitality units have problems because marketing objectives are not included in the design brief. Effective marketing is based on the design concept satisfying the needs of target markets and ensuring the service process is efficient. Marketers and operations personnel should be involved in developing the design brief and providing input into the planning stage.

The physical environment has also been described as a 'servicescape' (Zeithaml & Bitner, 2003) that is equivalent to the 'landscape' of the

natural environment. We will now discuss three elements that need to be considered when designing the physical environment.

1 Servicescape usage – how each area in the site plan will be used
2 Service space complexity – the level of complexity in the operation
3 Aesthetics – the creation of the design style.

Servicescape usage

Different hospitality product concepts have different servicescape characteristics, according to the level of service that is offered and the amount of interaction between customers and employees in the operation. Three categories of servicescape are self-service, interpersonal service and remote service (see Table 10.1).

A *self-service operation* relies on customers serving themselves. There are few (if any) employees, and the design of the physical environment focuses on ensuring that customers can conveniently and cost-effectively look after themselves.

An *interpersonal service operation* involves both customers and employees using the same physical environment at the same time. The design of the servicescape needs to ensure that customers are comfortable within the physical environment, and at the same that employees can perform their job effectively and efficiently. Sometimes poor design of the servicescape creates conflict between customers and employees. Small lobby and front desk areas, which are close to multi-purpose customer/service lifts to bedrooms upstairs, can inadvertently create conflict if large numbers of customers are arriving/departing at the same time as housekeepers are taking laundry up to service the accommodation.

Remote service, in this context, means a physical environment where there are no customers. The most common example of remote service in hospitality operations is in contract catering where food production takes place in large remote kitchens servicing multiple units. The key design issues focuses on employee needs and efficient

Table 10.1 Typology of the physical environment for hospitality and leisure

Servicescape usage	Complexity of the servicescape Elaborate	Lean
Self-service (customer focus)	Self-service restaurant	Vending machine dispensing food
Interpersonal services (customer and employees)	Cruise ship	Coffee shop
Remote service (employee focus)	Contract catering for airlines	Pizza home delivery

Source: Zeithaml et al., 2003, p. 285, reproduced with permission of the McGraw-Hill Companies.

production. Since customers never visit the servicescape, there is limited if any customer/employee interaction.

Service space complexity

There is a wide variety of different types of hospitality operations, ranging from small-scale, simple, single product units to large-scale, complex, multi-product units. The scale and complexity of the operation will influence the servicescape needs. Simple servicescapes are described as lean and complex servicescapes as elaborate.

Lean servicescapes have a limited number of variables, products, equipments and employees to control and only require a limited amount of space. The key focus in design is the effective use of this limited space.

Elaborate servicescapes have many variables and are much more complex. There can be different floor levels, different types of room usage and more equipment, which can be technologically very sophisticated. Elaborate servicescapes need more space, and the design issues can be complicated and intricate.

Aesthetics

Aesthetics is the study of form and beauty. In design, aesthetics is concerned with the tastefulness of the décor. The interior designer is given a design brief and the budget for a hospitality product concept, and invited to create the décor scheme. The scheme should include floor and wall coverings, lighting, fabrics and furniture and artefacts. It is the interior design that provides the tangible elements of the atmospherics in the hospitality product.

Marketing insight 10.2

Indigo – InterContinental Hotel's boutique brand

Indigo is one of InterContinental's newest brands and operates in the upscale boutique market. The first hotel opened in Atlanta, USA in 2004, and at the time of writing there are approximately 35 open, mostly in the Americas with another 50 in the pipeline. Each of the hotels is uniquely designed, located in 'culturespheres' (urban, mid-town or near urban markets close to local business, retail and cultural areas), and offers Indigo brand hallmarks to ensure the brand DNA is consistent. 'The soul of the brand is the retail-inspired concept of renewal'. This means that the Indigo Hotels' public spaces are adapted by changing the artwork, music, flora, murals and directional signage according to each season. Indigo claim that this renewal concept 'creates a sensory experience for guests with the scent, music, menu and wine pairings changing to reflect seasonality'.

Source: www.hotelindigo.com

Table 10.2 Innovative design concepts	
Hotels	**Examples**
Contemporary designer hotels	The Mondrian, Los Angeles, USA, designed by Philip Starck
Art hotels	Art'Otel, Dresden, Germany, designed by Rolf and Jan Rave and Dennis Santachiara
New business hotels	Sheraton Paris Airport Hotel, Roissy, France
New grand hotels	Park Hyatt, Tokyo, Japan and the Four Seasons Hotel, Istanbul, Turkey
Resort and theme hotels	The Palace of the Lost City, Sun City, South Africa and Kingfisher Bay Resort and Village, Fraser Island, Australia

Source: Riewoldt, 1998.

Designers are in the fashion business. At one time, hotels were considered to be boring, functional places with unimaginative décor. However, in recent years hotels and restaurants have engaged with the fashion industry and designers have been allowed to use their flair to create visually striking exteriors and interiors for hospitality product concepts in a wide range of different types of hospitality buildings. Visionary hospitality entrepreneurs, like Ian Schrager and Terence Conran, have championed this design revolution, and global hospitality chains have been influenced by the independents. The 'W' brand, Sheraton's boutique hotel chain and Indigo by InterContinental Hotels are chain-hotel responses to competition from independent boutique hotels. Table 10.2 illustrates the Indigo innovative hospitality design concept.

ELEMENTS OF THE PHYSICAL ENVIRONMENT

The physical environment for hospitality products comprises external features, the internal design, employees and customers. Table 10.3 provides a summary of the key components of the physical environment. Most hospitality businesses use professionally staged photographs of the unit's physical external and/or internal physical environment on their websites to present the hospitality offer attractively.

External

The external environment for hospitality products is the equivalent of a shop window in retailing. The visual display in a shop window sends powerful messages about product and service quality and price. The shop window reinforces the positioning and brand image. The surrounding environment, the external appearance of the building,

Table 10.3 The physical environment in hospitality premises

External	Internal	Employees	Customers
Surrounding environment	Internal spatial layout	Appearance	Appearance
External appearance of the building	Décor, furnishings and furniture	Dress (uniform)	Dress
Access	Equipment	Attitude	Attitude
Landscaping	Signage and point-of-sale material	Behaviour	Behaviour
Parking	Temperature and air quality		
Signage and logos	Music		
Lighting	Smell		

landscaping, access routes, car parking facilities, signage and logos and lighting are the shop window for the hospitality business.

We discussed the surrounding environment in Chapter 6, within the context of site selection criteria, and emphasized that the surrounding area must be compatible with the product concept. When the surrounding environment does match the hospitality product, potential customers will more likely be attracted to the physical environment. However, through no fault of the hospitality operator, the surrounding area can change over time; neighbouring properties can be sold and the new owners might change the use of buildings in a way that changes the character of the area. When the surrounding environment becomes incompatible with the existing hospitality product, then the operator will have to make a strategic decision whether to sell the property or reformulate the product concept.

The external appearance of the hospitality premises – the building, its size, age, architecture and, in particular, the quality of maintenance – sends cues to customers. Attractive, well-maintained properties inspire confidence, but buildings that appear neglected can actually deter potential customers. Effective landscaping can transform the visual appearance of a property. Well-maintained grounds, attractive lawns and gardens, pretty flower boxes and elegant outdoor swimming pools contribute towards a positive image of a hospitality property. The availability of sufficient secure car parking, close to the property, is important for all hospitality businesses that depend on customers travelling by road. Well-maintained attractive signage, including brand logos and effective external lighting send out positive signals to customers, whereas tired and damaged signage and poor lighting send out negative signals. Investment in the external physical environment can help to attract customers into the premises.

Internal

Although the external environment creates the first impression for potential customers, it is the internal environment that is most significant in determining whether customers are going to enjoy the hospitality experience. Internal factors include the layout, décor, furniture and furnishings, equipment, internal signage, temperature and air-quality, music and smells, which, combined together, convey the all-important atmosphere of the premises.

The internal layout refers to floor plans of the lobby area, front desk, lifts, bedrooms and bathrooms, restaurant, bar, conference, function and leisure areas. Although an architect is responsible for drawing the room layouts and making sure all the services (electrics, heating, ventilation and air-conditioning, communication systems, water supplies and drainage) comply with local building and safety regulations, it is up to the hospitality management team to ensure that the layout actually functions effectively to meet the requirements of employees and customers. Numerous new-build hotels and restaurants have design faults caused by inexperienced architects and management who have failed to understand the key operational details.

Décor is really a matter of personal taste; but in hospitality it is a crucial ingredient in creating the 'feel' in a property. Décor reflects the product concept, and impacts on the mood and style of the hospitality experience. Creating a décor scheme is a job for a professional interior designer. Every element of the hospitality product that is visible to the customer should be designed professionally. The interior designer ensures that the floor and wall coverings, the curtains and lighting, the seating, beds, desks and tables, and the pictures, bric-à-brac and ornaments deliver a consistent style. For the product concept, décor is another tangible cue.

Equipment, in this context, refers to equipment that customers actually use – for example, the air-conditioning system in the bedroom or the shower in the bathroom. It also includes equipment that employees use in front of customers. Customers expect equipment to work. Faulty or dirty equipment, especially in the bedrooms and bathroom or slow computer systems at check in/out, is a serious problem for customers and a major source of complaints.

Customers also expect the internal signage to provide clear directions throughout the property. Getting lost in a large hotel complex is embarrassing and frustrating for customers. The quality of the signage is another indicator of image.

We discussed the role of point-of-sale material in Chapter 9. From a physical environment perspective, point-of-sale material should be current, professionally presented and relevant. Unfortunately, hospitality businesses can suffer from dated and tired point-of-sale material, which is counterproductive in generating a positive image.

Air quality and temperature in hotels, clubs and restaurants are governed by local responses to climate and cultural conventions. In guest bedrooms, customers need to be able to control air-conditioning and heating systems for themselves. Customers who experience extremes of heat in bedrooms and restaurants, compared to their normal environment, can be very uncomfortable. If the management does not respond quickly to solve the problem, customers may even leave to find a competitor with a more comfortable temperature.

Background music, live music or no music is another matter of personal taste. However, when designing the hospitality product, music plays a key role in complementing the décor and creating atmosphere in public areas. In particular, bars and restaurants use music to attract target markets and to generate atmosphere. Indeed, sound is such an important atmospheric tool that many hospitality concepts stream music to outlets to ensure that employees cannot interfere with the ambience. W Hotels stream the music in synchronized time to all their properties – so the same music is played at the same time, regardless of time zones, in every W property whether it is located in Hong Kong, Paris, New York or Sydney.

Smell in hospitality is mainly associated with food and beverage outlets. Attractive cooking smells can stimulate the taste buds and attract customers. Foul bar and cooking smells – the combination of stale beer, cigarettes and fried food sometimes found in bars – are a powerful disincentive to many customers.

The combination of all these internal factors creates an overall atmosphere that should, if properly designed, appeal to the target market. However, if some of the key internal environmental factors fail, or do not fit, the customer's expectations, then customers can be dissatisfied.

Employees

The appearance, attitude and behaviour of employees should complement the positioning, product concept and physical environment. Employees' cleanliness, deportment and dress should reinforce the design theme and send a consistent message to customers. In formal, business-orientated hospitality operations, the staff uniforms reflect the business environment – professional attire in conservative colours and fabrics is the norm. In leisure and themed hospitality concepts, casual uniforms designed as part of the theme or no uniforms are appropriate. Contemporary boutique establishments often have contemporary designer-style dress for the employees' uniforms. Customers need hardly notice employees' dress and behaviour, when it matches the brand image and other elements of physical environment. However, if the employee's appearance, attitude and behaviour are inconsistent with the design concept, then customers will probably notice the inconsistency because it sends out a mixed message and confuses them.

Case study 10.1 **Hotel and restaurant uniforms**

Uniforms in fashionable hotels and restaurants are carefully designed to project the desired image. Nicholas Oakwell, Managing Director of No Uniform – a specialist British uniform design company suggests that 'the uniform tells the customer what the hotel is all about, especially since customers tend to be more fashion and design conscious today'. Uniforms need to be distinctive, easily recognizable and smart. Ideally, if there is a hotel or restaurant new build or major refurbishment project, the uniform designers will be involved 5 or 6 months before opening – to allow sufficient time to create a design, which reflects the interior designer's mood boards and the aspirations of the owners/managers.

Uniforms need to be practical as well as stylish. Table service staff need cool uniforms because they normally work up a sweat whilst running between the kitchen and the restaurant table; managers often need several pockets because they carry mobiles, keys, pens and memo pads. Uniforms also need a reasonable life span, Oakwell suggest 18 months, and to be available in a range of sizes to accommodate the different heights and shapes of employees.

Top Hat Imagewear is an American family business, founded in 1923, which also designs hotel and restaurant uniforms. Their client base includes most of the major hotel and restaurant companies including Four Seasons, Hilton, Mandarin Oriental and Marriott; and famous American hotels like the Pierre in New York and the Drake in Chicago.

Sources: Sims, J. (2009), The Chambermaid Wears Prada, Financial Times, Weekend 18/19 July 2009; and www.tophatimagewear.com

Customers

One of the distinguishing attributes of services is heterogeneity, which we discussed in Chapter 1. Hospitality experiences can be highly variable in content and quality due to the presence or absence, and behaviours, of other customers. Other customers in the physical environment can also contribute hugely to the atmosphere. Potential customers see and hear other customers. If what they see and hear conforms to their expectations, then other customers will feel comfortable. If other customers' dress seems inappropriate and their behaviour in terms of language, loudness, politeness and sobriety is inconsistent with the expectations of potential customers, then again an inconsistent message causes confusion. We have already discussed the problems caused by mixing incompatible target markets. Today's dress codes and expectations of behaviours are more relaxed than for previous generations. This makes it more difficult for hospitality management to control the dress and behaviour of customers. A number of exclusive clubs, restaurants and hotels still insist on a dress and behaviour code for customers. The Ritz, in London, makes the following statement on their website:

> *Befitting the elegant style of The Ritz, we observe a formal dress code in the public areas of the Hotel. With the exception of breakfast, gentlemen are required to wear a jacket and tie in The Ritz Restaurant, The Palm Court and The Rivoli Bar. Jeans and sport shoes are not permitted in any of these areas.*

(http://www.theritzlondon.com/tea/, downloaded on 7 July 2010)

Activity 10.2

If you can, visit the two hospitality units that you identified in Activity 10.1. Evaluate the external appearance of the units before entering, and then go into the units and evaluate the internal décor, employees and customers.

- Does the external environment match the internal environment?
- Do you think the physical environment is appropriate for the target markets?
- Does it match your expectations of a fast-food restaurant and a fine dining experience?

MAINTENANCE AND REFURBISHMENT

In our discussion of the external and internal physical evidence, we referred to the problems caused by damaged furniture, faulty equipment and tired décor. The role of maintenance and refurbishment is to maintain the hospitality product at an acceptable level to ensure customer satisfaction and efficient operation. Unfortunately, the nature of the hospitality business means that both customers and employees accidentally, and occasionally deliberately, cause damage to the property. In particular, bathrooms and toilets suffer from abuse and accidental water damage. The costs of not maintaining a property (Lawson, 1996) include:

- The loss of future revenue streams from potentially loyal customers who choose to patronize a competitor with a better-maintained product
- Loss of revenue from current customers who take their business elsewhere
- Loss of revenue caused by the inability to sell rooms that are out of operation because of maintenance problems
- Inefficient performance caused by faulty equipment and a loss in employee productivity
- Liability for health, safety and other legal infringements.

Although the responsibility for maintenance and refurbishment is an operational issue, marketing tired brands and tired properties is extremely difficult.

The maintenance and refurbishment life cycle

Effective maintenance should be planned into a new property as part of the design brief. The financial planning of a hospitality business will include a depreciation charge to cover the costs of wear and tear, and this depreciation charge is calculated by estimating the reasonable life expectancy of the décor, fittings, furniture and equipment. The life expectancy will be dependent on the quality standards of the original décor scheme and the desired market position. Although the depreciation charge is a book-keeping transaction, companies will also provide a maintenance budget of approximately 2 per cent–4 per cent of sales to cover repairs and redecoration. Older inns and hotels that have been converted from other uses can have difficult and costly maintenance issues. New-build properties should have fewer maintenance problems during the first years of operation.

Maintenance and refurbishment planning can be categorized under four headings:

1 *Preventative maintenance* comprises the regular servicing of equipment, such as elevators, kitchen equipment and air-conditioning plant, to ensure they do not breakdown
2 *Breakdown maintenance* includes all the minor damage caused during the normal daily operations of the business
3 *Corrective maintenance* includes regular redecoration according to a planned schedule; when the hospitality product becomes tired, a major refurbishment program is needed

Designing out faults is necessary when design faults emerge during the operation of the facility, and can improve guest comfort, operational efficiency, or both.

The refurbishment of public rooms, bars and restaurants varies according to usage and product concept. A popular venue with a short product life cycle might be refurbished every 3 years; and an established product might need new carpets and furniture as part of a major refurbishment scheme between every 5 and 10 years. Hotel bedrooms should have a planned life cycle for maintenance as follows (Lawson, 1996):

Décor and fabrics	2–4 years
Carpets and electrics	5–8 years
Furniture	7–10 years
Bathrooms	Renovated or replaced every 10–15 years

The implementation of a refurbishment program can create problems for the hospitality business. Bedrooms and food and beverage outlets need to be closed whilst the work is undertaken, resulting in a loss of sales. Customers can suffer from the noise and mess and possibly a reduced service level. Seasonal hospitality businesses can carry out routine maintenance and major refurbishment when the property is closed or during the low season. However, managers of properties in prime locations that enjoy high sales throughout the year have to plan redecoration program carefully to minimize the disruption to the business. Unfortunately, financial constraints during economic downturns often mean that the maintenance and refurbishment budgets are cut first, when in fact this is an ideal time for investment because there is less likelihood of losing revenue and upsetting customers.

CONCLUSION

In this chapter we have discussed the importance of the physical environment in attracting customers into hospitality premises and in contributing to the customer experience during the service encounter. Hospitality businesses that continually invest in refurbishment are more likely to enjoy high repeat and recommended business and nurture customer loyalty. Hospitality businesses that fail to maintain the physical environment of their premises will eventually become tired and have to compete on the basis of lower prices to attract customers; and this will result in lower profitability.

In this chapter, we have explained:

- How the science of environmental psychology is useful for explaining customers' responses to the physical environment
- How individual behaviour, social interaction and the characteristics of the physical environment influence both customers and employees
- The role of sensory marketing in developing the brand offer
- The importance of design in the hospitality servicescape
- The role of servicescape usage, servicespace complexity and aesthetics in designing the physical environment
- The characteristics of the external and internal environments in hospitality units
- The maintenance and refurbishment cycle (preventive maintenance, routine maintenance, corrective maintenance and designing out faults).

REVIEW QUESTIONS

Now check your understanding of this chapter by answering the following questions:

1 Discuss environmental psychology and customers' response to the physical environment in a hospitality context.

2 Evaluate servicescape usage and servicescape complexity when designing a new hospitality premises for:
- a self-service concept
- an interpersonal concept
- a remote service concept.

3 Why is the physical environment hospitality premises?

4 Discuss the role of maintenance and refurbishment in the life cycle of a bar or restaurant.

References and Further Reading

Bitner, M. J. (1992). Servicescapes: the impact of physical surroundings on customers and employees. *Journal of Marketing*, *56*, 57–71, April.

Burr, C. (2006). The Park Hyatt Vendome turns its signature scent in to a signature dessert the Park Hyatt Vendome. *Nation's Restaurant News*, *5*, 30.

Heide, M., Lærdal, K., & Grønhaug, K. (October, 2007). The design and management of ambience: Implications for hotel architecture and service. *Tourism Management*, *28*(5), 1315–1325.

Hulten, B., Broweus, N., & Van Dijk, M. (2009). *Sensory marketing*. Palgrave Macmillan.

Krishna, A. (2010). *Sensory marketing: Research on the sensuality of products*. Routledge.

Lashley, C. (2001). *Employing human resource strategies for service excellence*. Butterworth-Heinemann.

Lawson, F. (1996). *Hotels and resorts: Planning, design and refurbishment*. Butterworth-Heinemann.

Riewoldt, O. (2006). *Hotel design*. Lawrence King Publishing.

Riewoldt, O. (2006). *New hotel design*. Watson-Guptill.

Sims, J (2009). *The Chambermaid Wears Prada*, FT Weekend (18/19 July 2009). Life and arts, page 5.

Zeithaml, V. A., Bitner, M. J., & Gremler, D. D. (2009). *Services marketing* (5th ed.). McGraw-Hill.

Zeithaml, V. A., & Bitner, M. J. (2003). *Services marketing* (3rd ed.). McGraw-Hill.

Zemke, D. M., & Shoemaker, S. (August, 2008). Sociable atmosphere. *Cornell Hospitality Quarterly*, 316–329.

CHAPTER

11

Managing service processes

INTRODUCTION

Although managing service production and delivery processes is the responsibility of operations management, marketing managers need to understand the principles of service operations management. Customer satisfaction is dependent on the hospitality operation delivering the promise that pre-encounter marketing has communicated. The key marketing role of managing demand is made significantly easier when the service process consistently delivers the experience and quality the customers expect. However, when the service process fails to deliver, marketing the hospitality property and the hospitality brand becomes much more difficult.

In this chapter, we discuss the importance of managing service processes effectively and then introduce the concept of service blueprinting, which is a customer-focused tool for specifying service standards, and the SERVQUAL 'gaps' model of service quality. We also review the crucial role of service recovery when a customer complains about the service received.

Activity 11.1

Reflect on your own experiences as a customer eating out.

- Can you remember an occasion when the service quality you experienced was disappointing? Can you explain what went wrong?
- Did you or somebody with you complain to the service provider?
  - If yes, how did the employees/manager respond to the complaint? Were you happy with their response? Did they offer you any compensation?
  - If no, did you talk to your family and friends about your disappointing experience? If so, how many people did you tell? And did you mention your disappointing experience online, for example, on a social networking site?

THE IMPORTANCE OF MANAGING SERVICE PROCESSES

In Chapter 1, we discussed the special characteristics of services (SIPIVISH) that present challenges in marketing the hospitality business and managing the service process. To recap, some of the key issues include the following:

- Intangibility – because the hospitality product is intangible-dominant, customers cannot be certain about the quality of the service they will receive until it has been consumed.
- Inseparability – in the vast majority of hospitality services, customers are present whilst the product is produced. More importantly, customers are themselves an essential component of the product

and the physical environment. Customers, therefore, help to shape the experience of other customers.

- Seasonality – all hospitality services have busy and quiet periods. The service process can be stressed, and fail, during extreme periods of demand, resulting in customer dissatisfaction. When the operation has too few customers, a vital ingredient of the hospitality product – atmosphere – can be missing, resulting in customer disappointment.
- Variability – the intangibility, inseparability and seasonality contribute to the variability that customers experience when consuming the hospitality product. Variability – the lack of standardization in service outputs – is endemic in hospitality services; it can confuse customers and create uncertainty.

A crucial issue for hospitality businesses is to try and deliver consistent service quality despite the constraints posed by intangibility, inseparability, seasonality and variability. All the academic research into hospitality practice suggests that delivering consistent service quality better than competitors is a significant antecedent of customer satisfaction. This means that if a hospitality business does not deliver service quality consistently, customers will not be satisfied and they will not return or recommend the brand to family and friends. Customer satisfaction is, therefore, dependent on service quality, and customer satisfaction is an antecedent for customer loyalty. We will discuss customer satisfaction in detail in Chapter 13 and loyalty in Chapter 14, but remember that effective hospitality marketing is predicated on delivering appropriately levels of service quality by managing service operations effectively.

UNDERSTANDING PROCESSES

Processes can be classified in a number of ways that help you to understand their importance from a customer perspective: vertical and horizontal, front-office and back-office and primary and secondary.

- *Vertical processes* are those that are located entirely within a function or department. For example, the food production process resides totally within the operations department. *Horizontal processes* are cross-functional. A major 3-day conference event for a blue-chip client will involve sales and marketing, reservations, operations, front desk, housekeeping and general management.
- *Front-office processes* are those that customers encounter. The check-in/check-out and complaints management processes are examples. Back-office processes are hidden from customers, as in, for example, the procurement process. Some processes straddle both front and back offices, for example, front desk provides the corporate customer with their bill to check and sign, whereas the back office accounting department will invoice the company and make sure the bill is paid on time.

- A distinction is also made between primary and secondary processes. *Primary processes* have major cost or revenue implications for companies. For example, the human resource management process in hospitality companies contributes significantly to the cost base of the business. *Secondary processes* have minor cost or revenue implications. Customers may have a different perspective on what is important: they typically do not care about back-office processes but about the processes they touch. In hospitality, these include the reservation process, the processes encountered during a meal experience and the billing process.

It is useful to understand service processes from a customer perspective and design these processes so that they contribute to customer satisfaction and customer retention. It is not just front-office processes that have an impact on customer experience; the same is true of back-office processes. If procurement people do not know the quality requirements of the offer promised to customers, they may source inputs of too high or too low a quality. Similarly, if operations people are not aware of the quality expectations of customers, they may create service encounters that are unacceptable. Clearly, a major concern for hospitality marketers is that front-office and back-office processes should work together to create service experiences that meet or exceed customers' expectations, especially in terms of quality.

Marketing insight 11.1 illustrates an unusual way of making the service process transparent to customers in luxury restaurants.

Marketing insight 11.1

A table in the kitchen!

Although many hospitality managers are nervous about customers seeing what goes on behind the scenes – and especially what goes on in the kitchens – one of England's most innovative hoteliers, Eric Marsh, actually encourages customers to dine in the kitchen! Since a 1980 refit, there has been a table for two customers in a corner of the main kitchen at the Cavendish Hotel, on the Duke of Devonshire's Chatsworth Estate in Derbyshire, England. Eric believes that if customers want to see the back of house operation, they can. More recently, the Gordon Ramsay Restaurant at Claridges, London, offers a similar 'Chef's Kitchen Table' for approximately six diners. Gordon Ramsay at Claridges also encourages all diners to visit the Kitchen after their meal and during service; and approximately 75% of new customers take up this offer.

Normally chefs are apprehensive at the thought of customers watching every aspect of the food production process in an award-winning restaurant. However, the truth is that chefs enjoy the opportunity to perform, and customers enjoy the excitement of watching the fine cuisine being cooked along with the frisson at the service encounter when the kitchen is busy. This approach sends powerful signals to customers about the high quality of the kitchen management service processes and is an interesting example of tangibilizing the intangible. This also demonstrates that effective marketing ideas can often have a long life.

SERVICE QUALITY

People can view service quality from a variety of different perspectives, according to the context of the situation.

- Operations-based quality focuses on meeting pre-defined service quality standards, such as you find in the Standard Operating Procedure manuals of chain hotel organizations. Operational quality is regarded as high when service outputs comply with the defined service standards. An operations focus that ignores customer requirements is unacceptable to marketers.
- Product-based quality views quality from an objective and measurable perspective. It takes a narrow product-based focus. For example, chefs may agree that fillet steak is a better quality cut of beef than sirloin, according to culinary definitions of quality. However, product-based quality definitions that fail to consider additional perspectives (e.g. some customers prefer the flavour of sirloin steak to fillet) are not always helpful to the marketer.
- User-based quality does take a consumer perspective and in particular recognizes that different consumers have different approaches in evaluating service quality standards.
- Value-based quality takes the customer's perspective and recognizes that value is expressed in an optimal trade-off between price and quality.

In most contexts, customer-perceived quality is determined by the customer's assessment of the service received against the service expected. A budget hotel can deliver poor value for money if the perceived quality is below expectations for the price charged, whereas a luxury hotel can deliver excellent value for money if the perceived quality is above expectations for the price charged, despite the actual amount of money paid for the service.

Dimensions of service quality

Delivering service quality has become a major concern of hospitality marketers. Measuring service quality is complicated, because service performance is not easily defined. Consumers judge service quality against many different criteria, and their own disposition can significantly influence their evaluation of the service process. Parasuraman, Zeithaml and Berry (1985) suggested that customers evaluate service quality across five dimensions: reliability, empathy, tangibles, responsiveness and assurance (see Table 11.1).

Table 11.1 The five dimensions of service quality

Dimension	Definition
Reliability	The ability to perform the promised service dependably and accurately
Empathy	The caring, individual attention given to the customer
Tangibles	The appearance of physical facilities, equipment, employees and communication materials
Responsiveness	The willingness to help customers and provide prompt service
Assurance	The knowledge and courtesy of employees, and their ability to convey confidence and inspire trust

Source: Parasuraman et al. (1985), reproduced with permission of the American Marketing Association

Reliability

Pre-encounter marketing makes a promise to the customer, and customers, therefore, expect the hospitality business to deliver on the promise. Customers expect the product, service quality and price to match the promise. When companies deliver on the promise, they are considered to be reliable; when they do not, consumers consider them unreliable. Sometimes promises are specific to individual customers; sometimes they are segment specific.

Empathy

In this context, empathy means understanding and treating customers as individuals and providing them with personalized service. Companies that are able to make customers feel important score highly on service quality. In hospitality, a smaller, independent operator can generally empathize with a customer more easily than a branded chain operation.

Tangibles

In Chapter 10, we discussed the physical environment and its impact on customers. Tangibles represent the physical environment in this model of service quality.

Responsiveness

Responsiveness refers to how effectively companies respond to customers. During the hospitality service process, customers will naturally ask lots of questions (how is the dish on a menu prepared? where are the washrooms? what time is check-out?), perhaps mention minor problems, and possibly even complain. How the service process system (and in particular the customer-contact employees) demonstrate willingness to help customers influences the customer's perception of service quality.

Assurance

This dimension refers to employees' courtesy, competence and product knowledge. In hospitality, customers expect the employees to be polite and to know what job they are meant to be doing. When employees are polite and knowledgeable, customers have more confidence that the company can deliver its marketing promise. Assured employees inspire customers to trust the company. Of course, when employees are rude, customers are offended, and when the employees clearly do not know how to deliver the hospitality service, customers understandably lose confidence in the company's ability to deliver.

Although this approach has been criticized for having either too few or too many service dimensions, consumers clearly judge service quality using a variety of process criteria as well as outcomes criteria. Process criteria are concerned with *how* a service is delivered; outcome criteria are concerned with *what* is delivered. For example, a meal that is exquisitely prepared and badly served would be high on outcome and low on process quality.

The gaps model of service quality

Parasuraman, Zeithaml and Berry (1992) also proposed an integrated model of service quality that explains why companies can fail to deliver the service customers expect. The model identifies four gaps, which are the principal reasons for service failure.

Gap 1: Management not knowing what customers expect

Hospitality managers often think that they know what customers want and develop the marketing offer on the basis of their own understanding of customer service expectations. For example, some independent hoteliers have aspirations for their restaurant operations that are considerably higher than the needs and wants of their customers. Poor (or no) marketing research into customer expectations can cause this misunderstanding. Effective marketing research, which should include both customer and employee perspectives, will identify the service expectations of the target market. When managers actually know what customers expect, they can then start to formulate an appropriate offer to match customer expectations.

Gap 2: Service quality standards do not match customer expectations

Assuming that management actually understands customer expectations, the second service gap focuses on the design of service quality standards. The design of service quality standards should match the customers' expectations; however, less professional hospitality companies do not set formal service standards. More professional hospitality companies can create formal service specifications that have been developed from an operations perspective but fail to take into account the customers' perspective. Sometimes the service system becomes internalized, and customer focus can be lost. Management needs to think creatively to overcome these service design problems and ensure that service standards match customer expectations.

Gap 3: Service-performance gap

This gap occurs when the service production and delivery processes fail to operate to the defined service standard. This type of service failure can be attributed to the human resource function in the hospitality business (poor recruitment, poor training and poor reward policies), technology problems (reservation system down, faulty TV), the special characteristics of services (SIPIVISH) and the customer's own mood. The role of customer-contact employees in delivering a quality service is discussed in Chapter 12.

Gap 4: Delivering the service promise

Gap 4 is the gap between what the service system (both people and technology) delivers and the promises made in advertising, PR and sales communications to customers. In Chapter 9, we discussed the importance of pitching promotional messages appropriately. If the hospitality marketer makes undeliverable promises, the customer will be disappointed. From a customer's perspective, it is crucial for the company and employees to keep promises. This includes customer-contact employees during the service encounter, who in their many dealings with customers inevitably make promises. Breaking a promise to a customer leads to customer disappointment.

Closing the gaps

When Gaps 1–4 are closed, the company will be promising and producing service experiences that meet clearly understood customer expectations. When there are significant gaps because the hospitality management does not know what customers expect (Gap 1), or service quality standards do not match customer expectations (Gap 2), or the service operations fail to match defined service standards

(Gap 3) or the marketing promise creates unrealistic expectations which the service operation cannot deliver (Gap 4), then these service quality gaps will be a major cause of customer dissatisfaction.

SERVICE BLUEPRINTING

A key concern for marketers is that service production and delivery processes should fulfil the desired quality standards. Shostack (1981) developed a pictorial method for designing service processes, called service blueprinting, which helps to chart and analyse the performance of service processes. Borrowing flowcharting techniques from manufacturing industries, a service blueprint is a map that provides a specification of how a service is (or should be) delivered.

In hospitality new-product development, a service blueprint is used to design and map the service processes that customers will encounter. From the moment customers arrive to the moment they leave, all the actions that the customer and/or employees carry out are mapped on a diagram (see Fig. 11.1). The actions are listed under the following headings:

Physical evidence	Represents the facilities and equipment used in delivering the service
Customer	All the activities/actions taken by the customer
Contact employees	Visible front-of-house employee actions and invisible front-of-house employee actions
Support processes	The back-of-house service support systems that help the front-of-house employees to deliver the service

The service blueprint has three horizontal lines, which separate the various types of activities. The first horizontal line separates customers from front-of-house employees and is called the *line of interaction*. When a vertical line crosses this horizontal line (e.g. when the customer checks a restaurant booking with the greeter), then a service encounter between the customer and a front-of-house employee takes place.

The second horizontal line is called the *line of visibility*; this separates those front-of-house employee activities that the customer can see from those that cannot be seen. For example, the restaurant order-taker walks out of the customer's sight and into the kitchen with the order. In the kitchen, the front-of-house employees are invisible to the customer.

The third horizontal line is called the *line of internal interaction*. When the vertical line crosses the line of internal interaction, then these are internal service encounters.

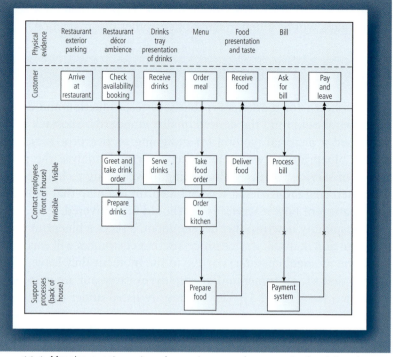

Figure 11.1 Mapping a restaurant service, customer service encounter (x = internal service encounter)

By mapping service processes from a customer's perspective, management can strive to set service standards and develop service production and delivery processes that meet customers' expectations. A crucial point about a service blueprint is that although the service process is analysed from the customer's perspective, both the employees' role and the service process can be evaluated at the same time. If you study Figure 11.1 and read this simplified version of a blueprint map from left to right, then you will know the service delivery from the customer's perspective. To look at the service from the customer-contact employees' perspective, read the horizontal lines above and below the line of visibility. In this way, the front-of-house employees' role can be evaluated and employees' job descriptions can be devised. The blueprint can also be used in training to show employees how their role links to other employees and functions in the organization. To review key elements of the overall service process, the blueprint can be analysed vertically. For example, the efficiency of the kitchen (back-of-house) service system is crucial in delivering a quality restaurant service. By critically examining the service encounters at the line of internal interaction, potential fail-points or bottlenecks can be identified and eliminated. Sometimes the fault can be attributed to kitchen production problems, and sometimes the fault is the front-of-house service staff efficiency. The blueprint enables the management to understand why the failure or bottleneck has occurred, which helps to establish strategies that correct the problem.

A blueprint can also be used to redesign an existing service. The first step is to map the current service process, and the second stage is to establish the desired service performance. The next stage involves comparing what actually happens with what the company wants to happen and identifying discrepancies. Finally, a solution will be proposed and mapped out on a new blueprint.

The benefits of blueprints can be summarized as follows (Gummesson & Kingman-Brundage, 1991):

- Service process weaknesses are identified, so that they can be resolved by improvement schemes
- Interdepartmental linkages are made transparent
- Employees are helped to understand their own role within the entire service process
- Blueprints help to facilitate internal marketing, where internal supplier–customer relationships are identified.

Case study 11.1 Baldwins' Omega, Sheffield, United Kingdom – 'Arguably, the Best Banqueting Venue in Yorkshire'

In 1980, David and Pauline Baldwin bought the Omega – a large, detached restaurant and banqueting operation with extensive grounds and car parking about 2 miles from the center of Sheffield. The Omega had suffered from changes in ownership and weak management in the 1970s, and consequently, the business was in a poor condition both financially and physically. However, David and Pauline were well known in the South Yorkshire community: they had already established a good reputation for high quality food and genuine hospitality by running several local inns and a banqueting house in Sheffield.

Over the next 30 years, the Baldwins transformed the Omega into one of the Britain's best banqueting venues. Today, the Omega has four interconnecting banquet rooms that can cater for several smaller functions or up to 300 covers at one sitting. Their business philosophy comprises three core principles:

- Excellent service quality in food operations is dependent on a deep understanding and passion for food products, cooking processes and kitchen management
- Fresh food, freshly prepared, cooked and served straight 'from the oven to the table'
- Honest, long-term, transparent relationships with customers, employees and suppliers.

David Baldwin believes that without high quality fresh ingredients, the menu will disappoint. All ingredients, apart from a small store of essential dry goods, are fresh and delivered fresh every day. There are two suppliers for each category of food – specialist farmers for poultry and meats, dairy, vegetables/herbs, fish (often from Yorkshire fishing towns such as Whitby). The relationship with a local farmer illustrates the attention to detail that the Baldwins invest in ensuring that the ingredients match the quality they expect. David Baldwin buys his own cattle at the market when they are 36 weeks old. The cattle are then reared by a local farmer in scrupulously clean, modern barns – indeed the cows sometimes relax with music playing in the background! This approach to farming can be described as 'caring husbandry' and all of Baldwins' suppliers subscribe to this philosophy. When a fresh turkey supplier changed hands, the new owners changed their rearing methods, and the Baldwins changed their supplier. Price is not a major factor in negotiations but, because there are always two suppliers, prices remain competitive. The Omega does not purchase organic produce primarily due to the difficulty in finding a suitable supplier who can source the high volume required for the operation. Because the Omega operates with a daily fresh food strategy, there are minimum storage facilities – despite the fact that more than 500 meals can be served in one day. There are small freezer facilities for emergencies, a very small dry good store and good refrigeration. All the meat is well hung to ensure quality flavour.

Many volume caterers use cook-chill, pre-plated production systems to enable kitchens to mass produce menu items up to 5 days in advance of service. In multiple-site businesses, outside contract operations and off-site event venues, the production can take place in separate premises – indeed, one central kitchen can serve several outlets. The premise underpinning cook-chill is to simplify the food production process, enhance quality and presentation and save costs. Cook-chill systems use specialized equipment including blast chillers to freeze the food quickly and safely. Then the meals are regenerated shortly before service. Although there are many advocates for cook-chill banqueting systems, especially from a cost-saving perspective, critics – such as David Baldwin – suggest that the process significantly reduces food quality. The Omega uses convection ovens that create a uniform temperature using internal fans to manage the hot air circulation. These ovens cook food faster and at lower temperatures, which help to seal in the flavour of roast meats and also provide energy savings.

Curiously, none of Baldwins' recipes are written down. The kitchen brigade, all personally trained by David Baldwin, has worked at the Omega for many years. For example, Head Chef Stephen Roebuck and the Sous-Chef have both worked at Baldwins for more than 20 years, and the most junior member of the brigade has worked for at least 3 years. The chefs are encouraged to constantly taste their cooking to ensure that the flavour and quality are correct. David Baldwin and Stephen Roebuck constantly carry out spot check tastings, and if there is a problem dish, it is discarded. The kitchen team starts the day by baking the fresh bread and preparing for lunches. All the vegetables are freshly peeled by hand, and all the desserts/puddings are made on the premises. Meats are roasted for 4 hours before service; after 2 hours of cooking, they are then rested for 2 hours. The banquet service is timed, and the chickens are roasted for 70 min before they are served. Refrigerated food, apart from salads and cream, is taken out of the fridges 30 mins before service to reach room temperature. This is what the Baldwins mean by their cooking philosophy of fresh food, freshly prepared and freshly cooked from the oven to the table, but it does require highly efficient kitchen management and good team work with the front-of-house employees. Although traditional Yorkshire food is always available, new menu items are introduced on a regular basis and recipes continue to adapt and evolve as consumer tastes change.

Efficient banqueting operations must know the number of diners at least 48 hours before the event, and all customers should have the same menu – except those with allergic, dietary or religious requirements. The best banqueting establishments ensure that customers with special diets also have a memorable dining experience. Despite Baldwins' generous portions including extra servings for those who want more, there is little waste, and any food that is not consumed by customers is used for staff meals.

At the start of his career in Sheffield, David Baldwin joined local business clubs such as Round Table and the Junior Chamber of Commerce. Networking at these events, he met many of his future customers who are still his customers today. David and Pauline have always been very involved in their local community and support many local charities. David is a regular interviewee on the local radio station and is widely recognized as a larger-than-life local character. All these activities help to promote the Omega.

Today, the Baldwins take 3 months holiday each year, but the Omega continues to deliver high quality food and service despite the absence of the owners. The operation's continued success is built on the long service record, professionalism and attitude of the key members of the management team and employees. Apart from the chefs – the General Manager, Janet Wilson has worked at the Omega for 30 years, the Operations Manager for 17 years, the Banqueting Secretary for 7 years and several front-of-house employees between 10 and 25 years. Indeed the children of older employees often work part-time in the business. David and Pauline Baldwin reward their key staff with appropriate financial packages and very generous 'thank you's', such as paying for them to eat out in some of Britain's highest rated restaurants. Because the business is so successful, the Omega closes for Xmas and New Year, so that the employees can enjoy their own holidays during the festive season – this is an unusual demonstration of employee welfare coming before profits. The Baldwins have very direct, honest relationships with their management team, employees and suppliers and even the customers. Over the years, this has developed into a mutual understanding and reciprocated loyalty. The Baldwins have created a strong team spirit that ensures that the service quality remains consistently high at the Omega.

- Explain why the Baldwin's business philosophy might be popular with customers, employees and suppliers.
- What are the differences between Baldwins' kitchen production process and cook-chill processes?
- How do the Baldwins maintain service quality?

Source: Pauline and David Baldwin

Complexity and divergence in hospitality services

Service processes can also be defined in terms of their complexity and diversity (Zeithaml & Bitner, 2009). The level of service complexity refers to the number of steps and sequences that need to be carried out to perform the service – the fewer steps, the lower the service complexity; the greater the number of actions required to perform the service, the greater the complexity. The level of divergence refers to the degree of tolerance allowed in performing the service process. Some service processes are highly standardized and consequently have a very low degree of diversity; other operations allow employees more autonomy in delivering the service, and therefore, there is greater diversity. The analysis of service processes against the criteria of complexity and divergence can help managers to understand key drivers in the service process. Figure 11.2 provides an example of the complexity/divergence matrix using a street vendor, a sandwich shop, a gourmet restaurant and customized event catering.

A person working on a mobile hotdog cart or an Asian street wok vendor has a very small number of actions to perform to serve a hotdog or stir-fry, so a hotdog cart or street wok has a relatively low level of complexity. Also, the service process for street cooking has a lower degree of diversity because it is a very standardized process with a limited number of ingredients. Conversely, a sandwich shop with an extensive menu and dozens of different fillings offering customers considerable choice has a relatively high degree of diversity, but the operation of making sandwiches is simple, and so the level of complexity is low. The kitchen skills and production processes required to deliver the highest quality menus in a gourmet restaurant are highly complex, but a gourmet restaurant must deliver high consistency, regardless of which chef is cooking, and so the level of divergence is low as the chefs follow the gourmet recipes. Some services are unique and encompass high levels of both complexity and divergence. For example, bespoke catering for special occasions, where the customer requires atypical cuisine

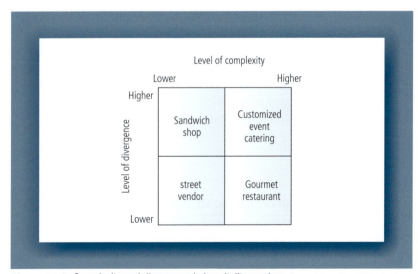

Figure 11.2 Complexity and divergence in hospitality services *Source: Adapted from Zeithaml and Bitner, 2003*

using unusual ingredients and exotic recipes prepared by highly skilled chefs to create a customized menu, is both highly complex and highly divergent.

Service process strategies

By mapping the service process using blueprinting, a company can establish the levels of complexity and divergence in its service operations. The service process can be changed either to increase or decrease the levels of complexity and divergence. There are four alternative strategies:

1 *Complexity reduction strategy.* To reduce the complexity of a service process, the number of steps and sequences used to produce the service are reduced, for example, reducing the number of items offered on the restaurant menu reduces the level of complexity. This might mean specializing in specific customer segments and narrowing the marketing offer. The reduction in complexity should improve consistency and cost control. However, such a strategy risks alienating customers who enjoyed the service standards of a more complex operation, and they might transfer their loyalty and patronage to a competitive establishment.

2 *Increased complexity strategy.* Increasing the complexity of the service process means adding more activities to the existing service and providing customers with an enhanced marketing offer, for example, introducing more items on the menu. By providing customers with additional services, the company should be able to generate additional revenue and/or enhance customer satisfaction. However, increased complexity might create service quality problems and increase costs, and some customers may not be interested in paying more for the new offer.

3 *Divergence reduction strategy.* Reducing the level of divergence in the service process implies a greater standardization of the services, for example, moving from a table service restaurant to a self-service restaurant operation. With a higher level of standardization, there should be increased productivity and cost reductions through economies of scale. This type of service process strategy is linked to a volume orientation and mass-marketing approach. From a customer perspective, the advantages might include greater consistency and reliability of service quality. However, some customers may resent the changes and react negatively to the standardized service offer.

4 *Increased divergence strategy.* Increasing divergence allows for greater customization of the service offer. This is associated with a niche positioning strategy, which in hospitality could be enabled by a human resource empowerment strategy where employees are encouraged to respond to customers' individual needs and wants.

However, increasing divergence can mean less control and could be linked to greater fluctuations in service quality. A customization strategy implies higher prices to cover the additional costs of an increased divergence strategy. In customized event catering, the customer will be prepared to pay the additional price for the uniqueness of the event.

REASONS FOR SERVICE FAILURE

Service failures occur when the service provided does not match the customer's expectation of the service promised in the pre-encounter marketing mix, word of mouth recommendation or from previous satisfactory consumption experiences. Typical hospitality service failures include the following:

- Facilities and services that have been promoted in marketing communications are not available
- The physical environment is disappointing (damaged furniture, tired décor, poor hygiene standards, inappropriate music, atmosphere not welcoming)
- The service is slower than expected
- The standard of cooking is poor (overcooked/undercooked food, too much/too little seasoning, food served at the wrong temperature)
- Employees who lack product knowledge, do not care or, even worse, are rude to customers.

Obviously, some service failures are relatively minor for the customer, whereas others are very important. Dissatisfied customers with serious complaints can litigate against hospitality companies. The characteristics of the product, the type of occasion, the price charged, the nature and seriousness of complaints and the personality of the customer influence how customers complain. Consumers have been categorized into passives, voicers, irates, activists and terrorists, depending on their propensity to complain (Singh, 1990).

Passives

Not all customers complain about the service, even when they have justifiable reasons for doing so. Some customers believe that it is simply not worth the trouble to complain and that perhaps the employees (and the company) do not really care about their service problems. Other customers do not know how to complain; this can be a problem for international visitors, who might not be familiar with the cultural norms when travelling in a foreign country. Passive customers are unlikely to tell others about their experience.

Voicers

Unlike passive people, some consumers believe that complaining is a positive action for both the customer and the company. They think that complaining helps the company to improve its service, and they give the company the opportunity to recover from the service failure. Voicers can develop a positive attitude to the company, if the employees or management responds appropriately to the complaint.

Irates

Irate customers will tell their friends and relatives about the service failure and spread negative word of mouth. They may also have complained to the company. They are likely to switch to a competitor.

Activists

Some people like to complain and even enjoy the confrontation either with service employees at the time of the incident or later by correspondence. Activists are more likely to complain to third parties, and they may become unreasonable in their demands for compensation. They are vociferous, telling as many people as they can about their poor treatment.

Terrorists

A tiny minority of customers who complain can become obsessed with what they believe to be the company's inadequate response to their complaint. These alienated individuals publicize the service company's failings in newspaper advertisements or online in blogs and social networking communities such as Facebook. They encourage other unhappy customers to complain, and by generating considerable amounts of negative publicity in the media, they can damage the company significantly. Companies such as McDonald's and Starbucks have suffered from this type of publicity. Today, the Internet provides low-cost opportunities for terrorist customers to set up anti-company websites to publicize their complaints to others.

Activity 11.2   Online search for poor hospitality service

In a search engine or social network site type in 'worst hotel in the world' and/or 'worst restaurant in the world'.

Review some of the entries, especially on the online hotel/travel comparison sites that might contain negative and positive customer feedback.

Make a list of the main reasons why angry customers complain.

What should the hospitality manager responsible for the unit do?

WHEN AND HOW CUSTOMERS COMPLAIN

Customers can complain to the company and third parties using a variety of approaches.

Concurrently

When a customer complains at the same time as the service failure occurs, this allows the customer-contact employees to respond and attempt to rectify the problem. From both the company's and the customer's perspective, this is the most opportune moment to resolve the service failure. It allows the customer to explain the nature of the complaint in detail. In hospitality services, this can include customers pointing out the defects in the quality of food or the lack of cleanliness in a bathroom. It also allows management and the customer-contact employees the opportunity to apologize to the customer immediately and to take appropriate corrective action. If the remedial action works the customer's initial disappointment can be turned into a positive incident, and customer loyalty can even be enhanced.

Subsequently

Customers can telephone, email, text or write letters of complaint. With the passage of time, even a few days, some customers can feel more strongly about the service failure. The details of the critical incidents can be magnified, especially if the complainer enjoys embellishing the description of the events. However, because the customer has contacted the company and provided details of the complaint, there is still the opportunity for the company to retrieve the situation and win back the customer.

Third-party complaints

Alternatively, the unhappy customer can contact other organizations, typically consumer affairs bodies or legal entities. Local or national governments, consumer protection bodies, tourist boards, motoring organizations, hotel and restaurant guide books all respond to customers' complaints by discussing the problems with the management of the hospitality business concerned. Normally, a hospitality company will agree a course of action with the third party and respond to the complaint satisfactorily.

Online complaints

Online hospitality distributors encourage customers to give both positive and negative feedback electronically. There are also third-party complaint sites where unhappy customers can report their complaints. Unhappy customers may be able to substantiate their complaint by uploading photographs or video. Effective managers will normally attempt to resolve the problem, thereby retaining the customer for future transactions. Some complaints go viral, meaning that they are communicated from person to person by email, perhaps as a result of having been uploaded to social networking sites. In other cases, customers may give the evidence to the media, which generally ensures extensive negative publicity for the company. This type of negative publicity is extremely damaging to the business's reputation and could even lead to a collapse in customer confidence, with disastrous consequences for the company (see Marketing insight 11.2).

Marketing insight 11.2

A negative response to customer complaints

In 2006, a controversial entrepreneur, called David Hattersley, built up a hospitality business in York, England, which included Marmadukes Hotel, Harvilles Steak and Oyster Bar, the Lamb and Lion and Guy Fawkes Inn. David Hattersley borrowed significant amounts of money to invest in the properties but seemed to adopt an abrasive attitude to customers when they complained about service quality in the hotels, restaurants and bars. Although a number of online customer comments were positive about the hospitality experience, many were not. It seems that when David Hattersley did respond to some customers' complaints, he did not apologize, wrote aggressive emails using bad language and created considerable controversy on travel comparison websites. In May 2009, the hotel company was put into administration and, at the time of writing, Marmadukes Hotel and the Guy Fawkes Inn are for sale. Because the administrators have taken over the management of the hospitality operations, online customer comments have been mostly very favourable. Although David Hattersley's business model was probably unsustainable, especially in an economic downturn, the service quality was clearly not consistent and the response to customer complaints did not send appropriate signals to potential customers visiting York.

Sources: Murphy, L. (2009, May 8). Yorkshire hotel group is hit by winding-up petition. Yorkshire Post; Laycock, M. (2010, March 5). Administrators put York hotels on market. The Press. www.tripadvisor.co.uk; www.sucks.co.uk

Negative word of mouth

Unfortunately, there will always be customers who do not enjoy the service and who will not communicate their dissatisfaction to the hospitality company. This means that the company does not have the opportunity to apologize and is not able to fix the problem and retain the customer. These customers tell their family, friends and acquaintances about the 'poor' service and create a difficult situation because of the power of negative word of mouth. Hospitality companies do not always know who spreads negative gossip and are not always able to respond.

SERVICE RECOVERY STRATEGIES

Given the inevitability of service failure, all hospitality companies should have a service recovery strategy. The more professional companies are acutely aware of the importance of handling customer complaints effectively and have procedures that are included in employees' training program. Major companies have customer retention teams in their contact centers who are skilled at complaint handling and resolution. Service recovery strategies include the following.

The zero defects strategy (or do it right first time)

The concept of zero defects is borrowed from manufacturing and is linked to Total Quality Management (TQM). The key principle is to design out every potential problem before it can occur. The special characteristics of services make the adoption of a zero defects strategy difficult to implement for a hospitality company, but the idea of TQM is to create a service culture within the company of 'doing it right first time'. By working to reduce operational service failures, perhaps by service blueprinting, companies can reduce the incidence of customer complaints.

Encourage complaints!!!

This might at first sound strange, but if a company can improve customer service by learning effectively from a complaint, then encouraging customers to complain can improve sales and service quality. One way of encouraging complaints is to tell customers exactly what they should expect and to encourage them to notify the company's staff if this does not happen. Most hospitality companies provide customer comment cards or questionnaires to encourage customer responses after the service transaction, and some companies email guests questionnaires to solicit prompt feedback. This helps those customers who want to make comments. Unfortunately, many companies do not respond to the critical comments from customer feedback and lose the opportunity to create a positive dialogue with the unhappy customer. Responsive companies write and thank customers for their observations and respond appropriately to the comments; such a response can turn a critical customer into a potentially loyal customer. Unfortunately, negative comment cards and questionnaires can be deliberately 'lost' by employees who do not want to be disciplined if they are responsible for the customer complaint. A key issue regarding encouraging customers to complain concerns unit managers who do not want to be seen as having a poor complaints record, even though a positive attitude to encourage complaints could mean that their unit is actually providing a better service than units with a lower level of complaints.

Treat customers fairly when they complain

Customers have a sense of 'fairness'. Following their complaint, customers look for three types of fairness from the company (Tax & Brown, 1998):

1 *Outcome fairness* refers to the tangible result the customer expects to receive after a complaint. Hospitality companies use a range of compensation options when customers complain, including apologies, replacing a menu item, providing a complimentary drink, providing a room upgrade, reducing charges or offering complimentary accommodation/meals, depending on the type of complaint. Most customers expect fair compensation relative to the magnitude of the complaint. If the outcome is 'fair', the customer at least feels that the company took the complaint seriously. However, when companies refuse to offer compensation, or the compensation offered is regarded as 'unfair', then the unhappy customer will be disappointed or even angry, making an already bad situation worse.

2 *Procedural fairness* refers to the company's policy and procedures for handling complaints. When a problem arises, customers ideally want the first employee they talk to be able to sort out the problem or find someone who can. Procedural fairness links to the company's policy and processes on responding quickly and efficiently to the complaint. Customer-contact employees and front-of-house management need to find out what the customer's problem is, apologize and take prompt, courteous and efficient action to provide a solution. This can significantly reduce or eradicate the complaint during the moment of truth.

3 *Interactional fairness* refers to customers expecting employees and management to treat them politely and honestly. Customers want companies genuinely to care about their problem. This might seem to be commonsense, but some hospitality companies do not provide training in customer care and do not allow front-line employees to take decisions. Some employees lie to customers and to management and do not take customer complaints seriously. When customers feel that they are unfairly treated because of the response from the customer-contact employees, they are more likely to defect to competitors.

Learning from customer complaints

Analysis of the pattern of customer complaints provides important evidence about the cause of service failure. If customers consistently complain about a certain problem, then management can develop solutions to the problem, reduce customer complaints and improve customer satisfaction. This is called root-cause analysis. By using customer complaint data, the service process and marketing offer can be much improved.

The service recovery paradox

It has been shown that customers who experience a service failure, complain and then are satisfied by the response from the company, can become even more loyal than customers who have enjoyed good service and not had cause for complaint. The service recovery paradox demonstrates that an effective service recovery strategy can redeem a potentially disastrous situation and turn customers with complaints into loyal customers. Excellent service recovery demonstrates two dimensions of service quality – empathy and responsiveness – that are less visible when service is delivered right first time.

Serial complainers

Hospitality companies are aware that some customers are vexatious in that they find cause to complain about service in the hope of obtaining compensation. Companies such as Hampton Inns and Premier Inn record all customer complaints in the CRS database. If a customer who makes frequent, dubious, complaints wants to book again, they may be advised that any complaints will not receive compensation. Tour operators that normally compete will sometimes share data on customers who are serial complainers.

CONCLUSION

Designing the service process to deliver what customers expect from the hospitality offer is a crucial component of encounter marketing. Companies need to develop a deep understanding of customer expectations to ensure that the service process delivers satisfaction. However, in the hospitality business, there will always be some customers who complain, so companies must have a service recovery strategy to respond to complaints. Indeed, managing complaints effectively can turn dissatisfied customers into very loyal customers.

In this chapter, we have explained the following:

- How processes can be categorized as vertical or horizontal, front-office or back-office and primary or secondary
- The importance of managing service processes to deliver customer satisfaction
- The five dimensions of service quality – reliability, empathy, tangibles, responsiveness and assurance
- The gaps model of service quality, which can explain the gap between customer expectations and customer perceptions of service quality after the service performance
- How to map a hospitality service using blueprinting
- The complexity and divergence in service process strategies
- The reasons for service failure in a hospitality context
- The characteristics of customers who complain – passives, voicers, irates, activists and terrorists
- When and how customers complain
- The role of service recovery strategies.

Activity 11.3

Reflect on the activity you carried out at the beginning of the chapter about your own experiences as a customer eating out.

- Can you remember an occasion when the service quality you experienced was disappointing? Can you explain what went wrong?
- Did you or somebody with you complain to the service provider?
- If yes, how did the employees/manager respond to the complaint? Were you happy with their response? Did they offer you any compensation?
- If no, did you talk to your family and friends about your disappointing experience? If so, how many people did you tell? And did you mention your disappointing experience online, for example, in a social networking site?

Do you now understand how your complaint was managed by the employees/management?

REVIEW QUESTIONS

Now check your understanding by answering the following questions:

1 Discuss the role of service process management in hospitality from a marketing perspective
2 Evaluate the gaps model of service quality, using examples from the hospitality industry
3 Map a hospitality service process that you know either as an employee or as a customer, evaluate the service from the view of a customer and make recommendations to improve service quality

4 Discuss the reasons for service failure in the hospitality business and suggest what companies should do when a customer complains.

References and Further Reading

Gummesson, E., & Kingman-Brundage, J. (1991). Service design and quality: Applying service blueprinting and service mapping to railroad services. In P. Kunst, & J. Lemmink (Eds.). *Quality management in services*. Van Gorcum.

Laycock, M. (2010). Administrators put York hotels on market. The Press. March 5, tripadvisor.co.uk; sucks.co.uk

Murphy, L. (2009). Yorkshire hotel group is hit by winding-up petition. Yorkshire Post, May 8.

Parasuraman, A., Zeithaml, V., & Berry, L. L. (1985). A conceptual model of service quality and its implications for future research. *Journal of Marketing*, *49*, 41–50.

Parasuraman, A., Zeithaml, V., & Berry, L. L. (1992). Achieving service quality through gap analysis and a basic statistical approach. *Journal of Services Marketing*, *6*(1), 5–14.

Shostack, L. (1981). Service positioning through structural change. *Journal of Marketing*, *51*, 34–43.

Singh, J. (1990). A typology of consumer dissatisfaction response styles. *Journal of Retailing*, *66*(1), 57–99.

Tax, S. S., & Brown, S. W. (1998). Recovering and learning from service failure. *Sloan Management Review*, *40*, 61–75.

Zeithaml, V. A., & Bitner, M. J. (2009). *Services marketing*. McGraw-Hill.

CHAPTER 12

Managing customer-contact employees

Chapter objectives

After going through this chapter, you should be able to

- Understand the importance of customer-contact employees in creating satisfactory or memorable customer experiences
- Evaluate service-orientated culture in hospitality companies
- Understand the concept of internal marketing and empowerment in a hospitality context
- Identify the sources of conflict for hospitality customer-contact employees.

INTRODUCTION

A defining characteristic of the hospitality industry is the crucial role played by employees during the service encounter with customers. It is the behaviour of customer-contact employees that creates impressions of high (or poor!) service quality. Furthermore, employees are the personification of the brand. Although recruiting, training and rewarding employees is a human resource management function, marketers need to understand employment strategies to ensure that employees are able to represent brand values and deliver the service experience promised by marketers to customers. At the same time, the human resource managers have increasingly adopted a marketing-like approach to employee recruitment and retention. This type of human resource management strategy is called internal marketing.

In this chapter, we discuss the role of employees in delivering appropriately high service quality during the hospitality encounter. We will then examine service culture, internal marketing and service encounters in hospitality organizations.

Activity 12.1

If you are working either full-time or part-time, or have worked, in a hospitality unit, reflect on your own experiences as an employee.

- Was the interview/selection process formal using a range of different methods (online application form/letter, several interviews and applicant tests) or was the process very informal?
- Did the company have formal induction and training?
- Were the managers and employees genuinely passionate about giving customers excellent service?
- What happened if a customer complained?

We will revisit these questions at the end of the chapter and see what you have learnt.

THE IMPORTANCE OF CUSTOMER-CONTACT EMPLOYEES

In Chapters 10 and 11, we repeatedly referred to the key role of employees in delivering appropriately levels of service quality. Considerable research has been undertaken in this area and has established the significant influence of employees on service quality and customer satisfaction. At the simplest level, W. J. (Bill) Marriott (Snr)'s famous quotation accurately summarizes the importance of employees – 'it takes happy employees to make happy customers and this results in a good bottom line' (Lashley, 2000).' At a more complex level, it is the customer-contact employees who deliver on most aspects of the five dimensions of service quality: reliability, empathy, tangibles (partly), responsiveness and assurance.

The service profit chain (Heskett, Jones, Loveman, Sasser, & Schlesinger, 1994) is a model that demonstrates the link between employee satisfaction, service quality, customer satisfaction and business performance. When employees are satisfied with their working conditions and relationships, they are more likely to work productively for the company. These employees know the company's service quality standards and should, therefore, be capable of meeting the quality standards that the company and customer expect. Customer satisfaction leads to repeat and recommended sales. Customers like to see familiar faces when they return, and when the same employees greet regular customers by name, this helps in the development of loyalty. Loyal customers are more profitable, so business performance improves.

If employees are not satisfied at work, the business can suffer from a cycle of poor employee retention, staff shortages and employees with limited company experience and limited product/service knowledge who deliver service quality below customers' expectations. Customers are less likely to return, and if they do return they are unlikely to be recognized. With fluctuating service standards and little continuity of customer-contact employees, the opportunity to develop closer customer relationships is lost. The business does not generate sufficient repeat and recommended sales, and profits can decline.

The service profit chain (Fig. 12.1) demonstrates the association between employee satisfaction and customer satisfaction. However, this relationship is complex, and there is no simple causal link. For example, some long service employees may fall into a pattern of poor customer service, especially in a hospitality unit that has changed

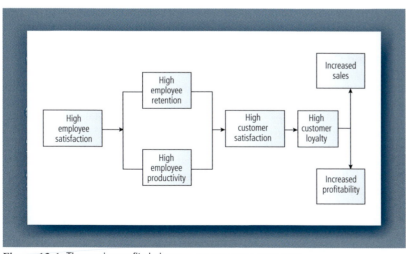

Figure 12.1 The service profit chain *Source: Adapted from Heskett et al., 1994*

ownership or management several times. Employees can become cynical and bored with their work environment, leading to indifferent service attitudes and lower standards of service.

DEVELOPING A SERVICE-ORIENTATED CULTURE

In this book, we have already mentioned how a hospitality company's formal Standard Operating Procedures can help or hinder an employee's relationship with customers. A company's culture has a powerful influence on how employees look after customers. There is a limit to management's ability to monitor and control service encounters, so customer-contact employees have enormous scope to interpret the company's rules. What guides customer-contact employees in choosing their behaviour towards a customer is the organization's service culture.

Each hospitality organization has its own culture – its own DNA. In everyday language, culture is what an employee describes when responding to the question: 'what's it like working here?' Culture, in this context, means the shared core values, beliefs and assumptions that underpin how the organization operates, including the way that it treats its employees. These cultural components are often deeply rooted in the organization's founding, history and recent development. Entrepreneurs such as Bill Marriott, whose strong Mormon faith provided the ethical foundation for treating employees in a positive, caring manner, still influences the Marriott Corporation's approach to human resource management. Companies that have been created through a series of mergers/acquisitions, and regard shareholders as the key stakeholders, can have a culture that values financial performance above all else. This can be less attractive to employees.

Case study 12.1 provides an illustration of service culture and service quality at Red Carnation Hotels.

Case study 12.1 Service culture and service quality at Red Carnation Hotels (RCH)

Company profile: The Red Carnation Collection comprises 13 luxury hotels and spas in London, the UK provinces, South Africa, Switzerland and the United States. These 4- and 5-star privately owned boutique hotels operate in intensely competitive environments such as London and Florida. The RCH mission is to provide exceptional, memorable hospitality by meeting or exceeding guest expectations. One of the RCH core values is to give personalized, warm and consistently exceptional service.

The challenge is how to ensure that 1500 employees from many different cultural backgrounds, working in four different countries and located in three different continents consistently deliver the RCH mission and core values.

The key idea is to invest above average resources in the company's people to deliver the exceptional and memorable guest experience which contemporary consumers of luxury products expect. RCH have developed a robust human resource strategy and monitoring systems to manage the recruitment, training and motivation of employees. Although RCH does have Standard Operating Procedures, the hotels are managed individually and the company service culture is customized at the property level.

Recruiting employees with open minds, character, energy and personality as opposed to technical skills is the critical starting point. Although skills can be taught, it is very difficult to change the behaviour of employees who have inappropriate service attitudes. RCH employs its own highly skilled trainers who conduct training in the hotel properties. Employees are empowered to deliver the RCH mission, but this empowerment is set within precise boundaries, so that employees, supervisors and managers all know what is expected of them. For example, if any guest checking-out has a problem with their bill, the front desk employees are empowered to immediately resolve the issue without having to contact their manager. When employees make mistakes, this is accepted provided the employee learns from their error. Employees are promoted within RCH properties and across the group, but unlike many hotel operators, newly promoted supervisors and managers are provided with additional training to support them in their new role.

Employee/customer ratios are an indicator of service levels in luxury hotels. In the RCH 4-star properties, the ratio is above the industry average at 1.5 employees to 1 customer, and in the 5-star hotels, the ratio of 2 employees to 1 customer is similar to other leading luxury hotels. To deliver memorable service, RCH carefully observes every customer *touch point* and strives to develop responsive policies that recognize the different types of customer (single, group, business and special occasion), the customer's culture (tourists from the United States have different needs and wants to Mediterranean customers) and what employees should, or should not, be doing. Two ideas help to focus the management thinking: first, to review the customer experience from a BDA perspective (Before, During and After) and second, to look to see how the hotels can deliver Tiny Noticeable Touches (TNT). For example, front desk employees are empowered to spend up to £ 50 on any guest to improve their stay. One couple who were regulars brought their dog to stay at one of the hotels; a front desk employee developed a good rapport with the customers. At the end of their stay, the front desk employee thoughtfully gave the owners an unusual present for the dog that cost £ 20. This low-cost gesture really delighted the guests.

One of the challenges is how to deliver consistent service quality in the European, American and South African hotels when each region has such different cultural attitudes to service. To ensure hotels such as the Twelve Apostles Hotel and Spa in Cape Town, South Africa deliver RCH service standards, many of the South African employees are sponsored to work in front office, bar, restaurant and housekeeping in the RCH hotels in Europe. This not only helps to develop the technical service skills of employees but also exposes the employees to the RCH service philosophy. Many of these employees are then promoted to supervisory and management levels when they return to South Africa. Clearly, this strategy is successful, because the Twelve Apostles Hotel has achieved significant recognition in several reader awards such as the 'Best City Hotel and Best Hotel Spa in Africa and the Middle East' in Travel and Leisure World and runner up in the 'Best Hotel in Africa' category by Trip Advisor's Readers' Choice Awards.

RCH employees have similar pay and employment conditions to competitor hotels. A key strategy is to ensure that employees are recognized, and this happens in a variety of ways. If an employee is interested in career development, then appropriate opportunities are provided to enable employees to progress. There are initiatives to involve employees in regular social events and many incentives and prizes. For example, up-selling at the front office is a major skill. Employees are encouraged to identify that customers might be interested in a room upgrade and then to sell the benefits of the upgrade. The front desk employee receives 10% of the upgrade as a bonus. Therefore, if a guest is up-sold from a £ 200 room rate to £ 250 and stays five nights, then the front desk employee will have a £ 25 bonus (5 nights × 10% of the £ 50 upgrade = £ 25). In 1 year, more than £ 250,000 of additional revenue was generated by employees' up-selling – and the front desk employees shared £ 25,000 in bonuses.

RCH monitors its human resource strategy in a variety of ways. Employees have catch-up meetings with their line managers every 3 months and an annual appraisal. Each year there is a detailed employee survey to track management performance. When employees choose to leave, there is a rigorous exit survey and interview. The monthly department and hotel employee turnover statistics for each property is reported, and an element of the general manager's bonus is based on achieving employee retention targets. The departmental/hotel comparative retention statistics are used as a tool to help unit managers to explore retention issues and identify any managerial/supervisory training requirements. Although there is a natural element of transient employment in the hospitality industry, the RCH employee retention statistics of between 20% and 39% are significantly better than most hotel companies.

The RCH human resource strategy helps to deliver high service quality and personalized exceptional service across a diverse portfolio of international luxury hotels.

Source: Jonathan Raggett, Managing Director Red Carnation Hotels and http:// www.redcarnationhotels.com

Employees learn the organizational culture by observing the behaviour and messages sent out by head and regional offices and through the unit's general manager – who represents and personifies the corporate culture. Employees' shared perceptions of the organizational culture, the visible manifestations of the surface layer of the company, are described as the 'climate' (Schneider & Bowen, 1995). Although the climate and culture in a company is not normally written down, it nonetheless influences both service culture and how customer-contact employees interact with customers and each other. Sometimes a company's senior management will draft a statement reflecting its vision, mission and values. This can encapsulate the culture of the organization.

In small- and medium-sized owner-managed hospitality businesses, the 'family' culture will be more visible to employees (see Marketing insight 12.1).

Marketing insight 12.1

The Blunsdon House Hotel, Swindon, England

Over the past 60 years, the Clifford family has turned a farmhouse bed-and-breakfast business into a major 4-star conference and leisure hotel, The Blunsdon House Hotel. Founders Zan and Peter Clifford have always been customer orientated, and their son John continues the tradition, stating: 'we are obsessive in our ambition to provide excellent service'. The founders live on the premises and still take a passionate interest in customers' welfare – demonstrating their commitment and leading by example. They also recognized the need for developing and looking after their employees as the business grew. Key employees, and members of their families, have worked with the Clifford family for generations. Most heads of department have long service awards, and the general manager was also appointed a director.

The service culture in a family business is often highly personalized and provides guests with a genuinely local hospitality experience.

Nearly, all major hospitality organizations claim to be good employers and suggest 'Our employees are our most important assets'. Employees might not believe these messages when the company's actual human resource practices are poor. Where employees hear company messages that promote a certain kind of behaviour but witness contradictory behaviours from management, then the organization suffers from a kind of cultural schizophrenia. Like a personality disorder, such inconsistency may undermines the organization's aim to deliver high service quality. Clearly, culture and climate reflect the philosophy of the senior management team. In some organizations, the senior management team may have a genuine ambition to provide high quality service, but middle managers, who are responsible for controlling costs, may thwart the company's intentions.

The general manager as a role model

Different units within the same hospitality brand can have different cultures and climates. Although the characteristics of a successful hospitality general manager (GM) will vary, the personality, behaviour and actions of the GM send powerful signals to the employees and help to shape the culture and climate of the unit. Employee morale and motivation are a reflection of the general manager; employees respond to the leadership provided and follow the example and direction set by the general manager.

Service myths, heroes and villains

Those hospitality companies aspiring to provide excellent service often use examples of extraordinary customer-contact employee actions in their advertising, publicity and newsletters. In publicizing these, the company is implicitly informing both customers and employees about the service experience it values. These stories influence employee and customer expectations. Over time, if repeated, these actions can become part of the dominant service culture. In the extraordinary service company, heroes become the personification of what is best about the company. However, some maverick companies employ characters (notably celebrity chefs) who become 'villains' through negative publicity, and enjoy their controversial reputation.

Support systems

Customer-contact employees are dependent on support systems, both human and technological, to help to deliver appropriate levels of service quality. In hospitality, there has traditionally been tension and conflict between front-of-house employees and back-of-house employees, especially between the restaurant and kitchen. If the organization wants to foster a service culture throughout the company, then back-of-house employees should think of front-of-house employees as partners or internal customers and not as enemies.

We have already discussed how the company's policies can either nurture or inhibit customer-contact employees' actions towards customers. Companies usually set boundaries to the authority employees have when dealing with customers. Some companies tightly restrict the authority of customer-contact employees, who must follow rules and regulations and report to the more senior managers who make decisions. A different perspective, which we will discuss in detail later, is the notion of empowerment. Empowerment gives customer-contact employees the responsibility, authority and tools for solving customers' problems. Technological support systems include the computer systems, equipment and infrastructure within a property or chain. Obviously, it is difficult for customer-contact employees to provide appropriate levels of service quality if computer systems are slow or food and beverage equipment does not function properly. No matter how pleasant customer-contact employees are, if the support systems do not work, the organization's claim to have a service culture will appear inconsistent to both customers and the employees. Finally, in a genuine service culture, all employees – regardless of their role and status – should be customer focused. Indeed, some experts, such as Gummesson (2008), contend that all employees in service companies are involved in marketing.

Activity 12.2

Building on Activity 12.1 – if you have worked in a hospitality organization, think about the service culture you observed whilst working.

- Evaluate the culture and climate of the company, the role adopted by the general manager, the service myths and company heroes and the adequacy of the support systems.

- What do you think the company did well? What could be improved?

INTERNAL MARKETING

The services marketing triangle (Zeithaml & Bitner, 2003; see Fig. 12.2) links pre-encounter marketing (also called external marketing) with internal marketing and marketing during the encounter (also called interactive marketing). The promises made to customers in pre-encounter communications have to be delivered during the service encounter. We have already discussed the role of employees, and specifically customer-contact employees, in the service encounter. Increasingly, human resource managers have adopted marketing-like approaches to recruit, communicate, motivate and retain employees. This is called internal marketing (Varey & Lewis, 2000).

The main driver of internal marketing is the recognition of the competitive labour market for hospitality employees by companies who compete for the best available talent. Because the success of the hospitality offer is significantly dependent on the quality of service, which is in turn highly dependent on employees, hospitality companies need to attract, train, motivate and retain the most appropriate employees

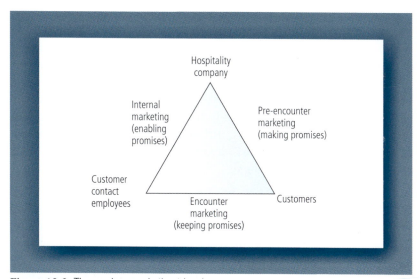

Figure 12.2 The services marketing triangle *Source: Adapted from Zeithaml and Bitner, 2003, Services marketing, p. 319, reproduced with permission of The McGraw-Hill Companies*

for their product concept. Internal marketing involves marketing the organization to current and prospective employees in much the same way as the organization markets its offer to external customers.

Recruitment

Societal perceptions of working in hospitality vary according to the importance of tourism to an economy. In societies where tourism is a key industry, such as the Caribbean, or where tourism is rapidly developing, such as in China, careers in hospitality are regarded favourably. Potential employees recognize that hospitality jobs are relatively well paid and enjoy high status. In these societies, employers can select potential employees from a large pool of available talent.

Marketing insight 12.2

The InterContinental Hotel, Phnom Penh

Thierry Douin's first appointment as a General Manager was the challenging task of opening a new InterContinental Hotel in Phnom Penh in 1996. Cambodia was just beginning to recover from 30 years of civil war, famine and disease, and employment prospects for local people were poor. The hotel needed to recruit 400 local employees, but more than 3800 eople applied for the jobs – working in a 5-star hotel represented, for many Cambodians, a unique opportunity to earn a good income.

In societies where hospitality is generally regarded as lower status with lower pay and prospects, the recruitment challenge is more difficult. The image and reputation of the company as an employer is crucial in attracting appropriate employees. Indeed, the strategic aim is often to be the 'preferred employer in the area'. As a Marriott brand, Ritz-Carlton has always nurtured a strong employee focus in their domestic operations and endorses the 'preferred employer in the area' strategy. The company won the USA Malcolm Baldrige National Quality Award back in 1992 and again in 1999 for service/performance excellence – the only hotel company to have achieved this accolade. In recent years, Ritz-Carlton has won many international 'Best Places to Work' awards in countries such as China, Dubai, Singapore and Portugal.

Service inclination

An essential quality that employers seek in employees is the 'right service attitude'. Some people seem to have a natural aptitude for service; they spontaneously respond to customers and co-workers and have a cheerful disposition. These characteristics are linked to

an individual's personality, interpersonal communication skills and initiative and are developed in life experiences over time. As such, attitude cannot really be taught as if it were a job-related skill such as operating a cash register. Unfortunately, one of the problems for hospitality employers in competitive labour markets is the lack of potential employees with the right service attitude. This means that unsuitable employees, who do not have an aptitude for service, are recruited, and these employees can undermine management's attempts to deliver appropriately high levels of service quality. Another important element in hospitality employment is teamwork – the ability to fit into a team and play a role. Some people enjoy working in a team, they are good team players and are supportive to those around them; however, other people are awkward in teams and are not good team players, which can be demotivating for co-workers.

Service competences

Employees need to have skills and knowledge to be able to perform their job effectively. Skills and knowledge in hospitality are called service competences. Historically, most hospitality managers had limited education and learnt service competences whilst working in the industry. Today, there is a well-established system of hospitality and tourism education in many parts of the world. Colleges offer craft training and diplomas and universities offer Bachelors, Masters and Doctoral program, and there is a range of study-mode options. The best institutions have very close links to the hospitality industry, for example, in Thailand, the Dusit Hotel Chain set up the Dusit Thani College to provide training and higher education for hotel, kitchen and restaurant and tourism management students. These educational institutions prepare students for the industry and provide them with core hospitality competences.

Training

Each hospitality company has its own service culture, operating systems and service standards. New customer-contact employees need induction training to become familiar with the product (product knowledge training) and service philosophy and to meet co-employees working in the same team. Induction training in larger organizations is more formal, whereas in the smaller hospitality firms, it is likely to be less formal. Continuous training and career development is a hallmark of successful hospitality companies. Companies with seasonal operations, such as Ski Olympic, have particular challenges when inducting their employees (see Case study 12.2).

Case study 12.2 **The training challenge for Ski Olympic**

Ski Olympic recruits more than 150 employees each year to work in its Alpine chalets and chalet hotels for a 5-month season. Approximately, one third of last year's employees return for the new season. Other employees are mostly recruited by word of mouth from the friends of recent employees and the families of customers. The challenge for each year is to train up to 100 new employees how to deliver the Ski Olympic experience, in less than 2 weeks. The training is conducted at the Ski Olympic chalet-hotel Les Avals. As soon as the employees arrive, they are greeted and treated like guests, following exactly the same schedule with breakfast, afternoon tea and dinner. The new employees adopt different roles, taking it in turns to be customers and then employees, and teams of chefs prepare the same meals that customers will eat on their holidays (one difficult challenge is cooking at Alpine elevations – it takes much longer to boil an egg!). Each employee learns his or her role during this intensive period, and departments have written job lists to help to ensure that Ski Olympic's operating standards, even in an informal, fun environment, are maintained. Gary Yates, an Area Manager, explained that treating the employees as customers was the most effective way to show them the customer experience. The success of Ski Olympic is built on customer satisfaction – 72% of sales are repeat business.

Source: Gary Yates, Ski Olympic

Empowerment

Customer-contact employees work within boundaries of authority allowed by their companies. We have discussed how some hospitality companies set clear rules about what any given customer-contact employee is allowed to do or not to do. An alternative approach is to empower employees to take responsibility for ensuring customers are satisfied with the service encounter. This responsibility needs to be matched with delegated authority and supported by appropriate resources such as technology, training and budgets. It is claimed that this approach, championed in hospitality by Marriott and their luxury brand Ritz Carlton, is more customer focused and motivates employees, involving them, to a greater or lesser extent, in self-management in the workplace. Table 12.1 illustrates various forms of empowerment in hospitality.

Table 12.1 Forms of empowerment in hospitality	
Form of empowerment	**Organization**
Quality circles	Accor Group
Suggestion schemes	McDonald's Restaurants
'Whatever it takes' training	Marriott Hotels
Autonomous work groups	Harvester Restaurants
De-layering the organization	Bass Taverns

Source: Lashley (2001, p. 6)

The concept that any customer-contact employee should take own-ership of and resolve customer problems, and respond empathically to customers' individual needs and wants, is attractive. Customers want speedy solutions, especially when complaining, and resent hav-ing to repeat their complaint to several different employees. How-ever, customer-contact employees do not necessarily want to take the responsibility for customer satisfaction because of the following:

* Employees may not be given genuine authority by the company to solve the problem
* Hospitality companies are traditionally bureaucratic and hierar-chical organizations, where the middle managers may resent cus-tomer-contact employees assuming their authority
* Employees may not receive the appropriate training and resources to make correct decisions
* Employees may feel that they are not paid enough to take this responsibility
* Some employees may not like the idea of taking responsibility at all and prefer to follow the orders of managers.

Though many companies talk about empowering employees, few have genuinely developed the organizational strategies and culture to support empowered employees. Marriott's training is recognized as a leader in the hotel industry with customer service as the core theme and empowerment as the strategy to encourage employees to show empathy towards customers' needs and wants (Lashley, 2001). The training involves 40–60 hours and looks at the guest experience by encouraging employees to participate in role-plays. Employees learn that guests need to be acknowledged whilst waiting; want to be treated as individuals; want to see employees who they know and who like their job and, most importantly, do not want 'hassle' when they are staying in a hotel or dining in a restaurant. Marriott continues to search for new ways to deliver the basic brand values through their associates (all Marriott employees are called associates).

Reward systems

Reward systems for employees include tangible and intangible ben-efits. Tangible benefits are pay, bonuses, tips, meals provided free of charge and discounted accommodation for live-in employees. The per-ceived 'fairness' of the distribution of the tips (and/or service charge) in hospitality businesses can be a controversial topic. Many of the intangible benefits of working in hospitality environment compensate for the unsocial hours and lower pay. Intangible benefits can include the excitement, fun and teamwork that many hospitality employees enjoy (and which many hospitality text-books forget!). There can be a sense of pride when customers make favourable comments about the hospitality service and when family and friends respect the company where employees work.

Communication

One important lesson that human resource management has learnt from marketing is the value of regularly informing employees about the company's current situation and future plans, as well as formal communications about company policy, most hospitality company employee magazines, newsletters or internal websites include career development opportunities, articles about social activities, fun events, competitions and long service awards and interesting anecdotes about individual employees. Important achievements are highlighted, and employees are meant to feel more involved with the company. From a marketing perspective, it is essential for customer-contact employees to be aware of new openings, new-product development and new marketing program, so they can inform customers during service encounters.

Criticisms of internal marketing

Critics of internal marketing challenge the theory and practice on a number of grounds (Mudie, 2000). For example, it is claimed that the champions of internal marketing (and in particular empowerment) have relied on rhetoric to promote an idealized workplace. The reality is that many hospitality premises are unpleasant, and sometimes hostile, places of work. There are often staff shortages, sometimes due to bad planning, which increase the workload for the remaining employees and create stress. Unfortunately, hospitality employees can suffer from physical and sexual abuse from customers and co-workers. Many owner-managers operate under conditions of high stress and can be abrupt, indifferent or aggressive towards with staff. Because managers are primarily interested in cost control and profits, they stand accused of poor communication with employees and of not genuinely caring for them. Indeed, many employees feel cynical about management and are suspicious of internal marketing innovations, such as de-layering, which appear to be more a cost-cutting exercise than genuine empowerment. Although there are poor employers in the hospitality industry, internal marketing theory incorporates the best practice and demonstrates the advantages of adopting a positive approach in managing employees.

Emotional labour

Customer-contact employees work long hours, at all times of the day and night, dealing constantly with customers. Working with people can be emotionally tiring, especially if there are staff shortages or if customers complain. Although working in hospitality can be great fun, it can also be very stressful. However, companies expect customer-contact employees to suppress their own feelings and their own identity to ensure that customers are satisfied. Some hospitality organizations even provide cues and scripts – especially in contact centers – to help customer-contact employees say the right words to customers. In particular, empowerment means that customer-contact employees are expected to take on more responsibility, which can lead to more stress. The term *emotional labour* has been used to describe the emotional demands that service-oriented work imposes on employees. Both hospitality managers and customer-contact employees can suffer from the long-term effects of emotional labour, resulting in minor illness, anxiety, depression and fatigue, which can lead to alcoholism, nicotine dependence, eating disorders and, ultimately, cancer, heart disease and nervous breakdowns.

Activity 12.3

Building on the other activities, if you have worked in a hospitality organization think about the service culture you experienced whilst working.

- Evaluate the company's recruitment and training policies, the service inclination and competences of the other employees. Did the company 'empower' employees?
- How valid are the criticisms of internal marketing in a hospitality company compared with your own experience?

SERVICE ENCOUNTERS

There is a wide variety of different types of hospitality service contexts, ranging from low customer-contact services to high customer-contact services (see Fig. 12.3 for an example of food service concepts). The importance of customer-contact employees rises as the level of contact between customers and employees increases. During each and every contact between customers and employees, the customer's perception of service quality is challenged or reinforced. There is an apt expression, popularized by Jan Carlzon (1987), which describes customer/employee contacts as 'moments of truth'. Even in a small independent catering operation, there are hundreds of moments of truth. These moments of truth may last for only a few seconds. Some hospitality experiences, such as staying in a holiday hotel for 2 weeks, can contain thousands of these moments of truth. The vast majority of service encounters between customers and employees can be described as routinized and, providing service standards conform to customer expectations, customers should be satisfied. However, in all hospitality operations, there will inevitably be occasions when customers experience disappointing service encounters. Many are

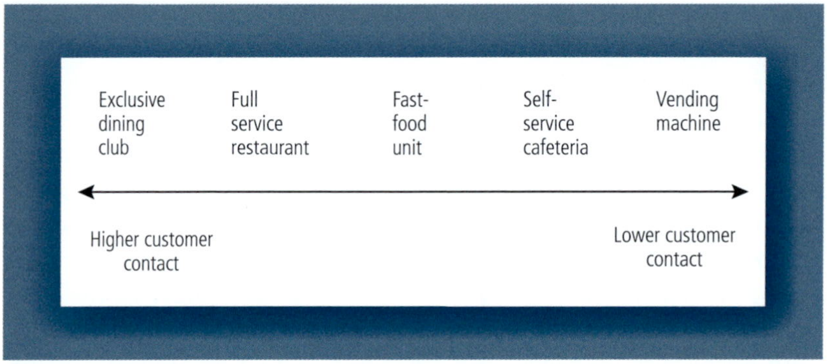

Figure 12.3 Higher and lower customer-contact service contexts – an example from food service

minor disappointments that do not adversely impact on customer satisfaction, but major disappointments can become critical incidents for hospitality organizations. How effectively the customer-contact employees respond to critical incidents will influence the customer's intention to repurchase.

Critical incidents

When a critical incident occurs, the response and actions of customer-contact employees can either save the situation or turn the incident into a significant source of customer dissatisfaction (Bitner, Booms, & Tetreault, 1990). Research suggests that there are three broad categories of critical incidents in service contexts:

1 The employees' responsiveness to service delivery system failures
2 The employees' responses to customer needs and requests
3 Unprompted and unsolicited employee actions.

Table 12.2 summarizes employees' responses to customer issues, which can result in either customer satisfaction or dissatisfaction.

Customers want service failures to be resolved quickly and politely. If the customer-contact employees apologize and provide a satisfactory solution to the problem at the time of the incident, then customers are more likely to forgive the company, and may even develop a more favourable attitude to the business. If the customer-contact employee fails to apologize or is unable (or even unwilling) to help, then the incident can become a source of a serious complaint.

Inevitably, some customers will have special needs and make special requests that are out of the ordinary sphere of the hospitality unit's operational norms. Customers who have special dietary requirements or who want to arrange a special event will ask for help and advice. By definition, these requests are unusual; indeed, they may even be contrary to the company's Standard Operating

Table 12.2 Positive and negative responses to critical incidents

Critical incident	Customer satisfaction	Customer dissatisfaction
Employee response to service delivery failure	Could be turned into incidents that employees use to advantage and generate customer satisfaction: an employee reacts quickly to service failure by responding sensitively to customers – by compensating the customer or upgrading the customer to a higher status service	More frequently, however, staff responses are likely to be a source of dissatisfaction – where an employee fails to provide an apology or an explanation or argues with the customer
Employee response to customer needs and requests	Employee responsiveness, flexibility and confidence that he or she can match whatever is required by the customer are important sources of positive customer responses	Employee intransigence, inflexibility and perceived incompetence are all likely sources of customer dissatisfaction
Unprompted and unsolicited employee action	This might involve employee behaviours that make the customer feel special, or where an act of unexpected generosity takes the customer by surprise	Customer dissatisfaction could be the result of a failure to give the level of attention expected or inadequate information, or might involve inappropriate behaviour, such as the use of bad language

Source: Lashley (2000)

Procedures. How customer-contact employees respond to these situations sends signals to customers. If employees can be flexible and have the confidence to adapt the service to the needs of the customer, then customers are likely to be highly satisfied. If, however, employees appear inflexible and are unhelpful, this can be a source of customer dissatisfaction.

Customer-contact employees can sometimes give customers delightful surprises by their unexpected behaviour, which exceeds customers' expectations. These unprompted and unsolicited employee actions are major sources of customer satisfaction. However, employees who demonstrate a lack of courtesy or use bad language in front of customers can be responsible for major customer dissatisfaction. Of course, unreasonable customers, who can be aggressive, insulting and even threatening, sometimes confront customer-contact employees, especially when customers under the influence of alcohol or drugs.

Good employers do not tolerate bad customer behaviour, and airlines such as British Airways have a 'zero tolerance policy' to protect cabin crew from abusive customers.

SOURCES OF CONFLICT

Customer-contact employees are confronted by both interpersonal and interorganizational conflicts whilst working for hospitality organizations (Lashley, 2001). Conflict at work can be a source and a symptom of employee dissatisfaction. Continuous or excessive conflict creates powerful emotional responses, including unacceptable levels of stress for employees. Understanding the sources of conflict can help managers to reduce stress in the work environment and promote positive working conditions.

Personal/role conflict

Employees have to perform roles at work that may sometimes conflict with their own values and belief systems. Young people may resent a strict dress and grooming code, vegetarians might have an ethical issue preparing meat dishes, people with a strong religious faith may have moral issues with the service and consumption of alcohol and the behaviour of customers (e.g. female near-nudity at resort hotels in some Muslim countries) can be offensive to social conventions. In these situations, the employee's values are challenged by the workplace. This is a personal conflict that individual employees need to resolve, or they may have to choose to leave the company.

Organizational/customer conflict

Organizations have policies, processes and Standard Operating Procedures that regulate the boundaries of employee conduct. Many of these regulations are designed to deliver the brand promise and to help customer-contact employees. Occasionally, customers will make what appears to be a reasonable request of customer-contact employees but which unfortunately breaks the house rules. For example, mid-market hotels with food and beverage facilities normally have opening and closing hours for their restaurant and bar; when customers want to eat or drink and the facilities are closed, customer-contact employees face a dilemma. Do they maintain the house rules and not serve the customer, which results in customer dissatisfaction, or do they break the house rules, serve the customer and deliver customer satisfaction? This type of organizational conflict with customers puts the customer-contact employee in a difficult situation. However, if a customer makes an unreasonable request, for example, asking the customer-contact employee to help in an illegal activity, then the employee should maintain the company's regulations and not help the customer.

Inter-customer conflict

Some of the most difficult situations for customer-contact employees arise from disputes between customers. In most hospitality services, customers are in contact with each other in a myriad of different ways, which can cause problems at times. Customers park their own cars in hotel and restaurant car parks, queue for service, drink with each other in bars and dance with each other in clubs. Conflict between customers can range from minor irritations, such as queue-jumping, to serious abuse and assault. Customer-contact employees need to remain professional and should try and calm difficult situations – but this is easier said, than done.

CONCLUSION

Hospitality companies must develop effective strategies to recruit and retain service-minded customer-contact employees. This is called internal marketing. Hospitality companies claim to be good employers. However, the industry does suffer from high employee turnover rates, and examples of poor treatment of employees are publicized in the media and spread by negative word of mouth.

In this chapter, we have explained

- The link between employee satisfaction, service quality, customer satisfaction and business performance (the service-profit chain)
- That during the hospitality encounter, moments of truth reinforce or challenge the customer's perception of service quality
- How each hospitality company has its own culture and climate, which guides customer-contact employees in their behaviour towards customers
- How human resource departments that use marketing-like approaches to recruit and retain employees are adopting an internal marketing strategy
- The three components of the services marketing triangle – pre-encounter marketing, marketing during the encounter and internal marketing
- That empowerment gives customer-contact employees the responsibility and resources for solving customer problems
- That critics of human resource management in service industries, and especially of empowerment, suggest that empathic employees can experience high levels emotional labour, resulting in stress and illness

- That when there is a critical service incident, such as service failure or unusual customer requests, the responses and unprompted actions of customer-contact employees influence customer satisfaction/dissatisfaction
- That customer-contact employees who experience role conflict, organizational/customer conflict and intercustomer conflict can suffer from work-related stress.

Activity 12.4

At the beginning of the chapter, we asked you to reflect on your work experiences in a hospitality unit. What do you now think about the management's approach in managing employees?

- Was the interview/selection process formal using a range of different methods (online application form/letter, several interviews and applicant tests) or was the process very informal?
- Did the company have formal induction and training?
- How did you learn about the service culture – from the management or the other employees?
- Were the managers and employees genuinely passionate about giving customers excellent service?
- What happened if a customer complained?

REVIEW QUESTIONS

Now check your understanding of this chapter by answering the following questions:

1 Discuss the role of customer-contact employees in delivering the hospitality offer
2 Discuss the sources of conflict for customer-contact employees whilst working in hospitality organizations. Provide examples to illustrate your answer.
3 Evaluate the role of culture and climate in hospitality companies
4 Analyse the theory and practice of internal marketing in the hospitality industry
5 What are the advantages of using 'empowerment' as a human resource strategy in a hospitality business, from each of the following perspectives?
    - the customer
    - the employee
    - the business.

References and Further Reading

Bitner, M. J., Booms, B. H., & Tetreault, M. S. (1990). The service encounter: Diagnosing favourable and unfavourable incidents. *Journal of Marketing, 54*, 71–84.

Carlzon, J. (1987). *Moments of truth*. Harper Collins.

Customer Management. (2000). Towards best practice. *Customer Management*, 6–11, July/August.

Gummesson, E. (2008). *Total relationship marketing*. (3rd ed.). Butterworth-Heinemann.

Heskett, J. L., Jones, T. O., Loveman, G. W., Sasser, W. E., Jr., & Schlesinger, L. A. (1994). Putting the service profit chain to work. *Harvard Business Review, 72*, 164–170.

Lashley, C. (2000). *Hospitality retail management*. Butterworth-Heinemann.

Lashley, C. (2001). *Employing human resource strategies for service excellence*. Butterworth-Heinemann.

Mudie, P. (2000). Internal marketing: A step too far, (Chapter 15). In R. J. Varey, & B. R. Lewis (Eds.). *Internal marketing: Directions for management*. Routledge.

Schneider, B., & Bowen, D. E. (1995). *Winning the service game*. HBS Press.

Varey, R. J., & Lewis, B. R. (2000). *Internal marketing: Directions for management*. Routledge.

Zeithaml, V. A., & Bitner, M. J. (2009). *Services marketing*. McGraw-Hill.

PART **D**

Post-encounter Marketing

CHAPTER **13**

Managing customer satisfaction

Chapter objectives

After going through this chapter, you should be able to

- Define customer satisfaction
- Understand the importance of satisfying customers
- Evaluate customer satisfaction guarantees in hospitality
- Describe tools for measuring customer satisfaction in the hospitality industry.

INTRODUCTION

The concept of satisfying customers is rooted deep in the philosophy of marketing and is a key element in most marketing definitions. Academics and practitioners agree that being able to create and maintain customer satisfaction is critical to business performance. In competitive markets where customers have choice, they may opt to take their business elsewhere in search of greater satisfaction. In this chapter, we explain why customer satisfaction is important; we then discuss customer satisfaction guarantees in hospitality and explain how companies choose between investing in improvements in customer satisfaction and investing in returns to the other, non-customer, stakeholders. Finally, we review measures for capturing customer satisfaction data and customer complaint processes.

Understanding and measuring customer satisfaction are important elements in the post-encounter marketing mix. Satisfaction has a significant influence on customer attitude and behavioural intention. Customers generally have pre-encounter expectations of hospitality experiences and after the encounter they evaluate the experience against those expectations, effectively asking: 'Did that experience meet my expectations?' If expectations are underperformed, dissatisfaction is likely to result. Dissatisfied customers are at risk of defecting to competitors and generating negative word of mouth comment. Satisfied customers, whose expectations are met or exceeded, however, hold out the promise of further business and positive word of mouth. Consequently, it is important for marketers to measure and understand the major influences on customer satisfaction.

DEFINING CUSTOMER SATISFACTION

Satisfaction is a complex phenomenon. In Chapter 3, we discussed consumer expectations, which are formed prior to purchase. Expectations are important comparison standards that help consumers to evaluate the perceived performance of the hospitality offer during and at the end of the service encounter. At the simplest level, customers are satisfied if the experience matches or exceeds their expectations and dissatisfied if the service performance fails to match their expectations. Customer satisfaction can therefore be defined as a positive attitude towards a supplier that is achieved when the customer's expectations are met. One situation that does not fit this definition is when customers expect that a service experience will be poor, and those expectations are met! Meeting these low expectations does not generate satisfaction. However, when expectations are positive, this definition of satisfaction is perfectly adequate. Because customers'

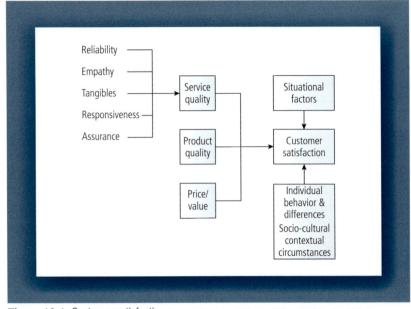

Figure 13.1 Customer satisfaction *Source: Adapted from Zeithaml and Bitner, 2003, Services Marketing, reproduced with permission of The McGraw-Hill Companies*

needs and wants change over time, consumer expectations of the hospitality also offer change over time.

In Chapters 11 and 12, we emphasized the strong linkages between delivering high-service quality, value and customer satisfaction (Zeithaml & Bitner, 2003; Fig. 13.1). Customers can enjoy a range of different types of satisfaction, including the following:

- Contentment, when a routine hospitality service is delivered satisfactorily
- Pleasure, when a hospitality experience makes the consumer feel happy
- Delight, when the experience surprises the consumer and exceeds expectations
- Relief, when a service overcomes a potentially difficult situation and delivers satisfaction.

Activity 13.1

Can you identify a number of hospitality experiences that have given you the following feelings:

- Contentment
- Pleasure
- Delight
- Relief.

Can you explain why you felt the way you did?

WHY CUSTOMER SATISFACTION IS IMPORTANT

Customer satisfaction is important to the success of hospitality businesses. Few hotels and restaurants will survive if they consistently deliver unsatisfactory experiences. When customers have alternative providers, they may choose to reduce the amount of business done or even not to return at all. They may also utter negative word of mouth, discouraging potential customers from visiting. Commonsense tells us that satisfied customers must be good for business. Research into a number of conditions supports this commonsense notion – the cost of acquiring new customers, the benefits of repeat purchases by satisfied customers and the impact of positive word of mouth recommendations.

Marketing insight 13.1

An example where customer satisfaction is less important

Hospitality units in prime tourist locations with transient visitors sometimes take advantage of tourists and can remain profitable despite delivering customer dissatisfaction. A restaurant close to the Rialto Bridge in Venice attracts tourists with a low-priced tourist menu and then encourages customers to eat local fish specialities at high prices. The dissatisfied tourists will never return, and the restaurant continues to trade profitably because of its prime location.

THE COST OF ACQUIRING NEW CUSTOMERS

Throughout this book, we have emphasized the competitive marketplace in which hospitality companies operate. Attracting customers carries significant marketing costs, the most significant being distribution, selling, advertising and sales promotion costs. Indeed, research suggests that the cost of attracting a new customer is five or six times greater than the costs of retaining an existing customer. At the same time, competitors are also striving to attract the same customers. Therefore, when a customer is initially attracted to your marketing offer your company is given a unique opportunity to make a sale and perhaps begin to develop a long-term relationship with the customer. Customer retention strategies are predicated on delivering customer satisfaction the first time a customer experiences the hospitality offer; customers who are not satisfied may never return, and the investment in the pre-encounter marketing activities will have been wasted.

Repeat customers

For the vast majority of hospitality businesses, repeat customers are an essential element of the customer mix. The cost of attracting repeat customers – providing they are satisfied – is significantly lower than and in many situations minimal compared with the costs of acquiring new customers (Reichheld, 1996). There are also non-economic benefits derived from repeat customers, including the following:

- Repeat customers know where and how to book, what to expect and how to find the premises
- Customers who return have expectations that can be met – they already know what the hospitality offer represents, and this indicates that they were relatively satisfied with their first experience
- Customer-contact employees greeting regular customers provide reassurance to first-time visitors regarding product quality and customer satisfaction
- Regular customers are less costly to look after because they know how the service operation works.

Indeed, repeat customers can become powerful advocates for the business, encouraging others to patronize the establishment.

Positive word of mouth recommendation

A word of mouth recommendation from a satisfied customer is simply the most cost-effective form of customer acquisition. When friends or relatives tell us that a restaurant served really good quality food at reasonable prices or that the atmosphere, drinks and music at a nightclub were excellent, then the next time when we book a meal or go clubbing, we will seriously consider following that word of mouth recommendation. Word of mouth has a positive influence on customers because the source of the message (our friends, relatives and associates) is highly trusted. They have no reason to lie to us, and we know them so well that we are likely to believe their advice. Customers who give positive word of mouth are also less likely to switch; they are more likely to be retained for the longer term.

Word of mouth recommendations are dependent on all the elements of the hospitality marketing mix working effectively. Helpful, smiling staff cannot win over customers when the prices are too high, a good product in the wrong location will suffer and wonderful food served by rude staff is normally counterproductive. Ultimately, it is marketing during the hospitality encounter that delivers customer satisfaction and generates word of mouth referrals.

BASIC PRINCIPLES OF CUSTOMER SATISFACTION

Effective management of customer satisfaction is based on several principles:

1 Identify which customers you are trying to satisfy. Not all customers or prospects are equally important.

2 Identify what is important to those chosen customers. Not all customers value the same components of the hospitality offer, and not all elements are equally important. For example, some customers value food quantity, whereas others value food quality. The same customers' expectations may change over time: customers generally want faster service at lunch but more leisurely service in the evenings.

3 Get it right first time. Customers' expectations, once understood, should be satisfied at the first opportunity. You should try to eliminate the causes of customer dissatisfaction, such as slow service, ill-informed contact staff and malfunctioning equipment.

4 Provide excellent recovery policies and systems. Accepting that occasionally even the best hospitality company will fail to meet customer expectations, you need to have in place recovery processes to mitigate customer dissatisfaction, pre-empt negative word of mouth and promote retention.

CUSTOMER SATISFACTION GUARANTEES

When consumers buy manufactured products, the manufacturer provides a guarantee and will normally repair or replace the product if the customer is not satisfied. Both consumers and manufacturers understand the concept of satisfaction guarantees, which play an important role in marketing manufactured products. However, many hospitality managers are intuitively opposed to the idea of customer satisfaction guarantees. They believe that too many guests will be dishonest and make bogus complaints, even when they have enjoyed their stay or meal. It is interesting to note that most hospitality providers do compensate customers when they have a genuine complaint. This approach to compensation for genuine complaints implies that companies do actually have some sort of customer satisfaction guarantee, even if they do not inform customers about it. This controversial topic can be better understood if we explain the different type of service guarantees that companies can adopt (Zeithaml & Bitner, 2003).

Implicit satisfaction guarantee

When customers book into a hotel or restaurant, they assume that they will receive a satisfactory outcome for the price they pay, even though the hospitality outlet has not given the customer any guarantee. There is an implicit understanding, grounded in experience, education and consumer protection legislation, that the hospitality provider will compensate a customer with a genuine complaint. Although there is no formal contract with the customer, most hospitality companies do compensate customers who complain. The problem with this informal type of customer satisfaction guarantee is that neither the customers nor the company knows what an implicit guarantee covers. There are no guidelines setting out what the company offers and how customers will be compensated if something goes wrong.

Explicit satisfaction guarantee

An explicit satisfaction guarantee is based on specific, measurable performance. Time-based promises, such as a maximum of 30-min wait for a room service delivery, are a good example of an explicit satisfaction guarantee. The length of time to deliver the service can be explicitly incorporated into the guarantee, and it is then simple to establish whether the service has been delivered as guaranteed – on time or not. These guarantees have been used with varying degrees of success. Unfortunately, Domino's Pizza had to withdraw a 30-min guaranteed delivery time because of problems caused by employees driving dangerously fast while trying to deliver pizzas on time. Ramada Jarvis Hotels offered an explicit money-back guarantee on their 'Summit Conference' package that included assurances that the conference equipment will be fully checked well in advance of the meeting, messages will be delivered promptly and a two-course meal would be served in just 35 min. Ramada Jarvis withdrew the guarantee implying either that the company could not deliver on this service promise, or that the guarantee was not valued by customers. Clearly, before a company introduces an explicit time-based satisfaction guarantee, the operation must be able to deliver the promise within the time agreed and at an acceptable performance level.

Marketing insight 13.2

Ibis 15 minute satisfaction contract

Ibis offer a '15 minute satisfaction contract' in their 800 hotels or guests stay free. Ibis states that 'if a customer reports a problem which is the hotel's responsibility, the teams are committed to finding a solution within 15 minutes maximum, 24 hours a day, every day of the week' (http://www.accorhotels.com/gb/brands/hotels-ibis.shtml). The 15-minute satisfaction guarantee applies to the breakfast, the room, snacks and the bar. The guarantee is promoted on the website, there is a leaflet in each bedroom called the Ibis 'Satisfaction Contract', and whenever a new Ibis Hotel opens, the guarantee is used as a key publicity tool.

Sources: Ibis 15 Minute Satisfaction Contract and www.accorhotels.com

Unconditional satisfaction guarantee

An unconditional satisfaction guarantee promises customers complete satisfaction or their money back. An unconditional guarantee makes a powerful statement about the confidence a hospitality service provider has in the integrity of the offer and the ability of the service delivery system – people, processes and technology – to deliver as promised. An unconditional guarantee gives consumers the following:

- Confidence to purchase the service (by reducing risk) in the knowledge that a 100 per cent refund is available if they are not satisfied
- Reassurance that the company can deliver on the promise, or it would not provide a service guarantee
- Preference over competitors who do not provide a similar guarantee.

Before a hospitality company can introduce an unconditional guarantee, the following conditions must be fulfilled:

- The target market must be clearly defined
- The company must understand the drivers of customer satisfaction for the products and services offered
- Product or service quality standards must be set that match customer expectations.
- Service delivery processes and enabling technology must enable the promise to be honoured
- Employees must be aware of the 100 per cent satisfaction guarantee and be capable of fulfilling their role in the service experience.

A hospitality company intending to introduce an unconditional guarantee must be prepared to invest significantly in marketing research to evaluate the drivers of customer satisfaction, competitive standards and consumer's perceptions of price and value, as well as investment in product quality and training; it must also ensure that there is an effective quality audit process. Most importantly, if a company cannot deliver consistent customer satisfaction, then it simply cannot afford to offer an unconditional service guarantee. In fact, very few hospitality companies offer unconditional service guarantees.

To successfully introduce an unconditional service guarantee, a company should do the following:

- demonstrate their customer orientation by viewing customer satisfaction from the consumer's perspective
- review the entire customer experience to eradicate failure points (areas of customer dissatisfaction)
- use the service guarantee as a differentiator in marketing communication campaigns to increase brand awareness and market share
- monitor the cost of consumer dissatisfaction by the cost of refunds to dissatisfied customers
- use customer complaints to identify and correct service/maintenance problems
- give managers and employees measurable customer satisfaction performance goals
- use the concept of unconditional guarantees in employee team-building exercises
- try to maintain a stable team of staff who understand the guarantee and the service standards that are required.

From a quality perspective, unconditional guarantees force companies to 'do it right first time' or the costs of complaints would be unacceptably high. However, despite all these advantages, few hospitality companies can seriously entertain the notion of providing a 100 per cent satisfaction guarantee. Many hospitality organizations do not have the product/service consistency to be able to offer an unconditional guarantee, and in these cases, the costs of compensating customers who might complain would be too high. Such companies should not consider introducing an unconditional guarantee policy.

Hampton Inns in the United States, and Premier Inn (formerly Travel Inn) in the United Kingdom, pioneered the introduction of unconditional guarantees in hospitality (Case study 13.1). Both operate in the budget accommodation market, with a price-led strategy, a relatively standardized product, simple pricing policies and few employees. This type of brand formula delivers a homogeneous marketing offer, which lends itself to an unconditional guarantee.

Most mid-market hotels target many market segments. They have a complex range of accommodation, food, beverage and leisure products, with a wide variety of prices and price bundles, and a relatively large number of employees, sometimes a multiple of the number of guests. This type of company delivers a heterogeneous marketing offer, and so it would be difficult to provide an unconditional guarantee, even if the management were interested in offering one.

Luxury hotels and restaurants providing high-quality service and well-maintained facilities do not need to introduce an unconditional guarantee. The reputation of Four Seasons Hotels, or the Savoy Hotel in London, carries an implicit guarantee of complete customer satisfaction.

Case study 13.1 **Customer satisfaction at Premier Inn**

The Good Night Guarantee money-back promise was such a successful marketing strategy that, when Travel Inn took over Premier Lodge and later became Premier Inn, the policy was retained as a key proposition and differentiator in the UK budget market. Premier Inn have made (and continue to make) a significant investment in their hotels to ensure that the 100% 'good night's sleep' satisfaction promise is deliverable and profitable. An interesting finding from Premier Inn marketing research is that customers who are aware of the 100% satisfaction guarantee are *more satisfied* with their experience than customers who are not aware.

Each of the 590 Premier Inn sites is audited twice each year to monitor cleanliness, comfort, décor, equipment, furniture maintenance and friendliness and service levels of its on-site team members. The audit, which is an example of mystery shopping, is performed by an external company and units do not know when an inspection is going to be carried out. Each hotel starts with a 1000-point scale, and points are deducted when performance in a certain area (e.g. bathroom cleanliness) is below satisfactory levels. The inspection checklist is used to identify areas for improvement, and if the overall site score is unsatisfactory, then the general manager needs to take action quickly to remedy the problem areas – before a new inspection is carried out.

Premier Inn sends customers satisfaction surveys to evaluate the performance of each site. These achieve a very high 33% response rate. The survey results are used to drive new marketing, product and investment initiatives.

Source: Premier Inn

Constraints on customer satisfaction

We have discussed the difficulties that hospitality companies have in delivering 100 per cent customer satisfaction guarantees. Although most companies could almost certainly improve their level of customer satisfaction, there are constraints that restrict such improvements. Customers want competitive prices, and there are limits to how much customers are prepared to pay for higher levels of satisfaction. Hospitality companies have other stakeholders who compete for the funds that could be invested in delivering higher customer satisfaction, for example, shareholders and owners want an increase in dividends, management and employees want higher wages and bonuses and suppliers want prompt payment. Therefore, investment in improving customer satisfaction has to be balanced against the needs of other stakeholders. Indeed, financial constraints frequently inhibit investment in the hospitality product and improvements in customer satisfaction.

Activity 13.2

Log on to the following hotel brand websites and evaluate their approaches in providing customer satisfaction guarantees:

- www.ibishotel.com
- www.premierinn.com

MEASURING CUSTOMER SATISFACTION

Hospitality companies use a combination of direct and indirect methods to measure and monitor customer satisfaction. Indirect methods included tracking sales and profit figures and monitoring them against forecast or previous period performances. Direct methods include customer research and analysis of complaints and compliments. Most hotels and many restaurants have customer comment cards or questionnaires that can be completed by customers on the premises. However, the industry does not have a standard approach to measure customer satisfaction, and companies use a variety of different methods to collect and analyse the data. For example, there is no common scale used in collecting customer satisfaction data – some companies use a numerical scale (1–5), others use word descriptors (poor, fair, good and excellent) and others rely solely on customer's own comments (see Chapter 2). Each organization will ask customers different types of questions according to their own needs and will rarely share data on such a commercially sensitive topic.

Delivering customer satisfaction consistently is dependent on listening to customers and customer-contact employees to make sure that service standards and performance are aligned with customer expectations. A number of different classes of customer can provide insight into the level and causes of customer (dis)satisfaction. Research can be conducted into current customers, lapsed customers, competitors' customers and potential customers. Techniques include the following:

- Collecting customer complaints and analysing them for insight into the root causes of customer dissatisfaction.
- Post-encounter surveys – customers are emailed questionnaires after they have experienced the hospitality service, when they have returned home or to work, with an incentive to complete and return them. The questionnaires obtain post-experience data about customer satisfaction. Many tour operators give customers a questionnaire to complete before or on the flight home, and this provides information about the hospitality service during their holiday.
- Key account customers, frequent guests and members of loyalty clubs understand the level of consistency across a hotel brand as well as many employees. Surveying the views of expert customers can identify underperforming units and highlight important brand inconsistencies.
- Employee surveys – encouraging employees to provide feedback on the service operation – are another technique used by progressive companies. Employees are acutely aware of service problems and often know the reasons why performance underperforms customer expectations.
- Focus groups of customers and employees allow the group moderator to explore customer satisfaction issues in depth.
- Mystery shopping is a key tool in auditing the service performance of hotels and restaurants. Mystery shopping uses a customer-centered approach to measure service performance. Researchers pretend to be customers and record their impressions of the service. Mystery shopper surveys measure both quantitative indicators (e.g. the length of waiting time for service) and qualitative dimensions (e.g. employee friendliness and courtesy). At the end of the visit, the mystery shopper survey scores are reported to the unit manager and to head office. In multiunit operations, the

management uses the scores to identify strong and weak performing units or as part of an internal benchmarking program. Some companies also use the results as part of the manager's bonus scheme, which emphasizes the importance of this auditing tool.

• Internal brand audits – hospitality chains employ their own staff or commission external firms to carry out brand conformance audits to ensure that the unit is delivering customer satisfaction (assuming that the brand standards do actually match customer expectations!). These inspections may be secret. If the general manager and employees know in advance when the audit will take place, they will obviously prepare for the inspection. Inspectors have detailed brand performance standards covering all major aspects of the operation and check the unit's performance against the company's benchmarks. In large hotels, several inspectors might stay for three or more days to produce a comprehensive review of the entire service operation. For franchise operations and hotels in consortiums, the brand audit provides the brand owner with evidence of operator compliance. This is used to make units performing below the minimum brand standards improve performance. Ultimately, if the unit continues to underperform, the brand owner can terminate the agreement and withdraw the brand name and support for the property.

Normally, both quantitative and qualitative research methods are used to collect data from customers. Research should be continuous, providing management with insight into changes in customer satisfaction and an explanation for increases or decreases. Processes for evaluating customer satisfaction include importance/performance analysis (IPA) and complaints capture.

Importance/performance analysis

IPA starts by identifying the elements of the hospitality experience that contribute importantly to customer satisfaction. Many companies conduct qualitative research, such as focus group interviews, to identify the important elements of the experience. The elements are then embedded into questionnaires that can be used to measure satisfaction. There are clearly dangers in using standardized instruments that have not been customized for a particular hospitality organization. The questionnaires are used to assess customer expectations of those elements as well as their perceptions of performance. The normal format is to ask customers to rate, on a 7-point scale, their expectations of an excellent hospitality company and their perceptions of the researched hospitality company's performance (see Table 13.1).

Analysis can then focus on identifying where the company falls short of meeting customer expectations. For example, if a customer

Table 13.1 Importance/performance questions							
Item	Strongly agree			Strongly disagree			
Expectation: Excellent budget hotels provide quiet sleeping accommodation	1	2	3	4	5	6	7
Perception: Hotel XYX provides quiet sleeping accommodation	1	2	3	4	5	6	7

were to rate an expectation item at 7 and the perception item at 4, this would mean a 3-point negative gap [perception score (4) less expectation score (7) = −3]. Customers are invited to identify the relative importance of each element or a group of similar elements, such as those relating to responsiveness of contact staff. It is a mistake to believe that every negative gap is equally important to customers. For most customers, a noisy bedroom is a much more important issue than a non-smiling employee. For this reason, many satisfaction questionnaires invite customers to identify not only expectations and perceptions but also the importance of each element. Typically, this is done by asking customers to distribute 100 points between the elements or groups of elements in a way that reflects their relative importance.

This information can be used to guide customer satisfaction improvement strategies. For example, where customers have identified a particular attribute as important and the company is not meeting expectations, there is a potential source of customer dissatisfaction and the gap should be closed. However, where the company is exceeding customer expectations on some attribute that is unimportant to customers, there may be a case for reducing expenditure on that attribute.

Results from this sort of analysis can be mapped onto an IPA matrix, as in Fig. 13.2. In the matrix, Cell I of the matrix represents a competitive strength – an area where the customer is satisfied with the company's performance on important attributes. Cell II is a threat – the company is failing to satisfy customers on important attributes. Cell III describes the situation where the company is meeting and perhaps exceeding customer expectations on attributes that customers think are unimportant. The options here are to educate the customer as to the attribute's importance or to reduce investment in that attribute. In Cell IV, the customer is dissatisfied, but the attribute is not a priority for most customers. It would make sense to monitor the importance of that attribute, because if customers come to regard it as important in the future, it will become a threat. Figure 13.3 provides an example of seven IPA attributes, for an upscale full-service hotel brand, mapped on an importance/performance matrix.

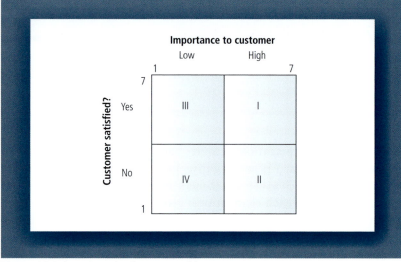

Figure 13.2 Importance/performance matrix

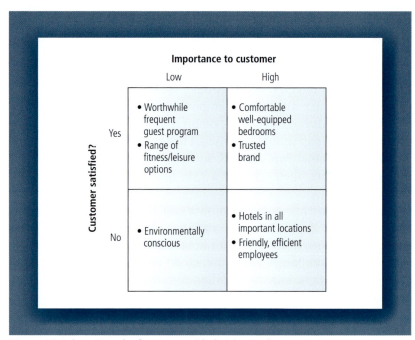

Figure 13.3 Importance/performance matrix, hotel example

Complaint capture and analysis

In Chapter 11, we explained that encouraging customers to complain and then responding effectively to the complaint helps to improve customer satisfaction. We also provided an example of an owner who responded to complaints inappropriately (see Marketing insight on page 321). Companies that take complaints seriously need to develop a policy and processes to capture and interpret customer complaints. These data can then be used to identify and correct failure points. In hospitality, one source of complaint data is the post-encounter questionnaire. Another source is complaint letters, which often describe a catalogue of critical incidents. Unless there is a formal process for recording complaints, those that are made face-to-face with a service employee may go unrecorded, meaning that the company has incomplete data on customer complaints. It also makes sense for companies to monitor travel comparison websites and social networks for complaint data. Complaints that go viral can be very damaging. Often, however, unit managers can address the complaint at the time it is expressed. Being empathic, courteous, honest and responsive are important behaviours in resolving complaints and retaining the customer.

These sources provided the management with important information about failure points. However, the problem with customer questionnaires and complaint letters is that they are unrepresentative of the majority of customers. Typically, they only represent very unhappy customers – those who are so dissatisfied that they are prepared to make the effort to complain. An effective complaint capture system will employ many channels, such as on-site questionnaires, email, fax, telephone calls, face-to-face and web form. It will also include a channel to facilitate employee feedback on customer complaints.

CUSTOMER SATISFACTION MAY NOT LEAD TO REPEAT BUSINESS

In highly competitive industries with commoditized products, low differentiation, many competitive or substitute offers available, low switching costs or consumer indifference, satisfied customers will still defect. Many hospitality sectors suffer from these characteristics; so while delivering customer satisfaction is essential for survival it is no guarantee of spectacular success.

In hospitality, completely satisfied customers may never return to the unit or to the destination for a variety of reasons. For leisure products, many of today's travellers want to explore the world and visit new destinations rather than returning to the same tourist area. They are variety-seeking customers. Given the industry's over-capacity, price-responsive consumers can choose from a wide range of competitively priced deals anywhere in the world. Customers attending unique events, such as wedding receptions, sports matches and exhibitions, will stay at or near the venue and may never have another reason to visit the area. However, this does not mean that customer satisfaction is unimportant to these customers. Hospitality businesses that take customer satisfaction seriously will not lower their service standards because of the transient characteristics of customers.

CONCLUSION

Customer satisfaction is a complex topic, which will continue to be the focus of research because of its important role in generating repeat sales, word of mouth recommendation and enhancing profitability. Although most hospitality companies have difficulty in offering 100 per cent unconditional guarantees of customer satisfaction, virtually all of them provide implicit service guarantees. The cost of improving customer satisfaction has to be balanced against the willingness of customers to pay more for enhanced satisfaction, and the needs of other stakeholders. Customer satisfaction is the foundation of a successful hospitality business, but satisfied customers may never return.

In this chapter, we have explained the following:

- A definition of customer satisfaction
- Four different types of satisfaction – contentment, pleasure, delight and relief
- Why customer satisfaction is important – because of the high costs of acquiring new customers and the economic and non-economic benefits of repeat customers
- The characteristics of an implicit satisfaction guarantee, an explicit satisfaction guarantee and an unconditional 100 per cent satisfaction guarantee
- The constraints on improving customer satisfaction due to the needs of other stakeholders
- Various tools for measuring customer satisfaction, including IPA and, complaint capture
- That some satisfied hospitality customers may never return.

REVIEW QUESTIONS

Now check your understanding by answering the following questions:

1 Discuss the importance of customer satisfaction to a hospitality business
2 Evaluate the concept of service guarantees in the following hotel market sectors:
   - budget
   - mid-market
   - luxury.
3 Discuss the role of customer satisfaction measures in improving customer satisfaction for a hospitality brand.

References and Further Reading

Kotler, P., Bowen, J., & Makens, J. (2009). *Marketing for hospitality and tourism* (5th ed.). Prentice Hall.

Lewis, R. C., & Chambers, R. E. (2000). *Marketing leadership in hospitality: Foundations and practice*. John Wiley.

Parasuraman, A., Zeithaml, V. A., & Berry, L. L. (1988). SERVQUAL: A multiple-item scale for measuring consumer perceptions of service quality. *Journal of Retailing*, *64*(1), 5–7.

Reichheld, F. F. (1996). *The loyalty effect: The hidden force behind growth, profits and lasting value*. Bain and Company.

Zeithaml, V. A., & Bitner, M. J. (2009). *Services marketing*. McGraw-Hill.

C H A P T E R **14**

Relationship marketing

After going through this chapter, you should be able to:

- Understand the differences between a relationship marketing strategy and a transactional marketing strategy
- Identify the components of a relationship marketing strategy
- Evaluate the concept of attitudinal and behavioural loyalty in the context of hospitality
- Analyse the role of frequent guest program in branded hotel chains.

INTRODUCTION

In the past, the usual focus of marketing managers has been on the acquisition of new customers. This traditional approach to marketing is often described as transactional marketing. Once a customer has bought the product, there is no strategic effort to develop the relationship further; the transaction is complete from both the customer's and the company's perspective; money has been spent and earned. This used to be the dominant approach to marketing practice.

The concept of relationship marketing takes a different perspective and looks at customers as a business asset that should be nurtured. This approach recognizes that some customers have the potential to generate significant value for companies over a period of time. Therefore, the focus of relationship marketing is to create, maintain and enhance customer relationships over the long-term.

In hospitality businesses, frequent or regular customers have always been recognized as important. The owners and managers of small hotels, bars and restaurants naturally develop a close rapport with regular customers, giving them a special welcome, knowing their preferences and making sure they are looked after well. However, for branded hospitality chains, this recognition of key customers at the unit level was not easily transferred across all the other units in a chain – until the ICT revolution provided the computer systems to create and distribute guest histories. Although independently owned and managed units can build on their traditions of hospitality and develop relationship marketing strategies for the unit, most of the discussion in this chapter is concerned with multiple-unit-branded chains.

In this chapter, we explain what relationship marketing is and discuss the economics of customer retention, the characteristics of relationship marketing and what multi-unit hospitality companies need to do to implement a relationship marketing strategy. Finally, we consider the role of loyalty and frequent guest program in hospitality.

WHAT IS RELATIONSHIP MARKETING?

Relationship marketing is both an approach to run a business that stresses the importance of customer retention and a marketing strategy with a set of tools and practices. Table 14.1 contrasts the traditional transactional approach to marketing with relationship marketing. Grönroos (1994) defines relationship marketing as:

> {to}identify and establish, maintain and enhance, and where necessary, terminate relationships with customers and other stakeholders, at a profit so that the objectives of all parties involved are met; and this is done by mutual exchange and fulfillment of promises.

Table 14.1 Relationship and transactional marketing	
Transactional marketing	**Relationship marketing**
Single sale focus	Customer retention focus
Focus on product features	Focus on customer value
Short-term promotions	Long-term relational marketing communication
Customers tend to be price-sensitive	Customers tend not to be price-sensitive
Short timescale	Long timescale
Discontinuous customer contact	Continuous customer contact
Token commitment to customers	High commitment to customers
Quality is an operations issue	Quality is an issue for all employees

The key point about relationship marketing is the recognition that customers who make repeat purchases have a high lifetime value (LTV). LTV is the present-day value of all historic and future profit margins earned from sales to a particular customer or segment. Building close relationships with key customers should be mutually rewarding for both the company and the customer. A relationship marketing strategy should be targeted at selected hospitality customers or segments. Not all customers want a relationship and not all customers merit a relationship. We mentioned in Chapter 13 that hotels and restaurants have a large number of customers who are unlikely to return, and therefore trying to build a long-term relationship with these customers makes no strategic sense and cannot be cost effective. There are two other customer segments that are unlikely or unwilling to want to develop relationships with a hospitality company. Some customers are aware of the wide choice of competitor products in hospitality markets, do not want to limit their options by developing a relationship with a single brand or provider, and prefer to switch their custom accordingly. Other customers are not interested in any type of relationship with any company and simply look at the most appropriate quality, value and convenience available at the time of purchase. Online search helps this type of customer to easily find low price, convenient hotel choices.

On the other hand, there are several circumstances when a business customer may want a long-term relationship with a hospitality supplier. These include the following:

- When the hospitality product is strategically important – for example, as a component of a bundled offer in a critical location for a tour operator or as a location for an international conference.
- To avoid switching costs – switching costs are incurred when customers change to another hospitality provider. Switching costs are

very low for individual business and leisure travellers who book their accommodation online, but the switching costs for a corporate client who arranges major conferences/hospitality events and for intermediaries who handle large volumes of bed-nights can be significant due to search, evaluation and negotiation costs. A strong relationship means that customers are less willing to incur switching costs. Provided the hospitality organization is delivering customer satisfaction at a competitive price, and the relationship is strong, then it is more convenient and cost-effective for the corporate clients and intermediaries to continue to purchase from their existing supplier.

- When reciprocity is expected. A food service company may want a close relationship with a hotel company. In return for guaranteed accommodation for its sales team, the food service company offers the hotel chain cheaper produce and processed food inputs for its restaurants. In many Asian markets, this type of reciprocal business relationship is more common – for example, a hotel might plan an advertising campaign on the local radio station at no cost in return for letting the radio station have an equivalent amount of accommodation, food and banqueting at no cost. Barter like this is a simple form of relationship marketing.

In a consumer context, relationships may be sought when the customer values benefits over and above those directly derived from the hospitality experience. For example,

- Recognition – a customer may feel more valued when recognized and addressed by name
- Personalization – for example, over time a restaurateur may come to understand a customer's particular preferences or expectations
- Risk reduction – a relationship can reduce, or perhaps even eliminate, perceived risk. For example, a customer may develop a relationship with a branded restaurant chain to reduce the perceived performance and physical risk attached to eating when away from home
- Status – customers may feel that their status is enhanced by a relationship with an organization, such as an elite health club in a hotel.

THE ECONOMICS OF CUSTOMER RETENTION

Hospitality companies lose customers each year, for many reasons. Customers grow older and move through the family life cycle, changing their employment, home, lifestyle and consumption habits. Corporate customers and intermediaries go through similar changes, with growth, mergers, takeovers, relocation, downsizing and demise. In addition to this natural loss of customers, competitors lure customers away with new-product initiatives, new openings, price deals and attractive marketing communication campaigns. For these reasons, hospitality companies traditionally have relatively high customer defection rates (also known as customer churn). Although companies need continually to attract new customers to replace lost ones, customer retention is critical.

The fundamental reason for companies wanting to build relationships with customers is economic. Companies generate better results when they manage their customer base in order to identify, satisfy and retain profitable customers. This is the core goal of relationship marketing strategies. Improving customer retention rates has the effect of increasing the size of the customer base. If competitors lose customers at the rate of 20 per cent each year and you lose customers at 10 per cent each year in a few years, other things being equal, you will have a significantly larger customer base. However, there is little merit in growing the customer base aimlessly. The goal must be to retain existing customers who have future profit potential or are important for other strategic purposes. Not all customers are of equal importance. Some customers may not be worth recruiting or retaining at all – for example, those who have a high cost-to-serve are debtors/late payers, or are promiscuous in the sense that they switch frequently between suppliers.

As customer retention rates increase (or defection rates decrease), so does the average tenure of a customer. Tenure is the term used to describe the length of time a customer remains as a customer. The impacts of small improvements in customer retention are magnified at the higher levels of retention. For example, improving the annual customer retention rate from 75 to 80 per cent grows average customer tenure from 10 to 12.5 years. Managing tenure by reducing defection rates can be critical for business performance. Research suggests that an increase in customer retention of 5 per cent increases profits from 35 to 95 per cent for some service firms (Buttle, 1995). One of the reasons why hospitality companies can increase profitability significantly by reducing customer defection rates is the high-fixed and semi-fixed cost structure of the industry. This means that the marginal costs of servicing a repeat customer are relatively small. Managing customer retention and tenure intelligently generates two key benefits:

1 Marketing costs are reduced. Less needs to be spent on advertising, distribution, selling and sales promotion to replace lost customers. In addition to reducing the costs of customer recruitment, costs-to-serve existing customers also tend to fall over time.

2 As tenure grows, companies better understand customer requirements. Customers also come to understand what a company can do for them. Consequently, suppliers become better placed to identify and satisfy customer requirements profitably. Over time, as relationships deepen, trust and commitment between the parties is likely to grow. Under these circumstances, revenue and profit streams from customers become more secure.

CHARACTERISTICS OF RELATIONSHIP MARKETING

Hospitality companies that want to implement a relationship marketing strategy successfully need a strong service culture, including a commitment to internal marketing, an effective segmentation strategy, an interactive relational database in all properties, trust from their customers and associated customer recognition and reward strategies. We will discuss each of these factors in more detail.

Service culture

The starting point for a successful relationship marketing strategy is the company's service culture. The company needs to invest in a genuine customer-orientated service philosophy that delivers the service quality customers expect. This investment requires a financial commitment to maintain and improve the quality standards and physical product and to provide systems and procedures that facilitate appropriate levels of service quality. If the company cannot deliver the service experience customers expect, it cannot hope to develop long-term relationships with them.

Internal marketing is an essential component of an effective relationship marketing strategy. In Chapter 12, we discussed the crucial role of customer-contact employees in delivering customer satisfaction, and the importance of internal marketing program to communicate with, upskill and empower employees. A service culture that fosters employee involvement and encourages employees to build close relationships with customers provides a strong foundation for a successful relationship marketing strategy.

Segmentation

The segmentation strategy should focus on customers who have a potentially high LTV or are strategically significant in other ways. For example, they might be reference customers (customers whom other customers copy) or customers who initially enable a hospitality company to enter a new market segment. The Pareto Principle (also called the 80/20 rule) can provide an effective criterion for identifying customers who are strategically significant. This principle suggests that the top 20 per cent of customers generate 80 per cent of sales and profits. In hospitality, these customers include frequent travellers, corporations and intermediaries. The branded chains are aware that frequent business travellers, who have a high LTV, are important customers and highly sought after. National and international corporations and key intermediaries also generate substantial volumes of

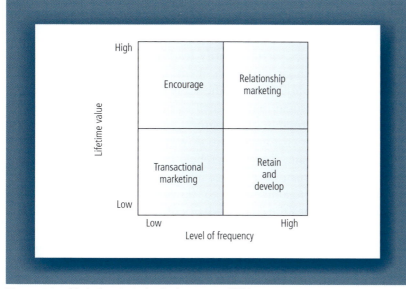

Figure 14.1 Marketing strategies for frequent and LTV customers

hotel bed-nights. Hospitality chains use their relationship marketing executives to liaise regularly with these key accounts, nurturing the relationship and trying to protect the business from competitors. Hospitality companies need to be careful in applying the 80/20 rule, as the key customers/distributors may not, in fact, be the most profitable – they may require costly pre-, during and post-encounter service as well as deeply discounted rates, thereby reducing their profitability.

Customers who have a relatively low spend per transaction but a high frequency of visits can generate a high spend over the lifetime of their patronage. In family restaurants, the average sale is considerably lower in value than staying in a hotel. However, research back in the 1990's discovered that a loyal American 'pizza' customer can have a LTV of US$ 8000 (Heskett, Jones, Loveman, Sasser, & Schlesinger, 1994); today the LTV would be considerably higher.

A transactional marketing approach is appropriate when the potential LTV of a customer is low and when customers will not benefit from a long-term relationship with companies. Typically, hospitality units in resorts where there are many transient visitors engage in transactional marketing, particularly if they have less well-known brands. Figure 14.1 illustrates marketing strategies for frequent and LTV customers.

Database

ICT is a prerequisite for multiple-unit companies interested in developing and implementing a relationship marketing strategy. Every customer's transaction history, demographic details, contact data and history and communication preferences are stored in the database and are used to implement relational marketing. Aggregated customer-related data can also be analysed to identify cross-selling and up-selling opportunities, or to identify lead indicators that a customer might switch. Regular customers mention their preferences to customer contact employees during their stay in a hotel. These preferences might include personal matters such as preferred salutation (formal: Mr Smith, or informal: Joe), a favourite newspaper, type of pillow or a food allergy. For customers who stay in several hotels belonging to the same hotel chain, these preferences can be recorded in the database and used to customize service interactions throughout the chain.

Hospitality companies need to track the sales pattern of key accounts and record the characteristics of their transactions in all the chain's properties. Monitoring consumption activity enables the company to identify potential new key accounts, reward those customers who maintain current high-value sales and track accounts that are declining in sales volume.

In Chapter 9, we discussed the role of the database in personalizing communications with key customers. The database is crucial in identifying key customers to target with specific promotions and in providing accurate contact information. Indeed many owner-managed units build simple, cost-effective email lists to provide regular communication with customers.

Trust and commitment

Trust and commitment are core concepts in relationship marketing. Customers must trust and have complete confidence in the company's competence and integrity. It does help the customer and the company to have shared values. It is less likely that a customer will develop a relationship with a company whose activities conflict with the customer's own values. Trust is built up over time and depends on the company being competent in delivering on its promises and not exploiting the customer. A long-term relationship provides opportunities for the company to demonstrate its values, competence and integrity to the customer. As trust develops over time, the customer feels secure in the relationship and the company earns the customer's commitment.

A long-term relationship implies that both parties have been prepared to make short-term sacrifices for longer term benefits. From a hotel company's perspective, this means that opportunistic behaviours to make short-term profits should be avoided – for example, the company will maintain a price commitment to key customers during high season periods, even though it could sell the rooms to a guest paying higher rates. Clearly, delivering consistent customer satisfaction is an essential condition for building a long-term relationship.

Customers who suffer from inconsistent service standards cannot give their trust to a company that is incompetent.

Case study 14.1 provides an illustration of successful relationship marketing at the local level.

Case study 14.1 **Relationship marketing at Sam's Brasserie**

Sam Harrison opened his first Brasserie in Chiswick, London, in 2005 and adopted a local relationship marketing strategy from the beginning of operations. Sam views high-service quality as a functional attribute for the hospitality business – it is a technically important function that employees can be trained to deliver. However, Sam thinks that the 'art of hospitality' is given by managers and employees who have an innate understanding of looking after people; and potential employees who do not understand the art of looking after people cannot change their behaviour simply through training. So Sam recruits employees primarily based on their personality – indeed 70% of the employees at the opening of his first restaurant had no formal hospitality experience. The starting point for selection is the CV, where successful applicants demonstrate a passion either for their previous employment or in their activities, hobbies and interests. Sam and his partners Rick Stein and Rebecca Mascaren bought a second site at Balham, London, called Harrison's and adopted a similar formula to Sam's Brasserie. One of the reasons for the expansion was to provide growth opportunities for his kitchen and front-of-house team.

Sam's Restaurants are local diners; open all day for multi-use customers, targeting business people, couples, families and small groups with a modern British brasserie style menu. Sam views the Restaurants as extensions of his private house and the employees as his family. All new employees have a personalized induction with Sam and are then encouraged to take ownership of their role in the Restaurants.

Both Restaurants share similar types of local communities, and a key element in Sam's marketing is to be closely involved in these 'London villages'. Sam undertakes detailed marketing research in the local areas to make sure he is aware of what is happening and to be involved wherever appropriate. Local charities, church and school organizations are supported with sponsorship and services – for example, providing a barbeque for the local summer fetes. Sam has also built up a database of the email addresses of 6000 local customers who are sent regular, monthly newsletters. The combination of Sam's employee recruitment and retention strategies and his focus on local relationship marketing helps to drive profits in these businesses.

Source: Sam Harrison and www.samsbrasserie.co.uk

Recognition and reward

Customers who have entered into a relationship with a company generally expect recognition. The customer information file on the database enables key customers to be identified as, or even before, they check in to the hotel. Bedrooms on executive floors and individually named suites easily identify key customers to all the customer-contact employees, who should be trained to recognize, greet and look after them appropriately.

A mutually beneficial relationship implies that there are rewards for both parties. We have already discussed how the company gains additional or more secure sales and profits by cultivating long-term relationships with key customers. Loyal customers should also be rewarded for their patronage. Although recognition plays an important role in rewarding customers, tangible reward systems can help build customer loyalty.

ATTITUDINAL AND BEHAVIOURAL LOYALTY

We will now discuss the concept of attitudinal and behavioural loyalty, the relationship marketing ladder of loyalty, frequent guest program in hospitality and customer disloyalty.

The concept of loyalty

Most hospitality companies are interested in encouraging customers to repeat purchase and generate positive word of mouth. However, there is a distinction between a frequent customer and a loyal customer. Frequency is not an indicator of loyalty – for example, a frequent business traveller might be compelled to stay at a particular brand because of his company's expenses policy. Other frequent customers may regularly patronize the establishment because there are no effective competitors in the area and these customers could easily defect if serious competition emerged in the neighbourhood. Indeed, some frequent customers might even be extremely dissatisfied with the offer, and complain, but still have to stay because of the lack of alternatives. This type of loyalty is described as behavioural loyalty, because it is simply based on frequent behaviour.

A loyal customer is true, faithful and constant. A loyal customer is completely satisfied with the marketing offer, emotionally committed and does not seriously consider competitor alternatives. This type of loyalty is described as attitudinal loyalty because of the strong preference the customer has built towards the brand or unit. Ideally, hospitality businesses want customers who have attitudinal loyalty and are frequent guests. There is evidence to suggest that totally satisfied customers are six times more likely to repurchase and probably have a greater propensity for loyalty than partially satisfied customers (Reichheld, 1993). Loyal customers will often take ownership of the relationship and refer to the brand in first person terms (e.g., loyal pub customers often describe their bar as 'my local'), they tune into the marketing communication messages sent out by the brand and shut out the messages from competitors. If there is a service problem, loyal customers are more likely to report it because they genuinely want to help. Price is less of an issue for loyal customers. Most importantly, loyalty creates a major barrier to switching behaviour and is strongly associated with relationship marketing. True loyalty can over-ride rational behaviour, as customers who are truly loyal to their hospitality brand have become emotionally involved with the brand, its persona and its values. Customer loyalty is therefore a powerful indicator of marketing success.

However, customer loyalty is a complex phenomenon. A key issue is to build loyalty with customers who belong to the target market profile; attracting loyalty from the wrong customers can be dangerous and embarrassing. Building customer loyalty to the brand, and to the unit, is important for the hospitality marketer. In hospitality, customers can be both brand-loyal and loyal to specific units from several brands. There is evidence to suggest that harder, more standardized brands generate customer loyalty to the brand, whilst softer, less standardized brands tend to generate loyalty towards individual units. What is certain is that frequent travellers who visit many destinations on a regular basis become hotel-loyal and not only brand-loyal. An international frequent traveller might therefore stay at first-choice hotels from a range of brands depending on the location, choosing the Hilton in New York, the Crowne Plaza at Birmingham, the Marriott in Athens, the Novotel in Sydney and the Shangri-La at Kowloon, Hong Kong.

Activity 14.1

Think about your relationships with hospitality brands.
- Can you identify brands where you have a transactional relationship?
- Are there any brands to which you feel emotional loyalty?
- If you work for a hospitality brand, has your relationship with the brand changed because of your experience as an employee?

It is a common misconception that all companies should adopt a relationship marketing strategy. There is a role for transactional marketing and in practice most branded hospitality businesses combine both relational and transactional marketing strategies according to the needs of different markets (Osman, Hemmington, & Bowie, 2009). Building frequency is a legitimate marketing objective and strategy, just as building loyalty is an appropriate objective and strategy for companies seeking to develop a relational approach to marketing. Table 14.2 presents the different marketing approaches that can be adopted when developing a frequent or a loyal customer base.

The relationship marketing ladder of loyalty

Research into consumer buyer behaviour has categorized customers into six different types according to their usage and loyalty (Peck, Payne, Christopher, & Clark, 1999). Different marketing strategies

Table 14.2 Marketing strategies targeting frequent versus loyal customers

Marketing activities	Frequent customer base	Loyal customer base
Objective	Build traffic, sales and profitability	Build brand desirability, sales and profit
Strategy	Incentivize repeat transactions	Build personal brand relationships
Focus	Segment behaviour	Individual emotional and rational needs
Tactics	Sales promotions, focus on free offers/discounts/ rewards; frequent guest program with incentives	Customized communications, preferred status, emotional rewards, added value upgrades; loyalty guest program with recognition and rewards
Measurement	Transactions, sales growth	Individual LTV, emotional responses and attitudinal change

Reproduced with permission from Lewis and Chambers, 2000.

are required for these different types of customers. The bottom of the ladder of loyalty starts with 'prospects', who need to be persuaded to make a first purchase and experience the offer. Once consumers have actually become 'purchasers', then the task is to encourage them to become regular 'clients', and then to turn clients into 'supporters' and supporters into 'advocates'. Finally, 'advocates' become 'partners' in the ultimate, mutually rewarding relationship (Fig. 14.2). The idea of the loyalty ladder is to progress appropriate customers further up the ladder. However, customers can also, of course, move down or off the ladder; and some customers will choose not to move at all. The loyalty ladder recognizes the need for segmenting customers in terms of the propensity for loyalty and their LTV. Although LTV can be calculated using the customer retention rate, achieved spends and variable costs, it is much more difficult to determine a customer's propensity to be loyal.

Frequent and loyalty guest program

Earlier in this chapter, we explained the crucial difference between frequency and loyalty. This distinction should also apply to any discussion of frequent guest program (FGP) and loyalty guest program (LGP). However, in everyday language, these expressions are virtually interchangeable, and hospitality companies use the term FGP to apply to any loyalty program.

The origin of rewarding customers for their patronage in tourism dates from the 1970s, when American Airlines introduced a successful Frequent Flyer Program (FFP) that was quickly imitated

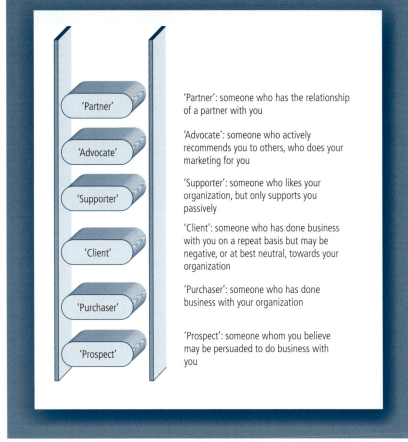

Figure 14.2 The relationship marketing ladder of loyalty *Source: Peck et al., 1999*

by competitors. The airlines' system of managing their FFP provided hotel companies with a template that they copied. Today's FGP enable frequent travellers to receive points and/or air miles whenever they stay at a hotel in the scheme. Although a number of chain restaurants have tried to launch frequent diner programs, few have been really successful apart from some simple coffee shop programs like UK-based Costa's Coffee Club. One of the reasons for the low take-up of restaurant loyalty program is that diners prefer immediate rewards whilst actually dining in the restaurant that day. In contrast, many restaurant brand managers prefer to offer a postponed points-based, non-monetary reward to encourage more frequent dining (Jang & Mattila, 2005). Therefore, the following discussion relates to hotel brands.

A FGP that adopts a transactional approach to marketing aims to build traffic by offering rewards from a wide range of services, including hotels and travel, retail and financial products. In contrast, companies that adopt a relational approach encourage regular customers to join a club to receive recognition as a privileged guest and focus rewards on added benefits during the stay at the hotel.

Table 14.3 The frequent guest program of international hotel brands	
Brands	**Programs**
Accor Hotels	A|Club
Best Western	Best Western Rewards
Hilton	HHonors
Hyatt	Hyatt Gold Passport
Intercontinental Hotel Group	Priority Club Rewards
Marriott	Marriott Rewards
Shangri-La	Golden Circle
Starwood	Starwood Preferred Guest

All the major hospitality brands recognize the importance of offering a guest program to reward regular customers (see Table 14.3), and the customers are very aware of their importance to the hotels. All these program provide different levels of membership, which are determined according to the number of nights a customer stays in the hotels. The higher the number of stays, the more generous the benefits become as a customer graduates to the top tier of VIP membership. Some program allow customers to 'double dip' – this means that a customer who has an airline FFP membership can earn air miles whilst staying at the hotel, and at the same time earn points from the hotel, which are credited to their FGP. We will review two different program here: Hilton's HHonors and Shangri-La's Golden Circle.

Hilton HHonors

The Hilton program is open to customers staying in any of their current lodging brands, ranging from the budget properties to luxury hotels. However, customers who are on discounted rates booked through channels such as wholesalers, tour operators, aircrew and Internet auction sites are excluded from the scheme. There are four levels of membership:

1 Blue – there is no minimum qualifying number of stays; benefits include expedited check-in, free newspaper, spouse stays free and express checkout.
2 Silver VIP – to qualify, a customer has to have a minimum of four qualifying stays or 10 qualifying nights. The benefits include 15 per cent bonus points and complimentary access to the hotel's health club where available.
3 Gold VIP – to qualify, a customer has to have a minimum of 16 qualifying stays or 36 qualifying nights. The benefits include

25 per cent bonus points, and upgraded accommodation when available, depending on the type of hotel/brand.

4   Diamond VIP – to qualify, a customer has to have a minimum of 28 qualifying stays or 60 qualifying nights. The benefits include 50 per cent bonus points, guaranteed reservations availability up to 48 hours before booking and a reward 'planner' service to help arrange all the customer's travel needs.

Each level of membership has to be earned in each calendar year. Because of the differences between each brand (market segment, product offer and rates), there are several exclusions and different rewards according to the brand and the location. For example, a Diamond VIP can choose a room upgrade at a Conrad Hotel, but only a bottle of water and one snack item at a Hampton Inn and there are no room upgrades at any of the Hilton hotels located in the Maldives. Indeed, the Hilton HHonors web pages explaining the benefits and exclusions for each brand are very detailed and quite confusing.

Hilton has agreements with more than 60 airlines, and encourages double dipping. Obviously, the rewards for staying in the budget brands are considerably lower in value than those in the mid- and upscale brands. Hilton has negotiated an extensive network of partners to provide customers with the opportunity to either earn HHH points when using their services or redeem points. The partners include AT&T Wireless for telephone services, Chase and Citi Mortgages for real estate finance, Critics Choice Video for DVD and VHS films, FTD.com for flowers, GMAC Insurance and several car hire firms including National Car Rental.

Although Hilton promotes its guest program as a world of 'recognition and rewards', the scale of the program, with many millions of members from a wide range of hospitality target markets staying at 3500 hotels and able to redeem their points from a variety of products and services, suggests that this is really a transaction-orientated FGP.

Shangri-La Golden Circle

Shangri-La's Golden Circle is for privileged guests who stay at Shangri-La Hotels, Shangri-La Resorts and Traders Hotels. The focus is on guest recognition and individual personal preferences. There are three tiers of membership: Classic, Executive and Elite. Each hotel has an exclusive Golden Circle members' floor, and other benefits include private check-in and check-out, complimentary breakfast, spouse stays free, free access to the fitness center and swimming pool and a suite upgrade if available at a small extra charge. Executive and Elite members enjoy additional welcome amenities, guaranteed reservations availability (72/48 hours prior to arrival) and early check-in. The only Golden Circle benefit that is not linked to hotel services is the air miles offered to customers, from approximately 30 airlines.

The Shangri-La program focuses on recognition and provides rewards linked to the hospitality offered by the hotel. With about 70 hotels, two complementary brands and focused target markets, the Golden Circle is a genuine relational marketing program aimed at recognizing guest loyalty.

Activity 14.2

Log on to Hilton Hotels (www.hiltonworldwide.com) and Shangri-La Hotels (www.shangri-la.com). Both the Hilton HHonors FGP and the Golden Circle FGP are accessible from the home page.

- Compare the language used by Hilton and Shangri-La to describe their FGP
- Review the rewards offered and the conditions in both schemes
- What differences can you identify between these hotel companies' approach to marketing their FGP?

Disadvantages of FGP

The main disadvantages of FGP include the following:

- Benefits are awarded to individual guests, and the most frequent guests are those staying on business – so their companies pay for the hotel accommodation but do not gain the rewards
- Potential guest liability for tax on the benefits accrued from an FGP
- Potential company liability of unredeemed rewards eventually being claimed
- Customers who stay in hotels frequently join the FGP of several hotel companies, which erodes competitive advantage and encourages customer switching behaviour
- Costs are incurred setting up and administering the scheme.

PROBLEMS WITH RELATIONSHIP MARKETING

Relationship marketing has been criticized for a number of reasons. First, there is a limit to the number of relationships a customer can sustain with companies. Consumers are bombarded with many competing messages and cannot possibly have a one-to-one relationship with every brand they buy. Hence, some hospitality companies may have unrealistic expectations about their customers' willingness to give them trust, loyalty and commitment. In reality, customers can only give their loyalty to a small number of brands. Some consumers are also concerned about organizations' use of personal information, which has to be disclosed when staying in a hotel. Unsolicited communication in the form of direct mail, email and text messages, which aim to build a relationship with customers, can actually be counter-productive and turn customers away. Other criticisms include the following:

- Hospitality companies want customers to be loyal, but often fail to deliver the services that customers expect
- Special introductory offers to attract new customers are not offered to existing loyal customers, who then feel that they have been treated unfairly
- Customers can change their preferences, and do not always want the same newspaper or drink every time they check-in
- Preferential treatment given to customers in the FGP can be upsetting, or even offensive, to other customers.

CONCLUSION

Despite the legitimate criticisms of relationship marketing, customer loyalty is an appealing goal. Those hospitality companies that can develop meaningful relationships with customers do gain a competitive advantage. However, a relationship marketing strategy is not appropriate for all branded hospitality organizations; companies developing a relationship marketing strategy must have a strong service culture that delivers high customer satisfaction, effective service recovery strategies and relevant recognition and reward policies, in order to create customer trust, commitment and loyalty.

In this chapter, we have explained:

- How relationship marketing strategies focus on customer retention and recognize the long-term value of loyal customers
- That transactional marketing strategies focus on customer acquisition
- That the LTV of regular customers is relatively high and increases in customer retention can enhance profitability significantly
- That all hotel companies are aware of the importance of repeat guests and have developed FGP to attract and reward frequent guests
- That frequency is not an indicator of loyalty
- That loyal customers are less price sensitive and more resistant to competitors' offers
- That frequent guests are loyal to individual hotels, as well as to hotel brands
- That there are limits to the number of relationships customers can have with companies.

REVIEW QUESTIONS

Now check your understanding of this chapter by answering the following questions:

1 Highlight the differences between a relationship marketing strategy and a transactional marketing strategy within the context of hospitality.
2 A hotel company is planning to develop a relationship marketing strategy. Explain what is required to implement an effective relationship marketing strategy successfully.
3 Discuss the concept of customer loyalty in the hospitality industry.
4 Evaluate the role of FGP in the international hotel industry.

References and Further Reading

Barsky, J., & Nash, L. (2002). Evoking emotion: Affective keys to hotel loyalty. *Cornell Hotel and Restaurant Administration Quarterly*, *43*, 39–46.

Buttle, F. (1995). *Relationship marketing: theory and practice*. Paul Chapman.

Dick, A. S., & Basu, K. (1994). Customer loyalty towards an integrated framework. *Journal of Academic Marketing Science*, *22*, 99–113.

Grönroos, C. (1994). From marketing mix to relationship marketing: Towards a paradigm shift in marketing. *Management Decision*, *32*, 4–20.

Hayward, P. (2003, February 13). Back finds himself in England set-up. Daily Telegraph.

Heskett, J. L., Jones, T. O., Loveman, G. W., Sasser, W. E., Jr., & Schlesinger, L. A. (1994). Putting the service profit chain to work. *Harvard Business Review*, *72*, 164–170.

Jang, D., & Mattila, A. S. (2005). An Examination of restaurant loyalty programs: What kinds of rewards do customers prefer? *International Journal of Contemporary Hospitality Management*, *17*, 402–408.

Lewis, R. C., & Chambers, R. E. (2000). *Marketing leadership in hospitality, foundations and practice*. John Wiley, p. 64.

Osman, H., Hemmington, N., & Bowie, D. (2009). A transactional approach to customer loyalty in the hotel industry. *International Journal of Contemporary Hospitality Management*, *21*, 239–250.

Peck, H., Payne, A., Christopher, M., & Clark, M. (1999). *Relationship marketing for competitive advantage: Winning and keeping customers*. Butterworth-Heinemann.

Reichheld, F. (1993). Loyalty based management. *Harvard Business Review*, *71*, 64–73.

Shankar, V., Smith, A. K., & Rangaswamy, A. (2003). Customer satisfaction and loyalty in online and offline environments. *International Journal of Research in Marketing*, *20*, 153–175.

PART **E**

The Marketing Plan

CHAPTER **15**

Marketing planning

Chapter objectives

After going through this chapter, you should be able to:

- Understand the contexts and types of marketing planning in hospitality organizations
- Describe a generic process for marketing planning
- Carry out the research needed to develop a strategic marketing plan
- Explain how analytical tools are used to evaluate a hospitality business's current and potential situation
- Recognize the limitations of marketing planning and the importance of contingency planning.

INTRODUCTION

Planning is widespread in businesses of all sizes. Larger companies have more formalized planning processes, but smaller companies also perform planning essentials. A plan can be thought of as a set of decisions about what a company wants to achieve and how it is going to achieve it. The essence of a plan is, therefore, a goal with accompanying strategy and tactics. The goal defines what the company wants to achieve, whereas the strategy and tactics set out how the goal will be achieved. A marketing plan sets out the marketing objectives that a company wants to achieve and the strategy and tactics that will be used to reach the objectives.

In this chapter, we build on your learning from the pre-encounter, encounter and post-encounter hospitality marketing activities discussed in previous chapters. We will explain how marketing plans in operational units consist of objectives, strategies and tactics across the three stages of a customer relationship: pre-encounter, encounter and post-encounter.

CONTEXTS OF MARKETING PLANNING

Although unit-level marketing plans are the major focus of this chapter, it is important to acknowledge that marketing planning is carried out at many levels in more complex hospitality organizations.

Corporate marketing planning

Complex hospitality organizations such as the Marriott Corporation produce strategic marketing plans at the highest corporate level. These are concerned with major strategic decisions such as which geographic markets to enter, which hospitality formats to offer in those markets and strategies for market entry – joint venture, acquisition or organic development. Decisions are also made on the allocation of resources to support the marketing activities of member divisions.

Divisional marketing planning

A divisional marketing plan focuses on the goals of a major division of a hospitality company. A division is a profit center comprised of one or more core businesses, run by a dedicated chief executive and management team. Major hospitality groups, like Whitbread, will produce marketing plans for each of its brands - for example Beefeater Grill, Costa Coffee, and Premier Inn. Each brand will set its own goals, often in terms of sales and profit growth, and develop strategies for goal achievement. These strategies will consist of decisions to open (or close) operational units, to focus on particular market segments, to position against named competitors and to compete by employing a particular set of competitive advantages.

Unit marketing planning

An operational unit may be a hotel or a restaurant that competes in a particular market. Strategies focus on issues such as targeting, positioning and developing strong pre-encounter, encounter and post-encounter marketing mixes. Goals can be developed for pre-encounter marketing (raise awareness, develop expectations, develop preference), encounter marketing (achieve revenue and average spend targets) or post-encounter marketing (satisfaction, intention to do repeat business, share of customer spend). Overarching marketing goals are also employed at unit level – for example, sales, occupancy, RevPAR.

Departmental marketing plan

Within a hotel, different departments (such as the rooms division or food and beverage) may produce their own marketing plans. The focus at departmental level is generally much more tactical. The core strategic marketing decisions of segmentation, targeting and positioning (STP) will have been made at divisional or unit level. Departments have to operate within the parameters of those strategic decisions. For example, the rooms' division manager may need to find a solution for an unexpected loss of business. If a tour group suddenly cancels, the manager needs to develop a rapid tactical response to win additional business from targeted customer groups, such as airlines, transients or meetings and conventions.

TYPES OF MARKETING PLAN

In general, a distinction can be made between strategic and tactical marketing plans. As the focus of marketing plans shift from corporate through division to unit and department, plans become much more tactical. Strategic plans set the broad goals for the company, whereas tactical marketing plans focus on the detailed planning required to achieve those goals.

Strategic marketing plans

Strategic marketing plans (SMPs) are generally established for a minimum 3- to 5-year term. They focus on long-term goals, such as developing market share, building yield and growing revenues. Core marketing decisions are made about market segmentation, target markets and market positioning, and these decisions establish the foundations on which tactical plans can be built. A company's decision to target the corporate travel market and the short-break leisure market and to position against certain named competitors in each of these segments influences the level of investment in developing offers to appeal to these markets, communication strategies to send messages to them and channels to reach them. SMP decisions have major cost consequences, and are not easy to reverse. A company that changes its strategic position in the marketplace too frequently runs the risk of confusing customers and alienating investors.

Two main approaches to strategic marketing planning have been developed by Porter and by Treacy and Wiersema.

Porter

Porter (1980) claims that there are three core generic strategies for success, whatever the industry – overall cost leadership, differentiation, and focus.

Overall cost leadership

Firms adopting a low-cost position relative to competitors need to pursue a strategy of cost control in every aspect of the business. In hospitality firms, this means that food and beverage costs, payroll costs, energy, maintenance, administration, marketing and distribution overheads, décor, fabrics and furniture costs, are designed to give the lowest possible running costs. The choice of location should be at the lowest possible land cost, and all these factors are critically examined to achieve and maintain the lowest cost position in the market.

Companies adopting a cost–leadership strategy need to generate high economies of scale in marketing and purchasing; this implies that the company should be seeking to obtain a high market share. A cost–leadership strategy is most suitable for commodity markets like the accommodation budget sector, where the product is hard to differentiate. This strategy is best delivered by designing new-build hospitality premises, for example, Formule 1, where the construction of the operation can be designed for maximum cost efficiency.

Differentiation

Porter's second generic strategy recommends that firms adopt a product–service differentiation policy that is perceived by customers as significantly different from competitors. In hospitality, differentiation is closely linked to branding and offer formulation. Firms adopting a differentiation strategy strive to deliver a clearly defined experience that differs from that of competitors'. We have already discussed the role of differentiation in Chapter 4 and have provided examples from the hospitality industry.

Focus

The focus strategy, Porter's third generic strategy, suggests that firms should concentrate on one narrow market segment, or one geographic area or one primary product. The benefits of a focus strategy are derived from serving one target segment more effectively than either differentiated or low-cost firms. A focused firm may also adopt a differentiated or low-cost strategy aimed at the chosen market segment. We discussed a focus (or niche) marketing strategy in Chapter 4.

If firms do not adopt any one of these strategies, Porter suggests that they will be 'stuck in the middle', losing cost-sensitive business to low-cost leaders and high-margin business to firms adopting a differentiated strategy. Porter claims that firms 'stuck in the middle' are not as profitable as firms that have adopted one of the generic strategies.

Treacy and Wiersema

Treacy and Wiersema (1995) identified three major approaches to marketing strategy that companies can adopt: operational excellence, innovation and customer intimacy. They call these market disciplines.

Operational excellence

This core marketing discipline calls for doing a limited number of things extremely well. It implies the development of a well-defined value proposition based on clearly understood customer expectations, and the repeated production and delivery of the product–service that complies with exact specifications of a Standard Operating Procedure Manual. Companies such as McDonald's, Taco Bell and Pizza Hut fit this model.

Innovation

The innovation discipline is founded on the belief that relevant, customer-focused innovation will win buyer preference. Companies that stress product–service innovation nurture ideas, translate them into product–service concepts and market them successfully. These companies experiment and think 'out-of-the-box'. The Yo! Company, which developed Yo! Sushi, YOTEL, Yo! Japan (a clothing brand) and Yo! Home, is constantly looking for innovative ideas in hospitality and retail to take to market.

Customer intimacy

The third marketing discipline, customer intimacy, is based on the provision of solutions that are customized for individual customers. In these companies, empowerment is pushed to the front line and the company is flexible, doing what it takes to produce satisfied customers. Marriott's Ritz-Carlton brand prides itself on being such an organization.

Tactical marketing plans

Tactical marketing plans (TMPs) differ from strategic plans in both their timeframe and content. The typical TMP operates within a short time-frame, normally no longer than 1 year. The TMP is subordinate to the SMP and, therefore, operates within the STP parameters established by the SMP. TMPs consist primarily of campaigns and events that may be unit or department specific.

A campaign is a promotion that runs for a short period of time. Campaigns are generally expressed in carefully targeted and timed customer or prospect communications. A campaign might be a sales promotion designed to fill rooms during the shoulder period or might be a sales blitz designed to generated prospects for a salesperson to follow-up. Typically, a campaign is designed to produce specific behaviours in the targeted audience – for example, to visit the website and make a booking – in the short term.

Event-based marketing is the term used to describe the creation and communication of offers to customers at particular points in time. The event that triggers an offer is typically something that occurs in the customer's personal or business life. For example, the scheduling of an 'automobile industry' trade show by a city convention center might trigger a timely offer by a hotel chain to accommodate visitors from exhibiting companies. Event-based marketers put together offers that are unique to the event, set the price and promote to a tightly defined target market. The success of an event can only be measured when all the costs and revenues have been computed.

A GENERIC MARKETING PLAN STRUCTURE

In this section, we present a generic framework for marketing planning. This offers a structured approach for establishing marketing objectives, strategies and tactics. Not all of the components of the framework appear in every marketing plan – for example, departmental plans may not incorporate a STP component. The framework consists of nine major elements:

1 Vision, mission, values
2 Situation audit
3 Objectives

4 STP
5 Marketing mix
6 Budgeting
7 Implementation
8 Controls
9 Evaluation.

This framework presents an analysis of where the company is now and provides direction for where the company wants to be at some predetermined future point. It focuses on the development of marketing mix strategies and tactics and addresses the questions of cost, implementation and control.

Vision, mission, values

Many leading hospitality companies have developed vision statements, mission statements or sets of values. These are enduring statements about what the organization is *en route* to becoming sometime in the future (the vision statement), why the organization exists (the mission statement) and how the organization shall act in relationships with its stakeholders, such as shareholders, customers, employees and local community (the values statement). Many organizations do have policies like these but merge them into a single generic mission statement that contains elements of all three. Increasingly, mission statements contain references to a company's corporate social responsibility (CSR) agenda to satisfy a range of different stakeholders. These statements serve as both a guide and constraint on marketing planning. The pursuit of diversity in employment might favour the recruitment of indigenous populations to work at all levels of a unit, whereas corporate values such as respect for the environment might rule out the development of a hotel resort close to an endangered reef.

Business mission statements are succinct 'philosophical' statements, at most a page in length. The mission defines the purpose of a business and the desired benefits that all the stakeholders should get benefits from the business.

Mission statements are, typically, published on corporate websites, featured in annual reports and displayed in prominent places for customers to view – for example, in reception and lobby areas. Mission statements are also given to new employees as part of their induction process. Smaller independent hospitality organizations are less likely to have a formal mission statement, although owners and managers may have a very clear vision of what they want their business to achieve.

The purpose of a mission statement is to enable top management to provide:

- A focus for the future direction of the company
- A link with the company's short- and medium-term objectives, and the long-term goals of the organization

- A tool for communicating top management's perception of the company's future with its various stakeholders.

A mission statement can include the following elements:

- A definition of the broad scope of the business, the markets served, the products and services offered and the distinctive benefits provided by the organization to its customers
- A summary of the distinctive competences the business has developed – for example, a service ethos (Marriott), quality (Savoy), product consistency (McDonald's)
- A description of the desired market position *vis-à-vis* competitors
- A clear statement about the company's values.

The Prêt à Manger's mission statement emphasizes the company's environmental ethics and passion for fresh, healthy and natural food compared to their fast-food competitors (Figure 15.1). Prêt à Manger's packaging emphasizes the natural ingredients provided by named suppliers and their good environmental practices. This concise mission statement established the company's competitive position in 1986, has provided a strategic direction for future planning for 25 years and retains its relevance in today's marketplace.

Figure 15.1 Prêt à Manger's mission statement *Source: Prêt à Manger*

Activity 15.1

Log onto the following hotel websites and evaluate their vision, mission and value statements in the 'about us' pages, using the criteria outlined above

- www.marriott.com
- www.shangri-la.com

Most hospitality companies have developed a unique set of values, expressed in their mission statements, which are often derived from their origins and built up over a long period of time. However, some hospitality companies produce bland corporate mission statements lacking originality (or even copied from another organization) to conform to societal expectations. Certainly, the development of a mission statement that does not reflect the company's historic values or its distinctive competences and that the employees clearly do not endorse, can be legitimately criticized. Indeed, meaningless 'motherhood' statements, providing solemn assurances of service and quality, are really faulty exercises in public relations and do not convince employees or customers.

Situation audit – 'where are we now?'

An early step in writing a marketing plan for a hospitality company is to carry out research into the company, and its environment, to answer the question 'where are we now?' Hospitality managers must try to be objective and rational about their company when evaluating the business's strengths and weaknesses. Too often, an emotional attachment to the business can influence owners and managers who see the weaknesses identified by customers as being minor, irrelevant or even attractive, rather than the negative attributes they really are. Although managers normally prepare their own marketing plans, the use of outside consultants can bring impartiality to the marketing planning process. Ideally, the situation audit for a property should be written up as brief factual statements covering all the key aspects of the hospitality business. The two sections of the situation audit are the internal audit and the external audit, and the key issues are summarized in a SWOT (Strengths, Weaknesses, Opportunities and Threats) analysis.

Internal audit

The internal audit assesses all aspects of the hospitality unit's operations, with the aim of establishing what the business is doing well – the strengths – and which parts of the business are performing poorly – the weaknesses. Managers can usually identify their business's strengths and, more often than not, know their weaknesses; but the difficulty is recognizing the difference between the symptoms of a problem (e.g. low food sales) and the cause of the problem (in this case, perhaps, unpopular menu items, high prices, poor service, unappealing décor or a combination of all of these factors). By identifying the causes of the problem, managers can plan action to correct the reasons for the poor performance and improve the offer to customers. Strengths and weaknesses can be identified in a rigorous way, first by vertical analysis (e.g. within business functions – finance, operations, marketing, human resources) and then horizontally, by looking at cross-functional processes and issues such as leadership and culture.

Most medium and larger hospitality companies are composed of a number of strategic business units (SBUs), some of which will be in the early stages of development and some of which will be mature. Some will be heavy users of cash to build market share, others will be powerful generators of cash surpluses. A healthy, well-managed company will have a balanced portfolio of SBUs and the internal audit should assess the health of the product–service portfolio. One tool that has been developed to help in this assessment is the Boston Consulting Group (BCG) matrix.

The BCG matrix is an analytical approach to assessing a SBU's cash flow, based on its relative market share and the industry's market growth. The rate of market growth indicates the attractiveness of a market – higher-growth markets are usually more attractive than low-growth markets. Relative market share indicates the degree of dominance a SBU holds in its marketplace and the share of the company in comparison to the market leader. For example, if Company X (the market leader) has a 20 per cent market share and Company Y has 5 per cent, then Y's relative market share is 0.25. The combination of these factors provides companies with a tool to evaluate possible strategic directions and, most importantly from a marketing planning perspective, to calculate the cash generation and cash usage of each SBU. This model's four quadrants have been labelled as follows, according to the characteristics of the SBU's performance (Figure 15.2):

1　*Star* (high market growth/high relative market share): A star is a hospitality brand that has a relatively high share of a high-growth market. The company will need to reinvest the cash generated from this SBU to continue maintain the brand's position by acquiring/building additional outlets. All the cash generated by this SBU is used within it.

2　*Cash cow* (low market growth/high relative market share): Cash cows operate in mature markets with low growth rates and high relative market share. They generate cash and high profits, because of their economies of scale and low marketing costs. The profits

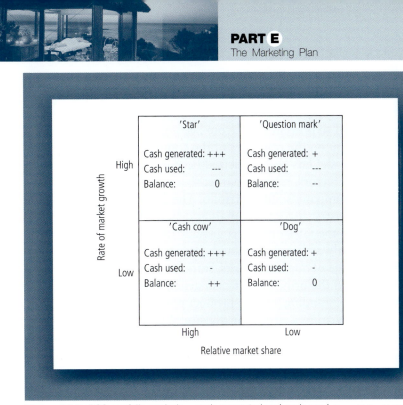

Figure 15.2 BCG portfolio analysis – cash generated and cash used *Source: McDonald, 1999, p. 185.*

generated are reinvested by the parent company to fund the development of the next category – question marks.

3 *Question mark* (high market growth/low relative market share): Question marks operate in high growth markets but suffer from a low relative market share. Most new products start out as question marks. Companies may develop many new product ideas and those that are retained require significant marketing support and, therefore, use more cash than they generate. If they succeed, they can eventually turn into stars and ultimately into cash cows to support additional innovation.

4 *Dog* (low market growth/low relative market share): Dogs operate in mature markets and have low relative market share. These businesses have to be tightly managed to ensure that they do not become a liability. Dogs can be cash-neutral; but if they start to make a loss they need to be disposed of quickly. Dogs are rarely able to generate the profits and growth expected by major companies. Although it does not generate sufficient return for its current owners, in the hands of new owners (who might have different performance measures) a dog may make a satisfactory return.

Marketing planners strive to achieve a balanced portfolio of SBUs with sufficient cash cows to generate profits to satisfy shareholders and fund investment in question marks. A good example is InterContinental Hotels Group's (IHG's) portfolio with the star (Intercontinental), the cash cow (Holiday Inn) and the question mark (Indigo), which may become a star in due course. The disposal of dogs is essential to prevent them from becoming a financial and time-consuming drain on the resources of the company.

The BCG model has been criticized because of its narrow focus in only using two factors, relative market share and market growth rate, to evaluate a company's SBU portfolio. The fragmented nature of the hospitality industry also creates market definition problems, and trying to establish the rates of market growth and accurate market share figures is not always easy. Although the BCG has limited practical use, the language of question marks, stars, cash cows and dogs is used in business, and the principles of cash generation and cash usage are helpful in understanding a multi-product portfolio.

Marketers writing a group or divisional plan also have to compile information on strengths and weaknesses, based on collecting data from the group's operational units. A key issue for head office marketers is delivering a consistent quality standard across hotels marketed under the same brand. A particular difficulty is when hotels under a single brand are a mix of owned, contracted and franchised units. The group marketing plan will also need to address the effectiveness of group sales and marketing activities in creating brand image and raising brand awareness, as well as building long-term relationships with key account customers and intermediaries.

External audit

Remember, the external environment includes all the factors over which the company has no control. The purpose of an external audit is to identify potential opportunities that might be exploited by the firm and any threats that might damage the business. The external factors are applicable to all companies operating in the same competitor set. The external influences impacting on a company can be classified under two headings: the macro-environment and the micro-environment.

The macro-environment

The macro-environment includes major regional, national and global trends influencing business and society in broad general terms. In Chapter 1, reference was made to these PESTE factors, which influence the demand and supply of hospitality services. The macro-environment analysis evaluates current and future PESTE factors to enable the hospitality business to adapt its operations to changes in the needs and wants of customers, and changes in trading conditions.

The micro-environment

Broad trends in the micro-environment influence all the players. A hospitality company's micro-environment includes external stakeholders and, most importantly, customers, competitors and suppliers. There is no doubt that local or regional influences in the micro-environment impact upon a firm's trading situation.

The SWOT Analysis

Although the situation audit requires considerable in-depth research and the accumulation of extensive data about the company, only a summary of the audit needs to be presented in the marketing plan. The situation audit, with commentary, focuses on the key factors influencing the current and future performance of the company. Appendices containing more detailed analysis – for example, the customer analysis, changes in consumer behaviour, competitor analysis – can be attached. A thorough understanding of 'where we are now' forms the basis of effective marketing planning and this is the function of the situation audit. Table 15.1 illustrates some of the key SWOT data that can emerge from a situation analysis. In this illustration, the internal audit data reflect the strengths and weaknesses of the marketing function; and the external audit presents the potential opportunities and threats facing a hypothetical hotel business.

The situation audit also helps to identify *critical success factors* (also called key factors for success), which are company specific (see Chapter 4).

Objectives – 'where do we want to go?'

Having conducted the 'where are we now?' audit, the next step in the marketing planning process is to set objectives. Objectives are statements that translate the hospitality company's mission into easily understood targets regarding markets and products, sales, occupancy and the marketing mix.

Objectives provide answers to the question 'where do we want to go?' Objective setting is an essential step in the marketing planning process. Companies that do not have objectives fail to provide managers and employees with a clear direction. Objectives should be Specific, Measurable, Achievable, Realistic and achieved within a set Timetable (SMART). SMART objectives provide managers with operational targets that measure the performance of the business and act as a control mechanism in determining whether management is effective. Examples of strategic and tactical hospitality marketing objectives are provided in Table 15.2.

SMART objectives are formed using quantified metrics like money, percentages and numbers. The timetable can either refer to the time period during which the target should be achieved ('to achieve £1 million sales within the next 12-month trading period') or to the date by

Table 15.1 Extract from hotel SWOT analysis

	Strengths (internal)	Weaknesses (internal)
Positioning	Brand image rating increased by 2% over key competitor according to independent research	Brand image suffers due to lack of consistency, caused by wide variety of standards in group's units
Location	Most convenient access to motorway network	Problems of noise from passing traffic
Product	Recently refurbished bedroom decor is superior to competitors	Standard bedrooms are smaller than those of two newly built competitors
Price	Customer questionnaires suggest very high 'value for money' ratings	Leisure-break family inclusive price 10% higher than competitors
Distribution	Contract with high profile international third party Internet (TPI) distributor has increased leisure bookings from three key source countries	Conference agents' high commission levels eroding profitability on conference bookings
Marketing communication	Recent online advertising and offline public relations campaign has raised brand awareness by 2% compared to our competitor set	Website design and photography dated compared to competitor's new website
People	Key heads of department have worked at the unit for 15+ years	High turnover of housekeeping staff is preventing effective staff training
Processes	Improved check-in/check-out at front desk, according to mystery shopper analysis	Banqueting suite does not have adequate hot food storage facilities
Physical evidence	Excellent landscaping and lighting and prominent signage on major road	Kitchen waste storage and bin area always untidy
Customer satisfaction	High (and increased) level of repeat business travellers staying compared to two years ago	Online customer questionnaires and in-room comment cards identify problems of inconsistent standards of housekeeping
Key relationships	Sales manager has successfully built close relationships with three key intermediaries in the conference market	Lost one key account due to inconsistent housekeeping standards

Table 15.1 Extract from hotel SWOT analysis—cont'd		
	Opportunities (external)	**Threats (external)**
Political	Changes in the Chinese government's approach to issuing tourist visas allow Chinese consumers more opportunity to travel to foreign countries	Changes in health and safety legislation mean that kitchen equipment specifications will have to be adapted
Economic	Increased consumer disposable income from Asian markets is generating more demand for long haul holidays in the Americas, Australasia and Europe	High exchange rate makes cost of foreign holidays relatively cheaper and negatively influences demand for domestic holidays
Socio-cultural	Demand for vegetarian meals is growing due to increased public concern about animal rights	Sophisticated consumers are bored with hotel restaurants
Technological	Growth of smart mobile technology creates opportunities to reach hospitality consumers whilst travelling	Business travel agents directing web links to corporate client's intranet is eroding customer loyalty to hotel brand
Environmental	Concern for environmental issues means consumers will value sustainable tourism initiatives	Concern about air pollution might discourage tourists from staying in downtown locations

which a target should be achieved ('to achieve one Michelin star for the restaurant by June 2014').

Marketing objectives will vary across the customer relationship from pre-encounter, through encounter to post-encounter. Managers need to think carefully about what is relevant for each stage.

- Pre-encounter objectives focus on achievements such as raising awareness, generating understanding and knowledge, creating expectations, building interest and stimulating first purchase
- Encounter objectives focus on generating customer satisfaction, influencing the level of spending, cross-selling and up-selling
- Post-encounter objectives focus on building repeat purchase intention, growing share of spend and promoting positive word of mouth.

Marketing planning in lifestyle and growth businesses

Marketing objectives will also vary according to whether the business is a lifestyle business that has no wish to grow, or a business with ambitious owners or investors who want to see the value of their investment

15

Table 15.2 SMART marketing objectives	
SMART strategic objectives (3–5 years)	**SMART tactical objectives (within 1 year)**
To increase sales from €165 million in the current year to €280 million in Year 3	To increase room occupancy from 69% to 72% within 12 months
To acquire 20 upscale, 100-bedroom properties in target European city center locations within 4 years	To acquire four upscale properties, with bedrooms ranging from 80 to 130, in Barcelona, Manchester, Prague and Stuttgart within 12 months
To develop a new food and beverage lifestyle concept suitable for residents and non-residents within 2 years	To test-market a new food and beverage lifestyle concept in Sydney between March and September next year
To increase brand awareness amongst European conference agents from a current level of 55% to 65%, in the BDRC Continental European Business Travel survey, within 3 years	To launch a new dedicated conference agent website for European distributors, in January, with new online booking options and video clips of key conference facilities

increase. Lifestyle entrepreneurs are content to see their restaurants busy with regular customers, their staff happy and secure and enough money coming in to sustain their lifestyle and repay any borrowings. Growth-oriented business people are more likely to set ambitious 'stretch' targets that, if achieved, will see the market value or capitalization of their business improve. Two tools enable the growth-oriented business to develop clear objectives and strategies: gap analysis and the Ansoff matrix.

Gap analysis

Gap analysis is an extension of the 'where are we now?' investigation. Company records should tell the marketer the level of sales achieved in the past and those currently being achieved. An examination of the SWOT conditions should give a good idea of what will happen to sales in the future if the identified threats and opportunities do actually impact on the business, and if the company continues to pursue the same strategies. Very often, companies finds there is a 'gap' between where they want to be in terms of sales objectives and where a forecast based on the SWOT analysis tells them they will be. Gap analysis is the art and science of computing the size of the gap. For example, a parent company of a budget lodging company could set a divisional objective of increasing room revenues from $175 million to $300 million within 3 years. The forecast shows that in 3 years' time, sales will be $200 million if the present marketing strategy is pursued. There is, therefore, a gap of $100 million ($300 million objective less $200 million forecast) that has to be filled through additional revenue

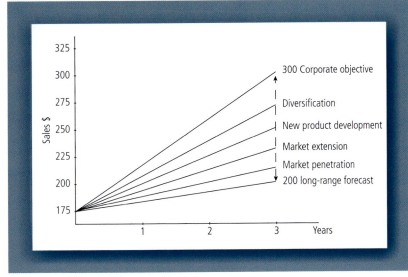

Figure 15.3 Gap analysis *Source: McDonald, 1999*

generation activity (Figure 15.3). The four alternative strategies for filling the 'gap' were developed into a matrix by H. Igor Ansoff.

The Ansoff matrix

Ansoff's four strategic options to bridge the revenue gap are:

1 Market penetration
2 Market extension
3 Product development
4 Diversification.

Using each of the Ansoff strategies, where appropriate, a company might be able to bridge the sales gaps but still not reach the objective. If this were to happen, then the company would have to re-evaluate the objectives and perhaps set a revised, lower objective.

A similar approach to sales gap analysis can be used to bridge 'profit' gaps. This approach includes an additional 'operational' strategy, improving productivity. The operations gap can be closed using strategies to reduce costs, improve the sales mix, increase prices and improve productivity.

Ansoff's four growth options are discussed here.

Market penetration strategy – existing markets/existing products

This strategy is based on the premise that the target markets are satisfied with the existing offer. A market penetration strategy aims to grow the business by increasing sales of the current offer(s) to current target markets. There are three ways to increase sales to existing markets. The first is to increase the frequency with which customers patronize the establishment (i.e. increasing repeat visits), increase customers' spend (i.e. increasing achieved room and meal rates) or, ideally, both. The second method is to attract your competitors' customers. The third route is to grow the market by convincing non-users to buy the product (Figure 15.4). Examples of strategies and tactics used for market penetration include:

- Brand loyalty and frequent guest programs
- Staff training to 'sell up'
- Sales promotions
- In-house marketing activity
- Email campaigns targeting ex-customers
- PR events for regular customers.

Providing that the market is not changing rapidly and the company is satisfied with profitability, a market penetration strategy is the safest and least risky strategy to adopt. The danger of relying on a market penetration strategy stems from the problems caused by dynamic changing market conditions, which can change customers' needs and wants and influence competitor activity, thus eroding a company's position.

Market extension or development – new markets/existing products

A market extension strategy features the roll out of existing product-service offers in new markets. In hospitality, there are different approaches to market extension, depending upon whether the strategy is focused on growth within existing units or on expanding the number of properties in the group. In existing units, market extension refers to promoting the existing property to new target markets. Most hospitality businesses will target the same primary markets each year, but secondary target markets can change in line with changing market trends. These secondary target markets represent new markets for which the existing product is suitable. Imaginative product/benefit bundles targeting new market segments can highlight the benefits of the company's products. A typical restaurant example is a competitively priced, all-inclusive meal promotion aimed at attracting 'early-bird' diners.

Another approach to market development that is particularly relevant to retail hospitality chains is geographic expansion of existing product concepts. There are numerous examples in hospitality of hotel and restaurant brands seeking to expand by rolling out new units. Because the product concept is proven, the key issue in expanding geographically is to ensure that the characteristics of the new target market are similar to those of existing successful markets. Hospitality companies also expand geographically by acquisition, which can be riskier, because the newly acquired properties may not conform to the requirements of the branded hospitality chain.

		Products	
		Existing	New
Markets	Existing	Market penetration or concentration (same markets/same products) Increase market share by: (a) Increase frequency and spend from existing customers (improve internal marketing; brand loyalty programs; frequent-stay promotions; in-house product/price bundles) (b) Attract competitors' customers (promote special offers, raise brand image/brand awareness) (c) Convince non-users to buy products (educate market by informing non-users of the product benefits)	Product development (same markets/new products) Introduce product improvement programs by: (a) Replacement and refurbishment of rooms, food and beverage, and leisure facilities – targeting existing customers (b) Introduction of new technology to improve service quality Introduce product extensions by: (a) Development of new menu items aimed at existing customers
	New	Market extension or development (new market/same product) (a) Target new customers: Identify new target markets and develop marketing communication program to promote existing product, e.g. early-bird diners (b) Target similar customers in different geographic areas: Identify geographic areas with similar demographic profile and roll out existing product (c) Use new distribution channels to reach new markets: e.g. work with intermediaries on joint-marketing initiatives	Diversification and innovation (new market/new product) (a) Intensive (inside the existing firm) Innovative, new bar and food concepts aimed at new target markets, e.g. new leisure center at hotel targeting new local customers (b) Extensive diversification (outside existing firm) Vertical integration (i) Forward (ii) Backward Diversification (i) Horizontal (ii) Concentrated (related) (iii) Conglomerate (non-related)

Figure 15.4 Ansoff or market/product mix

However, another approach to market development is to reach new markets via extensions of the distribution channel. Joint marketing initiatives with intermediaries who have access to new markets can be effective. For example, an independent hotel can join a consortium like Best Western Hotels to participate in their established domestic leisure break program and attract new markets by distribution through their international travel intermediaries.

Product development – existing markets/new products

Ansoff's product development strategy features enhancement of the product-service offers made to existing customers. Managers in hospitality operations are constantly looking for ways to increase customer satisfaction by improving the product offer. Product development strategies and tactics for existing customer markets include:

- Refurbishment programs to existing operations,
- Introduction of new menus,
- Introduction of new technology to improve the service operations,
- New leisure concepts aimed at existing customer markets.

Most 'new' product developments in hospitality operations are evolutionary rather than revolutionary. They are product improvements and product modifications, rather than radical new product-service concepts. Many new products are actually line extensions. For example, a new menu item may have been copied from a competitor, because it supplements a company's existing menu. The launch of new products primarily aimed at existing customer markets might also attract new customer groups. Providing the existing markets is profitable markets; product development is a proven strategy to retain customer loyalty.

Diversification – new markets/new products

The diversification strategy focuses on creating new product–service offers for new target customers. This is the riskiest growth strategy, because the company has no existing customer or product knowledge to exploit. Diversification within hospitality units is described as intensive diversification, meaning that new products are offered inside the existing unit. For example, intensive diversification might involve the building of a new facility on the premises, designed to attract new markets. Examples of intensive diversification in an existing hotel might include:

- A new restaurant concept aimed at new target markets (e.g. non-resident customers)
- A new leisure complex aimed at people living in the local neighbourhood
- New banqueting/conference and exhibition facilities aimed at new target markets.

Diversification outside the scope of the existing firm is described as extensive and can take many different forms:

- *Vertical backward integration* means acquiring suppliers – for example, a contract catering firm taking over food distributors
- *Vertical forward integration* involves acquiring intermediaries who have a direct relationship with customers – for example, tour operators acquiring travel agents
- *Horizontal diversification* is the acquisition of a competitor operating in the same market – for example, a mid-market hotel chain taking over another mid-market hotel chain
- *Concentric diversification* is the acquisition or start-up of companies that exploit the hospitality company's core competences – for example, a restaurant starting up a delicatessen using its kitchen brigade's skills;
- *Conglomerate diversification* is diversification into an unrelated area – for example, builders buying hotels.

The Ansoff matrix enables marketers to evaluate systematically the growth options facing the company. When management has decided which market/product options to pursue, then detailed marketing mix strategies have to be developed to achieve the market/product objectives. For example, in competitive hospitality sectors, companies strive to obtain competitive advantage by constantly investing in product development and continually improving the offer to customers. Once this strategy has been decided, the detail of the new product development strategies needs to be considered.

Segmentation, targeting and positioning (STP)

Having set objectives, the next step of this generic marketing planning process is to make the core strategic decisions about how to segment the market, which customer segments to target and how to position effectively against competitors in the same market. These issues have been addressed in earlier chapters, but it is worth stressing a few points here:

- Market segmentation involves dividing up the market into homogeneous subsets, so that marketing strategies and tactics can be developed for one or more segments
- Companies that are innovative in the way they segment a market can enjoy first-mover advantage as they exploit opportunities that have not been recognized by competitors
- Companies can choose to focus on one or more market segments, depending upon the attractiveness of the opportunities and the competences of the company
- Market positioning is concerned with selecting a competitive position in the market and determining how to compete effectively in that

position; for most hospitality sectors, this means choosing a competitive group and identifying how to generate sales from customers.

Until the STP decisions are made, companies cannot begin to develop strategies and tactics. Segmentation and targeting strategies are based on the findings from the situation audit, whereas the positioning strategy provides the core theme for integrating all the elements of the marketing mix to provide a consistent offer.

Marketing mix – 'how do we get there?'

Marketing strategies and marketing tactics are marketing mix decisions made by managers to achieve the agreed marketing objectives. Strategies and tactics are deployed to ensure that the company wins sales from the targeted customers (target market segments) against the identified competitors (market positioning).

Marketing mixes for both strategies and tactics will vary according to the stage of the customer relationship – pre-encounter, encounter or post-encounter. Table 15.3 provides a useful framework that can be used to construct appropriate marketing mixes. The eight elements of the hospitality marketing mix are listed vertically and the three relationship stages are listed horizontally. The check marks within the cells indicate the marketing mix elements that are more widely deployed at each stage of the relationship.

Throughout this text, we have explained the responsibilities of the marketing team and stressed how marketing needs to work with other departments to ensure the marketing offer is consistent and effective. The marketing team plays a major role in pre-encounter marketing to manage demand for the hospitality offer, and post-encounter marketing to build customer relationships and generate repeat and recommended sales. During the encounter, although marketing should

Table 15.3 The hospitality marketing mix matrix

	Pre-encounter marketing mix	Encounter marketing mix	Post-encounter marketing mix
Product–service offer	✓	✓	
Location	✓	✓	
Price	✓	✓	
Distribution	✓		
Marketing communications	✓	✓	✓
Physical environment	✓	✓	
Process	✓	✓	✓
People		✓	

provide input into the physical environment, service process and internal marketing, the primary responsibilities lie with operations and the human resource functions.

There are two different approaches to construct the marketing mix part of a marketing plan. In one approach, the strategy for each element of the marketing mix in the unit is discussed in turn – for example, the product strategy, the price strategy, the distribution strategy, the marketing communications strategy. In another approach, the marketing mix for each functional area of the unit is considered – for example, the marketing mix for the accommodation, the marketing mix for the restaurant operations, the marketing mix for the conference facilities. Either approach is acceptable.

Strategies and tactics need to be developed for each element of the marketing mix, but marketers must ensure that each strategy complements the other marketing mix strategies – inconsistencies between marketing mix strategies will send the target markets mixed messages and will inevitably be self-defeating.

Just as there is a choice of different marketing *objectives*, there can also be a choice of different marketing *strategies* that can achieve the same objective. For example, if an annual accommodation sales objective of £10 million has been set for a 200-bedroom hotel, there are different revenue management strategies that can achieve the sales objective (Table 15.4).

Unit and departmental marketing plans will normally include the detailed tactics that support the broad strategy. These will include events and campaigns that are scheduled for the year ahead. Sales and marketing personnel implement these tactical plans that typically include answers to the following questions:

- What action is going to be undertaken? (detailed list of events and campaigns)
- What is the event or campaign designed to achieve? (SMART objectives)
- Where will the actions take place? (locations, units, departments)
- When will the action take place? (timetable)
- How much will it cost? (budget)
- Who will run the events and campaigns? (responsibility and authority).

Table 15.5 illustrates the chart for a tactical marketing plan.

Table 15.4 Accommodation strategies	
Strategy 1 – lower occupancy/higher achieved room rate	**Strategy 2 – higher occupancy/lower achieved room rate**
200 rooms at 50% annual room occupancy and an achieved room rate of £273.90 = £10 million	200 rooms at 80% annual room occupancy and an achieved room rate of £172.23 = £10 million

Table 15.5 The tactical marketing plan

Objectives (SMART)			
• Target market(s) • Positioning • Financial • Marketing			
Actions	Timetable	Budget	Who is responsible?

Source: McDonald, 1999.

Budgeting

Companies need to create a budget for the implementation of their strategic and TMPs. Budgets include two classes of data: forecast revenues and costs. Revenues are generated by departmental sales (rooms division, food and beverage, entertainment, shops etc.), and these appear as forecasts on the top line of an income statement. The marketing plan needs to identify and quantify the cost elements that will be incurred in reaching the revenue targets. Not all cost elements are regarded as marketing costs – for example, food and beverage input costs are reported as operational department costs. The costs that are attributable to the marketing function are

- Market research expenses
- Distribution (commissions to intermediaries)
- Marketing communication activities
- Sales team (salaries, travel costs, support materials and training)
- Customer database management.

In Chapter 9, we provided a detailed discussion of the marketing communication budgets. Budgeting in the marketing plan is closely linked to limits set by the corporate financial plan, and marketers typically work within industry norms of 2–6 per cent of revenue.

Implementation

There are three main aspects to the implementation of any marketing plan:

1 Assigning the roles and responsibilities for resourcing and executing the plan to individuals, departments or external agencies

2 Engaging and obtaining the commitment of those individuals, departments or external agencies to ensure that the plan is successfully implemented

3 Designing a process to track the performance of the plan against revenue targets and costs assumptions.

Marketing plans do not simply involve marketing people. Operational units (such as food and beverage) and service departments (such as engineering or front office) influence customer experience and need to understand their roles in meeting the marketing objectives, delivering customer satisfaction and creating customer retention. Marketing plans also need the support of those who control the allocation of resources. A unit marketing plan might need to be endorsed by the division; a divisional marketing plan might need to go the corporate level for funding.

All the hard work in researching and compiling a marketing plan can be wasted if a company fails to communicate with the employees. Customer-contact employees are often unaware of the marketing plan's goals, strategies and tactics, and of their role in it. Chapter 12 emphasized the importance of effective employee/management communications. Involving employees in the preparation of the marketing plan provides a good opportunity to facilitate that communication process. Hospitality employees can – indeed they should – be involved in the situation audit. The employees can provide useful insights into how customers view the facilities and service, and often know the strengths and weaknesses of an operation better than management. Also, employees are very aware of competitors. They may have worked for the competition or have friends working in competitor organizations or even patronize competitors' food and beverage outlets. Finally, customer-contact employees need to be aware of what is happening during the implementation of events and campaigns, in case customers ask them any questions.

External persons and organizations may also need to be educated about their role in the plan's execution – for example, intermediaries, consortium partners, franchisees, management contractors, independent sales representatives and advertising and public relations agencies. Management also needs to communicate their SMPs effectively to other stakeholders, especially banks and any institutional shareholders.

Controls – 'how do we know we are getting there?'

The penultimate stage of this generic marketing planning process is to design a system to monitor and control the plan's implementation. The key concerns here are to ensure that there is no unacceptable variance between the plan's revenue targets and anticipated costs, and those that are actually achieved. When there is unacceptable variance, a tactical response may be initiated. Unfortunately, there is no such thing as a perfect marketing plan! External events beyond the marketer's control can have a major impact on both revenues and costs – for example, governments may alter their tax regime, resulting in lower consumer disposable income and reduced expenditure on leisure products; suppliers may increase prices, resulting in higher costs. Internal conditions can also influence performance against plan: key employees might leave the company or there might be publicity about a company's failure of a kitchen hygiene inspection. Controls are necessary to detect, correct and prevent unacceptable variances from the plan's objectives and cost profile. The key to control is setting SMART objectives. Without SMART objectives, managers have nothing against which to compare performance. There are five stages in the control process:

1   Set SMART objectives
2   Establish a reporting process to keep management informed of progress against targets
3   Monitor performance
4   Identify significant variations from target
5   Take corrective action.

Control measures can include financial performance – sales, achieved room rate, occupancy and RevPAR; customer mix ratios; changes in market share; changes in brand awareness and brand image; number of hits on the website; number of bookings (the conversion ratio from enquiries to bookings); changes in the customer satisfaction index.

Providing the objective is SMART then variance from the plan can easily be detected when it occurs. Marketing managers need to establish whether variance is minor or major, and whether it affects one market segment or all markets. If the variance is a minor underperformance for a short period in one market segment – for example, weekend leisure breaks in the North, in January and February, due to poor weather – then it might be tolerated. If it is significant and affects all markets, then urgent action needs to be taken. Appropriate actions might include adapting the tactics, revisiting the strategy or, in extreme circumstances, changing the SMART objectives if they are no longer realistic. Over-performance against plan can also be problematic. This happens when there is too much demand on a property. For example, a hotel might have a commitment to a TPI distributor for a 10% allocation of rooms, but changes in the exchange rate have made the location more popular than forecast. This could result in an overbooking situation leading to operational difficulties. Figure 15.5 summarizes the stages and monitoring and control mechanism in the marketing plan.

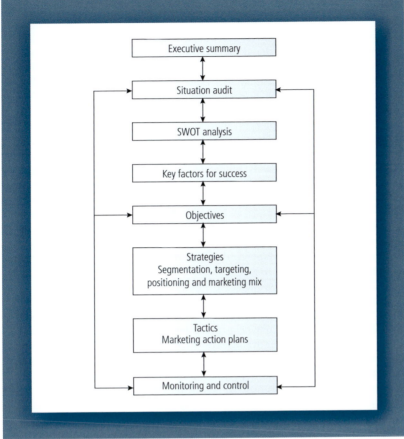

Figure 15.5 Summary of marketing plan

Contingency planning

Although the generic marketing planning process described above is founded upon a rigorous SWOT analysis, many companies also develop contingency plans. Contingency planning recognizes that the key assumptions upon which the marketing plan is formulated may be incorrect and contingency plans are formulated on 'what if?' scenarios – for example, what would happen if a serious environmental incident affected our business? Only major risks are considered in contingency planning.

Contingency planning can be linked to crisis management and has become more important as a result of dramatic events that have had a serious impact on hospitality companies. Environmental disasters such as the 2004 tsunami in South East Asia; health scares caused by epidemics such as SARS and terrorist incidents like suicide bomb attacks temporarily destroy demand for hospitality and tourism. In these circumstances, public health and safety are the most important issues and price does not influence demand. Hospitality companies respond to these crises by reducing costs as far as possible – especially

Case study 15.1 **Contingency planning at IHG**

On Thursday 15 April 2010, airspace across most of central and northern Europe was closed for 5 days due to volcanic ash clouds from Eyjafjallajökull in Iceland. Ninety-five thousand flights were cancelled and 5 million passengers were stranded not only in Europe but also around the world. The disruption to air travel was greater than that caused by the attacks on the United States on 11 September 2001.

Although some hoteliers simply thought of this incident as an immediate opportunity to fill their hotels at higher than normal prices, IHG recognized that this crisis was both an opportunity and a threat. On the Friday immediately following the closure of European airspace, IHG's crisis management planning team evaluated the potential threats from both a business and a consumer perspective. They soon realized that the long-term consequence of the disruption to their brands and customers was significant. An IHG corporate level virtual meeting of senior vice-presidents and executives on Sunday, 18 April, agreed a strategic and tactical response that was rolled out across all brands and hotels affected by the crisis.

The tactical response included the decision not to take advantage of stranded travellers by over-charging them on room prices and to even provide customers with discounted food offers of between 20 per cent and 25 per cent. To implement this response quickly, the IHG team had to ensure that all their franchisees were properly informed about the crisis and adopted IHG's policies. The fact that franchisees endorsed these pricing policies was in part due to the IHG's corporate values.

Although the widespread travel disruption due to the volcanic ash was limited to approximately 1 week, the effect of room cancellations – especially on conference business – created potential long-term negative financial consequences for some IHG hotel owners. IHG was sympathetic to hotel owners who experienced financial difficulty and supported them in a variety of ways. The IHG crisis management team had already identified the threat of business disruption to franchisees and initiated a special sales initiative to support the vulnerable hotels to help them re-build occupancy during the aftermath of the volcanic ash cloud incident.

IHG was able to respond quickly to the travel disruption and initiate an effective response because they had an experienced contingency planning team in place that identified the immediate and long-term issues confronting all their brands. The IHG corporate culture also enabled the team to implement the response strategy with the support of their franchisees.

Sources: IHG; Ash cloud chaos: Airlines face huge task as ban ends, Wednesday, 21 April, 2010 15:51 UK, http://news.bbc.co.uk/1/hi/uk/8633892.stm; Volcanic ash grounds Britain for days to come, Times Online, April 18, 2010, http://www.timesonline.co.uk/tol/travel/news/article7101162.ece.

payroll costs. As consumer confidence gradually returns, companies re-ignite their marketing activity to encourage customers to return, often using price-led promotions. The SMP should always include a budget item for contingencies. This provides funds to enable the company to take advantage of an unforeseen opportunity or to respond to a downturn in demand by increasing marketing activity.

Evaluation – 'how do we know we have arrived?'

This is the final step of the generic marketing planning process. Shortly after the conclusion of a planning period, event or campaign, the marketing team needs to evaluate results. The comparison of actual performance with the SMART objectives across all the areas of the business, with a commentary explaining the reasons for variance, provides useful information for the preparation of the next marketing plan. Companies repeat successfully tried and tested tactics of previous years and aim to learn from less-effective activities. Indeed, marketing is a continuous learning activity. The cycle of forward-planning the next campaign while implementing the current marketing action plan and evaluating recent activity is carried out simultaneously.

CRITICISMS OF MARKETING PLANNING

Critics of marketing planning claim that the uncertainty of the future makes long-term planning unreliable and costly and that marketing strategies should emerge as a management reaction to changes in the environment. Clearly, a SMP can be completely undermined when disease, terrorism or war suddenly break out. However, the planning methods and tools we cite here can be helpful because they provide a framework for organizing marketing activity on a regular basis. Other critics of formalized marketing planning portray examples of successful entrepreneurs (such as Sir Richard Branson of the Virgin Group) who use their flair, intuition and vision in building dynamic businesses and suggest that marketing is all about spontaneous ideas. However, companies cannot rely upon spontaneous thinking to solve all their problems, and the marketing planning process can allow opportunities for creativity and flexibility, via contingency planning, within a systematic framework. A valid criticism of organizational planning is the focus on financial matters. Although many companies pay lip service to the concept of a customer orientation, the reality is that budgeting, with its emphasis on sales generation, cost control and profit engineering, is dominant in the hospitality industry – and the influence of marketing always seems to be subordinate to financial imperatives.

CONCLUSION

Marketing planning provides hospitality companies with a structured approach to planning for the future. Although the future is uncertain, environmental trends can be identified and their impact on the hospitality company can be consequently evaluated. Although marketing planning has its critics, primarily because it can be a costly, time-consuming process, there is little doubt that such planning in any organization improves the chances of survival and success. However, marketing planning alone cannot be a guarantee of success.

In this chapter, we have explained:

- The contexts within which marketing plans are constructed – corporate, division, unit and department
- Two different types of marketing plan – strategic and tactical; strategic marketing planning typically takes a 3- to 5-year timeframe; whereas tactical planning covers a 12-month period or less
- A generic marketing planning process comprising nine stages – setting vision, mission, values; situation analysis; establishing objectives; performing market STP; developing marketing mixes; creating a budget; organizing the plan's implementation; setting controls and evaluation of the plan's performance
- That objectives should be *S*pecific, *M*easurable, *A*chievable, *R*ealistic, and carried out within a set *T*imetable (SMART)
- That contingency planning provides an alternative in the event of a major deviation from plan
- The key tools in strategic marketing planning, which include the BCG matrix, SWOT analysis, PESTE analysis, gap analysis and the Ansoff matrix
- Why marketing planning has been criticized as pointless, given the unpredictability of the future
- That marketing planning provides a structured approach to organizing marketing activity.

REVIEW QUESTIONS

Now check your understanding by answering the following questions:

1 Discuss the role of marketing planning in hospitality organizations.
2 Explain the SMP process, illustrating your answer with examples from the hospitality industry.
3 Explain why control is important in marketing planning.

References and Further Reading

Chan, B. (2003). Sharing the experience. *Hospitality Magazine (HCIMA)*, 18–19.

McDonald, M. (1999). *Marketing Plans*, Butterworth-Heineman.

McDonald, M. (2008). *Malcolm McDonald on marketing planning: Understanding marketing plans and strategy marketing plans*. Kogan Page.

Porter, M. E. (1980). *Competitive strategy: Techniques for analyzing industries and competitors*. Free Press.

Reich, A. Z. (1997). *Marketing management for hospitality and industry: A strategic approach*. John Wiley & Sons.

Treacy, M., & Wiersema, F. (1995). *The discipline of market leaders*. HarperCollins.

Index